D1561758

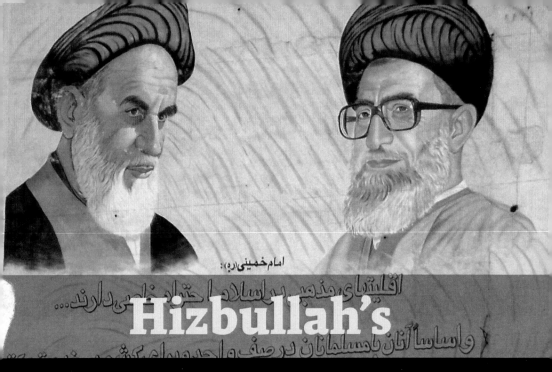

Hizbullah's

Identity Construction

Joseph Alagha

AMSTERDAM UNIVERSITY PRESS

For a better understanding of Hizbullah, *Hizbullah's Identity Construction* ought to be read in conjunction with Joseph Alagha: *Hizbullah's Documents,* Amsterdam: Pallas Publications/Amsterdam University Press (2011), ISBN 978 90 8555 037 2.

Both titles are fully searchable on Amazon.

Cover illustration: This unique propaganda painting, across the side of a huge building in Tehran contains an important saying of Imam Khumayni: "Religious minorities are accorded special respect in Iran. They stood side by side with the Muslims in serving their own country." Below stands the diagram of the "Star of Martyrs." In the middle, a Jew is depicted with his name inscribed in Hebrew and Farsi. To his right, a Zoroastrian with his name inscribed in Farsi and the Zoroastrian symbol intersecting it. To his left, an Armenian Christian with his name inscribed in Armenian and Farsi. On the top and bottom are Syriac or Aramaic Christians with their names inscribed in Syriac and Farsi. In the extreme left below, stands the emblem of the Martyr's Association with the Qur'anic verse (3:169) on top: "And do not think that those who have been killed ['martyred'] in the way of Allah as dead; they are rather living with their Lord, well-provided for." Picture taken by the author.

Cover design and lay-out: Maedium, Utrecht

ISBN   978 90 8964 297 4
e-ISBN   978 90 4851 395 6
NUR   697

To my family

Table of Contents

A Note on Transliteration

The transcribing of words and phrases in Modern Standard Arabic into English is in conformity with the transliteration system of the International Journal of Middle East Studies, with a few modifications that cater to the guidelines of the highly simplified transliteration system of Amsterdam University Press, where all diacritical marks have been omitted save for the ʿayn (ʿ) and hamza (ʾ). Concerning the translation of controversial terms, the author gave the English equivalent and included the original Arabic word in transliterated form in brackets beside each term.

Acknowledgements

I would like to profusely thank the entire Amsterdam University Press (AUP) team for all the hard work and dedication they invested in bringing this book to publication.

I wish to extend my deepest gratitude and appreciation to scholars Daniel L. Byman, Franck Salameh, Asher Kaufman, Seteney Shami, Armando Salvatore, William B. Quandt, Mark Levine, Bernard Haykel, Ibrahim G. Aoude, Anoush Ehteshami, Farhad Khosrokhavar, Michaelle Browers, Jonathan Benthall, and Robert G. Rabil, as well as AUP's two anonymous reviewers who read the manuscript and provided very constructive comments. Their critical reading and informed comments contributed to making this book a better read. Needless to say, any errors, weaknesses, omissions, or shortcomings are solely mine.

I would like to express gratitude to my informants and interviewees, without whom this book would not have been based on empirical research. I also owe a great deal to the editor and copy editor who exhibited unusual efficiency and professionalism in their work.

Last, but not least, I am truly grateful to my family for their patience and support throughtout the different phases of writing this book.

Joseph Alagha
March 2011, the Netherlands

List of Abbreviations

AFP	Agence France-Presse
BDL	Banque du Liban/The Central Bank of Lebanon
BKI	Babbar Khalsa International (of India)
CCSD	Consultative Center for Studies and Documentation (Hizbullah's think tank)
CEO	Chief Executive Officer
EU	European Union/Community
FI	Fatah al-Islam
FM	Foreign Minister
FPM	Free Patriotic Movement
GCC	Gulf Cooperation Council
GLC	Lebanese Labor Unions
IDF	Israeli Defence Forces
ISF	Internal Security Forces (Lebanese Police)
IT	Information Technology
LA	Lebanese Army
LAF	Lebanese Armed Forces
LBCI	Lebanese Broadcasting Corporation International
LCP	Lebanese Communist Party
LDP	Lebanese Democratic Party
LF	Lebanese Forces
LMCB	Multiconfessional Lebanese Brigades to Fighting the Israeli Occupation
LTTE	Liberation Tigers of Tamil Elam (in Sri Lanka and India)
MEA	Middle East Airlines
MP	Member of Parliament
NATO	North Atlantic Treaty Organization
NGOS	Non-Governmental Organizations

NNA	(Lebanese) National News Agency
OIC	Organization of Islamic Conference
PA	Palestinian Authority
PFLP	Popular Front for the Liberation of Palestine
PKK	The Kurdistan Worker's Party (in Turkey)
PLO	Palestinian Liberation Organization
PM	Prime Minister
POWS	Prisoners of War
PSP	Progressive Socialist Party
SLA	South Lebanon Army (now defunct)
SSNP	Syrian Social Nationalist Party
STL	Special Tribunal for Lebanon
UNDP	United Nations Development Program
UNICEF	United Nations Children's Fund
UNIFIL	United Nations Interim Force in Lebanon
UNRWA	United Nations Relief and Works Agency (for Palestine Refugees in the Middle East)
UNSC	United Nations Security Council

Summary

The Lebanese resistance movement Hizbullah changes as circumstances change. Since its inception, Hizbullah has been keen to control the Lebanese political system, initially through a top-down revolutionary process aimed at obtaining power by military force. This radicalism proved futile in the 1980s. From a *Realpolitik* perspective, Hizbullah reconstructed its identity, altered its political strategy, and recognized the 1990 Ta'if Agreement, Lebanon's new constitution.

Benefiting from the Syrian influence that controlled Lebanon militarily, Hizbullah played its cards well and was able to extract an important concession from the Lebanese government by being classified as a resistance movement and not a militia. This meant that it was able to keep its arms and continue resisting the Israeli occupation, while the militias of all the Lebanese political parties – which had participated in the sixteen-year civil war – had to disband and surrender their weapons to the Lebanese Army. This exception made Hizbullah the strongest military player in Lebanon, even more powerful than the Lebanese Army and security forces. Hizbullah continues to hold a considerable arsenal even after the nearly complete Israeli withdrawal from Lebanon in May 2000 and the Syrian withdrawal in 2005.

From the early 1990s onwards, Hizbullah readjusted its identity by endeavoring to control the political system through a bottom-up process of gradual participation and integration into the democratic system, starting with the parliament, the municipal councils, and the cabinet or council of ministers, the main executive body of the country. Thus, Hizbullah shifted to acceptance of, and engagement in, the democratic process under a sectarian-confessional political and administrative system that it previously regarded as an apostate. More dramatically, Hizbullah modified its demand from the abolition of political sectarianism to the adoption of the political Maronite (Christian) discourse, which stresses abolishing political sectarianism in one's mentality, before officially abolishing it in written laws. The party also called for upholding the principle of consensual democracy. However, based on its demographic strength, Hizbullah called for reducing the voting age from 21 to 18 and changing the electoral system to proportional representation, which the party believed would give the 18 ethno-confessional communities more equitable representation.

Hizbullah's identity has undergone a considerable transformation from the propagation of its first Manifesto in February 1985, passing through its eight clandestine conclaves, to the dissemination of its second Manifesto a quarter of a century later, in November 2009. The party has gone a long way in its attempt to display its new face. This book studies Hizbullah's identity construction and reconstruction within these contours by surveying timeless concepts and themes, such as tolerance and discrimination; interpretation and authority; political violence; as well as cooptation, integration, and empowerment.

Introduction and Analytical Framework

1 PROLOGUE: BRIEF HISTORY OVER THE PAST THREE DECADES[1]

The Lebanese Shi'ite resistance movement Hizbullah (Party of God) is going through a remarkable transformation, where its identity is constantly undergoing reconstruction. Hizbullah was founded in 1978 as an Islamic struggle (*jihadi*) movement of social and political protest by various sectors of Lebanese Shi'ite clergy and cadres, with Iranian ideological backing. Over the period 1985 to 1991 Hizbullah became a full-fledged social movement in the sense of having a broad overall organization, structure, and ideology aiming at social change and social justice. In the early 1990s, it became a parliamentary political party.

Hizbullah defines its identity as an Islamic *jihadi* (struggle) movement, "whose emergence is based on an ideological, social, political and economical mixture in a special Lebanese, Arab and Islamic context".[2] Its roots can be traced back to 1978, which coincided with the disappearance of Imam Musa al-Sadr[3] and the first Israeli invasion of Lebanon. By the efforts and under the auspices of leading Iranian hard-line clergy and military figures such as 'Ali Akbar Muhtashami and Mustafa Shamran, combined with the endeavors of the first and second Hizbullah secretary-generals, Shaykh Subhi al-Tufayli and Sayyid 'Abbas al-Musawi, Hizbullah's nucleus was established. With the victory of the Islamic Revolution in Iran in 1979, many Lebanese Shi'ites saw in Imam Khumayni their new leader. During the same period, Sayyid 'Abbas al-Musawi officially founded "The Hizbullah of Lebanon", supported by his students and other leading *'ulama* (religious scholars).[4]

The second Israeli invasion of Lebanon in 1982 was the spark that reignited Hizbullah and led to its formation as an Islamic *jihadi* movement. The Islamic Resistance, Hizbullah's military wing, made some breakthroughs in the face of the Israeli army that advanced towards Beirut and led a campaign of resistance against the Israeli forces after they occupied the Lebanese capital. Leading Hizbullah cadres such as Sayyid Hasan Nasrallah, the current secretary-general, Sayyid Ibrahim Amin al-Sayyid, the current head of Hizbullah's political council (Politburo), and Husayn al-Musawi[5] – currently a member of Hizbullah's parliamentary bloc after the 7 June 2009 legislature elections – were all Amal[6] members. These, among others, were later totally against Amal joining the Lebanese cabinet.[7] Therefore, these radicals abandoned Amal and joined the ranks of existing Islamic Shi'ite groups – including members of the *Hizb Al-Da'wa Al-Islamiyya* ('The Islamic Call Party'), *Itihad al-Lubnani lil Talaba al-Muslimin* ('The Lebanese Union of Muslim Students')[8], as well as independent active Islamic figures and clerics – and established Hizbullah to oppose the Israeli occupation, with the material support of Iran and backing from Syria.[9] These groups came together in fighting the Israeli occupation and built the backbone of the party, and most importantly its 'resistance identity'. Their later achievements in addressing the socio-economic grievances, resulting from the Israeli occupation, gained the party a solid ground among the grassroots of Lebanese society.

On 16 February 1985, Hizbullah became a noticeable player in the Lebanese political system when it publicly revealed its Political Manifesto or Open Letter, which disclosed its religio-political ideology, thus signalling its open engagement in Lebanese political life after operating clandestinely[10] for some years.[11] In the Open Letter Hizbullah disclosed a radical-militant approach that regarded the Lebanese political system as infidel by nature, and considered the Lebanese government as being an apostate, that should be uprooted by a top-down revolutionary process and be replaced by the rule of Islam.

Hizbullah's reputation as an Islamic resistance movement has been marred by the West's accusation of 'terrorist' operations of global reach; the majority of which were claimed by the Islamic Jihad.[12] Some of the attacks which made Hizbullah gain global attention were the US embassy suicide attacks on 18 April 1983[13] and 20 September 1984; the 23 October 1983 twin-suicide attacks that led to the death of 241 US marines[14] and 58 French paratroopers; the Buenos Aires bombing of the Israeli embassy on 17 March 1992[15]; and the holding of Western hostages. The Israeli government and the US Administration claim that Hizbullah's Islamic Resistance constitutes a semi-clandestine organization and that Islamic Jihad is its clandestine wing.[16] In an endeavor to ward off the charges of terrorism, Hizbullah's ideologues, leaders, cadres and intellectuals voice a consensus that has systematically and constantly denied any connection or link to Islamic Jihad or acts it has claimed as its own.

And so, in the 1980s Hizbullah became a closed sectarian social movement. Through heavy reliance on a strict application of Imam Khumayni's *wilayat al-faqih* (guardianship by the jurisprudent), 'Hizbullah – The Islamic Revolution in Lebanon' emerged as an internally strong organization with limited following. Al-Tufayli repeatedly stressed Hizbullah's aim of establishing an Islamic state in Lebanon as part of an all-encompassing regional Islamic state, headed by Iran. This unprecedented commitment to the Islamic state in Lebanese political discourse backfired domestically alienating Hizbullah from other political and social movements, and from an effective position within the Lebanese political sphere. Thus, Hizbullah's policies were counterproductive, leading to the failure of its integration into Lebanese political life.

Since the end of the civil war in 1990, Hizbullah has confronted major developments in Lebanon: most prominently, the emergence of a pluralist public sphere and increasing openness toward other communities, political parties, and interest groups in the Lebanese myriad. This resulted in a change in Hizbullah's discourse and priorities. The mixed confessional space in Lebanon led Hizbullah to move from marginalization to integration (*infitah* or 'opening-up') where the party became a major player in the Lebanese milieu, thus altering its stance and changing the political rules of the game from Islamization to 'Lebanonization' by propagating a down-to-earth political program. So since the 1990s, Hizbullah has shed its irredentist ideology and evolved, more and more, into an 'ordinary' political party, with an extensive network of social services (open to both Muslims and Christians), and participated in parliamentary, municipal, and governmental work. Although Hizbullah is still primarily an Islamic movement, it displays, more and more, the characteristics of a nationalist-patriotic political party pursuing *Realpolitik*, if this is required by the circumstances and serves its interest (*maslaha*).

Hizbullah shifted its political strategy from a gradual integration in the Lebanese public sphere in the 1990s, to attempting to manipulate the Lebanese public sphere after the assassination of PM Hariri and the Syrian withdrawal in 2005, and to endeavoring to exercise hegemony over the Lebanese public sphere after the 'Second Lebanon War' in the summer of 2006 by means of changing the political system through obtaining the one-third veto power in the cabinet, the main executive branch of government. Tensions reached unprecedented highs and the snowball exploded in May 2008 into violent military confrontations in the streets of the Lebanese capital and Mount

Lebanon. Hizbullah flexed its military muscle in order to gain veto power, which proved to be a short-term political gain. However, the experience was negative in the cabinet since it led to the paralysis of the state institutions, an eventuality that convinced the party to discard this newly gained political capital. The hegemony wave subsided after the Hizbullah-led opposition lost the 2009 legislative elections. Hizbullah took a reality pill and contended itself with minor political gains for the sake of upholding the fragile consensual democracy, the fulcrum of the political system. In an atmosphere of optimism, Hizbullah revealed its new face in November 2009 when it reconstructed its identity by forging a second Manifesto, which presents a complete overhaul to its 1985 founding document, the Open Letter.

1.1   A CONTINUOUS PROCESS OF IDENTITY CONSTRUCTION

In the 1980s, Hizbullah pursued the establishment of an Islamic state both from a religious ideology and a political ideology perspective. This era was characterized by Hizbullah's religious capital (Iranian *marja'iyya*, or authority of emulation); political and symbolic capital (Islamic Resistance's war and suicide ('martyrdom') operations against Israel in the south and the *Biqa'*, north-east part of Lebanon); economic and social capital (social institutions targeting only Shi'ite grassroots); and Islamic Jihad's acts as symbolic capital.

Fragmented public spheres existed in Lebanon as cantons – confessionally based mini-states within the Lebanese state. During the mid-1980s the issue of establishing cantons along sectarian lines was high on the agenda of many political parties, including the Christian ones. For instance, Habib Matar[17] stated in 1986 that his call to the Vatican of establishing a Christian state in Lebanon should not be viewed as a call for the disintegration of Lebanon; rather, he clarified that the Christian state would be erected on all Lebanese soil. Matar questioned, "Why don't the Christians in the East have a shelter or a small state?" When he was asked what the Muslims should do, he replied: "It's their own problem. There are a lot of vacant areas in the Arab world [where they can go], or let them be governed by the Christian state, and this is better for them".[18] A similar view was earlier announced by the Phalangist Leader, the late ex-President Bashir Gemayyel who said in 1982 that the Maronites were aiming at converting Lebanon into a Christian state where all the Christian Arabs could reside in.[19]

In Hizbullah's case, founding a Shi'ite canton in the areas under its control, would have implied establishing a replica of an Islamic state in miniature. For instance, unlike the Lebanese Forces and Progressive Socialist Party (PSP)[20], Hizbullah neither established a mini-state – with its own ports, airports, taxation, and civil administration – within the Lebanese state, nor did Hizbullah call for federalism. In 1986, Sayyid Hasan Nasrallah, Hizbullah's current secretary-general, stressed that the Muslims have no right whatsoever to even entertain the idea of a Muslim canton, a Shi'ite canton, or a Sunni canton… Talking about cantons annihilates the Muslims, destroys their potential power, and leads them from one internal war to another. Only the Islamic state upholds their unity.[21]

In the 1990s, Hizbullah's leading cadres took great care to ward off charges of the party being a state within a state. Hizbullah's leading cadres, most notably, Nasrallah and Hajj Muhammad Ra'd, *Shura* (consultative) council member and the current head of Hizbullah's parliamentary bloc, told me that the party never took part in the Lebanese civil war[22] and affirmed that it has never imposed (by force) its ideas, opinions, ideology or political program on anyone.[23] On the contrary, Hizbullah cadres claimed that the party has always respected the opinions, beliefs and ideas of others.[24] MP 'Ali Ammar told me that in parliament Hizbullah's MPs do not participate in the debates about the budget of *Casino du Liban* or anything that has to do with alcoholic drinks or legislations contrary to Islamic law (the *Shari'a*). He added that the party honors its parliamentary alliances in accordance with its religious obligations. The party is concerned about keeping civil order and does not intervene in the judicial process; it just advocates due process and helps the Lebanese state in conducting its work in a satisfactory manner.[25] Nasrallah added that the party views the existence of 18 ethno-confessional communities in Lebanon as an asset, and that it aspires to openness and dialogue among all the Lebanese. Hizbullah has repeatedly refused to be a social, political, judicial, or security alternative to the Lebanese state and its institutions.[26] If nothing else, intellectual Hajj 'Imad Faqih has said, a mid-ranking cadre, assuming functions of the state would eventually dirty the party's hands, which Hizbullah cannot afford, having spent years nurturing a reputation for probity.[27] So it would appear that the logic of operating within the bounds of the Lebanese state has prevailed over the logic of revolution. As such, Hizbullah's entry into Lebanese politics as a major player helped to bring back some kind of a coherent public sphere, which, more or less, existed before the civil war erupted in April 1975.

However, Hizbullah's Islamic state remained as a political ideology, a 'legal abstraction', but *not* as a political program. In the early 1990s, Hizbullah started promoting its Islamic identity and agenda by following a pragmatic political program, mainly to lull Christians and other Muslims who were opposed to the Islamic state. In the meantime, Hizbullah remained faithful to its Shi'ite constituency by employing a bottom-up Islamization process through working within the Lebanese state's political and administrative structures, while, at the same time establishing Islamic institutions within the civil society. Religious capital was consolidated when Khamina'i conferred upon Nasrallah and Yazbik[28] the *taklif shar'i* (religious and legal obligation) by nominating them as his *wakilayn shar'iyyan* (religious deputies in Lebanon); the addition of electoral politics to political capital (Sunnis and Christians on Hizbullah's electoral ballot); the disappearance of Islamic Jihad from symbolic capital; and the accumulation of more social and economic capital through the benefits for Sunni and Christian grassroots from Hizbullah's NGO services.

✦✦✦

By employing the analytical framework outlined below, my purpose is to give a better and clearer reading of Hizbullah's metamorphosis and identity overhaul throughout the whirlwind of changes.

2   ANALYTICAL FRAMEWORK

2.1   IDENTITY CONSTRUCTION

Working definition of identity
Since I am interested in examining the changing identity of Hizbullah, I will rely on concepts of constructed identities and their relationship with ideology as laid down by the constructivist theory of identity. Constructivists seek to construe the world in a better way "by listening to voices silenced by power – the voices… of oppressed ethnic minorities"[29], who as downtrodden people, found a sense of collective identity, which led them to mobilize in order to redress their grievances. This behavior seems to be warranted by the following analytical considerations. "Constructivism posits that social (and international) structures are alloyed with normative and material elements, that social structures constitute actors' identities and interests, and that the practices of actors embedded in the social structure not only reproduce the structure but also sometimes transform it".[30]

Collective (social) identity is defined as: "'An identity is the understanding of oneself in relation to others'. Identity is inherently relational – one defines oneself or groups define themselves in part by who belongs and, as important, by who does not belong."[31] In short, social identities are "identities that political actors generate through interaction with other actors."[32] As a working definition of identity construction, I employ Castells' definition:

"Identity is people's source of meaning and experience… [it is] the process of construction of meaning on the basis of a cultural attribute, or related set of cultural attributes, that is/are given priority over other sources of meaning."[33] In Castells' theory of identity, the concepts of 'resistance identity' and 'project identity' play a salient role in exemplifying resistance and defiance to established authority. His definition of resistance identity addresses the question of oppression and resistance, which influence the identity of a social movement.[34] According to Castells, conceptually, resistance identity is "generated by those actors that are in positions/conditions devaluated and/or stigmatized by the logic of domination, thus building trenches of resistance and survival on the basis of principles different from, or opposed to, those permeating the institutions of society."[35] He adds that empirically resistance identities are not confined to traditional values since they could be molded by progressive social movements that opt for the alternative to set up an independent communal resistance as long as they possess the strength and resources to launch an assault on the oppressive institutions they are resisting. However, according to Castells, these identities resist and hardly ever communicate with the state, except to struggle, negotiate, and bargain on behalf of their specific interests and values, so as to grant vital services to their constituencies. Castells concludes that communal (resistance) identity seems appealing to people resisting social, economic, cultural, and political oppression.[36]

Castells distinguishes between resistance identity and project identity. According to him, project identity is constructed "when social actors, on the basis of whichever cultural materials available to them, build a *new identity* that redefines their position in society and, by so doing, seek the *transformation* of overall social structure".[37] He explains how conceptually this process might take place, especially when social movements might acquire a leading role in the founding of a better society, a good life, and a good political order. In that case, the construction of identity is conducive to the realization of their project. Although their project might originate from or be based upon an oppressed identity, it aims at the construction and the subsequent *transformation* of society as an extension of this project identity on the basis of communal resistance[38], thus leading to a shared, reconstructed identity. Is Hizbullah capable of transforming itself from a resistance identity to a project identity?

Relationship between identity and ideology
Linking identity to ideology, Telhami and Barnett argue, "Identity appears most prominently as an ideological device to justify self-interested politics… [Identity] makes some action legitimate and intelligible and others not so."[39]

My working definition of ideology is that it is, "… 'world views' of any social groups which justify their actions but which cannot be counterposed to truth. However, they can be subject to re-description and thus do not have to be accepted… 'intellectual' ideology is understood as a [formal system of belief and] coherent system of thought: political programmes/manifestos, philosophical orientations and religious codification."[40] Thus, broadly speaking, I aim to analyze Hizbullah's identity by examining its mobilization activities focusing on depicting the religious or Islamic aspect of identity.

Hinnebusch's three levels and the dynamic between identity and state sovereignty
In order to accomplish that, I employ Hinnebusch's "three conceptually distinct environments", which distinguish among the "domestic level", the "regional systematic level", and the "global (or international) level".[41] In Hizbullah's case, the domestic level corresponds to Lebanon; the regional level comprises Israel/Palestine, Syria, and Iran; and the international level, in addition to pan-Islamism, refers to Hizbullah's stance towards the US. This is done in order to study why and how the three levels or environments effect Hizbullah's identity construction. In this respect, Hinnebusch argues, "Constructivists insist that interstate relations are contingent on the way identity is constructed; in the Middle East, sub- and suprastate identities compete with state identity, inspire transstate movements [transnational Islamic movements such as Hizbullah], and constrain purely state-centric behavior."[42] In a similar vein, Telhami and Barnett state that constructivism considers "that identity essentially constructs the world so that perceptions of one's state and others are defined by one's identity."[43] Likening this to resource mobilization, internationally and regionally, Hinnebusch argues that in the Middle East, "populations have remained mobilizable by transstate and irredentist[44] ideology."[45] In this perspective the effect of the Islamic Revolution's ideology is clearly salient on Hizbullah's ideology and identity. Domestically, Hinnebusch comes out with the following hypothesis: "the more the state system thwarted indigenous interests and identity [Shi'ite interests and Hizbullah's identity], the more status quo social forces inside the states were weakened [for instance, the Christian Lebanese Forces and Sunni political parties] and the more radical, middle class, or even plebeian forces were mobilized [for example, the Hizbullahis]."[46]

Since Hinnebusch based his argument on the distinction between identity and state sovereignty[47], an important challenge is to study and evaluate the dynamic between Hizbullah's Islamist identity and Lebanese state sovereignty. According to Hinnebusch, "the unique feature of the Middle East state system, specifically the uneasy relation of identity and state sovereignty, immensely complicate foreign policymaking in the Middle East… [because] Middle Eastern states lack impermeability and secure national identity."[48] Moreover, Hinnebusch adds, "loyalty to the individual states is contested by substate and suprastate identities. The resultant embedding of the state system is a matrix of fluid multiple identities."[49] And so, "built-in" anomalies of irredentist tendencies are characteristic of the region. They are reflected in the expression of the practices and worldviews of various ethnic and religious milieus, which challenge the immutability of territorial borders, thus simulating territorial conflict between states. Added to this is the immense and complicated power that political Islam possesses as a transnational, suprastate identity, which structures and commands the lives and worldviews of the people in the region. This makes the resort to the juncture of political identity and state sovereignty legitimate and wanting. Thus, the generated duality, which the ruling elite have to grapple with between asserting raison de la nation (pan-Arabism/pan-Islamism) and raison d'état (state sovereignty), is what has compelled them to treat the region as an arena of transstate political competition.[50]

2.2   RESOURCE MOBILIZATION AS A BRIDGE BETWEEN IDENTITY AND PIERRE BOURDIEU'S CAPITALS

In studying Hizbullah's identity formation, I mainly employ the concept of resource mobilization in relation to Ousmane Kane's interpretation of Pierre Bourdieu's notion of different kinds of capitals: religious, political, symbolic, social, and economic capitals. I do this in order to investigate how and why a shift in Hizbullah's identity is taking place. "The term resource mobilization is used to refer to the ways a social movement utilizes such resources as money, political influence, access to the media, and personnel. The success of a movement for *change* [identity reconstruction] will depend in good part on how effectively it mobilizes its resources… Unlike the relative-deprivation approach, the resource-mobilization perspective focuses on strategic difficulties [challenges] facing social movements."[51] Recourse mobilization plays a central role since the success of a social movement for change or identity construction depends on how well it mobilizes its resources in order to face strategic difficulties or challenges. I examine Hizbullah's use of resource mobilization focusing on how Hizbullah employs different types of capital in this process and the shifting balances among them.

Ousmane Kane[52] readjusted and applied Bourdieu's religious, political, symbolic, social, and economic capitals to the study of Islamic movements. In this book I follow Kane's formulation of Bourdieu's capitals.

1   *Religious capital:* According to Bourdieu, religious capital refers to the way religious knowledge is appropriated and disseminated.[53] Kane broadens Bourdieu's mandate by making the distinction between "ancient religious capital" and "new religious capital". He labels the former as "non formally certified cultural capital", and the latter as "formally certified cultural capital". According to Bourdieu, cultural capital refers mainly to education, culture, and related skills. Kane adds, "Non formally certified cultural capital refers to the religious expertise, which... includes a combination of both exoteric religious knowledge (Koran, Islamic law, Islamic exegesis) and esoteric sciences [Shiʿite theosophy for instance]... This capital is not based on the possession of a university degree, thus it is not formally certified. It tends to be the prerogative of traditional religious authorities..."[54] Kane continues, "formally certified cultural capital is based on expertise in exoteric knowledge, ... but it equally includes knowledge of the Koran (the mastery of the art of its recitation, knowledge of its conventional exegesis and Islamic jurisprudence) as well as knowledge of some secular subject matters (foreign languages, history, geography, mathematics, etc.). More importantly, formally certified cultural capital requires the possession of a degree delivered by a university or another formal institution of learning."[55] I adjust and apply Kane's analysis to Hizbullah's ʿulama who still play an important role in the crystallization and dissemination of the party's religious ideology. Thus, I study Hizbullah's religious ideology from the perspective of Kane's interpretation and use of Bourdieu's religious capital.

2   *Symbolic capital:* Simply stated, symbolic capital corresponds to 'your reputation and honor', distinction, and prestige.[56] Bourdieu defines symbolic capital as the "degree of accumulated prestige, celebrity, consecration or honour [possessed by someone and] founded on the dialectic of knowledge and recognition".[57] Since Hizbullah labels itself as an Islamic *jihadi* movement, symbolic capital acquires vital importance. According to Kane, "symbolic capital refers here to the status of a fighter for the cause of 'true Islam' whatever that means.[58] The Koranic verse [4:95]..., which states that 'God hath granted a grade higher to those

who strive and fight with their goods and persons' conveys this idea of symbolic capital. The more one fights with one's 'goods' or 'one's 'person', the more one accumulates symbolic capital."[59] Although symbolic capital is an indispensable component of Hizbullah's religious ideology, it acquired a substantial importance in Hizbullah's political ideology, and minor importance in the party's political program. This seems to be in conformity with Hizbullah's accumulation and conversion of capital (see below).

3 *Political capital:* "Political capital is everything that enables leaders to get anything done. It's their reputation, their ability to make the newspaper, their statutory role, their friends in the community, the amount of money they can raise, the number of people who support them, the length of time people are willing to pay attention to them and a lot more than that as well."[60] Thus, political capital is present in both Hizbullah's political ideology and political program.

4 *Social capital:* Social capital is "the network or influential patrons that you can use to support your actions".[61] Simply stated, social capital is contacts, acquaintances, and the practice of durable social networks. According to Kane, social capital "is what ordinary language calls 'connections'. By formalizing this concept, Bourdieu argues, one 'acquires the means of analysing the logic whereby this particular kind of capital is accumulated, transmitted and reproduced, the means of understanding how it turns into economic capital and, conversely, what work is required to convert economic capital into social capital, the means of grasping the function of institutions such as clubs or quite simply the family'."[62]

5 *Economic capital:* Economic capital corresponds to "stocks and shares but also the surplus present in very high salaries".[63] According to Kane, "economic capital refers to material wealth in the most common sense of the word."[64]

Readjusting Kane's interpretation of Bourdieu's theory, I classify and study his capitals (religious, symbolic, political, social, and economic) as forms of resource mobilization, mainly through accumulation and conversion of capital. "By accumulation of capital, is meant here the process through which social actors (or players) go in order to *obtain* a given sort of capital. By conversion, it is meant the act of *spending* one sort of capital and getting in return another sort."[65] (My emphasis). Thus, I endeavor to describe and analyze the interplay of the different forms of capital trying to study why and how there have been shifting balances among them. And so, by analyzing the changing balance of capitals, I hope to make statements about the different constructions of Hizbullah's identity.

***

In short, I am not going to discuss identity constructions on an individual level; rather, I will look at identity processes of Hizbullah as a socio-political movement in which the concept of resource mobilization plays a crucial role.

The concept of resource mobilization is pivotal to the survival of a social movement. Gramsci argued that "all the essential questions of sociology are nothing than questions of political science."[66] Paraphrasing Gramsci, social movements are nothing but political movements. However, "modern social movements are primarily social and not directly political in character. Their aim is the mobilization of civil society, not the seizure of power."[67]

As mentioned earlier, resource mobilization refers to the way a social movement mobilizes its resources and/or capitals in order to confront and survive strategic difficulties and challenges facing it. A social movement might reconstruct its identity in order to adjust to a world that is in incessant flux, or else it will risk demise or might not remain a viable social movement. By social movement is understood, "purposive collective actions whose outcome, in victory as in defeat, transforms the values and institutions of society".[68] Fuller notes that Islamism "represents the single most important [mobilizational] force for political change across the Muslim world."[69] He adds, "Islamists are good at identifying and articulating the grievances, but to succeed they must move beyond their present roles if they wish to remain relevant to societies' needs", and here comes the salient role of resource mobilization. Thus, according to Fuller, Islamism is "a religious-cultural-political framework for engagement on issues that most concern politically engaged Muslims."[70] It seems this religious-cultural-political framework constitutes the foundation of Hizbullah's ideology, political program, and cultural politics.

3   THE CONTROVERSY

The following describes some of the questions and themes that I intend to deal with in this book. Since Hizbullah labels itself as an Islamic *jihadi* movement, it is no wonder that Hizbullah's primary concern has been the preservation of its identity taking into account the dramatic developments and turmoil that rupture the Middle East. Can Hinnebusch's three levels and the dynamic between identity and state sovereignty furnish an explanation and a justification for Hizbullah's fluctuating identity, which seems to be permanently under reconstruction? Why does Hizbullah change as circumstances change? What is the role of resource mobilization in this regard? On the regional and international level, did Hizbullah broaden the mandate of the domestic concept of *mahrumin* (downtrodden) to the transnational concept of *mustad'afin* (oppressed), in line with Imam Khumayni's bipolarity of oppressors and oppressed? How can Hizbullah, which claims to be a Pan-Islamic and a Pan-Arab *jihadi* movement, be content with receiving more recognition and votes in local Lebanese politics?[71] At the domestic level, although social and economic capitals were mentioned in Hizbullah's political programs as ideological slogans, little was done to put them into actual practice. However, social and economic capitals acquired substantial importance in Hizbullah's political program through the sprouting of the party's NGOs and civil institutions. From this perspective, it is interesting to study to what extent Hizbullah was able to accumulate and transform (convert) social and economic capital into political capital, through integration into the Lebanese public sphere. What has led Hizbullah, which embraces an ideological-revolutionary version of Islam, to review its political ideology or to sometimes place it on the shelf and develop a secular political program? Is it the domestic level, i.e. the Lebanese status quo ante and specificities (*khususiyyat*)? Does the regional or international level have a bearing on this apparent change? What happened to Hizbullah's identity, as an Islamic *jihadi* movement, in this perspective? Why and how did Hizbullah revise and update its domestic, regional, and international identity in its second Manifesto of November 2009?

4   SYNOPSIS OF THE BOOK

The chapters in this book reveal different stages of Hizbullah's identity construction and are arranged in a thematic way. The first chapter surveys the concepts of tolerance and discrimination in relation to the status of minorities in the Islamic order. The second chapter deals with the thematic of interpretation and authority in relation to Hizbullah's adoption of the Iranian theory of governance and applying it in a pluralistic setting like Lebanon. The third and fourth chapters address the polemics of political violence from the stances of terrorism, 9/11, and suicide operations. The fifth chapter highlights how Hizbullah moved from integration in the 1990s to manipulation through empowerment in the early 21st century. The sixth chapter analyzes the new dynamics that resulted from the 2008 Doha Accord and its aftermath. The seventh chapter presents the proof par excellence of Hizbullah's identity construction by examining how the party employed its resource mobilization in such a way to survive domestic, regional, and international changes from forging its first Manifesto, the Open Letter in 1985, passing through all of its eight conclaves that culminated in a groundbreaking new Manifesto a quarter of a century later. The concluding chapter summarizes how Hizbullah negotiated its continuous renaissance in the whirlwind of change in Lebanon and the Middle East, highlighting the shift from resistance identity to project identity.

1 Tolerance and Discrimination: Ahl Al-Dhimma in the Islamic Order[1]

INTRODUCTION

This chapter highlights the shift in Hizbullah's relationship with Lebanese Christians from regarding them as potential *dhimmis*[2] within its conception of an Islamic state to citizens in a pluralistic polity. The author discusses in some detail, relying on primary sources and discourses, the place of Christians in Hizbullah's Islamic state, stressing points of agreement with and departure from the Prophetic tradition, and surveying how these influenced Hizbullah's policies in the 1980s. I will explain the seminal role of the 1990 Ta'if Agreement in helping to furnish these changes, in which the mixed confessional space led to the creation of pluralist politics and the emergence of a more or less 'open' public sphere. Hizbullah's second secretary-general laid the cornerstone of the party's transformation in his 1991 political program. Although Hizbullah's leaders and cadres paid lip service to an Islamic state, eventually Hizbullah dropped that notion from all its political programs by regarding it as a 'legal abstraction'. Even its November 2009 Manifesto has no mention of the Islamic state. And so, Hizbullah engaged in dialogue with the Lebanese Christians on the basis of the Vatican's Papal Guidance, and included Christians and Sunnis in its legislative and municipal election slates. Through a series of interviews with the party's intellectuals and policymakers, I demonstrate that, starting in the 1990s, Hizbullah dropped the *dhimmi* categorization and replaced it with the concept of *muwatana* (citizenship).

1.1 HIZBULLAH'S RELATIONS WITH THE LEBANESE MYRIAD: THE CHRISTIANS AS A PROMINENT EXAMPLE

Although there has been dialogue between Hizbullah and the Sunnis, most notably through the prominent role of the Union of Muslim 'Ulama[3], this was not the case with the Christians. From the early 1980s till 1990 hardly any political dialogue or high level contact was established between Hizbullah and Christians.[4] Although on face value it appears that Hizbullah's call (*da'wa*)[5] in its Open Letter was addressed to all Christians, in reality Hizbullah shunned any contact with political Maronism[6], Maronites, and any collaborator with Israel. Though some Hizbullah cadres had some low-level contacts with Christians living in the party's constituencies – especially in the *Biqa'* region, in the northeast of Lebanon and the *Dahiya*, Hizbullah's den in Beirut's southern suburb, which houses more than one million Shi'ites – nonetheless no tangible high-level dialogue materialized between Hizbullah and the Christians.[7] Indeed, Hizbullah's political ideology was selective in its treatment of Lebanese Christians. By addressing the Lebanese Christians in general and the Maronites in particular, the Open Letter set apart the Maronites from the rest of the Christians. The Open Letter also differentiated within Maronites on the following grounds: 1) the leading Maronite notables and their retinue who constitute the symbols of the then political system, i.e. representatives of political Maronism, or those with blatant connections with Israel; and 2) the rest of the Maronite notables and ordinary citizens. Hizbullah's 1985 Manifesto considered that the party's primary problem was with the symbols of the political system, i.e. political Maronism and the collaborators with Israel. The document called upon the chiefs of political Maronism to stop using their Christian militias to exercise 'oppressive' policies against Muslims. As such, Hizbullah contended that these policies would backfire on the Christians, endangering their peace and security, especially since such exploitation of force was based on "narrow-minded particularism, sectarian privileges, and collaboration with colonialism and Israel". Also, the Open Letter enjoined Christians to liberate their thoughts, minds, and hearts from what it described as "the despicable sectarianism, fanaticism and parochialism".[8] In addition, Hizbullah clarified in its 1985 Manifesto, that its views against political Maronism do not imply that it is seeking revenge against all Christians, stressing that it does not wish any inconvenience or harm, neither to the Christians who live peacefully in the areas that are under its control nor to those who are 'patriotic' and live elsewhere.[9]

1.2 PHASE I: THE PLACE OF THE CHRISTIANS IN THE ISLAMIC STATE

In the 1980s, Hizbullah considered the Christians as *dhimmis* or *ahl al-dhimma* who would have to pay the poll tax (*jizya*) as residents of an Islamic state.[10] This attitude might have been based upon a specific interpretation of the Prophet's political constitution of Medina, and might also have been inspired by the constitution of the Islamic Republic of Iran. In conformity to the Open Letter, Hizbullah's 1985 Manifesto, in one of its political declarations Hizbullah stated that it saw in the presence of the peace-loving Christians, residing in the areas under its control, the credible possibility of its 'opening-up' (*infitah*) or becoming more inclusive as permitted by the tolerant values of Islam. Hizbullah stressed that *ahl al-dhimma* share with the Muslims the social values of overt and purposeful tolerance such as love, fraternity, and solidarity. However, Hizbullah clarified in its political declaration that political Maronism is exempted from such tolerance since they were regarded as hypocrites:[11] "When the hypocrites came to you, they say: 'We bear witness that you are indeed Allah's Apostle.' Allah knows that you are indeed his Apostle and Allah bears witness that the hypocrites are liars." (63:1)[12]

The late Ayatullah Sayyid Muhammad Husayn Fadlallah (died 4 July 2010)[13], who was the 'godfather' of many Lebanese Islamists, might have left his imprints on Hizbullah's thought, especially in the 1980s. Sayyid Fadlallah explained that the first constitution of Islam, the Constitution of al-Medina (*al-Sahifa*), stressed the security as well as the protection of the persons and property of *ahl al-dhimma* as long as they were not treacherous. Fadlallah clarified that in the Medinan Islamic state the relations between the Muslims, on the one hand, and the Jews and Christians, on the other, were governed by the '*dhimmi* contract', which, based upon mutual consent, regulated those relations and enforced specific contractual obligations, by which the Jews and Christians held the same rights and duties as Muslim citizens. Fadlallah added that justice[14] in Islam has always been closely related to freedom, the freedom that grants benefits and precludes harm[15], and the *dhimmi* contract granted *ahl al-dhimma* such freedom, especially freedom of religion and the protection of their religious practices.[16]

In turn, 'Ali Kurani, a Hizbullah middle-rank cadre, stated that the freedom accorded to *ahl al-dhimma* in an Islamic state is within the confines of the safeguards of Islamic *shari'a*. He clarified that the Christian minorities who live under Muslim governance are accorded all their civil and religious rights, but not their political privilege since they are governed and not ruling anymore, as was the case with political Maronism.[17]

According to Muhammad Z'aytir[18], the Islamic republic that the Muslims are striving to establish in Lebanon does not impose a duty upon the Christians, in general, or the political Maronites, in particular, to convert to Islam because Islam has no need for them to be in its ranks; rather, he believed, they need Islam. He warned that governance and administration of the *umma* (Islamic community) should be the prerogative of Muslims, and the Muslims must not allow others authority in their affairs:

> O believers, do not take as close friends other than your own people [co-religionists]; they will spare no effort to corrupt you and wish to see you suffer. Hatred has already been manifested in what they utter, but what their hearts conceal is greater still. We have made clear our signs to you if only you understand. (Q.3:118)

Based on this Qur'anic verse, Z'aytir posed the following question: since it is a religious imperative not to allow the Christians to participate in government, then how could the Muslims accept to be ruled by them?[19]

In this respect, Sayyid Abbas al-Musawi, Hizbullah's founder and second secretary-general, argued that compulsion in religion is not allowed since Prophet Muhammad would not have established the Constitution of Medina (*al-Sahifa*) if it were. Sayyid Abbas considered the Prophet as the interreligious arbitrator among the Muslims, *ahl al-dhimma*, and others. Sayyid Abbas emphasized that the Constitution of Medina confirmed that although that city consisted of many religious communities, Medina became a unified political community headed by Prophet Muhammad. Thus, non-Muslims had conferred legitimacy to the Prophet as the political leader and final arbitrator. Sayyid Abbas stressed that since the Prophet's religious authority over non-Muslims was restricted, *al-Sahifa* granted each religious community full rights to follow its own religion and to practice its own internal affairs as it deemed fit. Sayyid Abbas conveyed the belief that Hizbullah would treat the People of the Book in accordance with the Constitution of Medina, which distinguished between religious authority and political authority or leadership.[20]

Nevertheless, in the Open Letter, Hizbullah practiced its Islamic propagation by exhorting all the Christians to convert to Islam in order to have felicity in this world and the world to come: "Open your hearts to our Call, which we address to you. Open yourselves up to Islam where you will find salvation and happiness upon earth and in the hereafter". Hizbullah called on the Christians to rid themselves of narrow denominational allegiance and monopolizing privileges that disadvantaged other communities. Hizbullah stressed that the Christians should answer the appeal from heaven and have recourse to reason instead of arms; to persuasion instead of sectarianism. Hizbullah encouraged Christians to review their thinking and they might come to know that their best interest lies in what they decide, by their own free will and not by what might be imposed upon them: "Say: O People of the Book, come to an equitable world (*kalimat siwa'*) between you and us, that we worship none but Allah, do not associate anything with Him and do not set up each other as lords besides Allah".[21] In an attempt to convey Hizbullah's tolerance towards non-Muslims, Z'aytir argued that Prophet Muhammad always placed the Qur'anic verse 3:64 as a header on all the letters he addressed to them. Z'aytir stressed that this conveys the "absolute freedom granted to non-Muslims, freedom that ruptures the chains of slavery, freedom that is based upon human solidarity, intuitive trends, and the spiritual dimension of human existence"[22], i.e. religious and social freedom, but not unrestricted political freedom, as was explained in the previous section. The Open Letter added that if the Christians refuse to adhere to Islam, Hizbullah would not force them to do otherwise, rather they were expected to respect and honor their covenants with Muslims and not to aggress against them.[23] Most importantly, Hizbullah stressed in the Open Letter that there is "no compulsion in religion".[24]

Z'aytir refined his position and explained the reason for excluding some Maronites from the tolerance described in Hizbullah's policy by reasoning that Islam rejects dialogue between an oppressed Muslim and an 'oppressor crusader' (political Maronism), and claimed, somewhat figuratively, that these crusaders have been conspiring for centuries against the Muslims with the 'Zionists'. He stressed that it is a well-known fact that anyone who allies himself with the enemies of Islam becomes an enemy of Islam even though he was not classified as such originally. Thus, according to Z'aytir, the friend of my enemy is my enemy: "O believers, do not take the Jews and Christians as friends; some of them are friends of each other. Whoever of you takes them as friends is surely one of them. Allah indeed does not guide the wrongdoers (*al-zalimin*)".[25] He added that in reality the political Maronites do not aspire to dialogue; rather they need allies. As such, dialogue was only a contrived means for them to establish control over the Muslims:

> Neither the Jews nor the Christians will be pleased with you until you follow their religion. Say: Allah's guidance is the [only] guidance. And were you to follow their desires after the Knowledge that came down to you, you will have no guardian or helper [to save you] from Allah.[26]

Z'aytir affirmed that the political Maronites do not mind holding meetings, with all the militia leaders, that arrive at conclusions calling for political settlements and stress upholding, what they call, 'legitimacy' and 'constitutionality'.

By this, he saw, the political Maronites trying to deceive the populace, absorb the rising discontent against Maronism, and deceive God: "The devils shall insinuate to their followers to dispute with you; but if you obey them, then you will surely be polytheists."[27] He concluded by posing a rhetorical question, namely that if the political Maronites are responsible for the 'destruction'[28] of Lebanon, then why would anybody negotiate with them, and about what?[29]

Hizbullah echoed the Open Letter's views towards the Christians in its political declarations. In 1986 Hizbullah issued a political declaration stating that it does not find itself obliged to conduct dialogue with a political Maronism that is collaborating with its enemies; rather Hizbullah claimed that it opens its heart and extends its hands in dialogue and understanding towards Christians and other religious confessions based on the unshakable conviction of enmity to the US and Israel.[30]

Some writers claimed that Hizbullah was abiding by a political ideology that was not only intolerant towards the Christians, but served Hizbullah's aim of imposing its will and its version of Islam on all the Lebanese from whatever denomination, sect, or religion.[31] I acknowledge that there appears to be a certain tension between Hizbullah's two propositions: 1) Hizbullah's intention not to impose Islam nor coerce the Christians to adhere to its call; and 2) Hizbullah's mission of establishing an Islamic order. Maybe the confusion has to do with Z'aytir's denial of the need to convert Christians and the Hizbullah establishment's call for conversion through peaceful means. Nevertheless, in conformity with the Prophetic tradition, both Z'aytir and the Hizbullah establishment agreed that there should be 'no compulsion in religion' in accord with verse 2:256 and an 'equitable world' or common grounds, as stated in verse 3:64, should guide the relationship of Muslims with Christians.

1.3   PHASE II: THE 1990S TILL THE PRESENT

Background to Hizbullah's change in the 1990s
The Ta'if Agreement was adopted as Lebanon's new constitution in September 1990. The new constitution specified the need to share political office on a fifty-fifty basis between Christians and Muslims, most notably in the legislature and cabinet. The Ta'if Agreement officially marked the end of the civil war since it stipulated the disbanding of all militias and the surrender of their weapons to the Lebanese state. It also called for the integration of militia members into Lebanese civil society and Lebanese state institutions, most prominently, the Lebanese army. Nevertheless, the Ta'if Agreement also

allowed the militias to transform themselves into political parties. Since the Lebanese government classified Hizbullah as a resistance movement, and not a militia, it granted permission for it to keep its arms and continue its struggle against Israel.[32] By abandoning its irredentist ideology, Hizbullah adjusted to its new dual role of confronting the Israeli occupiers in the south and gradually integrating into the newly created Lebanese public sphere, which was a result of peace.

In May 1991 Hizbullah held its second conclave and elected Sayyid 'Abbas Al-Musawi as its second secretary-general. In his political program, Sayyid Abbas initiated the policy of *infitah* and dialogue, especially with the Christians. On 16 February 1992 Sayyid Abbas, his wife, and his son were assassinated by the Israeli airforce. Two days later, Sayyid Hasan Nasrallah, Hizbullah's third secretary-general, was elected together with Shaykh Na'im Qasim as deputy secretary-general.[33] Both Nasrallah and Qasim currently retain their posts.

Since the end of the civil war in 1990, Hizbullah has confronted major developments in Lebanon: prominently, the emergence of pluralist politics and increasing openness toward other communities, political parties, and interest groups. This has motivated a change in Hizbullah's discourse and priorities. The mixed confessional space led Hizbullah to move from marginalization to integration, during which the party became a major player in the public sphere. Thus by altering its stance and changing the political rules of its game from Islamization to integration and propagating a 'down-to-earth' political program Hizbullah has evolved, more and more, into an 'ordinary' political party, but with an extensive network of social services (provided to Muslims and Christians), and has participated in parliamentary, municipal, and governmental work.

By engaging in a pluralistic process, Hizbullah shifted its political strategy from cooptation[34] to contestation[35], and finally to exercising empowerment.[36] Hizbullah's participation in electoral politics might be regarded as cooptation, while its gradual integration into Lebanese politics may be considered as contestation. Hizbullah's move to the political scene and becoming a 'whole nation' political party may also be considered in terms of human empowerment (*tamkin*)[37]. The shift to electoral politics helped to foment a national politics, instead of the fragmented politics or 'states within the state', which each political party or denominational group endeavored to establish in Lebanon during the civil war era (1975-1990). Thus, Hizbullah moved from being a closed sectarian social movement to an open national actor employing the policy of *infitah* and engagement in Lebanese domestic political life.

Hizbullah's views on the Islamic State

None of Hizbullah's 1992, 1996, 1998, 2000, 2004, and 2005, 2009, and 2010 parliamentary and municipal election programs, including its 30 November 2009 Manifesto, mention, refer to, or advocate the founding of an Islamic state in Lebanon. Hizbullah emphasized that the establishment of an Islamic state could not be the result of the logic or adoption by a certain group or faction of people, who enforce it or enforce their own opinions on other groups or factions in society. Hizbullah neither applies nor accepts coercion in its project of Islamization; rather they propose that the establishment of an Islamic state should be the result of freedom, will, and direct choice of the people. Thus, Hizbullah asserts it will only move in the direction of implementing an Islamic State in Lebanon on the basis of a democratic, tolerant process sanctioned by the majority of non-Muslims and Muslims.[38]

It seems that due to a pragmatic change in political strategy, Hizbullah has put to rest, once and for all, the issue of the establishment or implementation of an Islamic state in Lebanon. That is why its political program can be regarded as pragmatic. This accounts for Hizbullah's participation in electoral politics, and its decision to take an active part in the Lebanese public sphere. There is a probability that Hizbullah embraced its down-to-earth and practical political programs since it is apparent that it was counterproductive and politically unwise to remain committed to its earlier conception of an Islamic order. However, there appears to be a discrepancy between these political programs and the discourse of its leaders who continue to give lip service to the old ideological commitment of establishing an Islamic order. It is most likely that Hizbullah was guided by political necessity since in its political programs it has accepted the fact that the majority of the Lebanese do not wish to opt for an Islamic order, and imposing it by compulsion is an unacceptable option.

Hizbullah's dialogue with the Lebanese Christians

In conformity to Sayyid Abbas's 1991 political program, which called for a Lebanization process, *infitah*, and dialogue, most notably, with the Christians, Hizbullah took the initiative in 1992 and visited the Maronite patriarch. The talks centered mostly upon Christian-Muslim dialogue and Hizbullah's gradual integration into the Lebanese public sphere. However, with the passage of time, Hizbullah's dialogue did not remain confined to Maronites and it was extended to encompass the rest of the Christians that comprise the Lebanese mosaic. Hizbullah conducted dialogue with the Christians and other groups on the basis of transparency in order to define common grounds. As to the content and subjects of the dialogue, Hizbullah tried to avoid engagement in theological or religious issues, which have specific and particular meaning for every sect of religion in Lebanon, and concentrated on nurturing dialogue dealing with political, socio-economic, civic and societal issues. In its political program, Hizbullah blamed political sectarianism for Lebanon's malaise, calling for its abolishment in line with Lebanon's 1990 new constitution. Hizbullah embarked on an open, peaceful, and constructive dialogue with all sects, political parties, civil society groups and organizations in order to tackle the source or origin of cultural, political, theoretical, and practical differences. The 2006 national dialogue sessions conducted by the fourteen leading politicians in Lebanon dealt with such issues, including taboos such as Hizbullah's weapons and its defense strategy. Nasrallah, in person, took care to convey Hizbullah's stance, being in a strong position after his party managed, on 6 February 2006, to strike a ten-point understanding with the Free Patriotic Movement (FPM) headed by the Maronite general Michel 'Aun, who claimed to have received 70 percent of the Christian votes in the 2005 legislative elections and 50 percent of the Christian votes in the 2009 legislative elections.[39]

Hizbullah tried to portray itself as a principal promoter of Muslim-Christian coexistence stressing the importance of pluralism through multi-confessional representation. It incorporated Christians, including Maronites, in its parliamentary elections lists and granted them the right to speak in its name as long as they do not deflect from the party's established doctrines. Also, it shared municipal council seats with Christians. Thus, Hizbullah made it clear that the only condition for a sympathizer to speak in its name is to abide by its policy guidelines. Hizbullah's dialogue with the Christians, as stipulated in its political program, garnered the party support for its resistance against Israel and its *infitah* policies, especially among the Christians. By adopting what many observers might consider a 'Christian discourse', namely, the abolition of political sectarianism in the people's mentality, before abolishing it in the texts, Hizbullah is portraying a progressive-liberal, and pragmatic view towards the abolishment of political sectarianism, which is in conformity with the stance of the Maronite church and the papal guidance. The late pope's call for fraternity and the inculcation of dialogue and tolerance among the Lebanese had a responsive cord in Hizbullah's circles since most of it was reminiscent of Imam Musa al-Sadr's discourse on Christian-Muslim understanding, mutual coexistence, and open and permanent dialogue.[40] Hence, in an endeavor of rapprochement towards the Lebanese Christians, Hizbullah based its political program of dialogue with them on the papal guidance.[41]

According to a Hizbullah ideologue Shaykh Shafiq Jaradi[42], the Rector of *Al-Ma'arif Al-Hikmiyya* College, the concept of the *ahl al-dhimma* – which constituted part of the Prophetic tradition in the nascent Islamic state and continued to be practised throughout Islamic history, and in which *dhimmis* were obliged to pay the poll tax (*jizya*) – no longer informs Hizbullah's ideology. He and the intellectual Abd Al-Halim Fadlallah[43] contended that Hizbullah replaced the *dhimmi* concept by the concept of citizenship (*muwatana*), where both Muslims and non-Muslims should be treated equally under the umbrella of promulgated standing laws. As such the concept of *jizya* became unnecessary due to the removal of the need that gave rise to it in the first place. Both stressed that, even in the Islamic state, the *dhimmis* enjoy the same rights and privileges as any Muslim citizen. Like Jaradi, Fadlallah reiterated that Islam is a tolerant religion: no compulsion in religion;[44] quoting the Prophet, "There is no difference between a Muslim and a non-Muslim except on the grounds of piety… all believers are brothers."

Jaradi emphasized that Hizbullah's discourse and practice convey tolerance and acceptance of the other. Quoting a saying attributed to Imam 'Ali, he stressed that Hizbullah is primarily concerned with the human being and humanity at large: "People are of two types: either a brother in religion or a peer in morality, either a brother in Islam or an equal in humanity". (*Al-Nass sinfan: imma ahkun laka fi al-din, aww nadhirun laka fi al-khalaq*). Building on Imam 'Ali's statement, Abd Al-Halim Fadlallah employed his own *ijtihad* (independent reasoning) stressing, "we are all brothers in humanity" ("*kuluna ikhwa fi al-insaniyya*").[45] Jaradi portrayed Islam as a way of life and a message (*risala*). He added that only through dialogue could a common understanding be reached. Jaradi cited verse 16:125 of the Qur'an:

> Call to the way of your Lord with 1) wisdom and 2) mild exhortation, and 3) argue with them in the best manner. Your Lord surely knows best those who stray from His path, and He knows well those who are rightly guided (*id'i ila sabili rabik bi al-hikma wa al-maw'iza al-hasana, wa jadilhum bi al-lati hiya ahsan…*).

So *da'wa* may only be with the Qur'an, not the 'sword'[46] or other compulsion (*Jadiluhum bi al-lati hiya ahsan*: debate with them on the basis of that which is better).

In the political sphere, Sayyid Ibrahim al-Musawi, a Hizbullah intellectual, argued that Hizbullah applies the concept of citizenship in actual practice since the party had agreed to participate in the political system *as it is*, abiding by the Ta'if stipulation of evenly dividing political office between Christians and Muslims, although demographically the latter constitute the majority of the population. As he puts it: "Hizbullah has accepted, and continues to accept, to give a larger share of the political representation to the Christians in Lebanon, more than their real proportion to the total population, as a way to ensure the social and political stability of the country." According to al-Musawi this demonstrates the party's ability to give priority to preserving the concept of citizenship and civil society through the practice of tolerance and acceptance of the 'other': "All people are the family of God, and the most cherished by God is the one who is good to them."[47]

It seems that the Hizbullah cadres quoted above agree with Gebran Khalil Gebran: "Pity the nation that is full of beliefs and empty of religion." Gebran regarded sects/denominations as social phenomena that rely on human interests. He considered belief/faith as love, the love of God.[48]

In its 30 November 2009 Manifesto, Hizbullah paid special attention to the plight of the Christian Arabs and admonished against discord and sectarian strife that are rupturing the *umma*:

> Our societal cohesion is threatened by heightened sectarian tensions and instigated confessional frictions, especially between the Sunnis and the Shi'ites. The fabrication of national contradictions between the Kurds, Turkmen and Arabs, and between the Iranians and the Arabs, *the intimidation of minorities, the continuous hemorrhage suffered by Christian Arabs in the East and especially in Palestine, Iraq, and Lebanon*, are all factors that menace our societal structure, reduce collective immunity, and intensify those barriers against renaissance and development.[49]

1.5 CONCLUSION: FROM DHIMMIS TO CITIZENS

In the 1980s, Hizbullah advocated the establishment of an Islamic state in Lebanon and maintained the potential of an *ahl al-dhimmi* category. In spite of Hizbullah's exhortation of the Christians to convert to Islam, it did not seek to impose this conversion by force. Rather, the party applied its theory of tolerance to those Christians living in its constituencies, as well as to other Christians, as long as they were not 'treacherous or aggressive'. In conformity with the Prophetic tradition and the Qur'an, Hizbullah stressed that there should be "no compulsion in religion" and an "equitable world" or common grounds that should guide relationships between Muslims and Christians. As such, Hizbullah stressed that the common grounds between *ahl al-dhimma* and Muslims are the social values of mutual tolerance, respect, brotherhood, and solidarity. On this basis, Hizbullah recognized the human freedom, i.e. social and religious freedom of Christians, but *not* the political autonomy as was the case in the 1926 French Mandate Constitution and 1943 Independence Constitution. Thus, in the 1980s, contrary to the Prophetic tradition that granted non-Muslims partnership in political structures, Hizbullah's tolerance or 'inclusiveness' excluded Christians from political life, which could be regarded as a discriminatory practice. Hizbullah's then policy seemed to imply that tolerance is the responsibility of the 'majority' and integration is the responsibility of the 'minority'. Most likely Hizbullah's attitude towards Christians as *dhimmis* was a specific interpretation of the Prophet's political Constitution of Medina, but it may also have been inspired by the Islamic Republic of Iran's constitution. It is a further possibility that Hizbullah might have been influenced towards change by the late leading Lebanese *marja'* (religious authority) Ayatullah Sayyid Muhammad Husayn Fadlallah who, grounding his argument in the Qur'an, argued that the Muslim stance towards Christians is anchored upon the horizon of mutual coexistence, cooperation, and dialogue that should be based on points of convergence and common grounds with which all parties agree.

Since the early 1990s, Hizbullah regarded founding an Islamic state as a 'legal abstraction' and dropped their demands for its implementation in Lebanon. This paved the way for the party to employ the concept of *muwatana* (citizenship) instead of *ahl al-dhimma*. Hizbullah's intellectuals based this current practice on a new interpretation of the Prophetic tradition as sanctioned by Shi'ite jurisprudence. And so, from the 1980s to the 1990s and into the 21st century, Hizbullah has made great strides forward in acknowledging the human, civil, economic, social, cultural, and most importantly the political rights of the so called ex-*dhimmis*, recognizing their right to full citizenship, citizens of equal status and rights. This is not a rhetorical shift, rather it is a major policy alteration being implemented and aimed at making the 'other' secure in a shared Lebanese polity that might one day be dominated by the Shi'ite majority.

2 Interpretation and Authority: *Wilayat Al-Faqih*[1]

ABSTRACT

After three decades of the 'victory' of the Islamic Revolution in Iran it is worthwhile to study how Imam Khumayni's initial theory of *wilayat al-faqih* has developed in the political thought of Hizbullah as regards to the framework of molding and interpreting the original theory to make it adaptable to the Lebanese social and political conditions. Hizbullah employed *wilayat al-faqih* as a cornerstone in its religious-political ideology from 1978 to the present. The party managed to mold the doctrine through the successive changes in the political system by shifting its ideology in order to become a key player capable of affecting the dynamic changes taking place in the Lebanese public sphere. Although it is assumed in many circles that Hizbullah is the proxy of Syria and Iran, concentrating on the assumed Iranian influence, this chapter argues that Hizbullah pursued an independent course of action in its attempt to influence the Lebanese political system.

2.1 INTRODUCTION

Most secondary sources brand Iran and its contended "brainchild", the Lebanese resistance movement Hizbullah, with militant revolutionary tendencies, which do not conform to the tenets of the international community's standards of democratic values that govern civil society. Is Hizbullah an Iranian party operating in Lebanon, or a Lebanese militant party supported by Iran, which has to obey Iran and be its tool of policy in the Middle East?

Hizbullah was able to modify its identity from its founding as an Islamic movement of social and political protest (1978-1985), to a full-fledged social movement (1985-1991), to a parliamentary political party (1992 to the present). Hizbullah tried to preserve its Islamic identity, and at the same time, work within the confines of the Lebanese political system. On these grounds, the party recognized the Lebanese state. In spite of being perceived as having a political-strategic partnership with Syria[2] and a strategic-ideological alliance with Iran[3], Hizbullah is not a mere tool of policy in Syrian and Iranian hands. On the contrary, the party has pursued an independent course of decision making in conformity with the specificities (*khususiyyat*) of the Lebanese political equation, until it succeeded in May 2008 in obtaining veto power in the cabinet, the council of ministers, the main executive body of the country, thus controlling the political system to a greater extent. After its defeat in the June 2009 legislative elections, it backtracked and contented itself with the participation of two of their ministers in a power-sharing cabinet, waiving its earlier gain of veto power for the sake of consensual democracy, as it revealed in its 2009 Manifesto.

After three decades of the 'victory' of the Islamic Revolution in Iran it is worthwhile to study how Imam Khumayni's initial theory of *wilayat al-faqih* (guardianship of the jurisprudent or jurisconsult) has developed in the political thought of the Lebanese Hizbullah regarding the framework of molding and interpreting the original theory to make it adaptable to the Lebanese social and political conditions. In the 1980s, Hizbullah regarded *wilayat al-faqih*, as defined by Khumayni, as its true Islamic cultural identity and adopted it, in its original formulation, under the motto of: "The Islamic Revolution in Lebanon". Hizbullah recognized Khumayni as the official *marja' al-taqlid* (religious-legal authority of emulation) of the Islamic Republic and as the first *faqih* (jurisprudent, jurisconsult) after *al-ghayba al-kubra* (Great Occultation), and in contemporary history, to assume the title of the deputy of Imam al-Mahdi and to establish an Islamic state. As such, Hizbullah followed the religious authority of Iran and paid homage and allegiance to Khumayni as the political and religious leader of the *umma*, and abided by his *wilayat al-faqih* as a major pillar in its religious-political ideology. Hizbullah clarified that from a religious and ideological stance, it regarded Khumayni with high esteem; after his death, the same allegiance and respect was accorded to Khamina'i, his officially chosen successor. Hizbullah based its argument, in the Lebanese context, on demographic realities (the fact that the Muslims constitute the majority of the population) and proposed that Lebanon become part of the overall encompassing Islamic state. Hizbullah's cadres argued for the necessity of establishing an Islamic order, stressing that social change must begin from the top by changing the political system and annihilating the ruling elite through a top-down revolutionary process.

With the end of the sixteen-year civil war in 1990, Hizbullah's post-Ta'if[4] discourse continues to portray a different image of its buttressing of civil society and democratic processes that encourage more social and political integration, rather than violence. Although the liberalization process in Iran might have affected Hizbullah's policies, it did not at the expense of Hizbullah's autonomy of decision making and the Lebanese specificities. Is the Lebanese political structure forcing Hizbullah to take decisions that are not popular to the rank, file, and leaders? Is the Lebanese public sphere dictating a new strategy on Hizbullah, or is it transnational influences from Iran, or a little bit of both?

Starting in the 1990s, Hizbullah portrayed a post-Islamist phase moving from exclusion to inclusion through interpreting the doctrine of *wilayat al-faqih* in such a way that allows the party to maintain authority in the Lebanese sectarian-confessional system, apparently without compromising its doctrinal foundations. Employing a bottom-up Islamization strategy[5], the party stressed that its religious and political ideology defends the establishment of an Islamic state, but as a political program it is not practical because of the confessional and sectarian nature of Lebanon, on the one hand, and opposition by the majority of the Lebanese, both Christians and Muslims, on the other. In other words, Hizbullah shelved its political ideology and practiced a down-to-earth pragmatic political program in an endeavor to reach out to the largest possible sector of the Lebanese populace. This resulted in a dramatic change in Hizbullah's involvement in the Lebanese political system *as it is*. It not only participated in the parliamentary and municipal elections, but also, in 2005 joined the cabinet.

In order to question the alleged 'democratic character' of political Shi'ism and the 'authoritarian nature' of political Sunnism an anecdote is invoked. This is followed by Khumayni's 1988 religious edict (*fatwa*), which suggests an authoritarian nature of *wilayat al-faqih*. Based on these insights this chapter is divided into three parts demonstrating how Hizbullah employed the *wilayat al-faqih* doctrine in Lebanon as a cornerstone in its religious-political ideology from 1978 to the present, and how the party managed to mold the doctrine through the successive changes in the political system by shifting its ideology in order to become a key player capable of affecting the dynamic changes taking place in the Lebanese public sphere. Although it is assumed in many circles that Hizbullah is the proxy of Syria and Iran, concentrating on the Iranian influence, this chapter shows that the party pursued an independent course of action in its attempt to control the Lebanese political system.

2.2   ANECDOTE: MICHEL FOUCAULT IN KARBALA'!

23 April 2003 coincided with the fortieth day in the commemoration of the 'martyrdom' of Imam Husayn that occurred centuries ago in Karbala' in 61 AH/ 680 AD. It was the first time in around 35 years that the Iraqi Shi'ites were free to participate in the pilgrimage to the holy city of Karbala'. A crowd of people estimated to be at least one million celebrated the occasion. Ritual is indeed a construction of the sacred[6]: the barefooted pilgrims beat their chests, slashed their scalps with swords, and whipped themselves with chains. They were not alone; Michel Foucault[7] was there!

Foucault's reading of the Islamic Revolution is noteworthy since he saw in it a spiritual-esoteric dimension embedded in the heart of the political realm, in the sense that spiritualism takes from politics an eventuality or a place in which to ferment. It seems that Foucault judged rather fast in his reading and vision of the revolution when he made the analogy between democracy and Shi'ism, on the one hand, and Sunnism and tyranny, on the other. Not only that, Foucault considered that there are safeguards militating against the Shi'ite *ulama* – the leaders of the theoretic republic – to keep it from transforming into tyranny. However, these bones of contention should not prevent the reader from seeing Foucault's new vision at the time; namely, his innovation of the concept of 'political spiritualism'. According to him, 'political spiritualism' is based upon the premise that the esoteric dimension of the revolution would, in the final analysis, outweigh its exoteric aspect, especially since the 'holy commemorational dimension' and 'political opposition' are intertwined. Foucault considered Shi'ism not only to be an ideological tool used by the revolutionaries against the authority[8], but also to be rooted in resistance and opposition to power and tyranny as such. He contended that Shi'ism contains a political stance different from any other because it is based on the desire of the self to be completely "different from what it is now."[9] Foucault's religious discourse gives room for humanistic ambitions since these ambitions are not only economical or nationalistic, but also based on a metaphysical dimension. This explains, across Shi'ite history, the transformation of mobilization to a political force, which became a model for an 'extreme desire' in social and organic solidarity, in the Durkheimian sense. The Islamic Revolution afforded fundamental importance to the Foucaultian problematic, even if it later on took a different twist than his original expectations. What can be expected today from the Karbala' populace? Could there be any materialization of either the esoteric dimension or 'political spiritualism'? On this occasion Sayyid Hasan Nasrallah, Hizbullah's secretary-general, argued, "The US wants us to witness only defeat", insinuating that the Karbala' populace would mark a 'spirited resistance' to the US presence in Iraq.[10] It is most likely that the aforementioned statement could be construed along the lines of Foucault's notions. Not surprisingly, Nasrallah's annual 'Ashura discourse embeds the esoteric dimension, especially spiritualism. In January 2009, he invoked what remains of God on earth: "*ya baqiyya min Allah 'ala al-ard*".

2.3 THE CONTROVERSY SURROUNDING THE INTERPRETATION OF WILAYAT AL-FAQIH DOCTRINE: KHUMAYNI'S 1988 FATWA

During Khumayni's final days, there appeared to be a kind of emerging problem vis-à-vis the prerogatives of the jurisprudent (*al-waliyy al-faqih*)[11]. Sayyid 'Ali Khamina'i, the president of the Islamic Republic at the time and the current *faqih*, declared in his Friday speech of 31 December 1988[12] his condemnation of the expanded prerogatives of the Minister of Labor, thus indirectly criticizing the theory of absolute *wilaya* (*al-wilaya al-mutlaqa*) or the comprehensive authority of the *faqih*. Khamina'i remarked that the comprehensive authority of the *faqih* is something separate from the function of the state. He added that it is still unclear, even to those who were supposed to preach it, let alone to rule according to it. The incident outraged Khumayni and prompted him to write a letter aimed at clarifying and defending his theory, thus introducing new prerogatives pertaining to the space of authority the *faqih* is entitled to.

Among other things, in his *fatwa* Khumayni stressed,

> it is incumbent upon me to clarify that government branches from the Prophet's absolute *wilaya* and is one of the primary injunctions of Islam, thus takes precedence over all secondary ordinances, even over prayer, pilgrimage, and fasting... the government can one-sidedly annul any *shari'i* [religious] treaties conducted with the populace, if it considers it in opposition to the interests [*masalih, sing. maslaha*] of the *umma* or Islam. Further, the government could thwart any religious or non-religious practice if it regards it detrimental to the interests of Islam or if it deems it so.[13]

Therefore, Khumayni stipulated that the *maslaha* of the Islamic order, or its agencies, gains priority over any other principle in social and political affairs.

As such, Khumayni developed the theory of absolute *wilaya* in a way that could perfectly serve his political ends through giving the *faqih* absolute political and religious power. Khumayni's innovation was to unequivocally and cogently transform *wilayat al-faqih* into a system of political administration. Thus, Khumayni in his capacity as the *faqih* and *marja' al-taqlid*, blended *Imama* (Imamate) with *wilaya* and *marja'iyya* (religious authority), which is a precedent in Shi'ite religio-political ideology. This is of vital importance since in Shi'ite jurisprudence "the ruler's injunction abrogates the jurist's *fatwa*" (*hukum al-hakim yanqud fatwa al-mujtahid*), if the *maslaha* of the Islamic order requires such a course of action.[14] Thus, Khumayni believed in and practiced absolute *wilaya*. And so, it seems that Khumayni's 1988 *fatwa* qualified Foucault's claim of democratic aspects and lack of tyranny in political Shi'ism.

2.4 FIRST STAGE (1978-1985)

Wilayat al-faqih
Khumayni's *wilayat al-faqih* was successfully imported to Lebanon, serving as a blue print of a progressive Islamic state that was emulated to the letter by Hizbullah in its constituencies. Illustrating the vital importance given to becoming a member of '*Ummat* Hizbullah', a Hizbullah cadre told me on condition of anonymity that a person, who tried to join the party but failed the process of screening (*ta'tir*) that Hizbullah's prospective members undergo three times, came with a bomb action assault rifle and killed his recruiting officer. Another member told me that as practice of indoctrination and as a baptism/initiation ceremony, new Hizbullah recruits had to repeatedly state: "If the jurisprudent told you to kill yourself, then you have to do it" (*idha qala laka al-waliyy al-faqih 'an auqtul nafsak, fa 'alayka dhalik*).[15] This not only illustrates indoctrination, but also the total obedience to the *faqih*.

In the early 1980s, Khumayni instructed Khamina'i, who was at the time deputy Minister of Defense, to take full responsibility of the Lebanese Hizbullah. Since then, Khamina'i became Hizbullah's 'godfather'. That is why, since its inception, Hizbullah, based on a religious and ideological stance, fully abides by the ideas and opinions of Khumayni as communicated by Khamina'i. During that period, the religious-ideological bond between the Islamic Republic of Iran and Lebanon could be examined from the following declarations by Hizbullah and Iranian officials. Shaykh Hasan Trad: "Iran and Lebanon are one people in one country"; Sayyid Ibrahim Amin Al-Sayyid: "We do not say that we are part of Iran, we are Iran in Lebanon and Lebanon in Iran";

Ali Akbar Muhtashami: "We are going to support Lebanon politically and militarily like we buttress one of our own Iranian districts"; Shaykh Hasan Srur: "We declare to the whole world that the Islamic Republic of Iran is our mother, religion, *Ka'ba*, and our veins".[16]

2.5   SECOND STAGE (1985-1991)

Wilayat al-faqih
In stages one and two, Hizbullah argued that during the early phase of its formation, it needed a unifying religious-political ideology, rather than an elaborate political program. So Hizbullah based itself on *wilayat al-faqih* and regarded Khumayni as the jurisconsult of *all* the Muslims.[17] In stage one, Hizbullah was, ideologically, completely dependent on Khumayni. In stage two this dependency witnessed some leeway in the sense that Hizbullah did not blindly follow the Iranian regime; rather it had some specificity (*khususiyya*), since in his capacity as the Supreme Leader (*Rahbar*) he was endowed with the sole right to determine the legitimacy (legitimate authority) to Hizbullah. Khumayni highlighted certain precepts within which Hizbullah could move freely; however, he left their implementation to the party's discretion. Thus, although Hizbullah was ideologically dependent on the Iranian regime, it had some room to maneuver in its decisions pertaining to some cases in Lebanese domestic issues. Even though the multiplicity of *marja's* among the Shi'ites continued after Khumayni's death, in Hizbullah's case the issue of *marja'iyya* has been determined on the doctrinal-ideological basis of following the official *marja' al-taqlid*, who is recognized by the Islamic Republic of Iran. Thus, Hizbullah's religious authority was, still is, and will continue to be the Iranian *faqih*. This made the transition after Khumayni's death smoother in the end of the second stage and the beginning of the third stage.

2.6   ISLAMIC STATE IN RELATION TO WILAYAT AL-FAQIH (STAGES I AND II)

In the first and second stages (1978-1991), Hizbullah considered the Qur'an as the constitution of the Islamic *umma*, and Islam both a religious as well as a governmental order (*din wa dawla*). Hizbullah enjoined the Muslims to strive, using all legitimate means, in order to implement the Islamic order, wherever they might be.[18]

In stages one and two, Hizbullah considered the Lebanese political system, which is dominated by the political Maronites, as a *jahiliyya* (pre-Islamic pagan) system. Hizbullah applied this classification to every non-Islamic system: be it patriotic, democratic, or nationalistic, even if it were to be governed by Muslims.[19] In other words, in the first and second stages, Hizbullah pursued the establishment of an Islamic state, respectively from the perspective of a religious and a political ideology. Religious ideology, as Hizbullah's leading cadres argued, was to instate God's sovereignty and divine governance on earth through *hakimiyya* and the execution of God's law by instituting an Islamic order as a *taklif shar'i* (religious and legal obligation).[20] As a political ideology, Hizbullah did not want to impose the Islamic order by force unless an overwhelming majority of the Lebanese voted in its favor through a referendum. This should be taken with apprehension since Hizbullah's rhetoric, in stages one and two, was different from what it was actually doing in reality; in the sense of being actively engaged in preparing the ground for establishing an Islamic order, at least in its constituencies.

2.7 THIRD STAGE (1992 TO THE PRESENT)

Wilayat al-faqih
The year of 1992 was a central year in shaping Hizbullah's evolving identity. The party faced a challenge in deciding whether to participate in the parliamentary elections or not. Hizbullah's 12-member committee took a positive decision after much heated internal debate and discussions,[21] followed by Iranian arbitration (*tahkim*). Since *the faqih* is the one who determines 'legitimacy' (even in practical political matters), Khamina'i had to intercede and grant legitimacy for participation.[22] This caused a considerable schism within Hizbullah because Subhi al-Tufayli, Hizbullah's first secretary-general, contested the decision and pursued a confrontational stance with both the party and the Lebanese state.[23]

By interpreting the doctrine of *wilayat al-faqih* in a new light, the committee recommended that participation in the elections be a beneficiary must, which is in harmony with Hizbullah's holistic vision that favors living up to the expectations of the people by serving their socio-economic and political interests. It added that Hizbullah's greater *jihad* and dedication to addressing the plight of the people does not contradict its priority of smaller military *jihad* for the sake of the liberation of occupied land. As such, participating in the elections leads to the achievement of good political results, and is also regarded as a leading step towards interaction with others. By this Hizbullah presents a novel experience in the *infitah* ('opening-up') of a young Islamic party. The committee stressed that this participation is in accordance with the Lebanese specificities as well as the nature of the proposed elections, which allow for a considerable margin of freedom of choice. In short, the committee concluded that the sum total of the pros (*masalih*) outweighs the cons (*mafasid*) by far. That is why participation in the parliament is worthwhile since it is viewed as one of the ways of influencing change and making Hizbullah's voice heard, not only domestically, but also regionally and internationally through the podiums made available to the members of parliament.[24] Thus, it seems that Hizbullah was forced by the political circumstances, the Ta'if Agreement, Lebanon's new 1990 constitution, and the end of the civil war, to change to a new phase in its history by propagating a matter-of-fact political program and by co-opting with the Lebanese system.

2.8 HIZBULLAH GAINS MORE INDEPENDENCE IN DECISION MAKING, CONSOLIDATING ITS FINANCIAL RESOURCES: NGOS AND CIVIL INSTITUTIONS[25]

A further shift occurred in the interpretation of the authority of *the faqih* in the third stage when Hizbullah argued that it does not consider the regime in the Islamic Republic of Iran as the jurisconsult of *all* the Muslims, and in consequence, not all Islamic movements have to abide by the orders and directives of the *faqih* or the regime.[26] Another shift occurred, when, in May 1995, Khamina'i appointed Nasrallah, and Shaykh Muhammad Yazbik, head of the religio-judicial council, as his religious deputies (*wakilayn shar'iyyan*) in Lebanon. This move granted Hizbullah special prerogatives and delegated responsibilities (*taklif shar'i*) that reflect a great independence in practical performance. Thus, Hizbullah consolidated its financial resources since the one-fifth religious tax (*khums*) imposed on those Lebanese Shi'ites who follow Khamina'i as their authority of emulation (*marja'*), as well as their alms (*zakat*) and religious (*shar'i*) monies have poured directly into Hizbullah coffers, instead of being channeled through Iran, as had been the case. Already before 1995, these monies had allowed Hizbullah to found an efficient network of NGOs and social welfare institutions that are open to the public irrespective of communal origin. These include the Martyr's Association, the Association of the Wounded, the Association of Lebanese Prisoners[27], the Islamic Resistance Support Association, the Institution of the Good Loan, the Association of Islamic Health, the Institution of Construction and Development, the Association of the Relief Committees of Imam Khumayni, and the Association of Islamic Pedagogy and Education, all established over the period 1982-1991. In addition, Hizbullah boasts its own media and research institutions. Its weekly mouthpiece *al-'Ahd*, established in 1984, was renamed *al-Intiqad*[28] (in 2001); it founded *Baqiyyat Allah* Journal in 1991 with the aim of inculcating Islamic values and culture. Its think tank, the Consultative Center for Studies and Documentation (CCSD), and its *al-Nour* satellite radio station were both founded in 1988. The flagship *al-Manar*[29] TV, the only satellite channel belonging to an Islamist movement in the Middle East, was watched by 18 million people in 2009.[30]

The interpretation of authority took another dramatic shift after the Syrian withdrawal in April 2005. In conformity with its policy to change when circumstances change, Hizbullah seems to switch from Iranian to local authority when it suits its purposes. Although the watershed decision to participate in the Lebanese cabinet ideologically required the *shar'i* judgment and legitimacy of the *faqih*, Hizbullah set a precedent by apparently securing the legitimacy from Shaykh 'Afif al-Nabulsi[31] – the head of the Association of Shi'ite Religious Scholars of *Jabal 'Amil* (*Ra'is Hay'at 'Ulama' Jabal 'Amil*)[32] in south Lebanon – and not Khamina'i, which indicates more independence in decision making. Thus, Hizbullah heeds Lebanese religious authority in addition to the Iranian one and therefore, Hizbullah's participation in the Lebanese cabinet was relegated to an administrative matter. As a consequence, Hizbullah's leadership was capable of taking independent decisions. Instantly, Hizbullah joined the cabinet with two ministers and proliferated in Lebanese state institutions and the administrative structure just before the conservative Iranian president, Mahmud Ahmadinejad, and his government were sworn to power in Iran. This led to increased Lebanonization that is more in line with the specificities of the Lebanese society, rather than blind adherence to Iran. And so, Hizbullah moved from complete ideological dependency on Khumayni in the first stage, to less dependency after his death in the second stage. Finally, in the third stage, Hizbullah gained more independence in decision making, not only in practical political issues, but also in military and doctrinal issues, to the extent that it seems as if Hizbullah exercised almost independent decision making, at least in some cases. Even in military matters Hizbullah does not always heed Iranian orders if they do not serve its overall interest (*maslaha*). Two cases in point that illustrate this trend are Sharon's 'April 2002 West Bank counterterrorism offensive' and Barak's December 2008-January 2009 'Operation Cast Lead' in Gaza. Iran strongly urged Hizbullah to open the northern front across the Lebanese-Israeli border in order to release pressure on the Palestinians[33], but Hizbullah adamantly refused because such a move was considered detrimental to its national interest.[34]

This trend continued after Ahmadinejad won a second term in the controversial June 2009 presidential elections.

Although Hizbullah was inspired by the Islamic Revolution, it operates like any ordinary political party functioning within a non-Islamic state and a multireligious, confessional, and sectarian state. While the Iranian Hizbullah was instrumental in building a state, the Lebanese Hizbullah cannot go beyond being a political party operating within the Lebanese public sphere. That is why, for instance, in the parliamentary elections, Hizbullah reached out and allied itself with secular parties and former enemies on the Lebanese scene, like any political party that accommodated its protest by negotiations and bargaining, making compromises on some doctrinal aspects. By engaging in a pluralistic process, Hizbullah moved from cooptation to contestation, and finally to exercising empowerment (*tamkin*). Hizbullah's participation in electoral politics could be regarded as cooptation. The party's gradual integration in the Lebanese public sphere falls under contestation. Hizbullah's ascendancy to the political scene becoming a nationalistic political party could be viewed from the stance of empowerment.

2.9 LEBANONIZATION[35] OR INFITAH ('OPENING-UP')

In the first two stages Hizbullah viewed its mission to liberate Lebanon from the shackles of political Maronism and the Lebanese sectarian-confessional political system that is based upon 'situational laws' – (*al-qawanin al-wad'iyya*), that is to say, positive (man-made) laws and legislations such as state constitutions – and establish instead the *shari'a* (Islamic law), which could only be instated by *hakimiyya* through a pure and uncompromising Islamic order. Hizbullah argued that abiding by *al-qawanin al-wad'iyya* instead of Islamic *shari'a* is entirely prohibited both from a religious and political ideological perspective. In stage one, under the influence of Khumayni, Hizbullah argued that abiding by al-*qawanin al-wad'iyya* instead of Islamic *shari'a*, is totally un-Islamic.[36] In stage two, in line with Khumayni, Hizbullah argued that abiding by *al-qawanin al-wad'iyya* instead of Islamic *shari'a*, is the second out of four ways colonialism seeks to distort Islam.[37]

The major shift in the third stage is that Hizbullah became satisfied with *al-qawanin al-wad'iyya* and even contributed to their legislation through its MPs in the parliament. Hizbullah stressed that although the Qur'an, Sunna, and the *shari'a* are the sources and bases of legislation, some issues in life could be referred to other sources, which stands in direct contrast to Hizbullah's interpretation of *wilayat al-faqih* in the first two stages. Hizbullah argued that the *shari'a*, as a socially constructed phenomenon is flexible and can account for all the complexities of modern life.

The shift that happened in the third stage could be attributed to the transformation of Iranian politics after the death of Khumayni as well as to a change in Hizbullah's own internal dynamics. For instance, there was a clear alteration in the Iranian stance from Khumayni's 1986 *fatwa* – which stipulated that the Lebanese system is illegitimate and criminal and Khamina'i's argument for the necessity of the Muslims to rule Lebanon since they comprise the majority of the population[38] – to Khamina'i's 1992 ruling in favor of participation in the parliamentary elections, which Hizbullah interpreted as its unequivocal right to proliferate in the Lebanese political system as a whole, including state institutions and administration. As mentioned earlier, Hizbullah made compromises on some doctrinal issues by allying itself, in the legislative and municipal elections, on the same election slate, with ideological enemies, like any political party that accommodated its protest by negotiations and bargaining with a wide spectrum of groups across the Lebanese myriad. Thus, Hizbullah compromised its ideology in such a way to interpret its authority by shelving its demand for the founding of an Islamic state, which might seem contradictory to the tenets of *wilayat al-faqih*.

2.10 STAGE THREE: AN APPLICATION OF THE PROGRESSIVE NATURE OF SHI'ITE JURISPRUDENCE

Lebanon is our country and the country of our fathers and forefathers; it is also the country of our children and grandchildren and all future generations. We want it sovereign, free, independent, strong and unified… we reject partition and federalism.[39]

Bearing in mind that there are multiple paths of modernity available to the emerging Muslim public sphere leading to the creation of a new civil society, where Islamic values can be created and injected into new senses of a public space that is "discursive, performative, and participative,"[40] Nasrallah clarified that Hizbullah benefits from its jurisprudential vision which believes in the doctrine of *wilayat al-faqih* that gives it the legitimacy of having a political program in a multicultural, multireligious country characterized by pluralist groupings and forces, without encroaching upon its doctrinal-ideological, Islamic-religious convictions.[41] In May 2008, after the Hizbullah-led opposition gained veto power in the Lebanese cabinet, Nasrallah reiterated, "I am honored to be a member of the party of *wilayat al-faqih*. The just, knowledgeable, wise, courageous, righteous, honest, and faithful *faqih*… *Wilayat al-faqih* tells us [Hizbullah] that Lebanon is a multiconfessional, multireligious (*mutanawwi*, *muta'adid*) country that you have to preserve and uphold".[42] With this unshakable commitment to *wilayat al-faqih*, Hizbullah reformulated what it meant by an Islamic state by making a categorical distinction between *al-fikr al-siyasi* (political ideology) that it maintained and *al-barnamaj al-siyasi* (political program) that it promoted. From an ideological perspective Hizbullah is committed to an Islamic state, and it will not be dropped as a 'legal abstraction'. However, Hizbullah's political program has to take into account the political status quo and the overall functioning of the Lebanese political system. Hizbullah characterizes the Lebanese political situation as a complicated mold of sectarian-confessional specificities that prohibit the establishment of an Islamic state, not only from a practical perspective, but also from a doctrinal one. Hizbullah's political ideology stipulates that an Islamic state should be established on solid foundations having full legitimacy and sovereignty from the people. Since the general will of the Lebanese people is against the establishment of an Islamic state, then it is not plausible to establish one.[43] On 30 November 2009, after revealing Hizbullah's new political platform/Manifesto, which neither mentioned the Islamic state nor referred to *wilayat al-faqih*, Nasrallah affirmed in answer to a question that there is no contradiction/opposition between belief in *wilayat al-faqih*, on the one hand, and the erection of a strong institutionalized Lebanese state, on the other. On the contrary, *wilayat al-faqih* sanctioned and allowed Hizbullah's integration into the political system. Not only that, in line with the Vatican's position and the papal guidance, Nasrallah added that Hizbullah believes that Lebanon is a blessing and has accomplished great historical achievements. He reiterated Imam Musa al-Sadr's stance that "Lebanon is the definitive nation to all its citizens (*Lubnan watan niha'i li-jami' abna'ihi*)", which is in conformity with the Lebanese constitution.[44]

Thus, Hizbullah shifted its position through its acceptance of and engagement in the democratic process under a sectarian-confessional political and administrative system. More dramatically, Hizbullah's political program modified its demand from the abolition of political sectarianism, to the adoption of the political Maronite discourse, which stresses the abolition of political sectarianism in mentality, before eradicating it in the texts.[45] In line with the Ta'if Agreement, its earlier election programs, and Nabih Berri's recent call,[46] Hizbullah's 2009 Manifesto, called for the establishment of the 'National Body for the Abolition of Political Sectarianism' since sectarianism is perceived as a threat to consensual democracy and national coexistence.[47] Although Nasrallah deemed the sectarian system a tribal system, he clarified:

Let us be realistic. The abolition of political sectarianism is one of the most difficult issues and cannot be accomplished overnight… nobody can dictate how to
abolish it in a sentence or two. Rather, if after years of debate, ranging from five to
thirty years, we find out that political sectarianism cannot be abolished, then let
us be bold enough to say that what we agreed upon in the Ta'if Agreement cannot
be realized. But till then, the Lebanese need to establish the 'National Body for the
Abolishment of Political Sectarianism' in order to initiate the debate in a constructive manner.[48]

On 13 January 2010, Berri laid down his vision on a gradual plan for the
abolition of political sectarianism by initiating the 'National Body for the
Abolishment of Political Sectarianism'. Michel 'Aun, the leader of the Hizbullah allied Free Patriotic Movement (FPM), voiced his opinion arguing that
the abolition of political sectarianism should be linked to an overall political reform that delineates the effective limitations of the political system.
According to him, an arbitrary abolition of political sectarianism amounts to
a complete overhaul in the political system. 'Aun added that there are many
constitutional articles that need to be amended before entertaining the idea
of abolishing political sectarianism or putting it into practice.[49] The Maronite
Cardinal Mar Nasrallah Butrus Sfeir weighed on the debate reiterating the
need to abolishing political sectarianism from Lebanese people's mentality
before removing it from legal texts, or else nothing was bound to change. In
turn, PM Sa'd al-Hariri stressed that such an issue required the consensus of
all the Lebanese.[50] Some Christian right-wing parties contended that such a
move constitutes a threat to consensual democracy. Ironically, others called
for the establishment of the 'National Body for the Abolition of Hizbullah's
weapons'.[51] Basing itself on its demographic strength, Hizbullah called for
reducing the voting age from 21 to 18[52] and changing the electoral system
to proportional representation, which the party believed would give the 18
ethno-confessional communities more equitable representation.[53]

As a political remuneration for its acclaimed 'divine victory' in the July
2006 war[54] with Israel, Hizbullah asked for the formation of a national unity
cabinet, where the party and its Christian allies, mainly the FPM, wield the
one-third veto power, thus attempting to dominate the national political arena, after wielding power over the legislature and the presidency. The tug of
war between the Hizbullah-led opposition (March 8 Group), on the one hand,
and the Lebanese cabinet and its supporters (March 14 Trend), on the other,
led to a bitter polarization, which plunged Lebanon into 537 days of stalemate
and political deadlock, from 1 December 2006 to 21 May 2008. The political
agreement of 21 May – known as the 'Doha Accord' between March 14 and

March 8, negotiated by the Arab League – granted Hizbullah veto power in the next national unity 30-member cabinet[55] by a margin of eleven ministers, while March 14 acquired sixteen ministers and the president three. Hizbullah ended its sit-in in downtown Beirut and dismantled its tent city. After six months of vacuum in the seat of the presidency, something unprecedented in Lebanese history, the consensus president army commander general Michel Sulayman was elected on 25 May by 118 votes out of 127 MPs. The next day Hizbullah celebrated the eighth anniversary of the nearly complete Israeli withdrawal from Lebanon through a fiery speech delivered by Nasrallah, who stressed that Hizbullah abides by the Ta'if Agreement and will honor the Doha Accord to the letter, and will continue to participate in the political system as it is.[56] Nasrallah's stance remained the same after the fiasco of March 8 to become the majority in the June 2009 legislative elections.[57] This culminated in the formation of a national unity cabinet on 9 November 2009, based on the previously agreed power-sharing formula: fifteen seats for March 14; five for the centralist coalition of the president; and ten for March 8. Thus, contrary to its military power and demographic strength, in an endeavor to uphold consensual democracy, Hizbullah contented itself with two ministers.

2.11 CONCLUSION

Through heavy reliance on a strict application of Khumayni's *wilayat al-faqih* in the 1980s, 'Hizbullah – The Islamic Revolution in Lebanon' emerged as a strong internal organization with a limited following. Subhi al-Tufayli's firm, uncompromising political discourse and his repeated references to the establishment of an Islamic state, which was unprecedented in Lebanese political discourse, backfired domestically, alienating the party from other political and social movements and from the Lebanese public sphere to a great extent. Thus, Hizbullah's policies were counterproductive, leading to the failure of integration into Lebanese political life, especially after the party's initial vehement criticisms of the Ta'if Agreement.

Since the end of the civil war in 1990, Hizbullah has been confronting major developments in Lebanon: prominently, the emergence of a pluralistic public sphere and increasing openness toward other communities, political parties, and interest groups in the Lebanese myriad. Through a new interpretation of *wilayat al-faqih*, Hizbullah altered its discourse, priorities, and overall political outlook. The mixed confessional space in Lebanon led Hizbullah to move from marginalization to *infitah*, which led the party to become a major player in the Lebanese public sphere by participating in the parliamentary and municipal elections, and even obtaining veto power in PM Sany-ura's cabinet of 2008-2009. In short, since the early 1990s, Hizbullah started promoting its Islamic identity and agenda by following a pragmatic political program, mainly to allay the fears of Christians and other Muslims who were opposed to the Islamic state. In the meantime, Hizbullah remained faithful to its Shi'ite constituency by employing a bottom-up Islamization process and working within the Lebanese state's political and administrative structures, while, at the same time, establishing Islamic institutions within civil society.

And so, in the third stage Hizbullah faced the problem of reconciling its political ideology with political reality. Thus, the Party shifted from a *jihadi* outlook to a more flexible *shari'a* perspective. Hizbullah portrayed a distin-guished expediency in its political program in an attempt to reconcile, as much as possible, among its principles, aims, and political ideology, on the one hand, and the circumstances and its objective capabilities, on the other hand, by relying heavily on the jurisprudential concepts of necessity, vices, and interests as a kind of Islamic prima facie duty. This is how Hizbullah's pragmatism was conducive in forging a marriage of convenience between political ideology and political reality, to the extent of pursuing a policy of *infitah* sanctioned by its political program.

Thus, the logic of operating within the bounds of the Lebanese state pre-vailed over the logic of the revolution. The party justifies and legitimizes its political program by resorting to Qur'anic and jurisprudential bases. Signifi-cantly, the Shi'ite religio-political heritage conferred upon Hizbullah all the authenticity it needed in order to derive from it a political program based on flexibility and pragmatism. Relying on the progressive nature of Shi'ite juris-prudence, Hizbullah remolded, constructed, and interpreted its authority in such a way to render legitimacy to its participation in a pluralist polity based upon the quota system and patronage. And so, through this heavy reliance on Shi'ite jurisprudence, especially the concept of *maslaha*, Hizbullah was able to change parallel with the circumstances, through its pragmatic interpretation and metamorphosis of *wilayat al-faqih*. This proved to be flexible, capable of functioning in a multiconfessional, multireligious society such as Leba-non, and not only in, more or less, monolithic Iran where the overwhelming majority of the population are Twelver Shi'ites.

3 Political Violence: Terrorism and 9/11[1]

ABSTRACT

Highlighting the long lineage between Islamic and national resistance, this chapter examines the interrelation between the process of Hizbullah's domestic integration and its regional militancy. It focuses on Hizbullah's discourse on terrorism, particularly after 9/11. The next chapter attempts to analyze Hizbullah's political and religious dimensions of 'jihad' and suicide bombing ('martyrdom') for the different levels of action (domestic and regional) and also discusses the party's view of martyrdom and jihad in relation to the terrorism charge.

3.1 INTRODUCTION

The first meeting, after 9/11, of the Organization of Islamic Conference (OIC)[2], a 57 consortium of Islamic countries currently comprising around 1.6 billion Muslims, was held on 11-18 October 2003 in Putrajaya, Malaysia. In addition to addressing issues such as the Palestinian *Intifada*, and the situations in Iraq and Afghanistan, what topped the agenda was the endeavor to "absolve Islam from terrorism". In its final declaration, the OIC condemned as "criminal terrorist bombings" the attacks that targeted the UN headquarters and the Jordanian and Turkish embassies in Baghdad. Also, the OIC "called for the signing of a convention to 'distinguish between terrorism and the legitimate struggle for the right to self-determination of people living under occupation or foreign domination' [resistance]".[3] In a similar vein, Shafiq Masri, a Lebanese international law authority, earlier maintained that the international community failed to reach a consensus on a unified definition of terrorism. He added that international law distinguishes between terrorism and legitimate resistance. The latter is considered a legitimate exception to the exercise of violence for political aims. From this perspective, national resistance is legitimized in international law in the following two cases: 1) self-determination, and 2) resistance to occupation.[4] In a similar vein, on 25 August 2003, the Arab League endorsed a proposal that distinguishes between resistance and terrorism, and adopted it as a resolution. As such, the "Arab Agreement of Combating Terrorism" was amended "in order to distinguish between resisting occupation (which is considered a legitimate right and a national-patriotic duty) and terrorist activities".[5]

I suggest the Arabs and Muslims, till now, did not critically think about or analytically reflect upon the issue of terrorism. The OIC attempted to do that, but fell into the trap of highlighting the cherished distinction between "terrorism" and "resistance", thus retracting the problem to a definitional one. On the one hand, while the Arabs and Muslims are still searching for a unified-universal definition of terrorism, the world moves ahead, while they lag behind. Knowing that it is very difficult, if not quite impossible, to reach a common understanding of the definition of terrorism between terrorists and non-terrorists (resistance or freedom fighters), Arab and Muslim elites portray an ostrich-like behavior by insisting that "terrorism" and "resistance" are mutually exclusive. The fear is that this reasoning might boil down in the end to the following formula: terrorism is idiotic resistance (9/11), and resistance is intelligent terrorism or, as Skaykh Qaradawi puts it, "legitimate terrorism"[6] (Palestinian and Lebanese resistance, for instance). Consequently, the Arabs and Muslims are shooting themselves in the foot. On the other hand, in the West there is a consensus in condemning terrorism as a means to reach any objective, a means that is not sanctioned by any right, goal, or logic since it "targets innocent civilians". The West defines terrorism in a logical, coherent way because the "terrorist" is a person who equates a prohibited, illegal, and immoral means (terrorism) to an end in itself, which is destruction for the sake of destruction, the annihilation of the other by obliterating the self. From a theoretical perspective, I propose that terrorism, in general, is defective-blind violence, a violence not sure of itself, a violence very careful in negating "the terrorism charge", a violence that negates itself through itself. Terrorism is defective violence because it always needs a rogue to support it, a money launderer to "cleanse" its money, in order to cleanse it from the label of terrorism. Terrorism is defective violence since it extols its own dead as well as taking pride in the number of victims it has killed. The rogue tries to prove the artificial nature of modernity. Terrorism is violence that has no role in history because it is the negation of the will to live, as well as the will to power. Terrorism is neither confined to a specific religion nor to a certain identity.

In light of what has been said, I question what Hizbullah's view of terrorism is. Why is Hizbullah considered by most Lebanese and almost all Arabs and Muslims as a Lebanese national resistance movement, while it is classified by Israel, the US, Canada, Australia, the Netherlands, and others as a "terrorist organization"?

Synopsis of the chapter

In this chapter, I am going to put myself in Hizbullah's shoes to expose the party's own discourse, views, and arguments[7] on terrorism and 9/11, and some of the responses and polemics dealing with these issues. I follow Hinnebusch's "three conceptually distinct environments", which distinguish among the "domestic level", the "regional systematic level", and the "global (or international) level".[8] Domestically, Hizbullah pursued cooptation by integrating more into the Lebanese public sphere and following liberalization or *infitah* policies[9], even by adopting what many observers would consider "Christian discourse", namely, the abolition of political sectarianism in the people's mentality, before abolishing it in the texts (*ilgha' al-ta'fiyya al-siyassiyya fi al-nufus, qabla al-nusus*).[10] This, along with other moves, sheltered Hizbullah with additional legitimacy and gave it a freer hand in the regional confrontation, especially after the Israeli 'Grapes of Wrath' of 1996.[11] Since then, among the Lebanese, irrespective of their denominations, there emerged a national consensus that Hizbullah is the Lebanese resistance, not a terrorist organization.[12] Regionally, contrary to Hizbullah's elite discourse that claims no alterations have been made in the party's doctrines as a result of 9/11, I suggest that Hizbullah moved from its vocal support of the *Intifada* to logistically assisting the Palestinians by all means, including training and smuggling guns, as well as intelligence penetration into Israel proper, as the Israelis conceded. Indeed, as Blanford puts it, "Hizbullah's geopolitical priority is still to defeat Israel, and it will not allow other crises in the region to deflect the organization's efforts from that central goal".[13] Internationally – in spite of the perpetual US policy of classifying Hizbullah, since its inception, as a terrorist organization – Hizbullah, Ayatullah Fadlallah, and Iran, all condemned 9/11 as suicidal-terrorist attacks targeting innocent civilians. On these grounds, I take issue with Saad-Ghorayeb's conclusion that Hizbullah's "continued subordination of its domestic political role to its geostrategic concerns",[14] arguing that Hizbullah's integration in the Lebanese public sphere is, in general, in accordance with its political program, while the party's regional militancy is in agreement with its political ideology.[15]

In 1974, Sartre stated, "Terrorism is the atomic bomb of the poor". Sartre made this remark in reference to the 5-6 September 1972 PLO attack on Israeli athletes participating in the Olympic Games in Munich that claimed the lives of 11 Israelis. He labelled this attack as a liberation act conducted by "freedom fighters", not terrorists. Sartre was an advocate of social violence in order to counter the violence of the state. Compared to Hizbullah's position, Sartre is extremely radical because Hizbullah refuses to use violence against occupying forces outside the occupied lands.

Norton defines terrorism as "the intentional killing of innocent people for political aims". Based on this definition, he argues, "that is why terrorism earns such widespread opprobrium; it is a gross assault on people who are by definition innocent. But what of an attack on soldiers of an occupation force, or soldiers in battle… There is not much difficulty winning widespread if not unanimous support against terrorism of the first sort, but agreement breaks down very quickly when the victims are uniformed soldiers and the context is war or occupation… In the case of Lebanon and Israel, Israel occupied southern Lebanon for more than twenty years and left only after relentless and effective attacks on Israeli occupation forces. Was this resistance to occupation terrorism? In the hands of propagandists, terrorism is a useful rhetorical bludgeon, but America is compelled to recognize that for many of its Arab friends in the Middle East, Hizbullah's resistance was legitimate. In 1993 and 1996, Israel accepted 'ground rules' that expressly permitted the Lebanese to resist occupation".[16] In line with Norton, Goldstein defines terrorism as "political violence that targets civilians deliberately and indiscriminately".[17] Goldstein argues, "beyond this basic definition other criteria can be applied, but the definitions become politically modified: one person's freedom fighter is another's terrorist. More than guerrilla warfare, terrorism is a shadowy world of faceless and irregular tactics marked by extreme brutality".[18] In this chapter, I adopt Norton's and Goldstein's definition of terrorism as a working definition because it seems to entail the essential part of the standard definitions[19] and it seems to be an acceptable definition to the international community.

Thus, even though the West and most Islamic movements consider 9/11 as terrorist attacks[20], the point of departure is the distinction between what the West classifies as suicide operations and terrorism, and Islamic movements and Hizbullah deem legitimate acts of resistance. And so, when it comes to the definitions of terrorism, it seems both parties are caught in a prisoner's dilemma[21] since neither side is willing to compromise. Knowing that conflict within discourse disrupts the tendency to reach a wide audience, each party insists on employing an implicit discourse that claims the absolute truth, leaving little or no room for dialogue and understanding. As such, truth is defined by the dominant discourse, rather than the demotic (alternative) discourse.[22] It seems that the Western discourse has the upper hand due to its media hegemony.[23]

3.3 THE TERRORISM CHARGE

Keeping in mind Moussalli's argument that jihad "is neither suicide nor a campaign of atrocities"[24] and bearing in mind Masri's argument that national resistance is legitimized under international law in the case of resistance to occupation, Hizbullah's jihad materialized through its legitimate acts of resistance[25] and martyrdom operations against the Israeli occupying forces in southern Lebanon and the *Biqa'*. Byman rightly argues, "in Hezbollah's struggle to expel Israel from Lebanon in the 1990s, much of its activity vis-à-vis Israel was best characterized as guerrilla warfare rather than terrorism. The vast majority of Hezbollah's actions were focused on Israeli military personnel on Lebanese soil and intended to drive Israel out of the country".[26] And so, Hizbullah's Islamic Resistance inflicted heavy casualties on the Israeli side and was instrumental in driving the Israeli Defense Forces (IDF)[27] out of Lebanon by 25 May 2000 after 22 years of occupation.[28] Hinnebusch acknowledges "all the Arabs shared Lebanon's euphoria at Israel's evacuation of southern Lebanon under Hizbollah's pressure in June 2000".[29] Byman adds, "Faced with ferocious Hezbollah resistance, Israel withdrew to a 'security zone' in southern Lebanon and, 15 years later, left Lebanon altogether".[30] Also, Israeli based sources seem to acknowledge this as a fact. As Levitt puts it, "Following the withdrawal of the Israeli forces from south Lebanon in May 2000 (*for which it rightly claimed credit*), Hezbollah was obliged to scale back its guerrilla warfare against Israeli forces…"[31] (Italics added for emphasis). Indeed, with the Israeli withdrawal, the resistance was concentrated in the Lebanese Shib'a farms[32], which are still occupied by the Israeli forces.

Thus, the claim that Hizbullah is a "terrorist organization"[33], as most Western media and some governments label it[34], fails to comply with Lebanese reality. In this connection, Sayyid Hasan Nasrallah, Hizbullah's secretary-general, argues that the US brands Hizbullah with terrorism[35] exoterically or on the table, while esoterically or under the table, it is doing its utmost best to establish contact with it. However, according to Nasrallah, Hizbullah is refusing contact from the perspective of its ideological stance, power politics, and the interest of the stronger party. He added that the stick and carrot as well as rationalization policies employed by the US administration to contain and curtail Hizbullah's activities are of no avail.[36] Knowing that Hizbullah has legitimate and recognized parliamentary representation[37], I suggest that labelling Hizbullah as a 'terrorist organization', implicates Hizbullah's parliamentary bloc entitled 'Loyalty to the Resistance' (which includes Christians[38]) with terrorism. Byman acknowledges that "at home, Hezbollah is as much a social and political organization as it is a terrorist or guerrilla movement; abroad... It is embedded in Lebanese politics and society, unlike al Qaeda, is a stakeholder in the existing regional order, not a force bent on destroying it. This position has made Hezbollah stronger but has also forced it to become more cautious, cunning, and subtle."[39] It is not surprising then that some Western scholars have changed their views and no longer regard Hizbullah as a terrorist party. This attitude lends more weight to Hizbullah's integration in the Lebanese public sphere.

At the beginning of his writings, Martin Kramer branded Hizbullah with 'systematic terrorism' as conveyed in his 'Calculus of Jihad'[40] theory. Kramer altered his stance when he conceded that Hizbullah, unlike the PLO and others, did not engage in worldwide terrorist attacks against Israeli and American targets, rather it confined its struggle to the 'legitimate' act of resistance and liberation in southern Lebanon.[41] In this connection, Sayyid Ibrahim al-Musawi[42] argues that Israel is a 'terrorist state'[43], not the Lebanese resistance. He contends that from 1948 till the founding of the PLO there was not a single attack carried out against Israel from the Lebanese borders, yet Israel killed more than 100 civilians and wounded many others. Al-Musawi adds, in 1968, Israeli commandos blew up 13 Middle East Airlines (MEA) airplanes at the Beirut International Airport as a reprisal for an attack in Athens, by what they claimed to be "Lebanese-trained Palestinian" freedom fighters. Norton argues that "since the late 1960s, hundreds of thousands of Lebanese have been repeatedly displaced from their homes in the South, more often than not as a result of Israeli military action".[44] He adds, "since 1992, 14 Israeli civilians have died as a direct or indirect result of Hizbullah's attacks, while over 500 Lebanese and Palestinian civilians have died".[45] Furthermore, Norton continues, "in April 1996 alone, hundreds of thousands of civilians were driven north by IDF bombing... Israeli strikes on Lebanese power plants darkened much of Lebanon in 1996, 1999, and twice in 2000, causing damages estimated at $ 300 million".[46] As Norton puts it, in the beginning, the classical image of Hizbullah as depicted by Western media was the following: middle-aged men, with long beards and machete knives, thirsty for murder and terrorism. This hyperreality was overridden by another one, namely, "a handful of fanatics and terrorists who are only concerned with blowing up, drinking, gambling, and entertainment sports...”[47] Ranstorp writes, “contrary to the image of a group of fanatics [the Islamic Resistance is portrayed as] fighting for the liberation of Lebanon against a vastly superior army”.[48] Husem adds that the Islamic “resistance became increasingly viewed as a legitimate movement internationally”, especially after the de facto recognition it acquired from Israel and the US in 1993 and 1996 in the wake of ‘Operation Accountability’ and ‘The Grapes of Wrath’.[49] Norton has already endeavored to shatter this hyperreality on various occasions. He writes, “the long-standing view the U.S. and Israel have of Hizbullah as an irrevocably hostile terrorist organization has changed. The party’s gradual entry into the political arena in 1992 and its subsequent attraction to middle class members of the Shiite community has led Hizbullah’s members to become ‘Lebanese nationalists par excellence’”.[50] In this connection, Viotti and Kauppi write, “despite couching their agenda in Islamic terms, organizations such as Hizballah (Party of God) in Lebanon, Hamas in the West Bank of Israel… are also fuelled by nationalist sentiment”.[51] More emphatically, Hinnebusch argues that “… radical Islamic movements such as Hamas and Hizbollah are primarily manifestations of Arab national resistance to Israel rather than promoters of religious agenda”.[52] According to Husem, “the [Islamic] Resistance was increasingly recognized as a *national* resistance. The increasing positive exposure for the Resistance and the Hizbullah in Western academia and media contributed too to their growing international legitimisation”.[53]

Norton added that “Hizballah forces displayed impressive discipline” when they took over Lebanese territories evacuated by the IDF during the withdrawal from southern Lebanon.[54] In fact, in a gesture aimed at easing any possible tensions in the south after the Israeli withdrawal, Nasrallah said that unsatisfied, aggrieved people with the South Lebanon Army (SLA)[55] trials have individually prepared their cases and are ready to file independent lawsuits in order to appropriate their rights. Thus, Hizbullah resorts to *due process*, rather than vendettas and revenge. Hasan Fadlallah argues that Hizbullah is doing its best to make sure that the perpetrators of war crimes face the Lebanese state’s *legal* criminal justice and punishment.[56] In fact, Hizbullah honors and upholds *promulgated standing laws*. Bashar al-Asad, the Syrian president, argues “when the causes that led to the resistance are gone, I believe its members will go back to normal life and will choose other ways to serve their country after achieving the long-cherished victory”.[57] Norton argues that “Hizbullah fighters are totally integrated into Lebanese society… They have family ties, jobs if not professionals, homes, networks of social support, and hopes and aspirations for Lebanon”.[58] William Burns, the deputy US foreign secretary for the Near East, during his meeting with the Lebanese president, thanked the Lebanese government for its cooperation in the "war on terror". He conceded, "Hizbullah is a political party with a strong social and political base, but we [the Americans] are worried about its 'terrorist' activities, which require a deep, calm dialogue".[59]

In spite of Hizbullah's apparent integration into the Lebanese political and social life, on 21 May 2002, the US State Department released its annual report entitled "Patterns of Global Terrorism"[60] that argued that Hizbullah "furthers terrorism to achieve its ends" and claimed that Iran is the most salient in buttressing terrorism since it supplies militant Palestinian groups and Hizbullah with money, arms, and logistics.[61] Although the next day Hizbullah released a political declaration in reply to the accusations, it took Nasrallah only two days to vehemently respond in his speech commemorating the "Second Anniversary of the Israeli Withdrawal" in the presence of Imam Khumayni's daughter. In answering the American contentions about meetings among al-Qa'ida, on the one hand, and Hamas, and Hizbullah, on the other, Nasrallah affirmed that these meetings never took place, and there is no need to deny these accusations because they are naïve and unfounded.[62] According to Nasrallah, other US accusations claimed that Hizbullah posits a stronger threat to the US's national security than al-Qa'ida.[63] Nasrallah ridiculed this claim forecasting that the Americans might later on accuse Hizbullah of having weapons of mass destruction. He added that the American Administration is not leaving any opportunity to tarnish Hizbullah's image and integrity by incriminating the party with drug trafficking, money laundering, and other "nonsensical charges"; while everyone knows that Hizbullah is "cleaner" and "purer" than such accusations. According to Nasrallah, the truth of the matter is that the Americans are distorting the image [the truth] in order to target resistance movements in the region and serve Israeli security interests. Byman seems to second Nasrallah when he argues, "in contrast [to al-Qa'ida] Hezbollah is widely viewed as a legitimate, and even admirable, resistance movement fighting an oppressive regional hegemon [Israel]".[64] Nasrallah adds,

> If inflicting defeat on the enemy [Israel] in Lebanon is a crime, and siding with the Palestinians is an offence punishable by the New World Order, then we [Hizbullah] are proud to be indicted with such a crime and ready to pay the price. We cannot be conquered, we will not yield; since the beginning we were dreaming [to become martyrs] of Karbala', but we attained victory [against the Israelis].

Nasrallah affirms,

What is the most that the Americans can do to us? Kill us? *Dignity is the opposite of humiliation, and death to humiliation*[65]. If in order to stay alive, they want
us to prostrate to Condoleezza Rice[66], [Donald] Rumsfeld, Dick Cheney,[67] and
that crazy-idiot George Bush,[68] then, for sure, *we prefer death, one thousand times
than to live such a life* [of humiliation]... But who said that death is waiting for us,
maybe victory is, while fatality is waiting for them because we are in our land, and
we know how we fight and whom we fight... I do not promise you martyrdom
in battle with the enemy; however, with full confidence, I pledge you triumph in
every battle, with any enemy, and we are ready for this victory...[69] (Italics added
for emphasis)

From the aforementioned, one could infer Hizbullah's response to these
charges through its counter hegemonic discourse and deeds: more confrontation with the 'Great Satan' (the US), and its 'representative' in the region,
namely, the 'Little Satan' (Israel).

3.4   THE REGIONAL CONFRONTATION: SUPPORTING THE
PALESTINIANS

With the inauguration of the *Aqsa Intifada* on 28 September 2001, Hizbullah turned its resource mobilization to the West Bank and Gaza. I argue that
in regional affairs, especially the issue of buttressing the *Intifada*, Hizbullah
became more and more radical, using hard-line pre-Ta'if[70] discourse that
labels the US as "Great Satan" and the "Mother of all Corruption"(*Um al-
Fasad*).[71] I contend that Hizbullah's stance towards Israel remained ideologically the same, but it was coined in very strong terms. In conformity to Khumayni's discourse Israel remained the "Rapist Entity" (*al-Kiyan al-Ghasib*),
the "Zionist Entity" (*al-Kiyan al-Sahyuni*) that is a cancerous gland (*al-Gudda
al-Sarataniyya*)[72] in the region and should be uprooted at all costs because
it is the "Absolute Evil" (*Sharrun Mutlaq*).[73] In theory, Hizbullah's political
ideology distinguishes between a Jew,[74] and a Zionist.[75] For instance, Finkelstein,[76] an American anti-Zionist Jew[77] visited Lebanon in December 2001.
In spite of the Lebanese government's policy of boycotting Jews and Jewish
goods, he was given a visa to enter Lebanon. Also, contrary to Hizbullah's
standard policy of not sitting with an American or a Jew at the same table,
the party's low-rank cadres were present at both lectures, maybe to affirm that
they are not against 'Jews who tell the truth'; on the contrary, they exercise
not only tolerance, but also appreciation towards such Jews.[78] This attitude
is warranted by Hizbullah's ideological concession that "a 'small number' of
Jews are not Zionists" and the distinction between "Zionist Jews and 'ordinary

Jews', who are actually assimilated into their respective societies and whose affiliation to Judaism is devoid of any political or nationalist implications".[79] Hizbullah's cadres – a great majority of whom are the product of the European system of education, rather than Islamic schools and universities – contend that Finkelstein and Maxime Rodinson[80] could be considered such Jews. On these grounds, I do not agree with Saad-Ghorayeb's contention that Hizbullah's distinction between Judaism and Zionism is "purely academic"[81]; rather, I contend that it has practical implications as the former exposition endeavored to demonstrate. However, according to Hizbullah, in the state of 'Israel' the distinction between a Jew and a Zionist does not hold because all the citizens are considered Zionists. According to Na'im Qasim, Hizbullah's deputy secretary-general, "Israeli society is a military society".[82] Nasrallah affirms that in Israel Hizbullah does not distinguish between a civilian and a military, a woman, a child, and an elderly.[83] Nasrallah argues with a strong qualification,[84] "in Israel there are no civilians: they are all conquerors, occupiers, rapists of the land; they are all taking part in the crime and the massacre... they are all Zionists and must be killed".[85] In this connection Saad-Ghorayed correctly argues that Nasrallah's previous statement clearly runs against "the Islamic and humanitarian principle which dictates that civilians should be neutral... Hizbu'llah rationalizes that it is not killing innocent Israeli civilians, but hostile militant Zionists".[86] Nasrallah adds that "killing them is a religious obligation, and the persons who do it are regarded as martyrs".[87] In spite of this vehement rhetoric, Hizbullah itself does not engage in such attacks; rather, as Saad-Ghorayeb remarks, "it would justify [martyrdom operations] if they were staged by Palestinian groups such as Hamas and Islamic Jihad and Al-Aqsa Martyrs." Thus, Hizbullah "clearly advocates the resort to terrorism by armed Palestinian groups".[88] As Nasrallah puts it, "the Palestinians do not need anyone to fight on their behalf. They are capable of fighting on their own using their rifles, bombs, and the bodies of their martyrs in order to rapture the Zionist *disgrace and humiliation*[89] and defeat the Zionist entity".[90] And so, Hizbullah's war-by-proxy strategy allowed it to indirectly wage a war of attrition against Israel in the Occupied Territories. Nasrallah affirms, "those who killed Za'ifi [the Israel Minister of Tourism] are the most noble people of the *Umma*... The war against the Zionists in Lebanon and Palestine is the embodiment of the consensus of the *Umma*".[91] I would like to end by stressing that – contrary to the Palestinians who have blown themselves up with Israeli civilians – Hizbullah has never done so. Hizbullah did not engage in any suicide operation against Israeli civilians in its eighteen-year struggle with the Israeli forces occupying south Lebanon. Rather, all its field and martyrdom operations targeted Israeli and military personnel. So far, Hizbullah has not conducted any suicide operation in Israel. As Levitt concedes, "over the last three years, Hezbollah has steadily intensified its involvement in the Palestinian-Israeli conflict, gravitating from the provision of material support and training for Palestinian terrorist groups to the direct *recruitment of Palestinian operatives* under its own command and control".[92] (Italics added for emphasis). In a similar vain, Byman argues, "Hezbollah has provided guerrilla training, bomb-building expertise, propaganda, and tactical tips to Hamas, Palestinian Islamic Jihad, and other anti-Israeli groups".[93]

When Muhammad Rida Khatami, the Iranian deputy speaker, was asked to comment on the Palestinian authority's decision to consider any operation carried out by the Palestinian resistance as terrorism, he said that: "In general, we do not support acts of violence, especially those targeting civilians. However, when we examine the situation, we see that one of the parties [Sharon] still carries out his criminal attacks towards the other party [Palestinians]. Thus, we cannot call on the latter party to waiver its inalienable right of self-defence".[94] I suggest the same rationale applies to the Lebanese Resistance. Husem affirms, "the [Islamic] Resistance was determined to extract the highest price possible for the [Israeli] occupation and imbue any form of Israeli withdrawal with the image of a military debacle routing one of the world's strongest armies would have great political gains for the Hizbullah on the domestic [and international] arena".[95] I think the analogy with the Palestinian resistance is not that far-fetched. Husem argues that the Israeli withdrawal from southern Lebanon under Hizbullah's attacks "would probably signal to the Palestinians that Israel could be 'defeated' by force"[96], which is a precedent in the Arab-Israeli conflict. As Byman puts it, Hizbullah is known "... for its successful resistance against the Israeli occupation of Southern Lebanon (the only time that Arab arms have forced Israel to surrender territory)...".[97] Concerning the spillover of the Lebanese victory of May 2000 on the Palestinian *Intifada* or what came to be known as the "Lebanese Model[98] [*namudhaj*] of Resistance", Hizbullah uses the following major premise: "We [Hizbullah and the Lebanese] liberated our land after 22 years of occupation, you [the Palestinians] can do it after 33 years; it is not an impossibility".[99] Thus, it is no wonder "Palestinians regularly cite Hezbollah's combination of skilled operations, willing sacrifice, and emphasis on long-term struggle as a guide to their own efforts".[100]

I would like to end this exposition by stressing that the formula of equating civilians to the military applies *only* to Israel, not outside its borders, or "is the particular case of the Zionist entity" as Muhammad Ra'd affirms.[101] That is why, as will be demonstrated later, Hizbullah, Fadlallah, and Iran condemned the 11 September 2001 attacks as suicide-terrorist attacks that have nothing to do with martyrdom operations that are carried out by resistance movements for the sake of liberating occupied land. In the wake of Nasrallah's fiery, uncompromising discourse, The 'Saudi Initiative' was propagated to cool down the situation and extend a hand to Israel in an attempt to end the Arab-Israeli conflict.

3.5   THE ARAB SUMMIT AND ITS REPERCUSSIONS

In response to a question on the Arab Summit to be held, back then, in Beirut on 27-28 March 2002, Nasrallah said that he does not expect much[102], maybe because "Israel's conception of itself as a besieged refuge for world Jewry afflicts it with both insecurity and an irredentist need for territorial expansion".[103] As it turned out, the Arabs offered a lot of ideological concessions, while "one should not expect much from Sharon", as Nasrallah stated. The Arabs officially endorsed and adopted the 'Saudi Initiative' that called for the full recognition of Israel and normalization of relations with it, if it withdraws to the 4 June 1967 borders.[104] The Arabs[105] did not ask for the return of all the four million Palestinian diaspora or so[106]; rather, they demanded a "just solution" to the refugee crisis[107] based on UN Resolution 194.[108] For the sake of argument, I strongly believe that if Sharon would have said "yes" to the Arab Summit's proposals, then the so called militant groups – such as Hamas, Islamic Jihad, Al-Aqsa Martyrs, and Hizbullah – could not have done much to curtail the process since they would be working single-handedly losing most, if not all of their support from Arab states and Iran. Blanford concedes, "[Bashar] Asad said that Hizbullah and the Palestinian groups would 'by definition fade away' once a regional peace settlement had been reached".[109] Moreover, from a theoretical perspective,

> while a complete and lasting peace and resolution to the Israeli-Palestinian conflict is hardly a forgone conclusion, such a situation would drastically alter the dynamics of identification in most Middle Eastern countries. In part, a permanent resolution would alter the ability of transnational identities [Hizbullah as an 'Islamic *jihadi* (struggle) movement'] to influence the internal dynamics of states. Specifically, pan-Arabism and pan-Islamism have been important to identity disputes of the region.[110]

Although Hizbullah exploits both pan-Arabism and pan-Islamism in order to buttress the *Intifada* and support the "oppressed", I think that in the event of a permanent peace settlement, Hizbullah's transnational influence will wane or gradually wither away since the party will, most likely, content itself with Lebanese domestic affairs.[111]

Since this utopian scenario did not materialize, explaining Hizbullah's doctrinal stance sheds some light on its behavior on the ground. Knowing that Hizbullah is totally against the Oslo Agreement and any peace negotiations[112] with Israel, it is no wonder that Hizbullah rejected the 'Saudi Initiative' because it gives back only 22 percent of the historic Palestine – the 4 June 1967 borders – while Hizbullah demands the return of all of Palestine, namely, 1948 Palestine, from the Jordan river till the Mediterranean Sea, and the repatriation of all the Jews who came after the 1916 Sykes-Picot Agreement that divided the Middle East among the British and French after the demise of the Ottoman Empire, putting Palestine under British Mandate.[113]

In turn, Sharon's[114] response to the Arab Summit initiative was his "obliterating incursion" into the West Bank in order to uproot "terrorism"[115] and "isolate" Arafat. In the wake of these events, eighteen months after the start of the *Intifada*, Nasrallah threatened Sharon[116] to open a new front on Israel's northern boarder if the events of 1948 would be repeated and Sharon would fulfil his irredentist ambitions or what is known as the 'transfer policy'[117] of banishing the Palestinians from the occupied territories to Jordan and permanently annexing the land. In that case, Hizbullah's retaliation would not be confined to Shib'a; rather, Hizbullah would cross the redline and enflame the whole line of control along Israel, Syria and Lebanon.[118] Nasrallah added that not only Hizbullah, but also all the Arabs would stand firm and support the Palestinians if Israel would "massacre" them and wage a massive evacuation war against them.[119] Hizbullah blatantly admitted that it would keep on supporting the *Intifada* with all possible means, come what may, including smuggling guns and rockets through Jordan[120], as Hizbullah is a local Lebanese political party that has no branches in Palestine.[121] A few days later, Nasrallah's intimidation was substantiated by Fadlallah who argued that any Israeli attack on Lebanon would be met by massive retaliation from Hizbullah reaching "at least as far as *Haifa*".[122] In this situation, calls for restraint came not only from the us and the eu, but also from Iran.

During Sharon's massive incursion into the West Bank, specifically from 30 March till 12 April, Hizbullah kept on attacking the Shib'a farms[123] in spite of the Iranian call for restraint through the Iranian foreign minister, Kamal Kharazi, who visited Beirut 11-13 April. Hizbullah did not respond and kept its war of attrition against the Israeli forces still occupying Lebanese land.[124] Hizbullah's media and other affiliated or sympathetic media institutions criticized Kharazi's remarks, which came in the wake of Colin Powell's mission in the Middle East. A day later, Kharazi replied, arguing that "wisdom and vigilance dictates self-restraint against the Israeli provocations… the Lebanese resistance has the legitimate right to liberate occupied land."[125] As if this was not enough, the Iranian embassy in Beirut issued a memo affirming Kharazi's latter interpretation.[126] Thus, Hizbullah does not always respond to Iranian calls; rather, it follows the course of action that benefits its policies domestically and regionally. Hizbullah stopped attacking the Shib'a farms as of 13 April 2002, when Sharon's incursion waned. In the wake of the Shib'a attacks, Hizbullah sent its political council member and head of Hizbullah's Christian-Muslim dialogue, Ghalib Abu Zaynab, to tour Christian religious and political leaders explaining the situation and asking for their support, which he unconditionally got, including the backing of the Maronite cardinal who argued that what is happening to the Palestinians is "abhorrent", and that the Resistance (Hizbullah) has the right to liberate Lebanese occupied land. He added that he had great confidence in the Resistance and its rationalization in managing the conflict.[127] In addition, John Kelly, the ex-US ambassador to Lebanon, stressed "both Syria and Lebanon has affirmed that Shib'a farms are Lebanese and send a written memo in this regard to the UN. That is why Shib'a farms are Lebanese."[128] In turn, Asher Kaufman, an Israeli academic, demonstrated that Shib'a farms are Lebanese.[129] Also, a survey conducted by "Delta Centre" conveyed that 75 percent supported the opening of all Arab fronts with Israel; 63 percent supported the Lebanese Resistance; 74 percent buttressed the continuation of the *Intifada*; 63 percent refused peace with Israel; and 84 percent espoused the existence of an Arab Union, along the lines of the EU.[130] Even the Christian extreme rightist banned 'Lebanese Forces' issued a declaration supporting the *Intifada* and the Lebanese resistance.[131]

In spite of all of Hizbullah's efforts to buttress the *Intifada*, a Palestinian student wrote an article attacking Nasrallah arguing that he betrayed his word of "you [the Palestinians] can count on us [Hizbullah] when the time comes".[132] The student claimed that the "propaganda" attacks against *Shib'a* did not help the Palestinians in *Jenin*; rather, they were for public consumption. He felt that the Palestinians were left alone to be "massacred".[133] The student continued slamming Nasrallah, arguing that instead of supporting Palestinian freedom fighters who fired Katyusha rockets [into the occupied Syrian Golan Heights far away from *Shib'a*], Hizbullah curbed their activities by helping the Lebanese government to catch them. The student added, concerning Hizbullah's buttressing of the *Intifada*, that there was a gap between the "motto" and "reality". He concluded that the *Intifada* was helping Hizbullah and the Arabs, not the reverse.[134] This incident is an indication of Hizbullah's *infitah* policy and, more or less, of the existence of an "open public sphere"[135] in Lebanon.

In this milieu, the Lebanese responses were communicated with regard to 9/11 and the US stance towards Lebanon.

3.6 RESETTING THE CLOCK

The international confrontation and the domestic response: The US stance towards Lebanon after 9/11 and the Lebanese response

Since only in the state of Israel, Hizbullah does not distinguish between civilians and military personnel, Hizbullah, Fadlallah, and Iran all condemned 9/11 as suicidal, terrorist attacks targeting innocent civilians. The ideological explanation behind this is that Hizbullah "'does not pursue martyrdom as an end in itself', but as a means of achieving victory... without the imperative need for a defensive *jihad*, martyrdom becomes suicide, which is clearly proscribed in Islam and thereby not rewarded with an everlasting life in paradise, as is true martyrdom... [Nasrallah argues] 'Maybe some people think we crave martyrdom because we like to die in any way. No, we like to die if our blood is valued and has a great impact [on Israel]'".[136]

Fadlallah's and Hizbullah's response
Ayatullah Fadlallah denounced the 9/11 operations as criminal, suicidal acts that constitute an ugly human genocide in all respects. These, according to him, are not martyrdom acts. He added that neither offensive nor defensive *jihad* justifies such acts that are denounced religiously (*shar'an*). These are vicious acts that are not sanctioned by any religion, civilization, or human logic. It is not right to use innocent, peaceful civilians as bargaining chips and means of leverage to change a certain [US] policy. Islamically speaking, it is wrong to engage oneself in such acts because there is no *shar'i* justification for such acts. 9/11 is a horrendous act that is not authorized by any religion or approved by any "heavenly message". Thus, Fadlallah is adamantly against targeting civilian means of transportation because their safety and security is a worldly humane concern from a *shari'* perspective.[137]

In conformity to the Iranian stance[138] and that of the leading Lebanese *Marj'a* Fadlallah, Hizbullah, after five days of silence, condemned the 9/11, 2001 attacks against the US. Bearing in mind that Hizbullah's animosity is towards the US administration, not the US people, Hizbullah issued a political declaration entitled, "Hizbullah regrets lives lost and warns the US not to resort to unjust policies", which runs as follows:

After many Muslim clergy men stated their position toward the bloody attacks which recently occurred in New York and Washington, we call for caution and not falling prey to a state of fear and panic that was intended to be spread throughout the world to give the US administration free rein to practice all types of aggression and terrorism under the pretext of fighting aggressions and terrorism, Now the big question is whether what the American administration is planning really has to do with responding to the perpetrators of the latest attacks, or whether it wants to exploit those tragic events to exercise more hegemony over the world and practice more unjust policies which have led to this level of hate against the US by many peoples and governments in the world. The world, which is now waiting for the US response, must not forget that there are massacres carried out against the Palestinian people by the Israeli occupation, which feels proud, that the world is silent towards its crimes. We are sorry for any innocent people who are killed anywhere in the world. The Lebanese, who have suffered repeated Zionist massacres in Qana and elsewhere, massacres that the US administration refused to condemn at the UN Security council, are familiar with the pain and suffering of those who lost their loved ones in bitter events.[139]

It is worth mentioning that Hizbullah[140] complains of the US's unconditional support of Israel, including the showering of Israel with financial and military aid that are used to 'massacre' the Palestinians; the US's continual veto in the security council that encourages Israel's perpetual breaching of UN resolutions and international agreements. This attitude allows Israel to act with immunity above international law; on these grounds, Hizbullah accuses the US of practicing a double-standard[141] policy and of being a biased, unreliable moderator.[142] In this connection, Hinnebusch writes about "Washington's continued pro-Israeli bias… [and] Washington's tacit support for Israeli violations of UN resolutions in Lebanon and the occupied territories and its punitive measures against Iraq for similar violations".[143] Blum mentions, "… the habitual support of Israeli belligerence and torture, and condemnation of Arab resistance to it; the double standard applied to Israeli terrorism, such as the wilful massacre of 106 Lebanese at the UN base at Qana in 1996…"[144] In this connection, Huntington acknowledges the "West's failure… to impose sanctions on Israel for violating UN resolutions. The West… was using a double standard. A world of clashing civilizations, however, is inevitably a world of double standards: people apply one standard to their kin-countries and a different standard to others."[145] Hizbullah adds that in June 2002 the US lobbied for the international community to grant its personnel serving in peacekeeping operations immunity from prosecution by the newly established International Criminal Court (ICC), thus acting with immunity and impunity above international law. After the US threatened to use its veto power to curb all peacekeeping operations, the international community granted US personnel one-year immunity. Thus, for the second consecutive year, on 12 June 2003, and after a row with the EU, the US managed to get the international community to renew the immunity for one more year. Twelve members of the security council voted for Resolution 1487, while France, Germany, and Syria abstained. Arguing that all countries should be judged with the same law, Hizbullah questions why the US should be immune from war crime lawsuits when it is so much concerned with human right breaches and systematic abuses. As Hizbullah argues, it seems that the US advocates the application of justice, but does not want to apply it to its own citizens.[146]

The US stance towards Lebanon

> What do these Lebanese think? Do they think that the US would have cared for their problems if they were secluded from the problems of the Middle East and did not affect the region in one way or another? If we [the US] could totally isolate Lebanon and its problems from the Middle East, then we would not move our little finger even if the Lebanese slaughtered one another with old shaving razors.[147]

I claim that nothing has changed in the US position concerning Lebanon and Hizbullah before and after 9/11. As Byman puts it, "for most of the past two decades, Hezbollah has claimed pride of place as the top concern of US counter-terrorism officials."[148] Thus, ever since Hizbullah's inauguration, the US administration has considered the party as a "terrorist organization". Just before 9/11, in April 2001 the US listed Hizbullah on its terrorism list. Hizbullah released its own response entitled, "Hizbollah statement in response to the annual report of the US state department", which runs as follow:

> 1) The American administration, which considers the Lebanese resistance (terrorism), unveils once again its true face, which sees only from the Israeli eye. Now the whole world can easily differentiate between the terrorist who practices the most violent methods against civilians and the resistant who uses his legitimate right to liberate his land whether it is in Palestine or in Lebanon. 2) Adopting the Israeli perspective and considering the Palestinians who defend themselves as terrorists demonstrates the unfairness of the American administration, which keeps silent towards the Israeli massacres of our people in Palestine. 3) Distorting the hizbollah pure image and trying to pin the name (terrorism) on it, clearly shows the American and Israeli fear of the great example that the resistance provided specifically in terms of fighting the occupation. 4) The American administration

is trying to ignore the fact that there are Lebanese hostages in Israeli prisons who were kidnapped from Lebanese occupied land. It [is] also trying to ignore the fact that the three Israeli soldiers who were captured from Lebanese occupied land are aggressors not hostages. It is only honorable that we use them as a means to release our brothers in Israeli prisons. 5) We regard the hostile of the American administration as proof that we are following the right path. We are certain that the US government will consider whoever keeps the dignity of his people an enemy.[149]

After 9/11, the UN security council, under pressure from US lobbying, issued UN Resolution 1373 asking governments to file written reports within 90 days indicating the steps taken by them to curb terrorism and terrorist activities on their territories.[150] In turn, the US issued four terrorism lists after 9/11; two are binding issued through the UN, and two non-binding presidential decrees. These either included Hizbullah's members or asked the Lebanese government to freeze Hizbullah's assets.[151]

The Lebanese response
It is worth mentioning that Hariri, the Lebanese Prime Minister, was among the first Arab prime ministers, if not the first, to overtly condemn the 9/11 attacks by arguing that the Lebanese people sympathize with their fellow Americans because "they have suffered from terrorism for years".[152] The Lebanese official position concerning the US listing of Hizbullah as a 'Terrorist Organization' whose assets should be frozen was conveyed by the president Emile Lahud who told the four delegates of the US congress who visited Beirut that, "Hizbullah is a local Lebanese organization that has no foreign branches or ties with any terrorist organization operating outside Lebanon [no global reach]."[153] The Norwegian, Spanish, and Italian ambassadors in Lebanon remarked that Hizbullah is a resistance movement, not a terrorist one. The latter ridiculed the US and Israeli claims of the presence of terrorist camps in the Biqaʻ.[154] Chirac, the French president, told Hariri during his official visit to France that the US's fourth terrorism list, the third one after 9/11, which asks the Lebanese government to freeze Hizbullah's assets, is not binding to Lebanon because it was issued as a presidential decree, not as a UN or security council resolution.[155] In this regard, Salamé[156] argued that Lebanon has its own fiscal and monetary legislations that prohibit and control money laundering as well as the flow of 'terrorist' money. He added that Lebanon has a special understanding with the US ambassador in Beirut concerning that matter.[157] In turn, N'im said that the US list is a breach of the UN's Universal Declaration of Human Rights as well as the US's Fifth Amendment, namely, "Rights of those accused of crime; any deprivation of life, liberty, or property

requires due process of the law". He added that Hizbullah and the Resistance are a "continuation" of the Lebanese State, and only the Lebanese judicial system has the right to deal with Hizbullah's assets;[158] any other call to do so by another party is denied.[159] At that time, there seemed to be some kind of a consensus among many Lebanese political (including the Christian right-wing Phalangists), religious (including the Maronite cardinal), and social leaders that Hizbullah is a resistance movement, not a terrorist one. Thus, the Lebanese mosaic myriad conveys not only a consensus on this issue, but it also turns out to be a fundamental 'pillar' of national unity and solidarity, as such a 'shared public sphere'.

On 13 December 2001 both Lebanon and Syria individually sent a written response to the UNSC resolution 1373, dated 28 September 2001, which gave 90 days for countries to take constructive measures to curb terrorist activities on their territories, thus meeting the dealine of 27 December 2001.[160] Knowing that Article 40 calls for the formation of an international army to take military action and curtail terrorism, I think that considering Lebanon as a possible target of the US's war on terror is far-fetched. Lebanon has signed ten out of the twelve treaties and international agreements to curb terrorism, and is preparing to ratify the other two.[161] Also, Lebanon has already signed the Arab Agreement of Combating Terrorism. Faruq al-Shariʿ, the Syrian Foreign Minister at the time, remarked – on the doorsteps of the Lebanese presidential palace, during his visit to Lebanon on 26 November 2001 – that the common ground with Syria is the joint definition of terrorism, which clearly distinguishes between terrorism and resistance giving legitimization to the latter.[162] Shaykh Yusuf al-Qaradawi, who openly condemned the terrorist 9/11 attacks against the US, said that: "If jihad for the liberation of occupied nations is considered 'terrorism', then God raise me as a terrorist, and martyr me as a terrorist" (*Idha kana al-jihad fi sabili tahrir al-awtani irhaban, Allahuma ahyini irhabiyyan wa amitni irhabiyyan*). He added that martyrdom operations are the mostly extolled form of Jihad in the name of God, and that 'legitimate terrorism' is sanctioned in the Qurʾan: "And make ready for them whatever you can of fighting men and horses, to terrify thereby the enemies of Allah and your enemy" (8: 60). Thus, in this context, "terrorism" is welcomed.[163] In point seven of its final declaration, 'The Council of Muslim *Ulamaʾ* totally rejected the American lists of terrorism and their corollaries arguing that they are lies and allegations tarnishing the honesty and integrity of resistance movements in Lebanon and Palestine [Occupied Territories[164]]. They affirmed that "the resistance is the holiest and the noblest phenomenon in our modern history, and it is the lively embodiment of the will of the *umma* in defending its sanctified causes and rights against the Zionist entity." The *ulama* added that resistance movements symbolize by their *jihad* the honesty, dignity, and nobleness of the Muslims, and are an expression of the humanitarian aspirations of the *mustad'afin* (oppressed) everywhere in the world.[165]

In light of Hizbullah's 29 August 2002 attack on the Shib'a Farms that led to the death of one Israeli soldier and wounded two others, Richard Armitage[166], the US deputy secretary of state, on 5 September 2002, labeled Hizbullah as the "A-Team of terrorism" arguing that the time to deal with it had come. Vincent Battle, the ex-US ambassador to Lebanon, reiterated Artimage's stance affirming, "Hizbullah remains a terrorist organization." In turn, Hizbullah issued a political declaration attacking the US administration and its "fabricated and baseless political accusations [that are] no more than a stack of lies designated to mislead and divert the public opinion, in an attempt to justify the US Administration's hostile actions." Further, Hizbullah threatened the US by claiming: "We clearly announce to the Muslim *Ummah* that the American Administration will be held accountable for any offensive against Lebanon and we emphasize that we are in full readiness to confront any eventuality and defend our people."[167] This time, the new Italian ambassador, Franco Mistretti, came to Hizbullah's rescue: "The EU does not think that Hizbullah is a terrorist group[168]... there is no evidence that backs arguments that Hizbullah is engaged in terrorism."[169] On 11 December 2002, Canada placed Hizbullah on its terrorism list; Australia followed suit on 5 June 2003. A few days before the second anniversary of 9/11, the EU blacklisted Hamas' political wing.[170]

The Canadian and Australian ban: The interplay among the domestic, regional, and international dimensions

From the early 1980s through 9/11, 2001, and until the present, the Lebanese Hizbullah has been classified by the US State Department as a 'terrorist organization'. Since the inauguration of the party, the Israeli stance on Hizbullah coincided with that of the US. In 2002, Canada and Australia banned Hizbullah and added the party to their terrorism lists.

Canada placed Hizbullah on its terrorism list[171] because, in the event of commemorating 'Jerusalem Day' on 29 November 2002, Nasrallah called on the Palestinians to continue their "martyrdom" operations.[172] According to Nasrallah, the Canadian government's contention of Hizbullah's 'global reach' is based on an article in the 4 December 2002 issue of the *Washington Times* which claimed that Hizbullah's leader exhorted the Palestinians to pursue *jihad* against Israeli interests outside Israel, implying that Nasrallah called for a global campaign of suicide bombings.[173] Keeping in mind the fact that the speech was delivered in Nabatiyyé, not B'albak, as the *Washington Times* contended, Nasrallah argued this allegation is neither borne out by facts (since it is not present in the speech) nor warranted by discourse analysis. Moreover, the Canadian stance seems to be at odds with the earlier Canadian position, when Jean Chrétien, the Canadian prime minister, attended the Francophone Summit held in Beirut – from 18-20 October 2002 –although Nasrallah was present as an honorary guest.[174] At that time, only Hizbullah's military wing was banned in Canada, but not the party's civil and social institutions. Blanford contends that the move came "amid intensive lobbying and a threatened lawsuit by pro-Israeli groups."[175] In reference to the Francophone Summit, Byman argues, "In October 2002, Hezbollah operatives participated in the Francophone summit in Beirut with implicit French endorsement."[176]

In spite of the Canadian ban on Hizbullah and the prohibition of any official to establish contact with Hizbullah, on 26 June 2003, Tony Valeri, a Canadian MP, came to Lebanon to investigate the 'real reasons' (unearth the truth) behind the ban, which was considered, the least to say, as a breach to the ban. After a persistent request from Valeri to meet Hizbullah officials and listen to their viewpoints, Valeri met with the head of Hizbullah's parliamentary bloc, Muhammad Ra'd. Ra'd affirmed that Hizbullah was very much in favor of the continuation of normal and friendly relations between the Lebanese and Canadian people. He added that since the Canadian ban was not based on realistic data and that it was the result of great US pressure, Hizbullah could not find a justification for this decision. Ra'd stressed that Hizbullah is not a 'terrorist organization' with an alleged 'global reach' as the US labels it; on the contrary, Hizbullah does not have an 'outside branch' or activities outside Lebanon, neither in the form of security arrangements nor in the form of military and political presence. Rather, Hizbullah is a legitimate resistance movement operating within the UN principles and the Universal Declaration of Human Rights. Moreover, according to Ra'd, Hizbullah is a legitimate Lebanese political party with NGOs and civil institutions, which are functioning according to the stipulations of Lebanese law. Ra'd added that the aid Hizbullah receives is invested in performing socio-economic services for the needy, rather than sponsoring 'violent acts'. Ra'd argued that these 'facts' could be easily investigated; the burden of proof befalls those who filed those allegations. Based on my fieldwork and interviews I learned that in 2005 there were serious discussions between Hizbullah's NGOs (Social Service Institutions) and the Swiss government and NGOs to grant the party's NGOs Swiss licences so that they would be recognized by the international community as welfare NGOs and not 'terrorist organizations'. Before a deal was struck, the July 2006 war started. After the war, Hizbullah changed its priorities and had to channel all it resources to solve the refugee crisis and rebuild what had been destroyed. So what Hizbullah termed from the beginning as a matter of beating a dead horse, proved so, not because they gave up; rather because *Realpolitik* dictated another course of action. Valeri conceded the existence of US pressure; however, he argued for the necessity of finding a continuous mechanism to convey the aforementioned information about Hizbullah to the Canadian public, insinuating a role for the 'Lebanese-Canadian Parliamentary Friendship Committee' in this respect.[177]

In line with the Canadian position, on 16 June 2003, Daryl Williams, the Australian attorney general, announced that Australia decided to ban "Hizbullah's external military wing".[178] The draft legislation adopted by the Australian parliament was imposed retroactively as of 5 June 2003 in spite of the fact that the UN did not officially label Hizbullah as a terrorist organization. It is worth mentioning that according to Australian law in order to consider an organization as a terrorist one and to place it on a terrorist list, it must be deemed so by the UN; it seems that this law was not honored. *Reuters* conveyed the opinion of some analysts who argued Australia's ban on Hizbullah appears to have been as a result of the party's connection with international policies, rather than its link to terrorism. The analysts acknowledged that Hizbullah does not pose a threat to Australia. In turn, Cliff Williams, the director of 'Terrorism Studies' at the Australian National University, told the reporters that the ban on Hizbullah was most likely the result of pressure by the US on the Australian government because Hizbullah poses a potential threat to Israel.[179] On 17 June 2003, the Australian government announced that it placed Hizbullah on its terrorism list. In response, Hizbullah issued a political declaration addressed to the Australian prime minister and parliament, arguing that the decision lacks credibility because it is 'isolated' from any substantial evidence. Hizbullah affirmed that political pressure would not dissuade the party from giving any concessions with regard to its legitimate right of resisting the Israeli occupation to Lebanon.[180] Both in Canada as in Australia, the Lebanese immigrant community is of a considerable size. It was assumed that Hizbullah has a significant following among these communities – a conclusion, which is very doubtful and highly improbable. Political analysts argued the Australian move was based on the following three considerations: 1) The Australian government's acquiescence to the US's pressure after the war on Iraq; 2) The war on Iraq had its toll on Australian election interests, which resulted in the Australian Conservative Party having the upper hand and gave way to the pro-Israeli Australian lobby to express its will in the parliament; 3) The game of state's interests, especially economic, financial interests among Australian and US companies in terms of investments in the Middle East and Iraq, led the Australian governing party to reap rewards by officially branding Hizbullah with terrorism.

Almost two months after PM Rafiq Hariri's assassination, on 19 April 2005, a fourteen-member technocrat cabinet headed by PM Najib Miqati was sworn in. Hizbullah not only gave a parliamentary vote of confidence to the new cabinet, which received 109 votes out of 128 MPs, but also fielded Trad Hamadé, a Hizbullah affiliated sympathizer, for the first time in its history. Hamadé was accorded the Ministry of Labor and Agriculture, an appointment that was supposed to serve as a litmus test to Hizbullah's future ministerial work in the cabinet. Keeping in mind that the US administration brands Hizbullah as a 'terrorist organization', it neither voiced its opposition to such an appointment nor threatened boycotting him. On the contrary, in June 2005 Hamadé met, with Hizbullah's blessings, senior members of the US administration, including Elizabeth Dibble, the deputy assistant secretary of state for Near Eastern affairs, in his capacity as a minister representing Hizbullah in the cabinet.

That was not the only contact between Hizbullah and the US administration over the past few years. In an attempt to discuss the problematic that was impeding Muslim-European-US dialogue, a lot of unofficial meetings took place between the two parties in Beirut, Amsterdam, Rabat, Geneva, and Oman. Graham Fuller, a former intelligence officer at the CIA, conducted dialogue sessions with Hizbullah officials, most notably in March 2005 with the current MP and back then Hizbullah's foreign relations officer Nawwaf al-Musawi.[181]

Actually, in 2000 after the Israeli withdrawal from Lebanon, Hizbullah's leader Hasan Nasrallah met with Kofi Annan, the ex-secretary-general of the UN. Since then Nasrallah has also repeatedly met with Jewish intellectuals such as Norman Finkelstein, Noam Chomsky, US journalist Seymour Hersh, and British MP George Galloway. Not surprisingly, there has also been a European rush towards Hizbullah, especially after the June 2009 legislature elections, most notably by the EU foreign policy chief Javier Solana, French Foreign Minister Bernard Kouchner, British lawmakers, and other low-level contacts such as the British, Norwegian, and Danish ambassadors to Lebanon and other EU and US delegations.

Already before the elections, Britain re-established contact with Hizbullah's 'political wing' and met with MP 'Ali 'Ammar in March 2009 after it ceased contact with Hizbullah members in 2005, and listed Hizbullah's 'military wing' as a proscribed terrorist organization in 2008. In 2005 the European Parliament had already ruled Hizbullah as a terrorist organization. The resolution passed 473-33 in the EU parliament, but is not binding for EU policymakers. Senior US officials have mocked and publicly rejected the British decision. In May 2009 Jeffrey Feltman, the US deputy assistant secretary of state for Near East affairs and former ambassador to Lebanon affirmed: "Our position on Hizbullah remains unchanged… We see no distinction between the leadership and funding of the group's terrorist, military, political and social wings."

In line with the US stance, the Netherlands regards Hizbullah as a terrorist organization. Also, the resumption of talks with Hizbullah's political wing caused a row in the British parliament, with Labor MP Andrew Gwynne questioning the foreign minister on the wisdom of such a move, which, according to him, not only affects domestic Lebanese dynamics but also has a bearing on the peace process since the "British policy could undermine Arab moderates in the region who strive for peace through non-violent means." David Miliband, the UK foreign minister, begs to differ with Gwynne arguing that "Britain is willing to step-up contact with Hizbullah as they begin to play a bigger role in Lebanon's government." Miliband thinks that "carefully considered contact with Hizbullah's politicians, including its MPs, will best advance our objective of the group rejecting violence to play a constructive role in Lebanese politics… The UK strongly supports a comprehensive peace settlement to the Arab/Israeli conflict and this will need to include an agreement between Israel and Lebanon."[182] Hizbullah's unofficial mouthpiece, the daily newspaper *al-Akhbar*, boasted that secret meetings between senior Hizbullah cadres and the US administration are occurring all the time through the mediation of a third party, the hot item on the agenda being the naturalization of the Palestinian refugees in Lebanon, an eventuality that Hizbullah is adamantly against[183], as clearly stated in its 2009 Manifesto, the Lebanese constitution, and the latest Lebanese government's policy statement. In that very Manifesto, Hizbullah called on the EU to distinguish between 'terrorism' and 'resistance' and to dissociate itself from the 'unjust' US policies:

> Since some European people have a history in resisting the occupier, Europe's ethical and humanitarian duty – in addition to its political duty – is to acknowledge the right of the people to resisting the occupier, on the basis of distinguishing between resistance and terrorism.[184]
>
> The Bush Administration decided to establish a correlation between 'terrorism' and 'national resistance' in order to disarm the resistance of its humanitarian legitimacy and its righteousness of cause, and to justify the waging of all forms of wars against it… 'Terrorism' was transformed into an American alibi for hegemony.[185]

We think that the stability and cooperation in European-Arab relations require a European approach that is more independent, just, and objective (than that of the US).[186]

Not surprisingly, the US position remained the same regarding avoiding contact with the two Hizbullah ministers, while at the same time recognizing the Lebanese cabinet that was formed on 9 November 2009.

3.8 CONCLUSION

I suggest that after 9/11, the US policy towards Hizbullah has not changed. From the early 1980s up till April 2001, Hizbullah has been classified by the US State Department as a 'terrorist organization'. The same happened on 21 May 2002. After 9/11, the US issued three additional lists, which either included Hizbullah's members or asked the Lebanese government to freeze Hizbullah's assets. I further purport that in the Lebanese public sphere there has been no substantial alteration in Hizbullah's doctrines after 9/11, rather a re-evaluation of some priorities. Nasrallah argued, "In the light of the terrorist milieu propagated by the US on all the world after Sept. 11, I reiterated in more than one occasion, Hizbullah is as it is before and after Sept. 11; nothing has changed".[187]

Lynch notes, "... often public discourse reinforces the existing consensus rather than producing a new one".[188] From this stance, one can argue that there is a shared belief among most of the Lebanese that Hizbullah does not have branches in any part of the world, is not a political party in the traditional sense; rather is a local resistance movement that is "the embodiment of the people's will and sovereignty".[189] Thus, the response to the US terrorist lists was the consolidation of the earlier view that is shared among almost all Lebanese confessions, namely, a national consensus that Hizbullah is the Lebanese resistance, not a terrorist organization. And so, Hizbullah upheld its political legitimacy and capital, which springs from the support of the Lebanese government and people.

I dispute Saad-Ghorayeb's claim that Hizbullah's domestic agenda is subservient to its regional plan and that the party tends to stress the former at the expense of the latter.[190] It seems to me Hizbullah does not simply have to choose between either or emphasize one more at the expense of the other, as she contends, because the party can play its cards neatly or strike a balance between the two, at least sometimes. Further, I maintain that in the domestic sphere, almost nothing changed in Hizbullah's political program, which increasingly is targeting integration in the Lebanese public sphere through dovish policies aimed at pluralism and respect for sectarian differences in the Lebanese mosaic. However, in the regional sphere, especially after the 'April 2002 West Bank counterterrorism offensive' and the 2009-2010 'Operation Cast Lead' in Gaza",[191] Hizbullah became hawkish and more belligerent in its support of the Palestinian *Intifada*, to the extent that one can argue, "Hizbullah is more Palestinian than the Palestinians themselves"[192]; this made the party "a difficult number in the regional equation", as some political analysts remarked.

I contend that after 9/11, Hizbullah's support for the Palestinian *Intifada* became more confrontational both in discourse and deeds. This is due, in part, to the US administration's targeting of Islamic and resistance movements[193] labeling them as terrorist organizations, specifically the US's hostile attitude that accused Hizbullah of global terrorism[194], in spite of all of Hizbullah's integration policies. However, the catalyst that warrants such an attitude is Israel's 'aggressive' policies and its continual and devastating incursions into the Occupied Palestinian Territories that put Hizbullah's credibility and reputation at stake. This explains the resurfacing of the 'Great Satan' label of the US and the 'Absolute Evil' tag of Israel, both being used and exploited by Hizbullah in abundance for mobilization purposes. By this, Hizbullah is practicing its double-edged-sword theory, namely, domestic integration, and regional militancy: the former in conformity to its political program, and the latter in accordance with its political ideology. This leads us to discuss Hizbullah's views on suicide bombing or 'martyrdom', as they call it.

4 Political Violence: Suicide Operations[1]

ABSTRACT

After the nearly complete Israeli withdrawal from Lebanon in May 2000, Hizbullah had not committed a single martyrdom operation although it engaged, on many occasions, the Israeli soldiers in *Shib'a* and kidnapped three soldiers on 7 October 2000 and two on 12 July 2006. Contrary to what has been rumored, the party did not conduct martyrdom operations in the 'Second Lebanon War' or the July 2006 War since Hizbullah had the required arsenal to face the invading IDF and was able to inflict heavy casualties, killing more than 100 soldiers. In fact, Hizbullah's last martyrdom operation was conducted in 1999.

The basic question of this chapter is to study how religious, political, and national discourse is used to justify martyrdom for Islamic movements, in particular the Lebanese Hizbullah. (In other words, this chapter is about how nationalist and political discourses intermingle with a religious discourse on martyrdom, and how Hizbullah, an organization perceived as religious/fundamentalist, is relying, in addition to religious discourse, on nationalist and political discourses in its representation of martyrdom). My main concern is to analyze how the religious authorities of Hizbullah deal with this question, and how this discourse changes overtime. Thus, I endeavor to expose Hizbullah's religious-political discourse and analyze *fatwa*s (religious edits) and speeches dealing with the issue of martyrdom. I contest the commonly held view that regards martyrdom as a specifically Shi'ite phenomenon, arguing that, in addition to Sunni Palestinians, Lebanese nationalists, from all religious denominations, have also carried out such operations. I would like to debunk a few myths too, for instance the one regarding the social background of suicide bombers. I endeavor to rupture stereotypes and challenge the master narrative on the Islamic movements' constituency being "made up of poor desperate people who commit suicide so that they can enjoy the virgins in Paradise." The problematic is that although martyrdom has become the trademark of radical Islamic groups, it was not solely carried out by them. I purport that the icon that both parties, secularists and Islamists, embraced is that martyrdom operations were conducted in order to uphold the honor, pride, and dignity of the 'nation' (*'izzat wa karamat al-umma*). Thus, I argue that martyrdom operations – whether carried out by Islamic movements or resistance movements – are altruistic, self-sacrificial operations conveyed in the form of symbolic capital (honor and dignity).

4.1 INTRODUCTION

In conformity to its resistance identity as an Islamic *jihadi* movement, Hizbullah sanctioned martyrdom operations as a specific resistance strategy. Hizbullah clearly states in its "Identity and Goals"[2] that it "… also used one of its own special types of resistance against the Zionist enemy [Israel] that is the suicide attacks. These attacks dealt great losses to the enemy on all thinkable levels such as militarily and mentally. The attacks also raised the morale across the whole Islamic nation." Are suicide operations a legitimate tactic in a war for national independence? Does Hizbullah's quest for national freedom justify its resort to martyrdom operations? Is martyrdom incumbent upon men only, or is it the duty of women too? Is there an evolving understanding of the role of martyrs?

Background of the study
A survey conducted by *Reuters* on the Palestinian reaction towards suicide operations conveyed that 75 percent of the Palestinians supported the 4 October 2003 suicide operation, the sixth operation conducted by a Palestinian woman since the beginning of the *Intifada*. The operation was performed by lawyer Hanadi Jaradat[3] who blew herself up killing twenty Israeli civilians in the wake of the celebration of *Yum Kippur* (Day of Forgiveness) in Haifa, a city that is supposed to portray Israeli-Palestinian peaceful coexistence. The sample included 1,318 Palestinians from the West Bank and Gaza, out of whom 17 percent were against the operation, and 4.4 percent vehemently condemned it.[4] The late Shaykh Ahmad Yasin, founder of Hamas, argued, "I'm saying that in this phase (of the uprising [*Intifada*]), the participation of women is not needed, like men. We can't meet the growing demands of young men who

wish to carry out martyr operations".[5] On 14 January 2004, at the Erez crossing in Gaza, Reem Saleh Al-Riyashi, the seventh woman suicide bomber and the first Palestinian mother[6], blew herself up amongst Israeli soldiers, killing four and wounding seven.[7] In laying Reem to rest, Mahmud Al-Zahhar, a Hamas political leader, declared, "The martyr Reem is a heroine since she gave up everything. This was a young married woman who left behind a husband and children to go to *paradise*... She won't be our last."[8] (Italics added for emphasis). Although Shaykh Yasin earlier argued that it is not essential for women to participate in martyrdom operations, in spite of the growing number of male contenders, it seems he revoked his decision later on due to alterations dictated on the battlefield. In commenting on Al-Riyashi's operation, he said, "The operation is a watershed operation on two counts: first, because a woman executed it [first woman from Hamas to conduct such an operation]; second because it resulted from a joint endeavor between *Kata'ib Shuhada' al-Aqsa* [The secularist Al-Aqsa Martyrs Brigade, which is an offshoot of Arafat's *Fatah*], and *Kata'ib Izzeddine Al-Qassam* [the military wing of Hamas]." Yasin added that Hamas refuses any cease-fire with the 'Zionists' [Israel] because this is tantamount to capitulation. Yasin affirmed, "Hence, everyone knows that there is no road and no other choice save the road of resistance".[9] In justifying women's role in *jihad* and martyrdom, Yasin argued that when the enemy [Israel] occupied the land of the Muslims [Palestine], *jihad* became a religious duty incumbent upon all Muslims, men and women. He reiterated,

> We used to say in the past that we leave women aside unless there is an urgent need for them to conduct martyrdom operations. Thus, when our brothers in the *Kata'ib* found the need to perform an operation by resorting to a woman, they did so because, in my opinion, it is a new beginning for the woman. However, concerning jihad, it is not the beginning, rather the continuity of the road [*manhaj*] to martyrdom and struggle by recourse to both men and women.[10]

What has led to this apparent change in Yasin's thinking and discourse?

In the early morning of 22 March 2004, Israel silenced Shaykh Yasin (1937-2004) for good in what it calls "targeted killings". Yasin's assassination earned him the title of "the leading martyr" and sparked a wave of rage amid calls for revenge based on the slogan "an eye for an eye, and a tooth for a tooth".[11] His death strengthened the resolve of the Palestinian resistance and the 'ripple effect' of martyrdom operations was heavily felt, even in Israel proper. Likewise, Israel expected the assassination of Hizbullah's second secretary-general, Sayyid Abbas Al-Musawi, on 16 February 1992, would lead to the weakening of the party. However, the gap between Israel's prognosis and developments on the ground precluded this from materializing. On the contrary, it strengthened Hizbullah's mobilization and its resolve to end the occupation, after eight years, by driving the Israeli forces out of Lebanon through a relentless war of attrition. This analysis is substantiated by Nasrallah's farewell address to Shaykh Yasin issued on the same day of the assassination: "The martyrdom of the leader of the resistance in Palestine, Shaykh Yasin, is a rebirth and resurrection of the resistance… The martyrdom of the leader of the resistance puts the resistance on the final road to victory."[12] In less than a month, on 17 April 2004, Israel assassinated Yasin's successor 'Abd al-'Aziz al-Rantisi (1947-2004), the political leader and co-founder of Hamas. Hizbullah declined to retaliate military; rather it confined its condemnation of the incident to issuing, two days later, a political declaration pinning the blame and responsibility for the assassination on the US administration.[13] Interestingly, Ayatullah Sayyid Muhammad Husayn Fadlallah issued a communiqué condemning the assassination:

> This horrible crime is a result of the American free hand that was given to Sharon to eradicate the Palestinian people and end its cause, by killing its leaders and promoting political projects that would virtually cancel all its political rights including those that were articulated by the UN General Assembly. All these resolutions are meant to be sacrificed on the altar of the coming presidential elections…
> Those who killed Dr Rantissi are: Firstly, President Bush and his administration. Secondly, Arab and Islamic complicity or silence. Thirdly, Sharon and his government, having been given in his last visit to the US a green line and a readiness to provide a cover for any crime they might commit no matter how big it could be.
> The American Administration rushed to declare that it supports this criminal act in defiance of the Arab and Islamic World as well as the international public opinion and the stances taken by the European Union. It is suggesting to all of them that Sharon has the right to carry on in committing his crimes and massacres in Palestine in the same way American crimes are committed in Iraq, all in the name of 'fighting terrorism' and 'self-defense'.
> We say to the Palestinians that the American decision to commit massacres against them until the coming elections is final, and that the American-Israeli war against them is an open one. The only option they have is to endure, strengthen their unity and continue to hurt the enemy in a way that will make him cry first.
> To the Arabs and Muslims we say: Isn't that humiliation enough. Stop this fear that is about to kill what is left of the nation's dignity. One of the original peoples of the nation is being eradicated while you are discussing when you will hold the summit which we believe that it will not be in the near future so that you will not have to issue a communiqué condemning the murder just as is the case of killing Sheik

Yassin... Meanwhile, Sharon would commit additional crimes with the joy of the arrogant and the boasting of the haughty.[14]

Based on our religious capacity, we urge the Arab and Muslim peoples to take to the streets to voice their opinion, and erase some of the disgrace [religious capital], before the darkness spread and injustice dominates.

On 17 August 2005 Israel relinquished the Gaza strip after 38 years of occupation and started evacuating its settlers. Nasrallah termed this eventuality as the second victory for the model of resistance in five years: "The choice of resistance liberates Gaza." He added that this constitutes further proof for the utility of holding on to the weapons of Hizbullah's Islamic Resistance. On 12 September 2005 Israel officially ended its occupation of Gaza after the complete withdrawal of its military.

In four days – from 10 to 14 June 2007 – Hamas took control of the entire Gaza strip and established its Islamic Emirate after a bloody military coup that ousted Fatah and the Palestinian Authority (PA) from the Gaza strip and established its Islamic Emirate.

From 27 December 2008 to 20 January 2009 Israel conducted its military campaign 'Operation Cast Lead' in the Gaza strip aimed at stopping Hamas rockets from targeting southern Israel after a six months truce between the two parties expired on 19 December 2007. After almost five years of Yasin's and Rantisi's assassinations, on 1 January 2009, on the sixth day of 'Operation Cast Lead', Israeli war planes assassinated Nizar Rayyan (1960-2009). Rayyan, one of the top five decision makers in Gaza and the liaison between Hamas' leadership and the group's military wing, had threatened the resumption of suicide operations against Israel. Rayyan, a lecturer in Islamic Law and a preacher, dispatched one of his sons on a 'martyrdom' operation that killed two settlers and wounded fifteen in October 2001 in *Gush Katif* Gaza settlement *Elei Sinai*. Moreover, Rayyan planned and financed the 2004 operation at the *Ashdod* port, which led to the death of ten Israelis. The fourth major targeted killing claimed the life of Hamas's interior minister, Said Siam, who was killed with his brother Ayyad and another senior Hamas member in an Israeli airstrike on his house in the *Jabalya* district in Gaza City. These major targeted killings took place eight months after Hamas's Gaza coup of June 2007. According to Israeli sources, 'Operation Cast Lead' resulted in 1,166 Palestinian deaths and 11 Israeli deaths.[15] According to Palestinian sources 1,505 Palestinians died.[16]

Concomitant with the assassination of two other Hamas cadres, Rayyan's omen became a reality when, on 5 January 2008, a Hamas suicide bomber detonated himself in an Israeli tank wounding one soldier.

The problematic is that some social scientists have argued that the Shi'ites have cultivated a sense of martyrology. For instance, Cole and Keddie contend that Shi'ism constitutes a culture of martyrdom or is characterized by a "martyr complex"[17], while Fouad Ajami labels the Shi'ites as being "suicidal"[18]. Thus even though some authors regard martyrdom as a specifically Shi'ite phenomenon, nevertheless Sunni Palestinians and Lebanese nationalists, from all religious denominations, have also carried out such operations. If it is claimed that the Shi'ite discourse on martyrdom was adopted by the Sunnis, then in addition to the religious discourse, what other kind of discourse do the secularists embrace? If Hizbullah and the Palestinian resistance relied on their religious capital to sanction martyrdom operations, then how could one explain other secular political party's martyrdom operations, which were conducted by men and women of different religious denominations? Although martyrdom has become the trademark of radical Islamic groups, it was not solely carried out by them. For instance, secular Lebanese political parties have conducted martyrdom operations targeting Israeli occupation forces. The 'Lebanese Communist Party' (LCP) conducted a martyrdom operation carried out by a Christian female, while the 'Syrian Social Nationalist Party' (SSNP) has conducted twelve martyrdom operations evenly divided between six women and six men belonging to different confessions and religious denominations.

An anecdote: "Prologue in heaven", the martyr's mother[19]
(Martyrdom 1)[20]: On the sunny Sunday of 9 May 1999, Nynne Bjerre, Vibeke Toft, and the author went to interview the mother of a Hizbullah martyr[21] in the southern suburb of Beirut in a very humble, barely standing home. The two Danish journalism students experienced a 'cultural shock' when they learned that they had to congratulate the mother instead of offering her their condolences. As a Lebanese, I was not surprised myself, but the Danes were perplexed. They questioned how could a person congratulate a mother on the loss of her own son. How could a caring, loving mother give her own son willingly to death? The visible astonishment of the Danes, however, was a serious challenge for the illiterate martyr's mother. She said, "My daughters, if you are bitten by a snake and the poison is flowing in your blood stream, will you let it go all the way to your heart and kill you, or will you simply suck it out?" She gave another analogy; she said that if a person discovered a cancerous gland in his body would not he remove it from the root so as not to kill him? She showed us some pictures of her son without shedding a single tear; rather, she was cool in a heeding-up manner. In particular, she argued, "Dignity is the opposite of humiliation, and death [is preferable] to humiliation".[22] She

added that the martyr (her son) "acted as an anti-Destin, a bronze hawk, a hard-core altruist whose greatest duty and source of pride [honor and dignity] is to sacrifice himself for the well-being of his country by killing as many as possible of his enemies."[23] She stressed, "This is the greatest pride that can befall a mother."

(Martyrdom 2): In connection to this, even Sayyid Hasan Nasrallah, Hizbullah's secretary-general, felt 'embittered' when he was shaking the hand of a martyr's father – not because he felt ashamed, but because he nor his family were honored by any martyr. This is not the case anymore since he 'sacrificed' his own 19-year old son, Hadi, so that by his martyrdom, and that of many others, the cause will not die, Lebanon will survive, and Hizbullah will prevail: "Lo! The Party of God Is Victorious." (5: 56)[24]

4.2 JIHAD AND MARTYRDOM

The classical distinction between offensive and defensive *jihad* is well-known in the literature. It is adequately discussed in the 'manual' of *jihad* and martyrdom.[25] In a similar fashion, Khosrokhavar distinguishes between what he calls the "two forms of martyrdom", namely, "offensive martyrdom" and "defensive martyrdom", which respectively correspond to offensive and defensive *jihad*.[26] Moussalli illustrates the holy matrimony that exists between *jihad* and martyrdom. According to him,

> "*Hizbullah* adheres to the doctrines of *al-jihad al-akbar* (greater struggle) and *al-jihad al-asghar* (smaller struggle). Whereas the smaller *jihad* denotes the combating of activities against the enemies of Islam, the greater *jihad* was defined by the Prophet as that which encompasses the individual's service to the cause of religion. *Hizbullah* broadens the notion of greater *jihad* to include all efforts that an individual exerts to complete his duty as a believer... *Jihad* has basic characteristics like realism... Although struggle (*jihad*) aims at transforming any institution that opposes and does not allow Islam to be freely practiced, it is neither *suicide* nor a campaign of *atrocities*".[27] (Italics added for emphasis)

Nasrallah affirms, "Not all fighting is jihad". According to him, the Islamic-Qur'anic terminology (*mustalah*) or definition of *jihad*, is that *jihad* is the specificity of fighting in the name of God: "Oh believers, if you journey [fight with the sword] in the way of Allah be discerning... And he who kills a believer intentionally will, as punishment, be thrown into Hell, dwelling in it forever; and Allah will be angry with him, curse him and prepare for him a dreadful punishment." (4:94-93) According to Nasrallah, this is par excellence the toughest punishment in the Qur'an inflicted upon a person who intentionally kills a believer, for this a *kabira* (the worst sin). Nasrallah adds that *jihad* has its own religious injunctions and jurisprudence; there is *halal* (religiously sanctioned) and *haram* (religiously prohibited) in *jihad*. That is why he stressed the need to ask the jurisprudents about the jurisprudential details dealing with the *jihadi* work, or else this work will not be done for God, rather for some other end. Thus, *jihad* in the name of God should be governed by the God's Shari'a, God's legitimacy, and the total subjugation and obedience to God's volition. From here comes the devotion to martyrdom and the love of meeting God.[28] From this perspective, Nasrallah offered an outright condemnation of the 11 March 2004 train terrorist bombings in Madrid that claimed the lives of 191 innocent civilians and wounded around 1,400 others. Nasrallah said, "What has happened in Madrid is condemned by all standards and criteria... We in Hizbullah denounce it as a horrible crime and a blatant attack against innocent civilians and people. Every attack that targets innocent civilians to whichever country or religion or nation they belong to is a cowardly act that is vehemently censured from an Islamic, Qur'anic, and Muhammadi perspective".[29]

Although many scholars acknowledge that terrorism is the weapon of the weak[30], it seems that they do not adequately stress that 'relative deprivation', which is usually coupled with a loss of dignity and identity, is one of the main causes of what the West calls 'terrorism', and Islamic movements label as 'self-sacrifice' or 'martyrdom'. From the perspective of relative deprivation theories, "a group member engages in collective action any time that she or he is acting as a representative of the group and where the action is directed at improving the conditions of the group as a whole." Collective action seems to justify "why a person might forgo his or her personal interests and choose instead to take actions designed to the ingroup as a whole."[31] Thus, martyrdom could be classified as an altruistic act aimed at furthering collective action. The 'domino effect' of martyrdom operations in the West Bank, Gaza, and Israel seem to substantiate this conclusion. Sayyid Ibrahim al-Musawi[32] offers a religious-ideological explanation arguing,

[A] combination of frustration, anger, oppression, despair, a strong faith[33] and an unquestionable dedication all culminate to make the Palestinians what they are now: human bombs... the Lebanese victory against the Israeli Army provides the best example of how to liberate a people's land. The Lebanese have had experience of self-sacrifice operations, although they were not the first to carry them out... resistance fighters in southern Lebanon and occupied Palestine have marched relentlessly as human bombs toward their targets. Members of the Islamic groups in southern Lebanon and Palestine carry out their self-sacrifice operations on a basis of religious belief and courage in taking the ultimate test of faith. They believe this sacrifice will be compensated by God's ultimate reward: Heaven. Religion, however, forbids such acts in the presence of alternative actions that could attain the same results. In the face of a superior Israeli army and its great arsenal, and in the absence of any effective external support, Palestinians find themselves with little choice but to resort to such methods to fight against Israeli terror and subjugation. As such these actions become accepted by religion. Jihad in Islam is not assigned to women as a duty, yet Ayatullah Fadlallah has authorized women to carry out such operations under the current conditions in Palestine. Israelis have violated Palestinian rights and dignity. Recently, Bush issued a new '*fatwa*' proclaiming that a suicide bomber is a murderer and not a martyr. This is contrary to the Qur'an and to the Prophet's teachings... The answer is that the queue of self-sacrifice bombers [domino effect] is growing longer, as the rest of the world waits.[34]

Al-Musawi's explanation entails value-laden terminology reflecting, not only Hizbullah's understanding of concepts such as 'self-sacrifice', 'martyrdom', 'suicide', etc., but also the Islamic movements' perception of these concepts. In order to come to grips with Hizbullah's and the Islamic movements' insight into these concepts, I start by defining what martyrdom is. Then, I distinguish among the four senses of martyrdom; afterwards, I discuss the origin and causes of martyrdom, *fatwa*s and opinions on martyrdom, and I end up by differentiating between martyrdom and suicide. Since some authors use jihad and martyrdom interchangeably, thus blurring the distinction between the two terms, I start by offering, in the next section, the working definition of martyrdom that this chapter adopts.

4.3 MARTYRDOM

Definition of martyrdom
As a working definition of martyrdom, I adopt Momen's and Moussalli's definitions fusing them into one definition. According to Momen, "the ultimate in [self]-sacrifice [altruism] is martyrdom, in which a person sacrifices his or her own life itself for religion."[35] Thus in Islam, martyrdom is the highest and most extolled form of *jihad*.[36] According to Moussalli,

> *The martyr has a special place in Islam, because he is not punished on the day of judgment and is promised Paradise.* Although historically and *theoretically* Muslims have practiced martyrdom in defending their existence and land, it is not nor-

mally considered something that was acquired through fighting fellow Muslims. The fundamentalists believe that Islam has commended martyrdom as a way of uplifting the community and defending the weak [oppressed] and the community. For them, it is considered to be a sign of ultimate belief in God. Today, it is mostly practiced by fundamentalists, especially radicals, who use it as a distinguishing mark of their activism (*harakiyya*).[37] (Italics added for emphasis.)

Based on empirical[38] and theoretical research considerations, I suggest that the common definition of martyrdom among Muslims and non-Muslims, devout and secular, is that it seems to be regarded as a form of altruistic behavior. I propose that, for Muslims, it is based mainly on the Qur'anic interpretation of symbolic capital; for non-Muslims, the nationalistic dimension of symbolic capital seems to be the most salient.

Inspired by the martyr's mother[39], theorizing the debate, I argue that *jihad* and martyrdom, as carried out by Islamic movements resisting occupation, are forms of altruistic or self-sacrificial behavior, which is conveyed in the form of symbolic capital. (Altruism is a supererogatory act, i.e. an act done beyond the call of moral duty or obligation). Bourdieu defined symbolic capital as the "degree of accumulated *prestige*, celebrity, consecration or *honour* [*dignity*, possessed by someone and] founded on the dialectic of knowledge and recognition."[40] (Italics added for emphasis) Since Hizbullah labels itself as an 'Islamic *jihadi* movement'[41], symbolic capital acquires vital importance. "Symbolic capital refers here to the status of a fighter for the cause of 'true Islam' whatever that means.[42] The Koranic verse [4:95]…, which states that 'God hath granted a grade higher to those who strive and fight with their goods and persons' conveys this idea of symbolic capital. The more one fights with one's 'goods' or 'one's' 'person', the more one accumulates symbolic capital".[43] However, symbolic capital is not only confined to those who fight under the banner of Islam; it is also employed by nationalist and other resistance movements. For instance, the Syrian Social Nationalist Party leader said in justifying resistance and martyrdom: "Life is only a stance embodied in pride and dignity[44] (*Ina al-hayat waqfatu 'izzin faqat*)".[45] Building on the aforementioned, in the next section, I differentiate among the four senses of martyrdom, mainly among Islamic movements, but that could also be applied to non-Islamic ones. Thus, the next sections might answer the question why people martyr themselves. Does everyone will martyrdom, or is it sometimes 'accidental'?

Four senses of martyrdom[46]

The Messenger of God [Prophet Muhammad] said: "Nobody who dies and has something good for him with Allah will (ever like to) return to this world even though he were offered the whole world and all that is in it (as an inducement), except the martyr who desires to return and be killed in the world for the (great) merit of martyrdom that he has seen."[47]

According to Wensinck, "the essence of the later Muslim doctrine of the martyrs is already found in the Kor'an [9:20; cf. 47:4; 61:11]... The admiration of the martyrs expressed in Allah's book [Qur'an], is developed into a doctrine by tradition and dogmatics, a doctrine the centre of which is the close relation between martyrdom and paradise... Moreover the martyrs are elevated in rank above the other inhabitants of paradise."[48] Keeping in mind that the martyrs are absolved from the Day of Judgement and that "their sins have been cancelled by their meritorious life and death"[49], I distinguish among the following four categories of martyrdom basing myself on primary sources:[50]

Martyrdom 1): *al-istishhadi al-mujahid* (hard-core altruist, a supererogatory act): The word *al-mujahid* is implied, but not directly stated. 'The martyred fighter' corresponds to a Muslim person who – in performing jihad, or holy war – intentionally and willingly blows himself up in the battlefield or keeps on fighting in the battlefield till he dies (never surrenders) in order to inflict the highest amount of damage and fatalities on the enemy. According to Prophet Muhammad, this person is neither washed nor wrapped in a burial shroud (*la yughsl wa la yukaffan*)[51], although it is generally stipulated as a religious obligation to do so. As is acknowledged in the *hadith*, the "angels wash him". As interpreted by Qasim, this special treatment is done in recognition of his special status, or performed as a token of gratitude and a sign of special commemoration (*takrim*) for his great deeds. This corresponds, for instance, to the twelve Hizbullah fighters who blew themselves up targeting Israeli military and intelligence personnel during the occupation of Lebanon.[52]

Martyrdom 2): *al-shahid al-mujahid* (altruist, a supererogatory act): 'The martyr fighter' corresponds to a Muslim person who, in performing *jihad*, falls in the battlefield while facing the enemy. For instance, this is the case of Hadi Nasrallah and other Hizbullah fighters who confronted the IDF in conventional warfare without blowing themselves up. Like category one, the martyred fighter, the martyr fighter is neither washed nor wrapped in a burial shroud. The angels wash him. This corresponds, for instance, to the 1,281 Hizbullah fighters who had died in confronting Israel from 1982 till 2000.

Martyrdom 3): *al-shahid* (victim, not supererogatory act): 'The martyr' corresponds to an innocent civilian Muslim person who died without taking part in the fighting. He/she is washed and wrapped in a burial shroud because he/she died outside of the battlefield. However, the final evaluation is for God (*al-taqyyim 'inda Allah*). As Ayatullah Khamina'i puts it, "for every person martyrdom is a special prerogative. If God responded to his/her call (*du'a'*) and considered his death as martyrdom, then God has bestowed upon him/her the highest dignity and prerogative in return for his/her essence that has gone to heaven".[53] As Wensinck puts it, "whosoever demands martyrdom from Allah in uprightness obtains the place of a martyr, even if he should die in his bed."[54]

Martyrdom 4): *shahid al-watan* or *shahid al-qadiyya* (altruist, a supererogatory[55] act): 'The martyr of the nation-state' or 'the martyr of a cause' corresponds to a non-Muslim who died in the battlefield fighting for his country or the cause he believes in. God is the only one who evaluates whether he/she could take the remuneration (*ajr*) of a Muslim martyr and be elevated to the level of martyr fighter in the full Islamic jurisprudential sense of the word. This corresponds, for instance, to the non-Muslim Lebanese Army soldiers who died in the confrontation with Israel, the same day Hadi Nasrallah and his two companions died. Also, non-Muslim fighters of the September 1997 Hizbullah formed 'Lebanese Multi-Confessional Brigades' (*Al-Saraya Al-Lubnaniyya Limuqawamat Al-Ihtilal Al-Israeli*) fall in this category. They are buried according to the specific rites of their respective religions.

This classification leads us to inquire about the origin and causes of martyrdom. Is a sense of hopelessness the motivation behind martyrdom? Or is sexuality the motive behind such operations, I mean what some media portray as the alleged 70 or 72 virgin brides waiting for the martyr in heaven? If this is the case, then if the martyr is a woman, what does she obtain as a reward or receive in return?

Origin of martyrdom: Causes and motivation
Shedding light on the first martyrdom operation by a Palestinian mother, an editorial in *Al-Sharq* Newspaper entitled, "Martyrdom Resistance is the Culture of Downtrodden People" questioned the reasons for martyrdom operations in the Occupied Territories arguing that Israel and the US brand such operations with terrorism as a pretext to continue occupation and their 'iron-fist' policy. According to the editorial, these retaliating measures are incapable of eliminating terrorism; rather they are conducive to enflaming the so-called terrorists to sacrifice themselves. *Al-Sharq* stressed the need for a profound vision and thorough scientific study in order to find out the real causes that drive this growing number of educated youth to voluntarily enlist to conduct martyrdom operations, irrespective of the ideological, doctrinal, religious, or secular beliefs that they adhere to. The editorial concluded that popular resis-

tance or martyrdom is the only available and viable weapon that is capable of confronting "the arrogance that is fortified by shear power [Israel]." In other words, liberating occupied lands can be achieved by relying on the experiences of the Lebanese resistance [Hizbullah's model] and the victory that was achieved by forcing the 'Zionist occupation' [Israel] to withdraw from southern Lebanon. In short, the Israeli withdrawal encouraged the *Intifada* to adopt the martyrdom model in its resistance to the 'Zionist occupation.'[56]

Richard Antoun contends: "Passages from the Quran suggest that martyrs sit next to God with other righteous men, and *they enjoy multiple virgin brides.*"[57] (Italics added for emphasis.) I argue that the first part of the sentence is corroborated by the traditions attributed to the Prophet, but the second part is an unsubstantiated fiction that is neither warranted in the Qur'an nor in the *hadith*. Instead of validating his claim with the alleged Qur'anic verses, Antoun quotes Joel Greensberg's article in the *New York Times* issue of 25 January 1995. As far as I know, there are neither Qur'anic verses nor *hadith*s referring to 'multiple virgin brides' being offered as a reward for a martyr. On these grounds, I argue that Antoun's claim is an unsubstantiated myth that has no foundation in official religion whatsoever.

Condoleeza Rice, the US national security advisor at the time, tried to explain suicide operations arguing, "[A] sense of *hopelessness* provides a fertile ground for ideologies of hatred that persuade people to forsake university educations, careers and families and aspire instead to blow themselves up – taking as many innocent lives with them as possible."[58] (Italics added for emphasis.) Barbara Victor[59] subscribes to a similar view. In her study on Palestinian women suicide bombers, she contends that the main motive for this 'fatal cocktail' is that a 'culture of death' entered into the psyche of the Palestinian people as a result of hopelessness, social stress, and depression, which these relatively destitute women suffered from. Such a theory seems untenable, especially after a pregnant woman, a well-to-do lawyer, and a mother of two blew themselves up. Contrary to Rice and Victor, Harik rightly argues that "the fundamentalist rationale behind this tactic [martyrdom operations] stands at odds with the common belief that terrorists are raving lunatics who strike out blindly at those they hate."[60] In this respect Momen states,

> The theme of sacrifice and martyrdom stands uncomfortably in today's secular, hedonistic world. Most of the mainstream orthodoxies, in the Christian world at least, appear embarrassed by it and do their best to minimize its place in religion... In some new religious movements... there is a strong emphasis on self-sacrifice and arduous work to advance the cause. Perhaps its appeal to youth lies in the

commitment, intensity and idealism that it demands, which contrasts with their bland, cocooned existence".[61]

Keeping in mind Moussalli's argument that *jihad* "is neither suicide nor a campaign of atrocities", contrary to Rice, Ayatullah Fadlallah argued, "self-martyrdom is not the result of brainwashing, nor is it irrational or immoral. Those who interpret martyrdom in such a way are guided by the premises of psychology."[62] In refuting the psychological approach[63] to the study of martyrdom, Fadlallah argues,

> The problem with the discipline of psychology is that it attempts to study the phenomenon of martyrdom from the perspective of a pragmatic vocabulary and laboratory results. They [psychologists] refuse to admit that certain things can be understood only through labor and pain. You can never be capable of appreciating freedom if you do not come to grips with enslavement. You can appreciate the crises of the starved only when you come to grips with the pangs of starvation."[64]

In spite of Fadlallah's criticisms of psychological approaches to martyrdom, Antoun stresses that "the significant reward for martyrs are psychological or soteriological (gaining salvation), depending on one's worldview. The suicide bomber's death is described by militants as 'the martyr's wedding' (i.e., an occasion of joy and celebration). The martyr is said to become a saint and sit next to God in heaven. His family takes pride in his supreme achievement and receives the esteem of the community" [symbolic capital].[65] In a similar vein, Khosrokhavar postulates "three themes of the martyrs' predilection: (1) The mutation between sadness and joy; (2) The motivation to struggle against the oppressor; and (3) The identification of the martyr's death with marriage, which justifies the festivities, the refusal of sadness, and the necessity of a collective joy." According to Khosrokhavar, the martyrs do not die, but remain living and present in the midst of the people. As such, sacred death is not a duty, rather a realization of the most ardent desire. Also, Khosrokhavar adds that the theme of the martyr's blood is of vital importance; by being spilled on earth, blood enforces and revitalizes the sacred cause of combating the forces of evil. According to him, this miraculous, soteriological virtue originates from the sudden emissions of the (martyr's) body, emissions that liberate the combatant's body energy and causes the future victory against the oppressors. Khosrokhavar concludes that the martyr invokes the family, in particular the mother, in order to earn her consent and blessings for promoting the holy ideas in the service of those for whom the martyr has sacrificed herself/himself.[66] (My translation).

Whatever the case, psychological or not, according to Fadlallah,

> What gives the martyr the right to die is not merely a cause in a theoretical sense,
> but the practical conditions that gave rise to that cause. In a sense, Fadlallah seems
> to be saying that the *'ulama'* must sanction martyrdom only when the situation
> requires self-martyring acts… But the *'ulama'*, in Fadlallah's view… are the con-
> science of the suffering community. Suffering is mainly caused at the hands of the
> Israelis, and the only answer to this suffering is martyrdom.[67]

Concerning the Arab-Israeli conflict in general, and the Palestinian-Israeli
conflict in particular, the Muslim *'ulama* issued many *fatwas* sanctioning
martyrdom operations.

Fatwas and opinions on martyrdom
It is worth mentioning that Imam Khumayni was the fist to sanction martyrdom operations arguing that they constitute the highest level of self-sacrifice
for the sake of religion.[68] Khumayni added, "[A]s Shi'ites we welcome any
opportunity for sacrificing our blood. Our nation looks forward to an opportunity for self-sacrifice and martyrdom"[69]; as such, "red death is much better
than black life".[70] Khumayni added, "our leader is that kid who blew himself
up in front of enemy tanks."[71] In turn, the Iranian *'ulama* in *Qum* issued a
fatwa sanctioning martyrdom operations.[72]

Ayatullah Fadlallah argued that martyrdom operations are legitimate
because they are conducted under the banner of *jihad* in order to drive out the
Israeli occupation forces, which conducted a dynamic 'extermination' of the
Palestinian population that has no recourse except to deter the occupier by
shattering his security in any plausible way.[73] Fadlallah adds, "a person must
face power with equal or superior power. If it is legitimate to protect one's
life, land, and destiny, then all means of self-defence become legitimate."[74]
In explaining the basis of martyrdom operations, Fadlallah seems to offer
psychological and rational-political justifications in spite of the fact that he
openly blasted psychological interpretations of martyrdom. According to him
the psychological component of martyrdom is "spiritual happiness". In elab-
orating that, Fadlallah argues, to the mind of Muslim practicing resistance
against occupation, "the choice of martyrdom and death is in agreement with
the spiritual and doctrinal foundations of the believer. Death becomes a self-
willed process instigated by internal factors. Also, 'death is a step that leads
to reaching the martyr's goal. That is why the believer, when he achieves self-
martyrdom, lives through *spiritual happiness*".[75] In explaining the rational-
political component of martyrdom, which is "legitimate resistance", Fadlallah

adds, "Suicide attacks in occupied Palestine [Israel] are not the craven acts of the morally depraved as they are portrayed by Western Media, but a form of *legitimate resistance* amid escalating dangers."[76] According to Fadlallah, many Qur'anic verses support the view that killing oneself is similar to homicide, in the sense that both need God's permission. Fadlallah argues,

> 'Basically, it is *haram* (prohibited by religion) to kill oneself or others; but during *jihad* (holy war or struggle for the sake of Islam), which is defensive or preventive war according to Islam, it is accepted and allowed, as jihad is considered an exceptional case'.[77] In analysing the theological arguments legitimising suicide attacks, Fadlallah said that Allah did not identify a certain procedure to fight the enemy and defend the rights of the nation ['*umma*]. 'If achieving victory means that we have to go through a minefield, which necessarily and definitely means that many are going to be killed, then we would go,' he said. Fadlallah said that the Palestinian perpetrators of 'martyrdom operations' do not target civilians, but rather aim to defend their people by inflicting damage and losses on the Israeli side to maintain a kind of equilibrium with the high-tech arsenal used by the Israeli Army."[78]

In addition, Fadlallah issued a fatwa sanctioning the martyrdom ('self-sacrifice') operations of Palestinian women[79], which is revolutionary because in Islam *jihad* is not incumbent upon women.[80] As al-Musawi puts it,

> Fadlallah also contradicted views widely held by Islamic scholars on the role of women in jihad, saying women are allowed to participate and carry out 'self-sacrifice' operations. 'Nothing in Islam prevents women from embracing struggle and fighting for the sake of Allah. Women initially are not required to fight, for this is men's duty, but under certain circumstances [in the 'Occupied Territories'] it might be a women's duty as well'.[81]

Both Imam Khumayni and Sayyid 'Ali Khamina'i consider martyrdom as the highest level of self-sacrifice for the sake of religion, arguing that there is no difference between a man and a woman from a *shar'i* (religious) perspective.[82]

'The Council of Muslim *Ulama*' argued that self-sacrifice operations conducted against Israeli occupying forces [of Arab lands] are legitimate and they constitute the highest degree of martyrdom. They added that since martyrdom is conducted consciously, freely, and willingly, and since it is done out of a doctrinal belief in God, then it is one of the most important strategic weapons available to the resistance in order to enforce its will and try to counter the superior power of the Israeli forces.[83] The radical Shaykh Hamid al-'Ali argued that martyrdom operations are intended to kill the occupying 'infidels' in order to spread terror in their hearts, thus forcing them to relinquish occupation of Muslim land. If this process results in the inevitable death of some women and children, as a consequence, and not on purpose, then this is religiously (shar'an) sanctioned.[84]

It is interesting to note that these views on martyrdom are not only confined to Muslim discourse; rather, there seems to be a correspondence between Muslim discourse and Christian discourse, rendering the issue a nationalistic one. I take the late Edmond N'im, the Lebanese Maronite judicial, constitutional, and international law expert, as a case in point.[85] N'im gave a 'fatwa'[86] contending "the martyrdom operations in occupied Palestine [Israel] are certainly legitimate." He argued public international law sanctions the Palestinian people to face the Israeli superior military might by all available means in order to reach a balance with the means used by the Israelis. If the Palestinian people cannot find effective ways [to alter the Israeli military might], they have the right to blow themselves up in Israeli territories proper, in response to the Israeli destructive, sabotage, and killing operations perpetrated in Palestinian land. That is why, martyrdom operations are legitimate because they are the *only* means that the Palestinians can resort to in order to stand against the advanced weapons used against them by the Israelis. He conceded that targeting civilians in all violent confrontations is prohibited. However, this injunction holds only when there is, more or less, a balance of power among the warring nations. This is certainly not the case in Palestine. Therefore, when it comes to determining the aggressor; there is no difference among the military and the people of the aggressing nation. Since the military aggressing forces cannot be stopped by any weapon that the aggressed upon have, then the resistance has the right to resort to [Palestinian] human bombs against [Israeli] civilians. And so, there is no distinction between a settler, a civilian, and Israeli military. In short, N'im affirms that from the perspective of international law, "overwhelming power needs overwhelming resistance".[87] Thus, N'im mirrors Nasrallah's discourse offering, as he claims, an International law[88] justification in addition to the ideological one.

Acknowledging the problematic, Bin Eli'azar, the ex-Israeli Minister of Defense, conceded that there could not be any victory against Palestinian suicide bombers.[89] In a similar vein, Davis argues, "Lebanon's suicide bombers have been effective against Israel, according to Boaz Ganor, an Israeli terrorism expert and executive director of the International Policy Institute for Counter-Terrorism. In an article published by Ganor's institute on April 25, 1998, he said that suicide attacks during the 1980s led to the Israeli withdrawal from southern Lebanon and had even broader consequences:

This served as a proof for the Palestinian-Islamic organizations that a readiness for self-sacrifice, determination, and long-term vision, together with the correct use of terrorist strategies (and with the reliance on the influence of mass media on western opinion), can lead to far reaching military and political achievements. Activists in the Islamic organizations quickly learned that suicide missions are extremely effective. (A relatively small number of high-impact suicide missions succeeded in ousting from Lebanon the French, the Americans and eventually the Israelis.) The Palestinian-Islamic organizations, relying on a fundamentalist ideology similar to that of Hezbollah, started to learn and imitate the new terrorist methods, and preached daring and self-sacrifice in preparation for suicide missions".[90]

Bearing the aforementioned discussions in mind, the time has come to address the difference between suicide operations and martyrdom ones.

Suicide and martyrdom[91]

From the perspective of theoretical and practical ethics, the foundation rests on the distinction between what psychological egoism calls suicide: "All voluntary human actions are selfishly motivated", and what normative ethical theories label as altruism. Suicide is the opposite of altruistic or self-sacrificial behavior. As mentioned earlier, altruism is a supererogatory act, i.e. an act done beyond the call of moral duty or obligation.[92]

According to Kohlberg, Muslim authors "while unequivocally condemning suicide, ... attempted to define as precisely as possible the borderline between dangerous but praiseworthy behaviour [martyrdom] and foolhardy rush to perdition [suicide]."[93] Kohlberg tries to answer the question, "is it permissible for an individual warrior to attack a large enemy force?"[94] He comes to the conclusion that there seems to be a consensus among medieval Muslim jurists, belonging to different schools of law, that it is indeed the case: "jurists by and large upheld the principle of the quest of martyrdom placing only minimal restrictions on its realization."[95] Keeping in mind Kohlberg's argument that "modern ideas about martyrdom cannot be understood in isolation; they draw their inspiration from the past"[96], the analogy with contemporary suicide bombers is not that far-fetched. Kohlberg writes:

> In defending the actions of the suicide bomber, for example, some present-day writers compare him [her] to the individual soldier of medieval times who faced a large army: since the bomber's aim is martyrdom, and since he [she] is likely to cause damage to the enemy, his [her] action is not only licit, but conforms to God's will; it is not self-killing [suicide] but self-sacrifice [martyrdom]. These writers

maintain that if Muslims of the Prophet's days had been in possession of modern explosives, they would have used them in the same manner as today's fighters.[97]

From this perspective, Fadlallah, Qasim, and Nasrallah endeavored to set a line of demarcation between suicide and martyrdom for Islamic movements.

As mentioned in chapter 3, Ayatullah Fadlallah denounced the 9/11 operations as criminal-suicidal acts that constitute an ugly human genocide in all respects. These, according to him, are not martyrdom acts. He added that neither offensive nor defensive *jihad* justifies such acts that are denounced religiously (*shar'an*). These are vicious acts that are not sanctioned by any religion, civilization, or human logic. It is not right to use innocent, peaceful civilians as bargaining chips and means of leverage to change a certain [US] policy. Islamically speaking, it is wrong to engage oneself in such acts because there is no *shar'i* justification for them. 9/11 is a horrendous act that is not authorized by any religion or approved by any "heavenly message". Thus, Fadlallah is adamantly against targeting civilian means of transportation because their safety and security is a worldly humane concern from a *shari'* perspective.[98]

Why was Fadlallah so vehement is his condemnation of suicide attacks, while he blatantly supports martyrdom operations carried out by men and women? Fadlallah stressed a "linguistic distinction between 'suicide' and 'self-sacrifice'[99] operations. 'Suicide is considered a crime from the religious point of view.[100] One does not own his life to end it when he likes. Allah owns everyone's life and it is a great transgression to inflict harm as it is to others'. If one kills oneself or others without a religious permission, he will be punished in the hereafter by being immortalized in hell."[101] As I see it, there seems to be a concordance between Fadlallah's and Qasim's views.

Na'im Qasim distinguishes between suicide operations and martyrdom operations. In explaining the latter, Qasim exhorts parents to raise their children on the notions of *jihad* and martyrdom[102] or death in the name of God. According to him, the logic behind martyrdom is based on a religious understanding and belief in the hereafter where people live happily and realize all their dreams in addition to the fruits that behold the *umma* as a result of martyrdom. Qasim affirms that martyrdom, as the duty of defending and liberating occupied land, is an embodiment of the concept of obedience (*al-ta'a*)[103] to God and it is a "legitimate and religious responsibility" (*al-mas'uliyya al-shar'iyya wa al-taklif al-shar'i al-Ilahi*) that leads to eternal life. Qasim stresses that martyrdom is a voluntary, willed act that is based on the intellectual and theoretical foundations of a religious, psychological, and cultural upbringing embedded in the Qur'anic concept of *ithar*[104] or 'preference', preference of life in the hereafter, rather than the here and now, and preference of the *umma* over the individual. He concludes that martyrdom has specific religious safeguards (*dawabit shar'iyya*), meaning that, if inflicting injury, heavy casualties, or victory on the enemy cannot be done except by resorting to martyrdom, then it is welcomed as a religiously legitimate act. Contrary to Rice who does not distinguish between suicide and martyrdom, Qasim contends that suicide, not martyrdom, is an expression of *hopelessness*, frustration, and despair of life that usually occurs in the case of *non-believers* who are facing, for instance, economic, social, or political hardships. (Italics added for emphasis). Qasim is confident that while a believer surrenders to the will of God and knows that his/her patience will lead to rewards, a person who commits suicide will go to hell because he/she is not free to dispose his/her life as he/she deems fit. That is why understanding martyrdom and agreeing to it is not subordinate to international conventions or the enemy's and the 'oppressors' (*mustakbirin*) policies. Qasim continues to argue that it is quite natural that those wage an organized campaign against martyrdom in order to distort it and label it with demeaning connotations because it is a weapon that is tenable and cannot be under their control. That is why the West resorts to threats and intimidations that are of no avail to the martyrs, since "they live in this world, but are not part of it."[105] Qasim adds that martyrdom has given Hizbullah a special and extraordinary power that made the party's will to attain victory stronger, especially when power shifted in the direction of the 'enemies'.[106]

In this respect, Nasrallah has reiterated, on various occasions, that "victory is always the result of martyrdom." He also referred to the enormous pride and dignity in the hearts of the martyrs: "Our people in Palestine [West Bank and Gaza], as in Lebanon, possess a substantial power; they are lovers of martyrdom, lovers of meeting God, lovers of departing to the vicinity of God and the eternal gardens [garden of Eden]."[107] Harik notes that "this means that some [martyrdom] attacks will always succeed despite the most rigorous precautions taken to prevent them."[108] Nasrallah argues that martyrdom is as dangerous as non-conventional weapons because the target can never prepare a defense mechanism to deal with it, unlike the defenses that have been created to deal with almost any weapon. That is why martyrdom as a weapon is tenable and can never be controlled or contained by the 'enemy'.[109] As Saad-Ghorayed rightly remarks, Hizbullah

'does not pursue martyrdom as an end in itself', but as a means of achieving victory… without the imperative need for a defensive *jihad*, martyrdom becomes suicide, which is clearly proscribed in Islam and thereby not rewarded with an everlasting life in paradise, as is true martyrdom... [Nasrallah argued] 'Maybe some people think we crave martyrdom because we like to die in any way. No, we like to die if our blood is valued and has a great impact [on Israel]'.[110]

Thus building on what has been argued so far, one can claim that martyr-dom is the most efficient means available for the resistance to fight an out-numbered and outgunned occupation force. As Harik puts it, "martyrdom attacks are the means they have at hand to effectively confront the Israelis... if they had alternative weapons like the American-made Apache helicopter gun ships and the F 16 fighter planes used by the Israeli military establishment, they would use them instead."[111]

I would like to end by stressing that – contrary to the Palestinians who have blown themselves up into Israeli civilians – Hizbullah has never done so. Hizbullah has not engaged in any suicide operation against Israeli civilians in its eighteen-year struggle with the Israeli forces occupying south Lebanon. Rather, all its field and martyrdom operations targeted Israeli military and intelligence personnel. As Harik puts it,

> During the course of Hezbollah's seventeen-year struggle with Israel along the Lebanese/Israeli frontier in southern Lebanon, it has never been established by any party directly involved (including the United Nations contingent on the ground) that the Party of God has perpetuated a single terrorist attack against Israeli civil-ians... Hezbollah made an early strategic decision to exclude terrorist tactics from its jihad against Israeli occupation and stuck to it.[112]

Furthermore, Hizbullah has never conducted any suicide operation in Israel; rather, it has left it to the discretion of the Palestinians to do so. Nasrallah rationalizes this stance by arguing that "the Palestinians do not need anyone to fight on their behalf. They are capable of fighting on their own using their rifles, bombs, and the bodies of their martyrs in order to rapture the Zionist *disgrace and humiliation*[113] and defeat the Zionist entity."[114]

4.4 DO ONLY ISLAMIC MOVEMENTS ENGAGE IN MARTYRDOM?

It might be argued that the process of thought illustrated by the foregoing exposition on martyrdom, is that martyrdom operations are exploited by Islamic movements' leaders to grant religious capital to members and sup-porters who get killed in a political or military battle. Martyrdom, which is extolled as a religious (*shar'i*) injunction, is used by them as an instrument of mobilization, especially when these people are promised the ticket to heaven[115] if they conduct martyrdom operations. This might explain why Islamic movements and Hizbullah consider martyrdom as the ticket to heaven, while the West regards it as terrorist-suicide attacks.

It is worth mentioning that 'self-sacrifice', 'martyrdom', or suicide operations are not confined to Islam; there are 'nationalistic' types of martyrdom that have little or even nothing to do with religion, but with the struggle for national independence. For example, the Chinese communists during the insurrection in Shanghai in 1927; the Japanese kamikaze in wwii; the Liberation Tigers of Tamil Elam (LTTE) in Sri Lanka and India; the Kurdistan Worker's Party (PKK) in Turkey; Babbar Khalsa International (BKI) of India; and many others resorted to suicide operations.[116] As far as I know, the Chinese communists are Buddhists or Confucianists; the Japanese kamikazes are Shinto and Buddhists; the LTTE is mainly composed of Hindus and a few Christians[117]; and the BKI are Sikh. Gunaratna writes: "The LTTE has conducted one suicide operation in India. It is the only group to have killed two world leaders – the former prime minister of India, Rajiv Gandhi[118], and the president of Sri Lanka, Ranasinghe Premadasa – using male and female suicide bombers."[119] Qunaratna adds that between 1980 and 2000, for instance, the LTTE conducted 168 suicide operations, while the PKK conducted 22[120], which, I reckon, outweighed by far all suicide operations conducted in Israel and Lebanon during the same period.

In the Middle East, the Lebanese case exemplifies both trends: 'Islamic' and 'nationalistic martyrdom'. Compared to the Iranian and Palestinian case, Khosrokhavar classifies the Lebanese case as "ambivalent" wavering between 'martyrdom' and 'absurd death' because of the multiconfessional, sectarian nature of the Lebanese myriad. According to him, this along with the Israeli invasions created a "prosperous ground for martyrdom."[121] I turn attention to the fact that in the Lebanese case, Hizbullah was not the only political party that conducted martyrdom 1 operations against Israeli forces occupying Lebanon. Rather, Hizbullah had fierce competition from secular multiconfessional Lebanese political parties such as the rightist SSNP, the leftist LCP, the Ba'th Party, and the Naserite Social Party, especially in the years from 1985 till 1990.[122] While Hizbullah conducted 12[123] martyrdom 1 operations by Shi'ite males[124], SSNP and LCP performed martyrdom operations by both males and females of different religious denominations.

To begin with, I take the SSNP's martyrdom operations as a case in point. Although Khosrokhavar explains the 'religious motivation' behind Hizbullah's martyrdom operations, and the 'nationalistic' or 'political motivation' behind secular political parties' motivation[125], in the SSNP case, he seems to imply that, Sana Muhaydli[126], the seventeen-year-old Shi'ite SSNP girl, was the only SSNP martyr.[127] I argue that like Hizbullah, SSNP conducted 12 martyrdom 1 operations in total, which included, in addition to Sana, five other women. Thus, it seems that Khosrokhavar stresses religious capital[128], but is misinformed about or sidelines the eleven other SSNP martyrdom operations, which in addition to Shi'ites, were carried out by Sunnis, Druz, and even Christians.[129] I would like to stress the nationalistic aspect and the multiconfessional nature of nationalistic identity, rather than limiting it to one sect. My hypothesis is to try proving that, for instance SSNP and LCP, non-Shi'ite martyrs sacrificed their lives, not as 'absurd deaths', but as symbolic capital in order to uphold the *honor* and *dignity* of their nation and liberate their land, as was the case with Hizbullah martyrs, for example. Another contention and overgeneralization made by Khosrokhavar, concerning Muslim and secular martyrs, is that he argues that most of the martyrs come from poor, deprived classes (grassroots) of south Lebanon.[130] Based on fieldwork research, I found out that most of the martyrs were middle class; some even had university education.[131] Also, I have discovered that the martyrs came from different geographical locations in Lebanon, and not predominantly from south Lebanon as Khosrokhavar asserts. In the SSNP case, I was told that at least four martyrs had a university education and that they came from the middle class; one of them was even an aristocrat Christian.[132] As mentioned earlier, the SSNP martyrdom operations are based on its political ideology as stipulated by S'adé.[133] That is why, the SSNP martyrs were not only Lebanese, but included also Syrians and Palestinians. (This explains, why SSNP, unlike Hizbullah, sent martyrs to conduct martyrdom operations in Israel). The SSNP Sana Muhaydli[134], 'the bride of the south', is one of the most celebrated woman martyrs; she was only 17 when she blew herself up in 1985 in an Israeli patrol.[135] When I interviewed her father Yusuf[136], he argued that his daughter was a martyr and that she went to heaven even though she belonged to a secular political party. As he put it, "religion is for God, and the nation is for everyone (*aldin lil Allah wa alwatan lil jami'*)."[137] Sana's father reiterated S'adé's ideology: "Our martyrs are the indication of our victory."; "Our contact with the Jews is a contact of a foe to a foe." According to him, "Sana martyred herself to rid Lebanon and Natural Syria from occupation, so that the Syrian nation can live with honor and dignity." In highlighting the nationalistic will to power of the SSNP, Sana's father quoted S'adé, "In you is a power, which if actualized will change the course of history." In showing solidarity with the predominately Muslim Arab world, he quoted the SSNP leader: "We are all Muslims, some are Muslims by the Qur'an, others by the Bible, and still others by wisdom. There is no enemy fighting us in our religion, rights, and nation except the Jews."[138] He ended up by saying: "The blood that runs in our veins is not ours; rather it is the possession of our nation, when it requests it, it finds it." As such, "blood is the most extolled witnessing to life. It is a will that asks for death, when death is a road to life, it is a will expressed by our eternal martyrs." Thus building on S'adé, Sana's father links the concept martyrdom to the life and survival of the nation: "Our martyrs symbolize our great victories."

Another case in point is illustrated by the LCP upper middle-class Christian, Lola Abboud[139], the flower of the Biqa', "a courageous woman who fought for her land and for her people, and went to her death willingly... Abboud's avowedly devout Christian[140] family had already produced a long line of warrior-martyrs."[141] Lola came from the Lebanese village of al-Qar'un where Christians and Muslims live side by side in harmony and peaceful coexistence. According to Davis, Abboud became the "ideal martyr" for Palestinian women martyrs to emulate; "she had already paved that path in Lebanon."[142] According to her brother, Dr Fouad Elias Abboud, Lola was the "family's last martyr" when she blew herself up amongst the Israeli soldiers attacking her village on 20 April 1985; she was only 19 then.[143] According to him, the rationale for her martyrdom is that she was "fighting for the liberation of her own homeland", as a right and a duty and out of love for her country, in order to rupture the bitter humiliation and uphold the dignity and honor of her people. He argues that "a person is willing to die for his cause if it's a question of his very existence... All cases of martyrdom are cases of fighting for your existence... Every martyr of ours was a martyr who died in self-defence[144]. We never went to Europe or killed Jews there. We were defending our own children... Americans don't have that problem. They don't have to fight for their existence, and maybe that's why they don't understand or don't accept the concept of martyrdom".[145] Dr Abboud added: "The freedom fighter chooses death as a final choice. He doesn't choose it from the beginning. It's after he cannot fight anymore that he decides to kill himself... And she was fighting the Israelis within her own village. She was not fighting Israelis in Israel."[146] Davis alludes to the notion that martyrdom is an altruistic behavior of a supererogatory nature. Comparing Lola to "a modern-day Joan of Arc", she writes " it's fair to say that Loula Abboud's actions exceeded all expectations not only for women in war, but for men as well."[147] Since her martyrdom took place the day after Easter, it could be argued that her death served as a resurrection to her people. The Abboud's family patriotism was further conveyed when Dr Abboud acknowledged that he identifies with Hizbullah and regards Nasrallah "as a national hero". He added that Nasrallah "represents even me as a Christian. He represents my ideas, and I feel that he represents all Lebanese." Dr Abboud continued, "I am somebody who has put a lot of effort into liberating my country, and Hasan Nasrallah is somebody who was able to realize that dream for me. He was able to make it happen. He was responsible for the liberation of my country and I appreciate him for that."[148] Davis concludes that both Lola's mother and her brother did not perceive any antagonism between Lola's "death and their strong Christian beliefs, even though Christianity, like Islam, forbids suicide."[149]

A similar justification for martyrdom is offered by Munif Muhammad Ashmar, a father of two Hizbullah martyrs: Ali who blew himself up in the Israeli forces occupying Lebanon (*istishhadi*), and Muhammad who died on the battlefield fighting them (*shahid*). Before he conducted the operation on 20 March 1996, in his farewell address, Ali said, "… My body will become a fire that will burn the Zionist occupier, who everyday deliberately attempts to torture and humiliate you [the people]. However his [the occupier's] end is near, God willing, at the hands of the Islamic Resistance". The same rationale is offered by his father, Munif, who argues: "When duty calls and when there are dignities that are going to be downtrodden, when the pride and the honor of the *umma* is going to be downtrodden by the Jews, then we will not lay idle…"[150] I suggest that this discourse bears a striking resemblance to the SSNP slogan of "Life is only a stance embodied in pride and dignity", and that it is another indication of symbolic capital.[151]

And so, Khosrokhavar argues that the thematic (themes) and discourses of Lebanese martyrs, both secular and Shi'ite, are similar to the Iranian Shi'ite martyrs and Sunni Palestinian martyrs' discourses. The similarity is that all believe in the same values of combating the enemy through martyrdom, martyrdom that originates from a will to die and a desire of immortality. Khosrokhavar adds: "For the Shi'ites it is God's encounter that is realized by combating an infidel enemy. For the nationalists and the communists, immortality is achieved either by identification with the 'collectivité nationale' or by identification with all the poor [deprived] in the world."[152] (My translation.)

4.5 CONCLUSION

It seems that I subscribe to Reuter's[153] view, who stresses the individually driven nature of suicide bombers arguing that they "can be educated and uneducated; religious and secular; comfortably off and destitute; their link is the decision they make to transform their powerlessness into extraordinary power."[154] And so, in highlighting the long lineage between Islamic and national resistance (generalizing from my interviews with Sana's father and the martyr's mother of Hizbullah, as well as from the works of the aforementioned authors on martyrdom) I argue that martyrdom operations – whether carried out by Islamic movements or resistance movements – are altruistic, self-sacrificial operations conveyed in the form of symbolic capital (honor and dignity). This generalization seems to be warranted by a correspondence among the various discourses discussed above. Thus, I suggest that the common ground for both Islamic and nationalistic/secular movements is the agreement that living under occupation is tantamount to disgrace and humiliation. As such it is respectively a religious and nationalistic duty to end the occupation using all possible means, including martyrdom operations. In this chapter, I intended to express how both parties furnished a religious or secular political discourse to justify martyrdom, specifically to highlight how Hizbullah produced a religious discourse that became a model and a basis of justification for Islamic groups and movements, in particular the Palestinian ones. The icon that both parties, secularists and Islamists, embraced is that martyrdom operations were conducted in order to uphold *'izzat wa karamat al-umma* or the honor, pride, and dignity of the 'nation'; this being the main cause or motivation behind martyrdom operations. This value-laden expression of symbolic capital connotes different meanings of the word *'umma'* to the various adherents. Thus, for Hizbullah, the *umma* denotes the Islamic *umma*; for the SSNP the *umma* refers to the 'Syrian Nation'; and for the LCP the *umma* pinpoints to "all the poor [deprived] in the world." In its "Epilogue", Hizbullah's 2009 Manifesto accorded a high status to martyrdom and sacrifice:

> … for we are believers in righteousness; we speak in its defense and sacrifice in its quest until martyrdom… our deeds were… meant for the revival of virtue, the abolition of falsehood, the defense of your oppressed followers, the upholding of justice on your land and an appeal to your (God's) approval and nearness. For this our martyrs have died, and for this we continue to strive. You have promised us one of the two better goals/rewards (*husnayayyn*): either victory or the honor of encountering you through martyrdom.[155] (p. 71)

5 From Cooptation to Contestation to Political Power

ABSTRACT

The remaining chapters shift the tenor of the book to more practical matters of Hizbullah's political strategy in relation to its identity construction. Hizbullah altered its identity and militant character of the 1980s – when it anathematized the political system and regarded the Lebanese state as an apostate – to a gradual integration process in the political system, in particular, and the Lebanese public sphere, in general, since the end of the civil war in 1990 and the party's acceptance of the Ta'if Agreement, which became Lebanon's new constitution. This chapter suggests that Hizbullah adhered to its policy of cooptation and contestation from the early 1990s to 2005, the year PM Rafiq Hariri was assassinated and the Syrian troops withdrew from Lebanon after a presence of almost three decades, thus altering the rules of the game and even the geostrategic equation. This chapter argues that a bona fide policy shift, aiming at manipulation and obtaining more political power, picked momentum in the beginning of 2005, ensued with more vigour after the July 2006 War, and continues to be the norm till this day, through piecemeal socio-political engineering and identity reconstruction that allows Hizbullah to read and interpret events and react to these dynamic changes accordingly, dwelling on the complexity, flexibility, and pragmatism of Shi'ite jurisprudence, and thus rendering legitimacy to the party's behavior.

Hizbullah as an open national actor: The party's infitah policy
Since the public sphere "enables participation in collective choice, whether
about specific policy issues or basic institutions... [and since] the public
sphere is itself a medium of social integration, a form of social solidarity, as
well as an arena of debating others"[1], Hizbullah shed its irredentist ideology
and deemed it an absolute necessity to integrate into the Lebanese public
sphere, rather than to shun it by employing the policy of *infitah* (opening-up).
As mentioned earlier, in general, Hizbullah employs the term *infitah* or 'Lebanonization' to denote its political discourse, deeds, and policies in the era of
the political program[2], or to signify its enrolment in Lebanese domestic political life.[3] Thus, Hizbullah's *infitah* aims at inculcating an open dialogue policy
in a pluralistic setting through interaction and cooperation with all Lebanese
sects and communities that comprise the Lebanese myriad[4], in order to rid
Lebanon of its political and social problems, foster national unity, and build a
stronger, united Lebanon on shared common grounds.

Debates on the elections: An open public sphere?
Some changes that took place in the Lebanese politics illustrate the growing
importance of Hizbullah in the Lebanese public sphere. Although Hizbullah
initially regarded the political system, which does not take demographics into
perspective, as unfair and unjust, the party's integration into the Lebanese
system through electoral politics sheltered it with additional political legitimacy and a wider following. Hizbullah seems to have realized from the Iranian experience, as well as from the internal dynamics of the Lebanese public
sphere, that electoral politics (parliamentary and municipal elections[5]) is the
cornerstone of democratic practice. Hizbullah's participation in the elections
could be considered as a pivotal event in shaping its current identity.

    As mentioned in chapter two, after much heated debate and a lot of delib-
erations, Hizbullah took a favorable decision to participate in the 1992 elections, arguing that the interests outweigh the vices by far. Hizbullah presented
its findings to Imam Khamina'i and requested from him a formal legal opinion (*istifta'*) on the legitimacy of participating in the elections. As soon as
Khamina'i authorized and supported (*ajaza wa 'ayyada*) participation, Hizbullah embarked on drafting its election program and officially announced
its participation in the elections.[6] Thus, it seems that Hizbullah was forced by
the political circumstances, the Ta'if Agreement, and the end of the civil war,
to move to a new phase in its history by propagating a matter-of-fact political
program and by co-opting with the Lebanese system. Hizbullah shifted its

political strategy by accepting and engaging in the democratic process under a sectarian-confessional political and administrative system. Although Hizbullah is still primarily an Islamic movement, which changes its policies as circumstances change, it increasingly displays the characteristics of a nationalist-patriotic political party.

Hizbullah's advocacy of electoral politics
Hizbullah's election strategy is circumstantial and contextual, based upon and legitimized by the Shiʻite jurisprudential concept of public interest (*maslaha*): "For interests to be anything other than completely ephemeral preferences, they must be analyzable in terms of the identities of social actors."[7] Thus, in addition to its strategic alliance with Amal, speaker Berri's political party, Hizbullah reached out and allied itself with secular parties and former 'enemies' on the Lebanese scene, like any political party that accommodated its protest by negotiations and bargaining with a wide spectrum of groups across the Lebanese myriad, making compromises on some doctrinal aspects. It included Christians and Sunnis in its parliamentary bloc and the municipal councils it controlled.

All of Hizbullah's political programs from 1992 to 2010 stressed supporting the Resistance, even after the liberation of Lebanon from the Israeli occupation, which could be achieved through the enhancement of the Lebanese state's foreign policy. In the domestic sphere, Hizbullah called for the establishment of civil peace; the founding of the state of law and institutions; the promotion of political participation; political, administrative, social, and economic reforms; upholding public freedoms; *infitah* and dialogue among all the Lebanese. Hizbullah also stressed the need to address pressing social and developmental issues that deal with health, education and culture, as well as the environment. The party emphasized the need to attain social justice through constructive mechanisms that address the serious and pressuring socio-economic and financial crisis by finding a proper balance between material resources and human resources. This could be achieved, not only by defending and protecting the downtrodden and oppressed grassroots, but also by realizing socio-economic development, through projects targeting the deprived and dispossessed areas, aiming at a balanced development.[8]

In 1992, Hizbullah participated in the first parliamentary elections, which were frozen for a period of twenty years due to the Lebanese civil war. The party won all of the twelve seats on its election list: eight were reserved for party members, and four for affiliated sympathizers: two for Sunnis and two for Christians (a Greek Catholic and a Maronite).[9]

In the 1996 parliamentary elections Hizbullah managed to keep ten seats: seven were occupied by party members; two by Sunnis and one by a Maronite Christian, non-party members. Only the head of Hizbullah's parliamentary bloc, Sayyid Ibrahim Amin al-Sayyid, was a clergyman.[10]

Hizbullah won twelve seats in the parliamentary elections held in the summer of 2000. The party's nine candidates, along with two Sunnis, and one Maronite Christian, received the *highest number of votes in the country*. All Hizbullah's representatives in the parliament were civilian (no *'ulama*).[11]

Since its participation in the 1992 parliamentary elections, Hizbullah has played the role of a small but vocal opposition party in the legislature, which has grown increasingly powerful in recent years. Hizbullah participates in the legislature through the 'Loyalty to the Resistance Bloc', whose members have varied from ten to fourteen seats, and includes both party members as well as Sunni and Christian MPs not affiliated directly with Hizbullah, but sympathetic to the party's causes and issues. Between 1992 and 2009, prospective Lebanese cabinets received eleven votes of confidence from the legislature. Hizbullah's parliamentary bloc participated in all of these votes, exercising its voting behavior progressively according to the following pattern: from 1) voting against confidence between 1992 and 1996; to 2) abstaining between 1998 and 2004; to 3) voting for confidence since 2005, the year the party fielded incumbents to the cabinet. To wit, they gave their approval only after they participated.

By engaging in a pluralistic process, Hizbullah shifted its political strategy from cooptation to contestation, and finally to exercising empowerment. Hizbullah's participation in electoral politics could be regarded as cooptation. Its gradual integration into the Lebanese politics falls under contestation. Hizbullah's ascendancy in the political scene and becoming a nationalistic political party could be viewed from the stance of human empowerment (*tamkin*). The shift to electoral politics helped to foment a national politics, instead of the fragmented politics or 'states within the state', which each political party or denominational group endeavored to establish in Lebanon during the civil war era. Thus, Hizbullah moved from being a closed sectarian social movement to an open national actor employing the policy of *infitah*.

Hizbullah as a nationalist political actor

> Lebanon is our homeland and the homeland of our fathers, ancestors. It is also the homeland of our children, grandchildren, and the future generations. It is the country to which we have given our most precious sacrifices for its independence and pride, dignity and freedom.

We want a unified Lebanon for all Lebanese alike. We oppose any kind of partition or federalism, whether apparent or disguised. We want Lebanon to be sovereign, free, independent, strong and competent. We want it also to be powerful, active, and present in the geopolitics of the region. We want it also to be an influential provider in making the present and the future as it was always present in making the history.

One of the most important conditions for the establishment of a home of this type and its persistence is having a strong, capable and just state, in addition to a political system which truly represents the will of the people and their aspirations for justice and freedom, security and stability, well-being and dignity. This is what all the Lebanese people seek and work to achieve and we are a part of them.[12]

Since national identity "is commonly understood as being immutable, but in fact its salience varies... and its character is neither fixed nor the same for all nationals,"[13] Hizbullah expressed its Islamic legitimization in democratic form by portraying itself as a mainstream nationalist Lebanese political party while at the same time upholding its Islamic identity. Hizbullah's *infitah* and Lebanonization endeavored to convey how it was able to strike a balance between its Islamic identity and program, on the one hand, and its Lebanese national loyalty, on the other, through 'opening-up' to the various constituents of the Lebanese myriad. Although Hizbullah denies it, it seems its success in weighing between nationalist political commitments and its Islamic background was at the price of negotiations, bargaining, and compromises (even on some doctrinal issues), which characterize an open democratic system, a public sphere. Through buttressing civil peace, public freedoms, and a functioning civil society, Hizbullah attempted to preserve its Islamic identity while working within the domain of the Lebanese state's sovereignty, within a non-Islamic state and a multireligious, confessional-sectarian state.

In the post-Ta'if era, Hizbullah faced the problem of reconciling its political ideology with reality, so Hizbullah shifted from a *jihadi* perspective to a flexible *shari'a* perspective. The party became satisfied with positive (man-made) laws and legislations (*al-qawanin al-wad'iyya*) and even contributed to their legislation through its MPs in the parliament. Hizbullah argued that the *shari'a*, as a socially constructed phenomenon, is flexible and can account for all the complicities of modern life. And so, the party portrayed a distinguished flexibility in its political program in an attempt to reconcile, as much as possible, among its principles, aims, and political ideology, on the one hand, and the circumstances and its objective capabilities, on the other hand, by heavy reliance on the jurisprudential concepts of necessity, vices, and interests as a kind of Islamic prima facie duty. This is how Hizbullah's pragmatism was conducive in forging a marriage of convenience between political ideology and reality to the extent that Hizbullah was willing to place its political ideology on the shelf and pursue a policy of *infitah* as sanctioned by its political program. This dramatic change resulted in Hizbullah's involvement in the Lebanese political system *as it is*. Hizbullah justifies and legitimizes its political program and pragmatism by resorting to Qur'anic and jurisprudential bases. In fact, Shi'ite religio-political heritage conferred upon Hizbullah all the authenticity it needed in order to derive from it a political program based on flexibility and pragmatism.

Hizbullah developed a special relationship with Emile Lahud, the ex-general of the Lebanese army (1989-1998) and the then president of the Lebanese Republic (1998-2007). In 1993, when Lahud was general, he refused to obey the Lebanese cabinet and send the army to the south in order to uphold law and order and stop Hizbullah's resistance. Syria and Hizbullah were very pleased with this behavior. The relationship between Lahud and Hizbullah was further consolidated when Lahud visited Nasrallah in 1997 and 'congratulated' him on the 'martyrdom' of his son Hadi. In order to convey its nationalistic character, in November 1997 Hizbullah established the secular-patriotic Multiconfessional Lebanese Brigades to Fighting the Israeli Occupation (LMCB)[14], a move encouraged by Lahud. During Lahud's tenure as president, Hizbullah developed a strategic alliance with him as Syria's man in Lebanon who would not allow the Resistance to be disarmed.

Since the public sphere is defined by mutual participation[15], Hizbullah tried to portray itself as a big Muslim-Christian coexistence promoter stressing the importance of pluralism through multiconfessional representation. It incorporated Christians, including Maronites, in its parliamentary elections lists and granted them the right to speak in its name as long as they did not deflect from the party's established doctrines. Also, it shared municipal council seats with Christians. Thus, Hizbulah made it clear that the only condition for a sympathizer to speak in its name is to abide by its policy guidelines. Hizbullah's dialogue with the Christians, as stipulated in its political program, garnered the party support in its resistance against Israel and *infitah* policies, especially among the Christians. By adopting what many observers would consider 'Christian discourse', namely, the abolition of political sectarianism in the mentality, before abolishing it in the texts, Hizbullah is portraying a progressive-liberal, and pragmatic view on the abolishment of political sectarianism, which is in conformity with the stance of the Maronite church and the papal guidance. The Pope's call for fraternity and the inculcation of dialogue and tolerance among the Lebanese had a responsive cord in Hizbullah's circles since most of it was reminiscent of Imam Musa al-Sadr's discourse on

Christian-Muslim understanding, mutual coexistence, and open and permanent dialogue. Thus, in an endeavor of rapprochement towards the Lebanese Christians, Hizbullah based its political program of dialogue with them on the papal guidance.

Thus, it is most likely that the Lebanese public sphere is dictating certain policies on Hizbullah, and the Lebanese political structure seems to be co-opting Hizbullah to take decisions that may not be that popular to the rank, file, and leaders. On the whole, Hizbullah's decisions are based on *Realpolitik*, political expediency, benefit, and interest (*maslaha*). This calls into question the extent to which Hizbullah is willing to be co-opted into the Lebanese political system and state institutions as well as its possible diffusion in the public sector. Undoubtedly, the death of Rafiq Hariri along with the Syrian withdrawal and its aftermath played a major role in accelerating the political changes within Hizbullah.

5.2 ATTEMPTS AT MANIPULATION AND GAINING POLITICAL POWER

The strategy of manipulation after Hariri's assassination and the Syrian withdrawal

A major shift in the relations between Lebanon and Syria occurred after PM Rafiq Hariri's assassination on 14 February 2005.[16] This incident polarized the country into two main political groups. The predominantly Shi'ite March 8 Group comprising Hizbullah, Amal, and other pro-Syrian groups,[17] organized a demonstration in support of Syria. The other group known as the Cedar Revolution or the March 14 Trend[18] responded with an estimated demonstration of one million people, spearheaded by the 'Future Trend', the majority of whom are Sunni, in downtown Beirut to demand the withdrawal of the Syrian troops and the truth about Hariri's assassination. Under street pressure and UNSC Resolution 1559, Syria withdrew its military on 26 April 2005 after a presence of 29 years.[19] While March 14 hoped for the waning of Syrian influence in Lebanon, Hizbullah's strategic-political relationship remained strong with the Syrian regime.[20]

From 29 May to 19 June 2005, Hizbullah contested the first parliamentary elections after the Syrian withdrawal on the basis of a temporary four-partite alliance between Sa'd Hariri's 'Future Trend', Amal, and the PSP. Hariri's 'Future Trend' and his allies won 72 seats out of the 128. Hizbullah won fourteen seats[21], adding two seats to its previous gains.[22]

Hizbullah's leaders and cadres concede that the Syrian withdrawal hastened its joining the cabinet and proliferation in the Lebanese politics and state institutions. The party had resolved not to join the cabinet as long as the Syrians were present in Lebanon, since their presence accorded Hizbullah political patronage. After the Syrian withdrawal, however, Hizbullah felt that the Lebanese cabinet would be faced with decisions that might have grave consequences for Lebanon's future. Nasrallah has said that the 2005 parliament is the most important and most dangerous parliament since 1992, because it is obliged to decide the basic political and strategic choices for Lebanon in the decades to come.[23] The party deemed it necessary to seek a representation in the cabinet so as to influence its policy statement and its implementation.[24]

Nasrallah delivered a fiery speech in which he announced Hizbullah's intention to play a leading political and developmental role by fully integrating in the Lebanese politics through a complete enrolment in Lebanese political, economic, and administrative life, as well as the participation in all the Lebanese government's institutions, including the cabinet.[25] Capitalizing on the election results, Hizbullah participated in the cabinet with two ministers who were instrumental in drafting the section of the policy statement that grants Hizbullah the right to continue its resistance in the disputed Shib'a Farms. Sanyura remarked that he is "very pleased and honored" with Hizbullah's presence in the cabinet. Thus, Hizbullah was able to influence to its own advantage the cabinet's policy statement, as such manipulating the public sphere through the strong arm of the executive branch as represented by the council of ministers.[26]

Although two ministers cannot veto the Cabinet's decisions, it seems that Hizbullah gave up its older argument of refusing to be represented in the Cabinet because it rejected to hold responsibility for any dire decisions or unfavorable actions adopted by a 2/3-majority vote by the council of ministers.[27] Hizbullah thought that all decisions would take place according to the principle of 'consensual democracy', the principle of 'consensual democracy', whereby the unanimity of all the ministers would guarantee the passing of any legislation through Hizbullah's prudent tactics and forceful manipulation. In this case, Hizbullah thought that there would be no need for the 2/3-majority vote, which is only employed when there is a serious disagreement in the council of ministers. However, the precept of practice would prove Hizbullah wrong.

The setback: Hizbullah suspends its participation in the Cabinet; no to foreign tutelage & Nabulsi's religious edict (fatwa)

On 12 December 2005, the same day that *al-Nahar* anchor MP Gebran Tuéni was assassinated, the Lebanese cabinet met and referred this case, and other politically motivated assassinations, to the UN Commission investigating the Hariri murder, and asked for the formation of an International Tribunal (STL) to put to justice the perpetrators of these crimes. When the issue was put to the vote in the cabinet, as an apparent sign of disapproval, the five Shi'ite ministers walked out, including the two from Hizbullah, thus eventually suspending their participation in the council of ministers for a period of seven weeks. It was Nabulsi, not Nasrallah, who issued a *fatwa* barring any other Shi'ite from joining the cabinet in their absence.[28] Only after PM Sanyura reiterated Hizbullah's right to resist the Israeli occupation (in *Shib'a*), as stated in the policy statement, the five ministers returned to assume their duties.

A MAJOR STEP TOWARDS HEGEMONY: ALLIANCE WITH 'AUN

Saving Lebanon from civil war: Hizbullah's Understanding with the Free Patriotic Movement (FPM)

On 5 February 2006, after one day of the mobs torching the Danish embassy in Damascus as a protest against the cartoons of the Prophet, mobs attempted to set the Danish embassy on fire in the Christian East Beirut neighborhood. Mayhem erupted, and many shops, cars, and churches were vandalized, and the population cursed. Lebanese security forces failed to bring the matter to order, and as a result the Minister of Interior resigned, and Lebanon offered Denmark a formal apology.

In order to contain the negative repercussions of what happened and in order to prevent Christian-Muslim discord, not to say civil unrest or war, the next day, the leader of the FPM, general Michel 'Aun, and Sayyid Hasan Nasrallah, met in a symbolic church across the old 'green line' and signed a historic ten-point Understanding addressing political, economic, administrative, and security issues, as well as the relations with Syria. The Understanding also addressed domestic concerns such as administrative reform, election law, fighting corruption, and the investigations into the Harriri murder.[29] Interestingly, Article 7 entitled, "Lebanese-Syrian Relations", suggests four measures in order to ward off "foreign tutelage", including demarcating the borders between Lebanon and Syria[30]; uncovering the fate of the Lebanese detainees in Syrian prisons; and establishing diplomatic relations between the two countries. It is worth mentioning that the forgoing points represented the demands of the Maronite church, as well as the defunct Christian opposition group of 'Qrnet Shahwan'. Currently, these demands inform the policies of the March 14 Trend[31] in its entirety. Thus, Hizbullah succeeded in its manipulation strategy of weakening, splitting, or sowing discord in the March 14 ranks through its alliance with the FPM.[32]

Although the majority of the March 14 Trend are still Sunni and those of March 8 Group are still Shi'ite, the situation now is completely different since the four-partite alliance ceased to be. Most importantly, after the Understanding the FPM shifted its support to the March 8 Group. This escalated the tensions and the confrontations between the March 14 and March 8 groups.

HIZBULLAH LEADER MOCKED ON A LEBANESE TV COMEDY SHOW: CAN NASRALLAH CONTROL HIS FOLLOWERS AND CONSTITUENCY?

In the evening of 1 June 2006, LBCI aired its weekly political satire show entitled, *Basmat Watan*, which is a pun that could imply either 'The Death of a Nation' or 'The Laughs of a Nation'. Anyway, one of the actors, dressed like Hizbullah's leader in his black turban and religious attire, mocked Nasrallah as a political leader, and not as a religious leader. In spite of that, Hizbullah's constituency took to the streets chanting Imam Husayn's call in *Karbala*': "Death to humiliation" (*hayhat minna al-dhilla*), intending to go all the way to the Christian heartland to 'burn down' LBCI. On their way they wreaked havoc in Sunni and Christian areas, almost physically engaging the youth residents of these areas. After Hizbullah's MPs and middle-rank cadres failed to contain their crowds, in an unprecedented call, Nasrallah in person, by way of Hizbullah's media, called on the demonstrators to return to their homes. Although they immediately obeyed, the riots tainted Hizbullah's image as an advocate of free speech and expression.

NATIONAL DIALOGUE ENDS IN A FIASCO

The 2006 national dialogue[33] sessions among the fourteen leading politicians in Lebanon dealt with sensitive issues, including taboos such as Hizbullah's weapons and its defense strategy. Nasrallah, in person, took care to convey Hizbullah's position. The first session took place in March where a consensus was reached on two important issues: 1) the affirmation that *Shib'a* farms[34] are Lebanese, and thus Hizbullah has the right to continue its resistance against the occupying IDF; 2) the formation of an International Tribunal[35] to put to justice the perpetrators of the Hariri murder. The last session was supposed to take place on 25 July, but due to the 'Second Lebanon War' it never took place. This led to an eventual halt to national dialogue.[36]

The 'Second Lebanon War' or the July 2006 war between Israel and Hizbullah was triggered when Hizbullah kidnapped two Israeli soldiers on 12 July in a cross-border raid.[38] Hizbullah's strategic mistake might have been that it never anticipated such an action would spark a large-scale conflict that would ultimately lead to the destruction of almost all of Lebanon's postwar achievements. Although some Lebanese question the wisdom of Hizbullah's action that was used by Israel as a pretext to inflict so much damage on Lebanon, Hizbullah emerged from this crisis enjoying much more popularity than before, at least in its main constituencies.[39]

The media war: psychological warfare
Although the main role of Hizbullah's media was to mobilize its constituency and raise its morale, *al-Manar*[40] kept on portraying its regional and international outreach to the Muslim *umma* and its members worldwide through its motto, 'the channel of the Arabs and the Muslims'. During the 'Second Lebanon War', Hizbullah's media displayed a remarkable will of survival. Even though Israel completely leveled the *al-Manar* building and that of *al-Nour* sustained substantial damage, they were not out of the air for a single minute because Hizbullah had already prepared for contingency measures and alternative places to broadcast. Both continued to broadcast from undisclosed underground locations.[41] Likewise, *al-Intiqad* was regularly published on time every Friday, even appearing twice in the second week of the war[42] in order to accompany Hizbullah's 'feats' on the battlefield.

Destruction of cultural capital
In and around Hizbullah's 'Security Square' (*al-Muraba' al-Amni*) fifty-one publishing houses were totally destroyed, most of which dealt with religio-political issues. Indeed, where religion thrives, publications flourish. Many of these publishing houses did not keep their records on microfilm. Hizbullah's think tank, the CCSD, was completely wiped out. Many Hizbullah-affiliated schools, universities, and institutions of higher learning were obliterated.

The Lebanese cabinet's pragmatic moves: Hizbullah approves UNSC 1701
In an attempt to stop the war, on 5 August 2006 the Lebanese Cabinet unanimously endorsed PM Sanyura's Seven Points[43], although the fourth point stressed that the state has absolute monopoly over the use of force. After rejecting the UN draft resolution that fell short of demanding an Israeli with-

drawal, and in an attempt to influence the wording of the new resolution to Lebanon's advantage, in an unprecedented move[44], the Lebanese cabinet unanimously approved deploying 15,000 Lebanese soldiers from the Litani river to the border with Israel. This seems to constitute a genuine policy shift rather than a rhetorical move, since Hizbullah's earlier discourse vetoed sending the army to the south "to protect Israel from the attacks of the Lebanese Resistance." The cabinet also approved the 11 August 2006 UNSC Resolution 1701, which calls, among other things, for the cessation of hostilities and Hizbullah's disarmament – like the 2 September 2004 UNSC Resolution 1559 called for. In these decisions, Hizbullah's two ministers voted 'yes'. Indeed, "choices are actions (individual and collective) that imply the availability of multiple possibilities."[45]

Hizbullah is fully conversant that the public sphere "opens the possibility that actors may redefine their interests in the course of public communication and shifting understanding of both collective good and individual and collective identity."[46] Employing this precept, and keeping in mind that as a survival strategy Hizbullah changes as circumstances change, Nasrallah asserted that accepting the deployment of the army to the south – which is a repetitive Israeli demand to the Lebanese government – and agreeing to the terms of UNSC Resolution 1701 "serve national interest since the strength of Lebanon is in its resistance and national unity." Although this policy seems to be aimed at more integration and *infitah*, the real goal was to exercise more hegemony.

The devastation of the July 2006 War
Lebanon paid a heavy price: Israel imposed an air, land, and sea blockade almost completely severing the country from the outside world for approximately eight weeks – from 13 July to 8 September. In terms of material resources, Lebanon's infrastructure and economy were destroyed, its industries and exports were curtailed, and foreign investments ceased to be. Israel dismembered Lebanon through the systematic destruction of its roads, bridges, airports, harbors, telecommunication facilities, fuel supplies and reservoirs, electricity facilities, factories, etc. It was estimated that the tourism sector alone would have provided a net income of $ 4.5 billion during the summer season. According to a UN report, Lebanon lost $ 15 billion in damages and revenues, and was losing $ 50 million a day on tariffs. An EU damage assessment revealed that, in the south, the IDF destroyed or damaged 1,489 buildings; 21 out of 29 bridges over the Litani river; 535 sections of road and 545 cultivated fields. In the *Dahiya*, Hizbullah's south Beirut stronghold, 326 residential buildings sustained partial or complete damage, 269 of these were located in the *Harit Hurayk* district, which housed Hizbullah's central

headquarters. All in all, 130,000 housing units sustained partial or complete damage. In addition, all the runways of the Beirut Rafiq Hariri International Airport as well as six strategic highway sections were damaged.

Reconstruction

While the late PM Rafiq Hariri has been regarded as the champion of recon-struction, after the July war, Hizbullah is considered as the hero of recon-struction, since the magnitude of the crisis and level of destruction was too heavy for the Lebanese state and its institutions to cope with. Out of the mil-lion displaced by the war, almost half immediately returned to their destroyed villages and cities to find them littered with unexploded ordinances and clus-ter bombs, most notably in the south.[47] Hizbullah's NGOs and civil institu-tions spearheaded the relief efforts and started rebuilding partially destroyed homes. As soon as the cease-fire came into effect, Hizbullah dispatched spe-cial assessment commissions that toured the devastated areas. While the Leb-anese state and its institutions suffer from chronic corruption coupled with nepotism and favoritism, Hizbullah is renowned for its probity, integrity, and transparency in conducting public services and affairs. At a time when the country was facing severe shortages in foreign currencies, Hizbullah honored its words with deeds and delivered its promises of handing out cash dona-tions ranging from $ 4,000 to $ 12,000 to all of the people whose houses or apartments were partially or completely destroyed. Whether the source of this money is Iranian petrodollars or not is irrelevant here.[48] What is impor-tant to note is that Hizbullah delivered its promise of fully compensating the owners of 15,000 completely destroyed households, not only by eventually rebuilding them, but also by handing every household enough money to rent and furnish an apartment till their original households were rebuilt again. If Hizbullah has not done so, then it would have lost much of its constituency. After all, people need a roof over their heads and a decent living; they cannot live on ideology alone. At a time when Hizbullah's main reconstruction body, *Jihad Al-Bina'*, is classified as a 'terrorist organization' by the US Adminis-tration, it accomplished a feat in urban planning when it founded the *Wa'd* (Promise) reconstruction project, which is shouldering the gigantic burden of rebuilding the *Dahiya* almost one year after the war. All in all, Hizbullah allo-cated an estimated budget of around $ 4 billion to reconstruction,[49] and so far spent around $ 400,000 million.[50] The $ 4 billion were allocated not only for reconstruction as such, but also for buying land north of the Litani river, mainly from Christians and Druz, even sometimes at ten times its original price, in order to link the party's constituencies in the south and the *Biqa'*. In some instances, Hizbullah succeeded in buying entire villages, making these restricted military areas. Although *Wa'id*'s ambitious plan faces a lot of challenges, Iranian generous funding – which, in the first place, allowed such a project to materialize – will in the end realize *Wa'd*'s motto: 'We'll rebuild it more beautiful than what it was.' Engineer Hasan Jishi, the CEO of Hizbullah's *Wa'd* project, held a press conference where he announced that *Wa'd* is rebuilding 244 of the 281 living complexes destroyed by the July war.[51]

NEW RULES OF THE GAME: ALTERATION IN HIZBULLAH'S MILITARY
STRATEGY

Hizbullah's military strategy is characterized by asymmetrical warfare in which the two belligerents are so mismatched in their military capabilities or accustomed methods of engagement that the military disadvantaged power (Hizbullah) must press its special advantages or effectively exploit its enemy's (Israel's) particular weaknesses if they are to have any hope of prevailing. This was the situation before the Israeli withdrawal of May 2000, and continued to be the case from May 2000 to July 2006; and from July 2006 onward.

Hizbullah's military strategy during the Israeli occupation (1982-2000)
Hizbullah's intelligence is of a high degree of efficiency; its military structure is characterized by a high and sophisticated degree of discipline. Its clandestine tactics render it very difficult to identify members of the Islamic Resistance, especially when some fight in civilian clothes, while others wear the same uniform as the IDF, and even speak Hebrew. Hizbullah's revolutionary Resistance employs guerrilla warfare, hit-and-run as well as blitz tactics, which do not immediately aim at occupying land; rather endeavor to drive out the enemy by continuously launching a war of attrition in order to inflict the highest number of casualties on the IDF. The Islamic Resistance's tactics resemble the Vietcong strategies that were effective in defeating the Americans in the Vietnam War. Actually, Israeli higher military command has compared the plight of the Israeli occupation of Lebanon with the US involvement in the Vietnamese quicksand.

Hizbullah's military strategy after the 2000 Israeli withdrawal
Hizbullah's deterrent military strategy, which was employed from 2000 to 2006, was put to the test in the July 2006 war. In fact, Hizbullah dwelled too much on its stock of 20,000 rockets, thinking that these would prevent Israel from attacking Lebanon again. During the six years that followed the Israeli withdrawal, Hizbullah transformed southern Lebanon into a hi-tech bunker of sophisticated anti-tank rockets, as well as near-, middle-, and long-range

rockets. Hizbullah built elaborate fortifications and oversaturated these with armaments. The July war will prove that Hizbullah dwelled too much on its presumed balance of power with Israel, or what it calls 'balance of terror', invoking the Qur'an (17: 8): "If you come back, we will come back, and we will make Hell the resting place of the infidels." Thus, Hizbullah overestimated its deterrent strategy since it had no contingency measures to fend off a massive Israeli attack, except its heavy reliance on its cache of missiles.

The July 2006 war: Miscalculation on both sides
The July 2006 or the 'Second Lebanon War' was the most destructive war Israel launched against Lebanon. Israel kept heavily bombarding Hizbullah's constituencies in the south, *Biqa'*, and the *Dahiya* systematically, in an attempt to sow discord among the residents and diminish Hizbullah's following. Although Hizbullah's 4,000 rockets had limited destructive capacity on the material level, on the psychological level these rockets 'terrorized' the Israeli population and forced more than two million Israelis either to live underground in bunkers or to leave the targeted areas to safer places. A BBC documentary[52] claimed that Israel sustained the heaviest aerial bombardment since its creation in 1948.

Though Israel initially aimed at eliminating Hizbullah and releasing its two kidnapped soldiers, it gradually watered down its expectations to destroying Hizbullah's infrastructure and curtailing its capability of firing rockets on Israel, an eventuality that did not materialize either. Tzipi Livni, the Israeli Foreign Minister, conceded that the strongest army in the world could not disarm Hizbullah.[53]

By the concession of its leadership, Hizbullah was taken by surprise and miscalculated the Israeli reaction to the abduction of its two soldiers. Hizbullah's strategic mistake might have been that it never anticipated such an action would spark a large-scale conflict that would ultimately lead to the destruction of almost all of Lebanon's postwar achievements. On 27 August 2006, Nasrallah acknowledged that Hizbullah would not have kidnapped the two soldiers if it had known the devastating outcome: "We simply would not have done it."[54]

Thus, it seems that the July war resulted in a zero sum game since both Israel and Hizbullah claimed victory. Nasrallah dubbed it as "the most fierce battle in Lebanese history", hailing it as "a strategic, historical, and divine victory for Lebanon and the *umma*." Olmert stressed that in addition to its military victory, Israel won a great diplomatic victory by UNSC Resolution 1701. He purported that Israel was able to change the rules of the game that resulted from the 1996 'April Understanding'. Although Hizbullah kept on firing rockets into Israel till the last day, even in areas that were occupied by the IDF, the war proved that both Hizbullah's defense strategy and that of Israel need serious revisions.

Although the party was not well prepared for it, the July war did not pose an existential threat to Hizbullah's survival. After one year of the war, through the concession made by Ehud Barak, the Israeli Minister of Defense, Hizbullah has not only rebuilt its arsenal, but has also acquired more capabilities and power than ever before. Hizbullah constructed elaborate fortifications for its newly acquired long-range missiles above the Litani river so as not to conflict with the international community for breaching the 1701. The party is successfully linking its main constituencies in the south and the *Biqaʿ* by buying land and entire villages, making these restricted military areas. However, from the Litani river to the Israeli border, Hizbullah's fighters would remain invisible and their weapons would be out of sight, but not out of reach. Nasrallah warned Israel that if it considered attacking Lebanon again, Hizbullah would not hesitate to use unconventional weapons that could target any location. The 24 August 2007, UNSC Resolution 1773 – which extended UNIFIL's mandate till 31 August 2008 – reiterated what was achieved a year earlier by the 1701: no cease-fire, rather a 'cessation of hostilities'. Likewise on 27 August 2009, the UNSC renewed, to Israel's dismay and Hizbullah's relief, 1701 for one year under the same rules of engagement. And so, the cessation of hostilities was not coupled with a comprehensive political solution or settlement of the conflict, rendering the situation immensely fragile, like a volcano that can erupt at any time.

Hizbullah's military strategy after the July 2006 war
The major change after the July 2006 war is that Hizbullah shifted from a defensive to an offensive military strategy that aims at occupying all the Northern Israeli settlements, thus moving the war to Israeli soil if Israel attacked Lebanon. This new Hizbullah strategy was put to the test in November 2007 when, apparently in preparation for its upcoming third war on Lebanon, Israel conducted a military drill, which involved 50,000 military personnel, across its northern border with Lebanon. Hizbullah immediately responded with a three-day military drill, which involved the mobilization of 120,000 of its elite fighting force, dressed in civilian clothes, south of the Litani river, where around 12,500 UNIFIL and 15,000 Lebanese army soldiers were stationed. This unprecedented move aimed at sending a three-fold strong message to: 1) Israel in case it entertained the idea of attacking Lebanon again; 2) the international community, namely that Syria and Iran would use the Hizbullah card as a stick and a bargaining chip; 3) local Lebanese politics if

Hizbullah's demands were not met, as Nasrallah affirmed in his 11 November 2007 fiery speech. In that same speech Nasrallah defiantly challenged the implementation of the UNSC 1959 Resolution, affirming that all the armies in the world cannot disarm Hizbullah. In 2008-2009 Nasrallah reiterated that all of Israel is within Hizbullah's missiles reach. On 14 September 2009, commemorating the third anniversary of Hizbulllah's 'Divine Victory', Nasrallah boasted that the party's military capabilities were three times stronger than those in 2006. He introduced a new 'balance of terror [power]' formula aimed at deterrence, namely if Israel would bomb Beirut or the *Dahiya*, Hizbullah would then strike Tel Aviv, thus setting the new rules of the game.

HIZBULLAH'S 22 SEPTEMBER 'DIVINE VICTORY' PARADE[55]

Nasrallah's speech was attended by Lebanese MPs, cabinet members, politicians, clergy, many Arab dignitaries, and an audience of around 800,000, who guaranteed a perfect human shield, and barred Israel from executing its threat of killing Nasrallah as soon as the opportunity loomed.[56] Nasrallah stressed that Hizbullah would surrender its arms if Israel relinquishes the *Shib'a* farms, releases the Lebanese prisoners of war, and submits the landmines maps: "We will not keep our weapons forever." Nasrallah affirmed that Hizbullah's rockets increased from 20,000 before the war to 33,000.[57] Many March 14 cadres criticized Nasrallah[58], arguing that there is nothing in the military dictionary called a 'divine victory'.

In turn, Israel mocked Hizbullah's "divine, historic, and strategic victory", arguing that Hizbullah was only showing off while Nasrallah had been in hiding since 12 July, and he would return to his dungeons after finishing his speech. According to Israel, this claim was made by a person who conceded three weeks earlier that if he had known Israel's devastating response, he would not have kidnapped the two soldiers. Israel accused Hizbullah of being a Syrian-Iranian agent executing their policies in the Middle East.

TURNING THE TIDE: THE POLITICAL PRICE OF THE VICTORY

Keeping in mind that choices "are shaped by social imaginaries – that is, more or less coherent socio-cultural processes that shape actors' understanding of what is possible, what is real, and how to understand each other"[59], as a political price of the victory, Hizbullah demanded getting hold of the required one third veto power in the council of ministers, after wielding power over the legislature and the presidency, at the time.[60] This could be accomplished through an alliance with the FPM, which received the highest number of votes in the 2005 legislative elections.[61] For this to take place, Hizbullah demanded the formation of a representative national unity government and the holding of earlier legislative elections based upon a more representative election law that all the Lebanese would agree upon, preferably one based upon proportional representation and small electoral districts, as Hajj Mahmud Qmati later clarified.[62] Indeed, "participation in public life can accordingly be itself a form of social integration or solidarity." Broadening the mandate of Habermas's notion of 'constitutional patriotism', Calhoun emphasizes "the importance not only of loyalty to created institutions but in participation in the process of creation and recreation... [because] democratic choice is inherent in the public sphere".[63]

This calls for some explanation. The Ta'if Agreement divided political power, according to the quota system, evenly among the Muslims[64] and the Christians, both in the cabinet and the parliament. Thus, the 128 seats in the legislature were split 50-50 between the Muslims and the Christians, so were the 24 seats of the current Sanyura cabinet. As such, all the Shi'ites are entitled to five ministers out of the 24; even if they all resign, the cabinet can still meet and take decisions by a 2/3-majority vote. This definitely does not reflect Hizbullah's demographic strength nor its big political force. Since Hizbullah decided to participate in the political system *as it is*, it can only exercise hegemony over it and the public sphere through alliances based on negotiations, bargaining, and even compromises.

In the legislature, at the time, Hizbullah[65] and its allies had 57 MPs[66] out of a total of 128, or 44 percent control of the parliament, which implies that the Hizbullah-led opposition was entitled to more than thirteen ministers out of the 30 of the future national unity cabinet. Aiming at obtaining veto power, the Hizbullah-led opposition asked for eleven ministers. Thus, there has been a visible change in the balance of power to Hizbullah's advantage after its alliance with the FPM.[67] This strategy of attempting to manipulate and exercise hegemony over the public sphere through its integration into the political system is conducive to Hizbullah's bottom-up Islamization project. Already the president and the speaker were on their side (not to say that the Hizbullah-led opposition virtually controls the institution of the presidency and that of the parliament). Thus, all they need to control the Lebanese political system is to have the veto power in the council of ministers, which, if granted, were a precedent since the founding of the Lebanese Republic in 1920, and its first constitution in 1926.

Since in the public sphere "culture – and identities – will be made and remade in public life… [and since] citizens need to be motivated by solidarity, not merely included by law"[68], Nasrallah gave the cabinet a one-week ultimatum, starting from Monday 6 November, for the formation of a national unity government where Hizbullah and its allies would wield the one-third veto power, or else, the Hizbullah-led opposition would take to the streets until the cabinet yielded to their demands. It is interesting to note that an editorial in *al-Safir* criticized Nasrallah for not mentioning Israel once in his three-hour interview. The Mufti of Mount Lebanon, Shaykh Muhammad 'Ali Al-Jusu, accused Nasrallah of nurturing Sunni-Shi'ite discord and of unfounded accusations towards the PM to the extent of indirectly branding him with treason. In turn, on 4 November, MP Pierre Gemayyel said in reference to Hizbullah's one-week ultimatum: "We will not allow those who determine war and peace to have the final say in state building."[69]

ATTEMPTS TO REVIVE THE DIALOGUE END IN A DEADLOCK

The sessions of the 'National Consultations Conference' ended with the resignation of the five Shi'ite ministers from the cabinet, on the symbolic day of 11 November, which marks Hizbullah's 'Martyrs' Day'. After a few days, an ally of president Lahud, Jacob Sarraf, the Greek Orthodox Minister of the Environment, followed suit.[70] The resignation of the six ministers did not lead to the collapse of the Sanyura cabinet since eight should resign for this to take place. In the wake of these tensions, the assassination of Pierre Gemayyel took place on 21 November 2006. This implies that the resignation or assassination of one minister could deal a fatal blow to the Sanyura cabinet. Since then, tensions rose to a new high and a political deadlock got hold of the Lebanese public sphere.

THE ROLE OF MEDIA[71] IN THE PUBLIC SPHERE

Quoting John Stewart Mill's concept of the 'tyranny of the majority', *al-Intiqad* labelled Sanyura's government as tyrannical, claiming that it only has an 'artificial' majority. In turn, Sanyura replied that granting the Hizbullah-led opposition veto power in the cabinet amounts to the 'tyranny of the minority'.[72] It is worth noting that the political deadlock between the two parties lasted for

18 months since the launching of the protests on 1 December 2006; as Qmati clarified, "the sit-in is a symbol of political opposition."[73]

Al-Intiqad had a face-lift in order to accommodate Hizbullah's new image as the leader of the Lebanese opposition. Starting issue 1192, exactly one week after Hizbullah took to the streets, the left banner read: "Lebanon 1: The Popular Movement for National Unity". *Al-Nour* dubbed itself "the voice of national unity", followed by the national anthem, then songs by Marcel Khalifé, a popular Christian Lebanese nationalist singer.

HIZBULLAH'S SOCIO-RELIGIOUS COMPROMISES

In addition to its earlier doctrinal compromises[74], Hizbullah socio-religious beliefs apparently gained some flexibility. Hizbullah was accused of mixing and sleeping in tents in order to achieve narrow political gains. Hizbullah's cadres took care to refute these claims by contending that it upheld its ethical and Islamic values and norms, and that other members of the Lebanese opposition might be committing such acts, but definitely not Hizbullah's members. In spite of their attempts to ward off such accusations, Hizbullah's cadres sounded speechless when asked to comment on pictures showing Hizbullahis hugging members of the FPM who were sipping champagne on New Year's Eve. This came at a time when the Maronite patriarch admonished against the mixing of the two genders in tents. And, most importantly, the caricature of Future TV, Hariri's media outlet, on Christmas Eve: "Merry Christmas (*milad majid*, which also means happy birth), but in which tent?" The implication is that the youth were sleeping around in tents.

HIZBULLAH'S POPULARITY

On 6 January 2007, a survey conducted by the Saudi funded *al-'Arabiyya* cable TV tested Hizbullah's popularity. The results revealed that the party's popularity plummeted from 74 percent to 54 percent[75]; 53 percent pinned the blame of the war on Hizbullah, Iran, and Syria; and 51 percent considered the demonstrations of the Hizbullah-led opposition conducive to increasing the sectarian tension (Sunni-Shi'ite discord). Although this survey should be taken with a grain of salt, it sheds some light on the situation. For instance, in Egypt, during the war and its aftermath, Hizbullah flags and Nasrallah's posters where visible everywhere, but after Hizbullah's attempts to topple the Sanyura cabinet, these signs of support dwindled, not to say ceased to be. This might suggest that when it comes to Sunni-Shi'ite discord, the parties forget about their commitments to nationalism, pan-Islamism, and pan-Arabism, and seek narrow confessional interests.

HIZBULLAH TAKES TO THE STREETS

In spite of dangerous precedents[76], which suggested that no one can guarantee the security of the street, on 1 December 2006, Hizbullah, the FPM, and other members of the Lebanese opposition took to the streets in downtown Beirut – filling completely Martyr's Square and the *Riyad al-Solh* Square – demanding the formation of a national unity cabinet, where the Lebanese opposition wields the one-third veto power. PM Sanyura admonished Nasrallah by saying: "Do not waste your military accomplishments and victories on Israel in Beirut's alleys." Hizbullah failed to deliver its promise of a fast collapse of the government.[77] Addressing the demonstrators over a big screen, Nasrallah delivered his second promise: "We will defeat (topple) the Lebanese government, like we defeated Israel in the 34-days war".[78] In the early days of the sit-in, Hizbullah frontline *jihadis* besieged the council of ministers' headquarters in downtown Beirut. However, behind the scenes contacts resulted in ending this blockade. The tug of war between the Hizbullah-led opposition (March 8 Group), on the one hand, and the Lebanese cabinet and its supporters (March 14 Trend), on the other, led to a bitter polarization that put Lebanon in a stalemate and political deadlock for over a year.

SLIPPING TOWARDS CIVIL WAR: 23 AND 25 JANUARY 2007 CIVIL UNREST: NASRALLAH'S FATWA

This tension resulted in serious civil unrest. On 23 January, after 53 days of sit-ins and protests in downtown Beirut, the Hizbullah-led opposition crippled the country through a general strike, coupled with the blocking of main roads, burning wheels, etc. Three people died and 150 were wounded. This was not the end of it. Two days later, during the proceedings of the Paris III Conference[79], a Sunni-Shi'ite confrontation erupted in a populous Sunni neighborhood of Beirut. This resulted in four deaths and 300 wounded, including thirteen Lebanese army soldiers, and 216 arrests. Dangerous scenes reminiscent of the civil war erupted: sniping, automatic weapons, gunfire, mayhem, burning cars, destruction of property, etc.; it was a real battle zone. In an unprecedented move, Nasrallah issued a *fatwa* calling on his supporters – and by extension all the Lebanese – to immediately vacate the streets: "From the stance of a national, patriotic, ethical, religious, and *shar'i* duty…, I call on you to fully cooperate with all the measures that the Lebanese army is taking

in order to ensure and uphold peace and stability... this *fatwa* is in the interest (*maslaha*) of our country, its civil peace, and peaceful coexistence... we
insist on using civil, democratic, and political means in expressing our political differences, and any recourse to arms, from whichever party, is considered
treason."[80] Similar calls were made by speaker Berri and Sa'd Hariri, the parliamentary majority leader.[81] Nasrallah added: "Even if 1,000 Hizbullahis die
we will not be led to *fitna* (discord) or take recourse to our weapons in the
domestic infighting."[82] After these bloody confrontations, Hizbullah labeled
the Sanyura cabinet as "the government of the armed militias".[83]

Most likely, if civil war erupts, then it would lead to the total destruction of
Lebanon since – unlike the 1975-1990 civil war, where mainly Muslims fought
Christians and vice versa – the whole country is polarized in such a way, that
both camps (the March 8 and March 14) include parties from all religious
denominations and sectarian affiliations.

SHI'ITE OPPOSITION ALLIED WITH THE MARCH 14 TREND:
INDICATORS OF AN OPEN PUBLIC SPHERE OR A FREE PUBLIC
SPHERE?

It seems that Hizbullah does not completely hegemonize or monopolize the
Shi'ite public sphere since it does not muffle or put the lid on dissident voices
such as Sayyid Hani Fahs[84] (a Shi'ite intellectual); Sayyid 'Ali Al-Amin, the
ex-Mufti of Tyre and Jabal 'Amil[85]; Shaykh Muhammad Al-Hajj Hasan[86], the
leader of the Free Shi'ite Movement (*Al-Tayyar 'Al-Shi'i Al-Hurr*); Shaykh
Yusuf Kanj; and Shaykh Subhi Al-Tufayli. How much power do they wield on
the ground, and do they have a substantial following?

Sayyid 'Ali Al-Amin[87] – a graduate of the Najaf seminary who descends
from an influential family[88] of religious scholars (*'ulama*) – was one of the
main wielders of authority in *Jabal 'Amil*[89], the historical den of Shi'ism in
Lebanon. Most importantly, when Shaykh Muhammad Mahdi Shamseddine,
the head of the Islamic Shi'ite Higher Council[90], died, al-Amin was a serious
contender to succeed him. However, Hizbullah placed a veto on al-Amin,
accusing him, as it has done with Berri, of deflecting from Imam Musa al-
Sadr's path. This incident poisoned the relationship between Hizbullah and
al-Amin. Although Fadlallah still maintained his contacts with Hizbullah
and occasionally met Nasrallah, it seems that al-Amin and Fadlallah are on
the same wavelength, but since they are both Sayyids and wield substantial
authority and following, they do not put their hands together. So, it boils
down to a matter of contestation of authority. Who wields more power and
following? To whom shall the *khums* go?[91]

Sayyid Hani Fahs is a member of the Shi'ite establishment, the pyramid structure that holds the bulk of the Shi'ite community, which is mainly composed of Hizbullah's constituency, and, to a lesser extent, Amal's constituency. Although he is vocal against Hizbullah's *taklif al-Shar'i*, he neither sides with the March 14 Trend, nor appears in anti-Hizbullah public events.

Unsubstantiated reports claim that Shaykh Yusuf Kanj[92] studied in the religious seminary of Shaykh 'Afif al-Nabulsi, but he parted company with him and established his own seminary. When Nabulsi told him that you need a certificate of *ijtihad* (*ijazat ijtihad*), Kanj replied: "I'm the one who should give you an *ijaza*."

The renegade Shaykh Subhi al-Tufayli contends that Hizbullah is protecting the Israeli border by preventing *jihadi* groups from attacking Israel, and he accuses Iran of serving the interest of the US. In an interview on Future TV on 27 January 2007, Tufayli vehemently censored Hizbullah's leadership, accusing Nasrallah of executing Khaminai's policies in Lebanon.[93] It is worth mentioning that al-Tufayli is the only one among the above who has armed followers and controls several villages in the *Biqa'*, which are off-limits to the Lebanese state's security apparatuses. Thus, Hizbullah managed to exercise hegemony over the Shi'ite representation in Lebanon.[94]

NASRALLAH'S EASTER SPEECH[95]: 8 APRIL 2007

Addressing 1,734 Hizbullah university and school graduates, Nasrallah stressed that Hizbullah is a viable and vital political movement in its early youth: "We were never defeated, and we will never be defeated... we are a viable party... we survived more than a quarter of a century and we're there to stay; the future is ours."[96] Not mentioning Israel in his discourse and speeches became folklore; instead, he concentrated his attack on the Sanyura cabinet[97], "Feltman's[98] government", as he repeatedly labeled it, admonishing against "foreign tutelage".[99] Nasrallah communicated Hizbullah's official position on the International Tribunal, namely, that the party is going to hand in its reservations, but only to a national unity cabinet, and not to the UN or any other mediator. This seems to stand in sharp contrast to the consensus of all the parties, including Hizbullah, on the Tribunal during the first dialogue session in March 2006. It seems Hizbullah retracted its earlier position.

LEBANON ON THE VERGE OF SUNNI-SHI'ITE DISCORD

On 23 April 2007 two Sunni members of the PSP – Ziad Ghandur (12 years old) and Ziad Qabalan (22 years old) – were kidnapped from *Shiyyah*, in

Dadiya, Hizbullah's stronghold in southern Beirut. On 26 April, Lebanese security forces found the two bodies of the victims, who were shot at close range, in *Jadra*, a Christian village of *Iqlim al-Kharrub*. *Iqlim al-Kharrub*, a predominantly Sunni area situated in the heartland of the Druz mountains, votes for the PSP and Jumblatt. It seems quite obvious that the abhorrent crime meant to sow discord among the Druz, Sunnis, and the Shi'ites, since the assailants were the brothers of Yehya Shamas, one of the Shi'ite victims belonging to Amal who fell in the Thursday, 25 January 2007 civil unrest in the predominantly Sunni area of *Tariq al-Jadidé*. In order to ward off discord, Jumblatt took the initiative to calm down the situation arguing that the crime was a vendetta crime, and not a politically motivated one. Jumblatt's call for national unity was well received by the March 8 group, including Hizbullah, who on 2 May met with the March 14 trend while the parties were paying their respects to the families of the victims in their birthplace of *watah al-Msaytbé*, a predominantly Sunni area, as well as in *Dar Al-Fawa*, the residence of the Sunni Mufti of the Lebanese Republic. Even during the funeral procession on 27 April, members of the March 8 group were present, including, members of Berri's parliamentary bloc. These initiatives helped to break the ice between the parties, paving the way for Nasrallah's new initiative.

SANYURA'S INITIATIVE

Reaching out to the Hizbullah-led opposition, Sanyura came up with a proposal aimed at ending the deadlock. He conceded to the opposition's demand offering them two seats more than they asked for (13 out of 30[100]), on condition that reaching an agreement on a common political program, which is based upon the Seven Points, the implementation of the decisions reached in the national dialogue sessions, and, most importantly, full implementation of UNSC Resolution 1701. Although Berri, the speaker of the parliament and the leader of the Amal movement, agreed, naturally, Hizbullah rejected the offer because this would eventually lead to its disarmament. However, Hizbullah did not put it bluntly; rather it argued that it was unwilling to participate in a government headed by Sanyura, whom the opposition holds responsible for the economic crisis since he served as the Minister of Finance for twelve years in the previous Hariri governments. It seems that the Sanyura initiative fell on deaf ears.[101] Unfortunately, after the 'Second Lebanon War', in its bid to monopolize the public sphere, Hizbullah's leaders, cadres, and intellectuals failed to "read and hear alternative points of view."

Since "modern ideas of legitimacy depend on the notion that a government or political power [should] serve the interests of its people",[102] and because Hizbullah's aim is to maximize aggregate interests, on 5 May 2007, Hizbullah revoked its earlier acceptance of the Seven Points. Hizbullah's intellectual par excellence Sayyid Nawwaf Al-Musawi, the political council (politburo) member and foreign relations officer, and the pragmatist MP Muhammad Fnaysh, the Minister of Power[103], argued that the party did not approve the Seven Points, "which were Condoleezza Rice's orders to Sanyura", as al-Musawi contended.[104] On the same day, Nasrallah affirmed the contentions of al-Musawi and Fnaysh.[105] This runs contrary to the minutes of the council of ministers and Nasrallah's earlier public declarations[106] in support of the Seven Points, which were also publicly endorsed by Berri. Two days later Sanyura categorized the Hizbullah establishment as 'oppressors'. Was Hizbullah's initial aim behind its gradual integration into the Lebanese public sphere the sheer exercise of power?

MORE DIALOGUE

On 14-15 July 2007, attempts were made at breaking the standoff during dialogue sessions in Saint Cloud, France, among second class cadres of the March 14 and March 8 groups, formally invited by the French foreign minister, Bernard Cuisenaire, through his special envoy ambassador Cousseran. 31 representatives of Lebanon's fourteen leading parties participated in closed door talks. Cuisenaire was scheduled to visit Beirut on 28 July in order to follow through the French initiative aimed at breaking the political deadlock that had been rupturing the country for more than eight months. No substantial or tangible results were reported from either the dialogue sessions or Cuisenaire's visit. In addition to the representatives of the leading politicians in the country, the French introduced representatives of civil society organizations, although they do not yield much power on the ground.

5.3 CONCLUSION: THE TUG OF WAR

The *al-Akhbar* columnist Nikolas Nasif said[107] that there are three main junctures in the tug of war between the Sanyura cabinet and the Hizbullah-led opposition: the International Tribunal[108], the national unity cabinet[109], and the presidency. Nasif purported that Hizbullah lost the first two, and the third is not determined yet. He questioned what would happen to Hizbullah's credibility following these "defeats". What seems to substantiate Nasif's analysis is that the discourse of all the parties shifted to the issue of the presidency, which dominated the public sphere. Qasim admonished that the president[110] should be elected by a 2/3-majority of the parliament, and not 50 + 1, as the March 14 Trend were lobbying for. In turn, 'Aun proposed ratifying the constitution once so that the president could be directly elected by the people. Since the March 8 Group did not recognize the legitimacy and constitutionality of the Saynura cabinet, it proposed either holding early legislative elections or obtaining the one-third veto power in any future cabinet. In turn, the March 14 Trend insisted on electing the president first before discussing the formation of the national unity cabinet and the agreement on a new electoral law to base the June 2009 legislative elections upon. Although both parties (March 14 and March 8) agreed on the Lebanese army commander, general Michel Sulayman, as a consensus candidate to the presidency, the tug of war did not end. Indeed, a distinctive feature of the public sphere is that "it is created and reproduced through discourse... public sphere exists uniquely in, through, and for talk."[111] And since a public sphere could be "shaped by struggle against the dominant organization of others"[112], every party is trying to manipulate the constitution and interpret it to its own advantage. How could a zero sum game, or the late PM Sa'ib Salam's statement of "no winners and no losers" be achieved in this regard remains to be seem.

On 24 July 2007, in an attempt to pressure the two parties into reaching a compromise, general Michel Sulayman threatened to resign in case another cabinet was formed, whereby Lebanon would have repeated the negative precedent of 1988, when the country was split between two cabinets, where each one controlled a certain geographical area.[113] If this scenario materialized, it would have eventually led to the dissolution of the military establishment and the disintegration of Lebanon.

In his 17 August 2007 Friday prayer speech, Ayatullah Fadlallah admonished that the political crisis was so severe to the extent that the issue was not about Lebanon's future, but about the very existence of Lebanon. The Maronite patriarch reiterated the same concern in his 19 August 2007 Sunday sermon.[114] The late Gebran Tuéni's father, the 80-year old veteran politician and journalist, MP Ghassan Tuéni, depicted the sixteen-year Lebanese civil war as a proxy war fought on behalf of others, rather than a war of others, as the title of his book suggests: A War for Others.[115] In this regard, Sayyid Fadlallah stated that Lebanon has become a battleground for regional and international struggles, struggles that have rendered the Lebanese as chess pieces.[116] Keeping in mind that since 1976 the Lebanese president has almost always been the result of mediation between Syria and the US, would the precept of practice prove Ghassan Tuéni right?

Even though it seems far-fetched that Lebanon is going to plunge into civil war in the near future, the country is not immune to discord (*fitna*)[117], especially after the assassination of two March 14 MPS.[118] In the wake of the war that erupted on 20 May 2007 between Fatah al-Islam militants and the Lebanese army in the *Nahr al-Barid* Palestinian refugee camp near Tripoli and its vicinities[119], the former conducted its retribution assassination of Lebanese army brigadier general François al-Hajj.[120] In its bid to power Hizbullah was endeavoring to exploit its military triumph in the 2006 July war by seeking a substantial slice of the pie, at least equivalent to its demographic strength. The party was buying time till the tide turned in its favor. Hizbullah exercised patience for more than one year to affect change. Did it wait for another year till the next legislative elections of June 2009, as Nasrallah said in one of his speeches, or did it attempt to change the political system by force?[121]

6 The Doha 2008 Accord and its Aftermath

6.1 COUPS D'ÉTAT: FROM 8 MARCH 2005 TO 8 MAY 2008

Hizbullah's bid for power laid the cornerstone for a new phase in which it seeks to dominate the public sphere and national political arena. Under the slogan of partnership and the reformulation of the political system (*al-musharaka wa i'adat intaj al-sulta*) and after eighteen months of a wavering political stalemate, Hizbullah affected change by force on the ground gaining its long awaited veto power in the Lebanese cabinet. In a politically charged atmosphere, the cabinet decided to confront Hizbullah for the first time since *Ta'if*. After a long meeting on 6 May that went on till the early hours of the morning, the council of ministers deemed Hizbullah's telecommunications network an "onslaught against the state's sovereignty and its financial resources" (*i'tida' 'ala siyadat al-dawla wa al-mal al-'amm*) or as illegitimate and a threat to the state's financial security. The cabinet affirmed that it was going to bring to justice all those who participated or were involved in deploying this network, which was tantamount to an arrest warrant against Nasrallah. Also, the cabinet dismissed the pro-Hizbullah-Amal Beirut Airport head of security, Lebanese army general Wafiq Shuqayr,[1] who had been serving in this post since 2000, accusing him of deploying cameras across Beirut International Airport's lane number 17 in order to monitor the travellers. Hizbullah exploited a general strike called on by the Labor unions on 7 May and the aforementioned two governmental decisions as pretexts to storm and occupy, by military force in the night of 8-9 May, West Beirut, where most government ministries are located. By 12 May Hizbullah was able to control the *Shuf* region, a Druz den. The party managed to strike a 'silent consensus' deal with

the Lebanese army not to interfere in the crisis. Knowing that at least 60 percent of the army are Shiʿites and that it is made up of a further seventeen
confessions that form the Lebanese myriad, involving the army in the clashes
would have led to its disintegration, as was the case during the civil war. The
Hizbullah-led opposition waged a campaign of civil disobedience blocking
vital routes and key arteries to the Lebanese economy such as the national
airport and the Beirut port. In scenes reminiscent of the civil war, turf bat-
tles between the warring factions left more than 65 people dead[2], including
at least sixteen Hizbullah fighters, as Nasrallah conceded in a press conference.[3] In an unprecedented development – which did not even take place
during the Israeli fourteen-day occupation of West Beirut in 1982 – Hizbullah cracked down on the media supporting the cabinet silencing Future TV,
al-Sharq Radio, al-Mustaqbal and al-Liwaʾ newspapers, and al-Shiraʿ weekly
journal, threatening them with total annihilation if they resumed broadcasting or publication. In fact, Future TV's old offices were ransacked and burned,
and many TV and radio antennas and transmitters belonging to Future TV
and al-Sharq Radio were destroyed. This situation continued till 14 May, when
Hizbullah handed the aforementioned media outlets to the army. Although
Hizbullah's al-Manar TV and MP Hasan Fadlallah, the head of the media and
communications parliamentary committee, paid lip service in condemning
such events, such a condemnation did not revoke the damage caused by Hizbullah's actions, which again tarnished its image as an advocate of free speech
and expression.

   With the arrival of the Arab League delegation on 14 May, the cabinet
annulled its two decisions as Nasrallah demanded in his 8 May press conference, thus setting the pace for an end to the crisis. The guns were completely
silenced on 15 May after the Arab League delegation was able to negotiate a deal
between the warring factions. The 'Beirut Declaration' stipulated the traveling
of the warming factions' representatives to dialogue sessions in Doha, Qatar,
aimed at reaching a final settlement to the eighteen-month deadlock. After
five days of intensive negotiations, Hizbullah obtained its long awaited veto
power in the cabinet. This was consolidated by the political agreement of 21
May known as the 'Doha Accord' between March 14 and March 8, mediated
by the Arab League, granting Hizbullah veto power in the next national unity
30-member cabinet by a margin of eleven ministers, while March 14 acquired
sixteen ministers and the president three. The considerable achievement of
the Doha Accord is that it barred the use of weapons in domestic feuds. Hizbullah ended its sit-in in downtown Beirut and dismantled its tent city after
537 days. The party was very pleased with the performance of the army and its
commander Michel Sulayman, who had been in his post since 1998. After six

months of vacuum in the seat of the presidency, something unprecedented in Lebanese history, the consensus president Sulayman was elected on 25 May by 118 votes out of 127 MPS.[4] On the next day Hizbullah celebrated the eighth anniversary of the nearly complete Israeli withdrawal from Lebanon through a fiery speech by its secretary-general, Nasrallah, who stressed that Hizbullah would abide by the Ta'if Agreement and would honor the Doha Accord to the letter.

Although the Hizbullah-'despised' PM Sanyura headed the new cabinet, the formula of a zero sum game between March 14 and March 8 did not materialize as the secretary-general of the Arab League 'Amr Musa contended. Instead, Hizbullah obtained, by force[5], its long awaited veto power in the council of ministers, the main executive body that runs the country. Since the cabinet conceded to Hizbullah's demands and revoked its two earlier decisions – although it was adamant in its initial stance not to do so – it seems that Hizbullah appropriated more political capital from its coup d'état and its campaign of civil disobedience more than it has appropriated after the July 2006 war, in the sense that it can, from now on, veto government decisions that might reflect negatively on it or its constituency or that are deemed against its interest, strategy, and policy. Will the Doha Accord constitute a springboard for another Ta'if Agreement, whereby the Lebanese Shi'ites wield more political power, especially after Mufti Qabalan, the deputy of the Islamic Shi'ite Higher Council, called for instituting the post of a Shi'ite vice president, which unequivocally runs contrary to the present Lebanese constitution? Thus, Hizbullah succeeded in exercising hegemony over the Lebanese public sphere and political system through a bottom-up process by engaging in the political game through alliances, mainly with the FPM as well as other members of the Lebanese opposition, as long as such alliances suit its purposes and serve its policies, until the political system falls prey to its whims or it manages to produce a complete overhaul. Aiming at more hegemony, on 18 August 2008, Hizbullah reached out to its ideological enemies, the Salafists, and signed with them an understanding aimed mainly at warding off Sunni-Shi'ite discord (*fitna*) in the future.

6.2 THE UNDERSTANDING WITH THE SALAFI MOVEMENT[6]

After less than three months, at a time when tensions were still running very high and people did not forget about their lost blood and destroyed possessions, Hizbullah's public relations campaign paid off when an understanding was reached with the Salafi movement. After intensive negotiations that lasted for months, on 18 August 2008, Sayyid Ibrahim Amin al-Sayyid, the current head of Hizbullah's political council, representing Hizbullah, and Shaykh Hasan al-Shahhal representing the Salafi movement in Lebanon, signed an understanding aimed at organizing the relationship between the two parties, defusing the chronic tensions in the Islamic sphere, and warding off any prospect of *fitna*. In a well-attended press conference, the Salafi Shaykh 'Abd Al-Ghaffar Al-Zu'bi, the political aide of the Islamic Heritage Endowment, read the eight points of the understanding below:

1 Starting from the prohibition of shedding the blood of a Muslim, we prohibit and condemn any aggression committed by any Muslim group on another Muslim group. In case of any aggression or onslaught, the aggrieved party has the right to recourse to any legitimate means to defend itself.

2 Avoiding sedition and provoking the public because this ultimately leads to discord, thus slipping the carpet from underneath the feet of the religious scholars (*'ulama*) and placing the decision in the hand of the rash, vile people or the foes of the Islamic *umma*.

3 Standing firm in the face of the Zionist-US project, which aims at disseminating discord through the dictum of "divide and conquer".

4 Doing our utmost best to uproot infidel (*takfiri*) thinking that is existent among both the Sunnis and the Shi'ites because branding all Shi'ites as infidels is rejected by Salafis and vice versa.

5 If Hizbullah or the Salafis are oppressed or attacked by any domestic or foreign actor, then the other party must stand firm with the aggressed party as much as its capabilities allow.

6 Forming a committee from Hizbullah's *'ulama* and those of the Salafist movement to discuss points of contention between the Sunnis and Shi'as, which contributes to confining disagreement among the members of the committee, thus avoiding any spillover to the public, to the street.

7 Every party is free in what it believes in. No party has the right to impose its ideas and its jurisprudential concepts on the other.

8 Both parties (Hizbullah and the Salafis) regard this Understanding as a means to ward off discord among Muslims, and promote civil peace and coexistence among the Lebanese.

Although the Understanding did not survive long after Hasan al-Shahhal's cousin, Shaykh Da'i al-Islam al-Shahhal – the head of the largest puritan Salafi movement in Lebanon – vehemently criticized Hizbullah's move as an attempt to place a wedge between the Salafis, in particular, and divide the

Sunnis, in general; the eight points above are telling since they portray the possibility of finding a common ground between Sunnis and Shi'ites if jurisprudential differences are set aside and common political, ideological points are addressed.

6.3   THE RUN-UP TO THE JUNE 2009 ELECTIONS

On 7 June 2009, Lebanese voters went to the polls to elect a new parliament. These were the fifth legislative elections since the end of the civil war in 1990 and the first time they were held in one day. The Lebanese state deployed around 50,000 army and security forces, almost two-thirds of Lebanese military capabilities. Forecasts expected the Hizbullah led-opposition (March 8) to win the majority of seats, thus gaining almost complete control of the country. One week before the elections, the Hizbullah leader delivered an empowering speech in which he promised to strengthen the Lebanese state by fortifying its army through acquiring Iranian weapons. The results of the elections would affect the domestic tug-of-war between the two opposing camps in Lebanon, and was expected to have a bearing on the regional dynamics in the Middle East and geopolitical implications, in light of the Special Tribunal for Lebanon (STL) or the UN-backed internationalized tribunal investigating prime minister Rafik Hariri's assassination in 2005, as well as the Iranian nuclear file.

Hizbullah's 2009 elections program
In this context, Hizbullah announced its 2009 election program on 1 March, aimed at reaching out and allaying the fears of the other. Shaykh Na'im Qasim, deputy secretary-general of the party, highlighted the most salient points based on the slogan 'we resist [Israel] together and together we build Lebanon'. The program was divided into two parts: one on the resistance (Hizbullah's military wing), the other dealing with socio-economic development. The former included: a) total independence and rejection of foreign tutelage in any form; b) liberation of the land still under occupation and standing firm to 'Israeli dangers and aggression'; c) development of a viable defense strategy with the Lebanese army to fend off any aggression against the country, and commitment to the principle of non-violence in respect to domestic rivalries: "our central enemy is Israel…We do not have domestic foes and we will not respond to violence with violence." The latter section included: a) prioritization of the economic situation, especially agriculture and industry; b) social security and healthcare for everyone; c) urban development concomitant

with rural development; d) the stamping out of corruption in all aspects of life; e) a meritocratic approach to governmental institutions.[7]

However, this positive program contrasts sharply with political developments. Two international events weighed in. First, on 27 April 2009, the International Criminal Court (ICC) ordered the release of the four generals detained four years ago on suspicion of having a role in the 2005 Hariri assassination. Second, the UK resumed the dialogue with the political wing of Hizbullah. Both events seem to have boosted the electoral prospects of the Hizbullah-led March 8. Mass firing of MK47s in the air to celebrate the former event contributed to an atmosphere of confrontation and defiance. Meanwhile, March 14 was waiting for a balancing act from the international community to pressure Israel to withdraw from the border *Ghajar* village, which was occupied after the July 2006 war. Instead, there was another Israeli goodwill gesture, with the release of the cluster bomb maps as stipulated under UNSC resolution 1701. However, March 14 considered this move insufficient to turn the tide to its favor.

Meanwhile, on the domestic scene, on 13 May 2009, the supposedly neutral president of the Lebanese Republic entered the debate and announced that the March 8 camp would win a narrow majority in the legislature. It is not clear if this was a tactical move aimed at calming the March 8 camp so that the elections would pass without violence, or if it reflected his own opinion and preferences. Nasrallah's fiery 15 May 2009 mobilization speech in celebration of the first anniversary of the 8 May 2008 show of force further antagonized the situation. March 14 interpreted this as March 8 camp's expectation of imminent power – either through electoral victory or another 'coup'.

According to the Doha Accord, the 2009 election law is based on an appended version of the 1960 election law, which divides the country according to 26 small election districts (*aqdiya*) instead of the previous five election districts (*muhafazat*). March 14 claim that the elections in all districts were scheduled on the same day (7 June), unprecedented since the Ta'if Agreement, in order to disadvantage Sa'd Hariri in his bid to win in both Beirut and Tripoli as he did in 2005. It is worth mentioning that in 2005 the Hariri-led March 14 was able to secure the 28 seats in the north where Hizbullah has no constituency. This was conducive to obtaining a majority in the legislature after Hariri also secured Beirut, leaving only one seat vacant for Hizbullah. The prime minister was then inevitably selected from the March 14 bloc, as the constitution requires that the legislature names the prime minister. Past practice and the situation on the ground made it doubtful whether Hariri would be able to do the same in 2009.

In an interesting turn of events, a recent article in the German weekly *Der Spiegel*, which implicated Hizbullah's role in the 2005 Hariri assassination, led indirectly to a diffusion of tensions. One of the most notable in a wave of domestic condemnations of the article was by the March 14 leading cadre and head of the PSP, Druz MP Walid Jumblatt. Jumblatt's statement was well received by Nasrallah, who reiterated it to the letter in his 25 May speech, leading to rapprochement between the two parties after tensions erupted in violent military confrontations in May 2008. In a reconciliatory discourse – aimed not only at defusing tensions with the Druz, but also with the Sunnis – Nasrallah reached out to the Sunnis of Beirut and explained what he meant when he termed 8 May a 'glorious day' in the sense of warding off Sunni-Shia discord (*fitna*). Nasrallah also conceded that it was a 'sad and painful day' since people died and others lost their possessions.

Nevertheless, in the countdown to the 7 June 2009 elections, the war of words between the opposing parties reached an unprecedented high, which ran contrary to the détente presented in Hizbullah's election program and agreed upon at the national dialogue sessions, headed by the president. But this is to be expected in Lebanese politics in such decisive elections, which might herald the inauguration of the 'third republic', namely, the Hizbullah-led opposition governing on its own. The March 14 camp voiced this concern in a poster that represented Hizbullah as holding the ministries of defense, foreign affairs, and labor, in a cabinet headed by the late Shaykh Fathi Yakan.[8]

Hizbullah's strategy and internal policy

There seems to be no tension between Hizbullah's domestic and regional ambitions, since the party has stuck its feet deep in the Lebanese domestic quagmire and flexed its military might in May 2008 in order 'to impose certain shares and conditions', in other words attaining veto power by force. This has tarnished Hizbullah's record of not having participated in the civil war, and also risks it being labeled as a militia, shattering the halo of the Resistance, all for short-term political gain. Nasrallah had promised in a speech that if the Hizbullah-led opposition would win a majority in the parliament, it would grant veto power in the cabinet to March 14, a proposal vehemently rejected by Sa'd al-Hariri and March 14 cadres. More recently, Nasrallah extended a hand to March 14 to join the March 8 group in forming a national unity government. Will Nasrallah honor both promises or will he backtrack, as was the case with his earlier assurance that the party would never use its weapons domestically, come what may? If so, then a real change in the status quo is unlikely, since whichever scenario materializes, the political system will remain an easy prey to Hizbullah's ambitions. Knowing that the Christian vote is the determinant vote that will impact the whole result, on the eve of the elections cardinal Sfeir indirectly admonished the voters not to vote for Hizbullah and especially the FPM, warning that a March 8 victory poses an existential threat to the Lebanese entity and compromises Lebanon's identity.

The Israeli government has made direct references to this election, with Ehud Barak, the Minister of Defense, warning the Lebanese of dire consequences if they voted for the Hizbullah-led opposition, while foreign minister Avigdor Lieberman has called for an international arrest warrant against Nasrallah. These calls coincided with Israeli military drills and the charging, by the Lebanese military prosecutor, of more than 100 people for spying for Israel, a charge punishable by death according to the Lebanese penal code.

Election results

To the dismay of the Hizbullah-led opposition, 71 seats were won by March 14 and 57 seats went to March 8, in an election that witnessed 54,8 percent turn out.[9] Hizbullah won twelve seats: ten for party members and two for Sunni allies. Due to its alliance with the FPM, this time Hizbullah had no Christians on its election list.[10] The results put the veto power to the test and kept it hanging on the balance after its inefficiency in achieving its presumed goal of hegemony. Thus, one year after the Doha Accord, March 8 failed to affect change by democratic means and, most likely, will be forced to work under the status quo ante that prevailed after the 2005 legislative elections.

The elections were neither an epitome of disorder nor did Hizbullah close the door to compromise with its opponents. On the contrary, one day after the elections, the party's secretary-general, Sayyid Hasan Nasrallah conceded defeat, called for burying the hatchet and placing skeletons in the closet, congratulated and extended a hand to the victorious March 14 ruling coalition to form a national unity government, and stressed that bygones were bygones. Rapprochement between Nasrallah, the March 14 Druz leader and seasoned politician Walid Jumblatt, and the parliamentary majority leader Sa'd al-Hariri seemed to be inevitable after the elections. In marathon meetings, after a freeze of almost three years, many misunderstandings and mutual fears were addressed.

So, many tensions were defused. In accordance with the dictum of 'I'll scratch your back, if you'll scratch mine', Nabih Berri was elected as speaker for a fifth consecutive term since he first assumed office in 1992. Since he received 90 votes out of 128, when the Hizbullah-led opposition controlled only 57 seats, it meant that 33 MPs from March 14 voted for him. This was reciprocated when on 28 June Sa'd al-Hariri was nominated as incumbent prime minister by 86 MPs, when March 14 only controlled 71 seats of the legislature, which implies that the thirteen members of the Berri parliamentary bloc along with two Armenians from the Hizbullah-led opposition nominated Sa'd al-Hariri. In this atmosphere, 'Aun toned down his demands from seven ministers to five after he previously argued that since he won 50 percent of the Christian vote, he should be entitled to half the Christian ministers. This along with the groundbreaking meetings between Nasrallah, Jumblatt, and al-Hariri serve as indicators of a tendency towards national unity and reconciliation. In a positive turn of events, Jumblatt dispatched his son Taymur and MP Akram Shihayyib, and Sa'd al-Hariri and PM Sanyura sent MP Muhammad Qabbani to represent them in Hizbullah's third 'divine victory' celebration on 14 August. March 14's gesture was well-received by Hizbullah, where Nasrallah delivered a reconciliatory speech trimming down March 8 demands on the cabinet formation to ten ministers, thus wavering its earlier demand for veto power. Nasrallah classified the Israeli rhetoric in the domain of impeding the cabinet formation, pressuring Hizbullah not to participate, and trying to change the UNIFIL's rule of engagement, something that did not materialize when the mandate was renewed for a third time without any alterations. Nasrallah added that the best response to Israeli threats would be to promptly form a national unity cabinet in which his party would play a constructive role in defusing Israeli threats. In the same speech, Nasrallah introduced a new 'balance of terror [power]' formula aimed at deterrence, namely that if Israel were to bomb Beirut or the *Dahiya*, Hizbullah would then strike Tel Aviv.[11]

The longwinded formation of the cabinet
This atmosphere of optimism was shattered after 72 days when Hariri submitted a 30-seat cabinet line-up to the president on 7 September 2009, but March 8 rejected it, prompting al-Hariri's resignation on 10 September as a political maneuver and tactical move. This warrants some explanation. In light of the May 8 coup, Hizbullah considers the Telecommunications Ministry and the Ministry of Interior as 'security ministries'. Since March 14 is unwilling to hand these to Hizbullah, the party's only bid is on the FPM to get these. Already, 'Aun's son-in-law MP Gebran Basil was the Minister of Telecommunications in the outgoing Sanyura cabinet. So in the proposed ministerial line-up, Hariri appointed Basil as a minister of state and kept the ministry of interior with Ziad Barud on meritocracy, in recognition for his 'outstanding performance' before, during, and after the elections.[12] Naturally this move angered 'Aun, prompting Hizbullah and the speaker to side with him, which ultimately resulted in a rejection. Again, Cardinal Sfeir weighed in on the debate siding with the March 14 argument, namely, that those who failed in

the elections cannot become ministers, since this would be against the 'popu-lar will of the people'.[13] In turn the Association of Catholic Schools called on 'Aun to support the ministerial line-up since the ministry of education was given to a Christian from the FPM, when it was handed in for decades to a Sunni. After mandatory consultations, on 16 September, Hariri was renamed with 73 votes, 71 from the March 14 coalition and two Armenians from March 8. However, conceding to its March 8 allies, most notably Hizbullah, the FPM, and Berri's parliamentary bloc did not nominate anyone, which unprecedent-edly prompted the ex-PM Salim al-Hoss to vehemently bash them for not exercising their duties as MPs, questioning how they were going to partici-pate in a national unity cabinet, when they refused to nominate anyone. It is worth mentioning that in 1969 Lebanon remained without a cabinet for nine months from April till December, when during the 'constitutional crisis' the late PM Rashid Karami was conducting the affairs of the country as deputy PM.[14] Al-Hoss's criticism prompted Berri's parliamentary bloc to assert that not naming anyone amounts to a vote of confidence (tazkiya) to al-Hariri.[15] Nasrallah's 'Jerusalem Day' speech of 18 September, which is always primar-ily dedicated to supporting Palestine and the Palestinian people, stressed the need for national reconciliation, dialogue, and cooperation, wishing al-Hariri success in forming the cabinet. Nasrallah clarified that March 8's move of not nominating anyone should be viewed in the positive light of fending off any civil strife, calling on everyone to remain calm and release the tension through democratic, constitutional practices, as was the case after the elec-tions. He said that it was better to take our time in forming the cabinet than hastily forming one that would lead Lebanon into 'the unknown'.[16] Nasrallah's views were in line with Ayatullah Fadlallah who calmed the waters stressing that the national unity cabinet would take a long time to be formed, assuring the citizens that Lebanon would not remain without a cabinet indefinitely.[17]

Consociational democracy: Hizbullah's reading of Arend Lijphart
What is the real problem behind this political bickering? More likely, each party has its own understanding and conception of what democracy is. It seems that the predicaments characterizing the Lebanese cabinet formation process have little to do with pro- and anti-democratic tendencies. For almost all political parties, the question was not whether democracy was desirable, but what kind of democracy should be preferred, and what sort of political system should be connected with it? While March 14 promoted a majoritarian democracy (50%+), March 8 preferred a consensual democracy, proportional representation, and lowering the voting age to eighteen, which, in practice, boils down to demographic majority rule since, as mentioned in chapter two,

Muslim voters number around 75 percent, while the Christian voters number around 25 percent.

The Lebanese system, which is based on the philosophy of elite accommodation, is the most well-known example of consociationalism. Arend Lijphart, who coined the term, proposes that a consociational democracy has to fit four main criteria. First, the elites representing the leading societal groups should participate in an overarching decision-making structure. Second, this structure should incorporate a veto mechanism for each of these groups. Third, proportionality should be the guiding principle in all forms of political representation. Finally, every group should be allowed to arrange their internal matters independently.[18] March 8 and March 14 agree on Lijphart's first and fourth point, but disagree on the second and third. Hizbullah was able to obtain veto power in Sanyura's 2008-2009 cabinet, a short-lived experience that impeded the proper functioning of the cabinet, but was not continued in the 2009 Sa'd Hariri cabinet. Nevertheless, March 8 still calls for proportionality to give Lebanon's eighteen ethno-confessional communities more equitable representation. So, in Lebanon, contrary to Lijphart's stipulations, veto power seemingly does not work, while the issue of proportional representation remains debated. However, as 'Ali Fayyad noted, the institutionalization of structures fostering consensus between the societal elites remains the core of Lebanon's political system and its success – political stability – depends on the extent to which elites manage to agree on structural political dilemmas.[19]

The views of the Shi'ite opposition and cardinal Sfeir
Both Sayyid 'Ali al-Amin, the head of the Shi'ite opposition, and cardinal Sfeir attributed the current deadlock in forming the cabinet to foreign intervention, more than local dynamics. Sfeir called on Hizbullah to surrender its weapons and stop promoting the Syrian-Iranian relations in the region: "March 14 and March 8 cannot coexist in one government." In reference to 'Aun's FPM, Sfeir argued: "Domestically there are those who are empowered by foreign players in order to seek more parliamentary and ministerial gains." Concerning Hizbullah, Sfeir argued that it is working more for Iranian interest than the interest of Lebanon. In spite of that, he said that other foreign players than Syria are delaying the formation of the cabinet. In reference to the party's arms, Sfeir affirmed that militia weapons and democracy do not match: "The arms should be in the hands of the army. We fear that we will reach a stage where everyone will have recourse to arms, an eventuality that will ignite another civil war."[20]

Sayyid 'Ali al-Amin, the ex-Mufti of Sour and Jabal 'Amil[21], questioned how could the institution established by Imam Musa al-Sadr further the interest of armed militias that confiscate the Shiʻite public space and stifle the freedom of expression.[22] Al-Amin attributed the deadlock more to Syria and its stance from the international Hariri tribunal. He said that Iran is aiding a militia that constitutes a state within a state, in a country with weak security forces. He admonished that when the cabinet is formed by March 14 under the fake banner of national unity it would be the best pretext for March 8 and Hizbullah to further the Iranian agenda. He added that such a cabinet would be a legal cover for a minority that will actually rule by the power of weapons. He said that the Lebanese state is still unable to enforce the results of the 7 June elections, i.e. the majority (March 14) to take the helm of things and form an efficient cabinet. He did not hide his fear of an explosion of *fitna* (Sunni-Shiʻa discord), especially in light of the international community's will to naturalize the Palestinians in Lebanon and Hizbullah's ambitions to control the political system. Al-Amin stressed that political differences neither sanction fighting between the Shiʻa and Sunnis nor the destruction of the Lebanese state and its institutions. According to him, in May 2008 Hizbullah illegitimately spilled innocent blood without due cause.[23] He ended up by stressing that his intellectual and political thought is totally against Hizbullah deciding the fate of Lebanon and the Shiʻa sect.[24]

On 8 November 2009, Shaykh Muhammad Al-Hajj Hasan[25] – the leader of the Free Shiʻite Movement (*Al-Tayyar ʼAl-Shiʻi Al-Hurr*) and member of the Unified Nationalistic Union (*Al-Tajamuʻ al-Qawmi al-Muwwahad*) – stated that the atmosphere of optimism surrounding the formation of the new cabinet amounts to nothing after March 14 succumbed to the demands of the minority (March 8) that is reaping its political capital resulting from its 'military coup' of May 2008. He added that May 2008 cannot be forgotten even though the politicians seem to give lip service to the dictum of 'bygones are bygones', in direct reference to Sayyid Hasan Nasrallah. The "paralyzed cabinet", as Al-Hajj Hasan termed it, amounts to a bowl of stone soup fed to the miserable Lebanese people. He questioned how the loser (March 8) could enforce its conditions on the winner (March 14) of the 7 June 2009 legislative elections. He concluded that there is no democracy in Lebanon; rather just power politics that started with the May 2008 Doha Accord. In a reference to legitimizing Hizbullah's weapons – the "plague" as he called it – al-Hajj Hasan called on March 14 ministers and MPs not to give in; rather to fight any policy statement contrary to the cherished values of the Independence Uprising or Cedar Revolution and to remember and give tribute to the martyrs of independence. Finally, he lashed the "hypocritical discourse" of ʻAun, the leader of the FPM – who had a big hand in persuading the US administration in imposing the 'Syria Accountability Act' and UNCR 1559 – arguing that if he had had the chance he would have fought the Shi'a till death.

After five months of the elections, the 24th cabinet since independence saw the light. The national unity cabinet was based upon the previously agreed political framework and power-sharing formula: fifteen seats for March 14; five for the centralist coalition of the president; and ten for March 8: five for the Shi'a (two ministers for Hizbullah, two for Amal, and one neutral); and five for the FPM. Although March 8 insisted on obtaining the two security ministries of interior and telecommunications[26], the ministries of interior and defense were included in the president's share and the ministry of tele-communications went to Hizbullah's ally, the FPM. The cabinet included sixteen old faces and fourteen new, including two women.[27]

According to the NNA, on 25 November 2009, Shi'ite opposition figure Ahmad al-As'ad met with Sayyid 'Ali al-Amin to discuss current developments. Al-As'ad was unhappy with Hizbullah's founding in October 2009 of its NGO 'Qiyam [Values]' and its 'Order is an essential part of Faith' campaign which aimed at giving a facelift to al-Dahiya by inculcating civic education, specifically teaching the people about keeping law and order and obeying the state and its institutions. Al-As'ad claimed that Hizbullah was incapable of stopping drug trafficking and addiction, as such manipulating the government and using it as a scapegoat in facing the drug problem, claiming that Hizbullah was not genuine in its collaboration with the Lebanese state in that area. He contended that Nasrallah's affirmation in his 11 November 2009 speech of exposing felons was just a charade. Al-As'ad ended by posing the fundamental question on Hizbullah's weapons, which, according to him, were heavily deployed in the Dahiya outside the framework of the sovereignty of the Lebanese state. He pointed out that these very weapons were aimed at fellow Lebanese in May 2008, thus shattering the claim that their only purpose is to fight Israel. Al-As'ad wondered whether the state would only monitor the party's weapons from a distance, knowing that certain areas are off limits to the security forces.[28] Rhetorically, al-As'ad questioned whether Hizbullah's weapons would dictate on the Lebanese state what is right and what is wrong.

These statements echoed the March 14 worries one day before the cabinet's 22-page policy statement saw the light after ten[29] extensive, marathon sessions of the drafting committee. The result was that there were no drastic changes to the post-2005 security statement which continued to balance the dynamic between Hizbullah's resistance identity and the Lebanese state's sovereignty. Article six read: "From the stance of the duty to uphold Lebanese sovereignty and territorial integrity, the cabinet affirms the right of Lebanon, its government, its people, its army, and its resistance (Hizbullah) to employ all legitimate means in order to liberate all Lebanese territory."[30] As such, the cabinet stressed its commitment to the full implementation of UNSC Resolution 1701 and the need of finding a unified stance at the dialogue sessions towards reaching a national defense strategy. As a ritual practice and from the stance of upholding state sovereignty par excellence, five March 14 ministers registered their reservations to the policy statement: the two Lebanese Forces ministers Ibrahim Najjar and Salim Wardé ; the two Phalangist ministers Michel Phar'un and Salim al-Sayyigh; and Butrus Harb. A day earlier Shaykh Na'im Qasim made it clear that Hizbullah's weapons were not open to discussion, not even on the national dialogue table.[31] On 22 November 2009, the president announced in his independence day address the resumption of the national dialogue sessions as soon as the cabinet is confirmed by the parliament. President Sulayman admonished against the national-dialogue body taking the prerogatives of the cabinet while attempting to enact reform. This sentiment was echoed by the ex-PM Salim al-Hoss who argued that the body, which was formed under special circumstances that have changed now, should be dissolved in favor of the cabinet that is supposed to be the ultimate arbitrator. If needed, thorny issues could also be referred to the legislature for adjudication.[32]

6.4 CONCLUSION: MENDING THE TIES, RAPPROCHEMENT, AND MORE POLITICAL POWER

Tensions were defused after a series of groundbreaking reconciliatory meetings. On 25 November 2009 a reconciliatory meeting took place at the presidential palace in B'abda between 'Aun and Jumblatt, the first since Jumblatt's visit to 'Aun in Paris mid-April 2005. While the cabinet officially approved the policy statement, a watershed reconciliatory meeting between 'Aun and cardinal Sfeir took place after the two exchanged bitter rhetoric for over three years.[33]

After the policy statement was approved by the drafting committee and the 'Id al-Adha holiday was over, on 30 November 2009, Nasrallah dropped a bomb: he held a press conference in order to introduce Hizbullah's new Manifesto or 'Political Document (al-wathiqa al-siyasiyya)', which resulted from its eighth conclave that was held in the summer-autumn of 2009. This is most likely the best proof of Hizbullah's continuous identity construction and reconstruction, bearing in mind the dictum that the party changes as circumstances themselves change.

7 The Eighth Conclave: A New Manifesto (November 2009)

This chapter surveys Hizbullah's identity construction from the time of the propagation of its first Manifesto, the Open Letter in 1985, passing through all of its eight clandestine conclaves, to the publication of its second watershed Manifesto in 2009. I begin by analyzing the Open letter.

7.1   THE SALIENT POINTS OF THE OPEN LETTER

Hizbullah's political declarations, *al-'Ahd*, the discourse of its leaders and cadres, and most notably the Open Letter specify the constituents of the party's political ideology: oppressors and oppressed; Islamic state; relations with Christians, anti-Zionism, pan-Islamism, anti-imperialism, and jihad and martyrdom.[1] Hizbullah employs Qur'anic legitimization of its political ideology in the form of Qur'anic verses to justify its stance. One may notice that only the first section of the 'Open Letter' explicitly refers to Hizbullah's religious ideology: belief in Shi'a Islam, *wilayat al-faqih*, and *jihad* in the way of God.

OPPRESSORS AND OPPRESSED

The concept of oppressors (*mustakbirin*) and oppressed (*mustad'afin*) is central to a proper understanding of Hizbullah's political ideology. Although Hizbullah seems to employ an exclusivist discourse[2] in which it classifies people according to the Qur'anic classification/dichotomy of Hizbullah (The Party of God) (5:56) or *Hizb al-Shaytan* (The Party of the Devil) (58: 19), Hizbullah uses the Qur'anic term or Islamic expression of oppressed and reproduces it as an all-inclusive concept in order to uphold political and social justice. On the face of it, it appears that Hizbullah is using Marxist terminology, which is translated or interpreted in Islamic terms along the lines of economic, political, and social justice, thus producing a kind of Islamic socialism, as some scholars have claimed.[3]

However, Hizbullah clearly argues in the Open Letter and its political declarations that its friends are the oppressed of the entire world, irrespective of their color, race, or religion. The party interprets and applies the contemporary concept of *mustad'af* by stressing that it is a Qur'anic concept that came to prominence with the advent of the Islamic Revolution. Hizbullah emphasizes that this usage conveys and is in conformity with its identity as an Islamic *jihadi* movement struggling to address and redress the injustices that the oppressed suffer from. However, the party clarifies that its usage of the term *mustad'af* is different from the political concept that is used by the socialists to refer to the poor peasants or the proletariat, the Qur'anic concept being more encompassing and holistic in its orientation because it touches upon the existential level of oppression and offers prescriptions and remedies in dealing with the oppressors and warding them off. Hizbullah emphasizes that *mustad'afin* applies to the wronged, unjustly treated, tyrannized, and impoverished who do not own their daily bread, and who are oppressed in their freedom, dignity, and endeavors without any consideration whether they are Christians or Muslims. Therefore, Hizbullah's political ideology stresses the universality of the Qur'anic concept – as opposed to the specificity of the Marxist concept – that cuts across class, cultural, and religious cleavages.

Even though Ayatullah Fadlallah is not part of the main establishment of Hizbullah, Hizbullah might have been influenced by Fadlallah's views on oppression. The point of convergence is that both Fadlallah's and Hizbullah's Islamic theory of oppression differ from liberation theology. Although liberation theology places the oppressed, marginalized, discriminated minorities, women, workers, etc. at the center of its discourse, siding with the oppressed in their struggle for their rights, it does not call for an overall Christianization of society nor does it aim at establishing a religiously based society and political system. Rather, liberation theology builds on religious sources reinterpreting them for secular-Marxist aims by supporting the struggle of the oppressed "wretched of the earth" for social justice. In spite of that, there seems to be a considerable difference between the two views since Fadlallah's political-ideological legitimization conveys specificity in his characterization of oppression that is at variance with Hizbullah, especially his Qur'anic legitimizations that distinguish between two groups of the oppressed. It seems as if Fadlallah is insinuating a distinction between negligent, idle oppressed who let grass grow under their feet and do not even exercise persuasive *jihad*, on the one hand, and committed oppressed who mobilize in order to confront their oppressors (smaller military *jihad*) or alter their condition of oppression by emigrating to the Muslim heartland, if they are capable of doing so, on the other.

ANTI-ZIONISM

Hizbullah's anti-Zionist political ideology often seems to conflate Jewish identity with Zionist ideology, thus equating Jews with Zionists. Also, there seems to be a contradiction between Hizbullah's views concerning the people of the book and how it treats the Jews in Israel. However, the Open Letter and the political declarations clearly state that Hizbullah equates all Israelis with Zionists. Further, Hizbullah's *al-ʿAhd* and the discourse of its leaders clarify that the party does not discriminate against the Jews as a race or religion and it would accord them their human and civil rights as the constitution of Medina had done, in spite of their discouraging Qur'anic and historical precedents of treachery, hypocrisy, and breaking the covenant with the Prophet and fighting him at *Khaybar*.

Hizbullah's doctrinal behavior is also warranted by Khumayni's ideology that distinguished between the Jews living in Muslim countries under Muslim rule and the Zionists in Israel. Simply stated, Hizbullah's political ideology considers that there are no Jews in Israel, only Zionists. That is why, the Zionists can be driven out and their country annihilated. From this stance, Hizbullah unleashed its venom towards the 'Zionist Entity' that has occupied Palestine by military force. Hizbullah characterizes Israel as an aggressive, racist, expansionist, anti-humanist, cancerous gland instated by Western colonial powers in Muslim heartland. Hizbullah's political ideology conveys no recognition of Israel, calls for wiping it out of existence, and stipulates a continual commitment to the liberation of Palestine. This political-ideological stance mirrors that of the Islamic Revolution: "Today Iran, and tomorrow Palestine", i.e. the liberation of Iran from the Shah would be followed by the liberation of Palestine from the Zionists. From a principal and doctrinal perspective, Hizbullah's political ideology seeks to restore Arab-Muslim historical rights in Palestine and is totally against any cease-fire, truce, land for peace, peace negotiations, or normalization of relations with Israel.

Hizbullah's political ideology heeds Imam Khumayni's call for pan-Islamism, especially in the wake of what he termed the worldwide conspiracy against the unity of the Muslims. Hizbullah's political ideology has always called for unity, both in the Islamic and domestic fronts, in order to avoid the dangers of discord. In its Open Letter, Hizbullah allotted section 22, entitled "God is with the Unity of the Muslims", to advocating pan-Islamism in order to render special attention to the dangers of discord, stressing a revolutionary distinction between upright Muslim religious scholars and the corrupt ones, or state jurists who follow the injunctions of the imperialist colonizers by applying the precept of divide and conquer. Hizbullah based its call for the unity of Muslims and warding off of *fitna* on a host of Qur'anic verses: (3:103); (6:159); (2:191); (2:193); (8:28); (8:73).

On the basis of what has been presented in section 2.5, it seems that the conspiracy theory has governed a lot of Hizbullah's visions. That is why Hizbullah considered any political or military dispute between Sunnis and Shi'as as an oppressor-colonizer's conspiracy aimed at spreading discord and dissention among the Muslims. Thus, Hizbullah blames internal discord on the West. Hizbullah has repeatedly warned against this and called upon the Muslims to uphold common grounds that ultimately lead to enforcing the power of the Muslims in the face of the mounting challenges facing the *umma*.

Hizbullah's discourse is general, in the sense that it does not give specific examples on Sunni-Shi'ite disagreements, since this would lead to discord, when Hizbullah's aim is to unite all the Muslims. However, Hizbullah's efforts to unify the Muslims remained on a theoretical level as a kind of persuasive smaller *jihad* by the tongue and heart, rather than real Sunni-Shi'a unity, mainly due to mutually branding each other with infidelity (*khutab al-takfir*) and the disintegration that the Islamic community was passing through. Nevertheless, in the local Lebanese context 'The Union of Muslim *'Ulama*'[4] has covered some grounds on the way to unifying Islamic work among the Sunni and Shi'a *'ulama* as well as their respective populace. Hizbullah argues that respecting the jurisprudential differences among the Sunni and Shi'ites does not preclude unity and cooperation among the Sunni and Shi'a Islamists on common political-ideological concepts such as anti-imperialism, anti-Zionism, 'the liberation of Jerusalem', etc. In fact, such political-ideological concepts forged a unity of interests and common goals between Hizbullah and Sunni Islamists such as the Lebanese *Harakat al-Tawhid al-Islami* and *Al-Jama'a Al-Islamiyya*[5], as well as Palestinian Sunni Islamists, who all receive material support from Iran.

Hizbullah stresses that it is exercising its legitimate right of defending the rights and the dignity of the *umma* by confronting its basic enemies: the US, France, and Israel. Imam Khumayni clarified that the sensitivity of the Iranians is not towards the American people, rather the American government.[6] Thus, Hizbullah is against Westoxification[7] and does not practice xenophobia (antipathy to the West and East). Nevertheless, Hizbullah's Westoxification is rooted in its hatred to the US administration, not the US people.

Hizbullah employs a specific reading of Khumayni since it took one aspect, namely reforming the individual before reforming others, and integrated it in another debate as a critique of Western concepts of revolution. By this, Hizbullah intended to convey the superiority of the Islamic order – that is holistically concerned with all aspects of life, especially the spiritual dimension – over the materialist outlook of the East and West, socialism and capitalism. Hizbullah does not address the assumption that Western capitalism is rooted in specific cultural and societal traits.

Thus, Hizbullah's political-ideology claims a sense of moral superiority vis-à-vis the West. By building a holistic, coalescent individual, Hizbullah purports that the project of the Islamic Revolution does not aim at modernizing Islam, but rather that Islam aspires to Islamize modernity, which poses a binary threat to materialism and rationalism that are found in the West. According to Hizbullah, this is what Islam has to offer in response.

JIHAD AND MARTYRDOM

Hizbullah distinguishes between smaller military *jihad* and greater *jihad*, relegating the role of the former to defensive *jihad* in the battlefield against the enemies of Islam and the latter to the internal struggle against one's self. Hizbullah practices the smaller military *jihad* against the local enemies of Islam, the political Maronites, as well as against the regional and international enemies – Israel, France, and the US. Hizbullah emphasizes the ideological-political dimension of greater *jihad* whereby mere membership of the Hizbullah amounts to engaging in the greater *jihad* in the generic, overall encompassing metaphorical sense of membership in the community of 'the son's of Hizbullah's *umma*'. By this Hizbullahis would accomplish their legitimate political responsibility (*taklif*). Therefore, Hizbullah amplifies the greater *jihad* to encompass all stages of membership in Hizbullah's activity. Employing a high-level theological discourse, Nasrallah distinguishes between greater *jihad* and smaller *jihad* arguing along the lines of Khumayni that the greater *jihad* should be practiced before engaging in the smaller military *jihad*. Based on Khumayni and Fadlallah, it could be inferred that Hizbullah's conception of greater *jihad*, as spiritual-transcendental *jihad*, aims at constructing a distinct Islamic identity of the individual.

Hizbullah consciously extolls martyrdom as a religiously sanctioned legitimate defensive *jihadi* act conducted in order to face a superior invading or occupying army equipped with a high-tech arsenal. While Hizbullah views the reward of martyrdom as eternal life in heaven, it vilifies suicide as a ticket to hell in a moment of despair, hopelessness, and frustration. Hizbullah legitimizes its martyrdom operations on the basis of religious edicts and reiterates its prohibition of conducting them if the same objectives could be realized by smaller military *jihad*.

THE OBSOLETENESS OF THE OPEN LETTER

The events that have occurred since 1985 changed some of the basic details of Hizbullah's vision, especially after the end of the Iraq-Iran war in 1988 and after the collapse of the Eastern Bloc and the Soviet Union in 1989-1990, which led to the emergence of a unipolar system and New World Order headed by the US. In Hizbullah's reading, this garnered more and more support for Israel from the US and the international community at the expense of the Arabs, and specifically the Palestinians in the Arab-Israeli conflict. All of these events acted as catalysts to change Hizbullah's orientation and tactics, as well as some of its near- and medium-range interests and targets. Indeed, the intellectual foundation and background to Hizbullah's Manifesto did not change much because it is based upon *jihad* against Israel and its allies, spearheaded by the US and the UK.[8] Also, Hizbullah's classification of foes and friends has undergone a radical revision dictated by domestic changes in Lebanon and the regional and international state attitudes towards the Islamic Revolution in Iran. However, Hizbullah's animosity towards Israel and its existence remains a fixity in Hizbullah's thinking, at least on the rhetorical level.[9]

7.2 HIZBULLAH'S EIGHT CONCLAVES

FIRST THREE CONCLAVES

Bearing this in mind, in 1989 Hizbullah held its first conclave and revealed the identity of its leaders and cadres. The conclave resulted in the creation of the post of the secretary-general and the election of Shaykh Subhi al-Tufayli as

Hizbullah's first secretary-general and the nomination of a *Shura* council that included Hajj Muhammad Ra'd, one of the founding members of the party.[10]

Starting 22 May 1991, Hizbullah held its second conclave and elected Sayyid 'Abbas Al-Musawi as its second secretary-general, and Shaykh Na'im Qasim as his deputy. Unlike the first conclave in which the seven-member *Shura* council was nominated, in the second conclave they were elected. The conclave set written moral precepts upon which dialogue would be conducted with the Christians.[11] Thus, the most salient decision of the conclave was Hizbullah's *infitah*. This development was reflected in Hizbullah's 1991 political program, authored by Sayyid Abbas al-Musawi. In the early summer of 1993, Hizbullah held its third conclave, in which it re-elected Sayyid Hasan Nasrallah as its secretary-general, and Shaykh Na'im Qasim as deputy secretary-general. It is important to note that the Islamic Resistance was rewarded by electing Hizbullah's 'Central Military Commander', Hajj Muhsin Al-Shakar, as one of the seven-members of the *Shura* council.[12]

FOURTH CONCLAVE

In July 1995, Hizbullah held its fourth conclave. Some of the basic organizational changes that Hizbullah made were the following: 1) The Politburo was renamed as the 'political council' and its jurisdiction was enlarged; 2) The creation of the *'Jihadi* council', headed by Sayyid Hashim Safiyyeddine, the only new member of the *Shura* council; 3) The 'executive council' replaced the 'executive *Shura*' with, more or less, the same jurisdictions; 4) In order to evaluate Hizbullah's experience in the parliament, the party formed a new body called the 'parliamentary bloc council'. In addition to its pledge to liberate Lebanese occupied land from the Israeli army, Hizbullah reiterated its commitment to continuing dialogue to consolidate ties with all the constituents of the Lebanese myriad. The secretary-general and his deputy were re-elected. Hajj Hasan Khalil was elected as Nasrallah's political aide or advisor and MP Muhammad Ra'd as the head of the 'political council'. Shaykh Nabil Qawuq replaced Sayyid Hashim Safiyyeddine[13] as Hizbullah's political representative in the South; MP Muhammad Yaghi was elected as the party's political representative in the Biqa'; and 'Ali D'un remained in his post as Hizbullah's political representative in Beirut. Nayef Krayyem replaced 'Ali Rashid as the head of the party's Central Information Office, while the latter became the head of a specialized committee within the political council; and Abdallah Qasir remained the head of the executive council.[14]

Shaykh Subhi al-Tufayli was officially expelled from Hizbullah by a political declaration issued on 24 January 1998. On 30 January a violent military confrontation erupted between the Lebanese army and al-Tufayli's supporters, who occupied Hizbullah's religious seminary in *'Ayn Burday*, near *B'albak*, by military force. The bloody face-off – which resulted in some casualties, the most important being the deaths of a Christian army lieutenant and ex-Hizbullah MP Khudr Tlays, Tufayli's son–in-law, and many others wounded – ended with the destruction of Tufayli's headquarters and the Lebanese state's issuing of an arrest warrant against Tufayli. However, till this day, he is still at large.

After solving the problem of internal discord, Hizbullah held its fifth conclave between 20 June and the end of July 1998. Nasrallah was elected for a third term. For this move to be made, Hizbullah had to amend its internal bylaws by deleting the stipulation that the secretary-general cannot serve for more than two consecutive terms. Shaykh Na'im Qasim was elected as deputy secretary-general; Hajj Hasan Khalil as Nasrallah's political aide; Muhammad Ra'd as the head of the political council; and Sayyid Hashim Safiyyeddine as the head of the executive council. Thus, out of sixteen incumbents, seven were elected to the *Shura* council, the ones who harmoniously and efficiently could work together, according to *Shura* council member Muhammad Ra'd. Ra'd clarified that the party evaluated its performance on four main junctures: 1) the 1996 Israeli 'Grapes of Wrath' and means to boost Hizbullah's military readiness in any future confrontation with Israel, especially in light of the deterioration in the prospects of a comprehensive peace settlement between Israel and the Arabs; 2) al-Tufayli's uprising and its repercussions; 3) the 1998 municipal elections; 4) the 1996 legislative elections. Ra'd added that the conclave also discussed the necessity of rehabilitating the party's cadres culturally and politically. Hizbullah's leaders also discussed the most efficient means to attract leading personalities in the social, economic, artistic, and intellectual domains to the party, without being organizationally tied to it, thus guaranteeing their independence. The *Shura* council is incumbent on following the progress on this matter and reporting to the rest of the cadres the progress achieved in this regard. Ra'd stressed that in domestic Lebanese politics, Hizbullah pursues 'the Lebanese national interest' over any narrow interest in its alliances and dealings with the state and the political groupings in the country. In answering criticisms about Hizbullah's alleged authoritarian nature of appointing its leadership and cadres, Ra'd claimed that making drastic changes or a complete overhaul to the leadership and cadres in every conclave would lead to instability, rather than being conducive to democratic practice.[15]

SIXTH CONCLAVE

Hizbullah's sixth conclave that ended on 30 July 2001 had a different flavor. The party evaluated its eighteen-year struggle against the occupying Israeli forces that withdrew in May 2000 due to the relentless Lebanese resistance and war of attrition spearheaded by the Islamic Resistance, Hizbullah's military wing. Concerning the party's organizational changes, Nasrallah was re-elected for life, and Sayyid Ibrahim Amin Al-Sayyid and Hajj Jawad Nureddine (Imad Mughniyyé's pseudonym) replaced Hajj Muhammad Ra'd and Hajj Muhsin Shakar in the *Shura* council. Hizbullah placed its media institutions under the direct command of Nasrallah, aided by the head of the political council and that of the executive council. This was done in order to upgrade the role of Hizbullah's media, and pursue its ideological hegemony. Also, Hizbullah abolished its central planning council, and strengthened internal audit and accountability mechanisms. From this perspective, the roles and duties of the municipal councils were expanded (horizontally) and upgraded (vertically).[16] Most importantly, the party took the decision to revise its Open Letter in light of the changing political arena and dynamics since 1985. This would only bear fruit in 2009.

THE CONTROVERSY OVER A NEW OPEN LETTER, MANIFESTO

Acknowledging the difficulty of implementing the stipulations of the Open Letter in the Lebanese public sphere and its clash with the political system, in October 1994 Nasrallah hinted at a possible rewording of the Open Letter: "The Open Letter conveyed general precepts and general guidelines of our identity... some time ago, we have reviewed the Open Letter and I do not consider that there are major alterations that have occurred to our overall doctrines and orientations although we should account for the changes and eventualities that took place in the previous years."[17]

In October 2002, rumor surfaced that Hizbullah was in the final phases of launching a new updated version of its Open Letter in conformity with an earlier decision taken in its sixth conclave. The rumor was substantiated by Qasim's interview in the *Daily Star* on 28 October 2002. Qasim argued, "Much has happened and much has changed between 1985 and now... Our basic principles remain the same because they are the heart of our movement, but many other positions have changed due to evolving circumstances developing around us." Locally, Qasim stressed that Hizbullah's position towards the Phalangists had obviously changed, stressing that they were now partners in dialogue. Regionally, concerning Hizbullah's stance towards Israel, Qasim affirmed Hizbullah's outright animosity towards the 'Zionist entity' and the 'Small Satan' from an immutable, doctrinal perspective: "Since many positions have changed, we need to be flexible and change ours too… But the resistance against Israel has been the core of our belief and that has never changed" since "the struggle against Israel remains the central rationale of Hizbullah's existence." Internationally, Qasim argued that Hizbullah's relationship with the West had witnessed many changes in line with its *infitah* policy and the West's changing perception towards the party, especially France: "The French were considered our enemy because they attacked our bases in the Bekaa… France's position has changed towards us, so we have to change ours." However, he added that Hizbullah's perception towards the US[18] was still the same, since the party still regarded it as the 'Great Satan'.[19]

Leenders observes: "Even earlier hints of a fundamental revision of the party's outlook – such as amending its now largely obsolete founding document – have failed to materialise."[20] Well, not quite. In February 2003, a leading cadre – who is currently a member of the *Shura* council – told that the newly reconstructed, updated, and modified Open Letter/Manifesto was ready but that its launching had been postponed due to the deteriorating regional and international situations and the imminent US-led invasion of Iraq (March 2003).[21] Keeping in mind that the Open Letter delineates Hizbullah's local, regional, and international stance, it seems that the regional dimension froze its launching for more than six years. Sobelman aptly remarks: "Today Hizbollah views the original platform [Open Letter] as outdated… [There is] an increasingly apparent metamorphosis [identity reconstruction] in the organization at the declaratory level and in the practical sphere… [Hizbollah] has traveled from the time of its founding and its more recent decision to choose pragmatic integration into the Lebanese system over pure ideology."[22] Sobelman attributes this stance to Hizbullah's *infitah* policy. He argues that Hizbullah's decision to publish a new and updated version of its Open Letter, "which according to Na'im Qasim will be more moderate in its relations with the Lebanese Christians and Western countries like France, a country understood to oppose against Hizbollah's inclusion on the European Union's list of terror organizations, is no coincidence."[23] Whatever the case, these instances illustrate Hizbullah's serious attempts to aim at identity construction and reconstruction, since over the years its ideology, political strategy, and future outlook has undergone drastic and dramatic changes.

From early June to 16 August 2004, Hizbullah held its seventh conclave. Unlike the previous conclaves where information was leaked to the media, hardly any information was disseminated. It seems that Hizbullah's extra clandestine tactic maybe had to do with the dismantling of a network of underground operatives allegedly linked to Israel as well as the assassination attempts the party's rank and file suffered from in the previous two years.[24]

It is worth mentioning that the followers of Subhi al-Tufayli released a political declaration chastising the conclave and asking to reinstate him and his followers to their 'natural, normal position of leadership' in the party after being ousted due to conspiracies that occurred a few years back. The political declaration added that the convening of this conclave offered a historical chance to conduct honest elections in Hizbullah's rank and file in order to choose leaders who would retain Hizbullah's earlier glory as a religious, Shi'ite social movement. The declaration accused Nasrallah of planting discord in the Shi'ite house (milieu) by his "total hegemony and tyrannical control" over the party and its capabilities and directing them in a way that was not conducive to the Shi'ites, for instance, as exemplified by the criticisms directed towards Ayatullah Fadlallah in favor of some (Iranian) personalities and *maraji'* (pl. of *marja'*).[25]

Hizbullah released a political document in the form of two political declarations. The first political declaration conveyed that no changes took place within Hizbullah's seven-member *Shura* council, which included the following members: Sayyid Hasan Nasrallah, Hizbullah's secretary-general and the head of the *Jihadi* council; Shaykh Na'im Qasim deputy secretary-general; Sayyid Hashim Safiyyeddine head of the executive council; Sayyid Ibrahim Amin Al-Sayyid, the head of the political council; Hajj Hasan Khalil, Nasrallah's political aide or advisor; Shaykh Muhammad Yazbik head of the religio-judicial council, or the one "responsible for the dossier of the *shar'i* matters and Islamic scholars' affairs"; and Sayyid Jawad Nureddine (Imad Mughniyyé's pen name/alias). In its second political document, Hizbullah listed four priorities and eight basic modifications or amendments. The most salient amendment was Hizbullah's division of the south into two administrative geographical areas: the first south of the Litani river, and the second to its north. Both function under the auspices of one central organizational leader in order to secure organizational structures that are capable of improving local administration and activate polarization. In addition, Shaykh Abd al-Karim 'Ubayd was appointed as the head of Hizbullah's social institutions and Shaykh Hasan Izzeddine, Hizbullah's spokesman at the Central Press Office, was appointed as Hizbullah's political representative in the south. He was replaced by Nasrallah's media aide or advisor, the engineer Hajj Muhammad Afif.[26]

FIRST WOMAN APPOINTED TO A PROMINENT POLITICAL ROLE

In the beginning of December 2004, and in light of the decisions taken in Hizbullah's seventh conclave, Hizbullah, for the first time in its history, appointed the head of its Women's Organization, Rima Fakhry, as a member of its eighteen-member political council (Politburo). Also, Hizbullah appointed Wafa' Hutayt, the person responsible for political programs in *al-Nour* radio, as deputy of Hizbullah's Central Information Office.[27] These two moves came as a result of internal debates among Hizbullah cadres and of amending some of the party's bylaws.[28]

As a practical political dimension, Hizbullah founded its *Jihadi* council in 1995 in order to closely monitor and supervise its *jihadi* activities. The *Jihadi* council gained more importance after the May 2000 nearly complete Israeli withdrawal, since in its seventh conclave, the secretary-general himself became its head. However, this turned out to be a hoax and a smart maneuver aimed at hiding the real identity and function of the infamous Imad Mughniyyé – Hizbullah's ex-military cadre on whose head the US put a $ 25 million reward – who was assassinated by a car explosion in Damascus on 12 February 2008.

HIZBULLAH'S EIGHTH CONCLAVE

The eighth conclave was supposed to take place in 2007 – in accordance with the every three years dictum – but, in conformity with *Realpolitik*, the situation on the ground dictated another course of action. The repercussions of the July 2006 War and fear of assassination of the leaders and cadres were conducive factors that kept on postponing the eighth conclave, till the leadership took the decision to hold it in spite of all the political and security threats. Starting the summer of 2009 and lasting for around four months, thousands of middle- and high-rank party cadres embarked on an intensive evaluation of previous policies through a long and thorough political, organizational workshop that witnessed, in conformity with the party's scalar principle, the election of the primary electoral college that elects its representatives to the *Shura* council.[29] On 19 November 2009, the party released the following political declaration:

Hizbullah ended its general congress, which lasted for several months[30], whereby a new political document was adopted, the second of its kind after the Open Letter of 1985. It also approved a number of organizational amendments commensurate with the nature of new developments in its movement over the last few years at various levels. The election of members of the *Shura* (consultative) council took place and their responsibilities were nominated for the new mandate. They are the following:

1. Sayyid Hasan Nasrallah, secretary-general.
2. Shaykh Na'im Qasim, deputy secretary-general.
3. Shaykh Muhammad Yazbik, chairman of the Religio-Judicial Council.
4. Sayyid Ibrahim Amin Al-Sayyid, chairman of the Political Council.
5. Sayyid Hashim Safiyyeddine, chairman of the Executive Council.
6. Hajj Husayn Khalil, political aide to the secretary-general.
7. MP Hajj Muhammad Ra'd, head of the Loyalty to the Resistance Bloc.

The secretary-general of Hizbullah will hold a press conference in the next few days, God willing, to announce the new political document.[31]

What the party did not reveal was that an eighth member was added to the *Shura* council. However, fearing assassination[32], the name of the leading resistance cadre in the council was not revealed. Electing Hajj Muhammad Ra'd is telling since it reflects an innovative trend that accords parliamentary work a great status. It could also be regarded as a personal recognition for all the hard work and dedication on his part since he represented the party in the national dialogue sessions after a failed assassination attempt on Nasrallah's life made the latter shun public events. This move is also indicative of the role Hizbullah is according to its MPs in order to reveal its new face in light of the new manifesto, since many of them have already met EU diplomats, including foreign ministers and ex-foreign policy chief Solana. In a similar vein, the party established a special unit in an attempt to boost its involvement in the cabinet's work and take an active role in the administrative apparatus of the state in an endeavor to stamp out corruption. The great achievement of the eighth conclave is par excellence the new Manifesto, rather than the slight changes to the party's organizational structure or structural formations.

Finally Hizbullah's decision in its sixth conclave bore fruit. After almost a quarter of a century, on 30 November 2009 the party revealed its new Manifesto/Political Platform delineating its domestic, regional, and international policy dynamics.[33] The party's spokesman, Sayyid Ibrahim al-Musawi, told me: "It will send waves of awareness about the party and help shatter negative, preconceived ideas."[34] The Manifesto also addresses issues such as the resistance; political, social, economic, administrative, and judicial reform;

and contains a stance on the abolition of political sectarianism and the implementation of the Ta'if Agreement. The Manifesto outlines the party's political and intellectual vision in light of a dynamic world.

From the perspective of the party's call to the establishment of a strong, capable, and just state, Hizbullah started to give the *Dahiya* a facelift a month before announcing the Manifesto, whereby law and order were being imposed by the Lebanese police and all breaches to public facilities and criminal offences were penalized. As part of its campaign, entitled 'Order is an essential part of Faith' and headed by the general coordinator Sayyid Husayn Fadlallah, the party founded a new NGO called '*Qiyam* (Values)' in order to spread and inculcate civic consciousness among the population through a combination of Qur'anic verses, *hadith* prohibitions, and popular sayings and aphorisms exhorting the masses to employ their religious discipline in order to uphold law and order. Some of the banners and slogans read: "It is prohibited to make use of water and electricity through illegal means; God has organized your daily dealings; encroaching on public order is a *haram*; abiding by traffic signs is a measure of intelligence; be careful in using water, etc."[35] The same message was reiterated again in a lengthy speech by Nasrallah on the seventh day of *Muharram*, where he stressed to his followers the religious duty to abide by law and order, citing a consensus among the jurisprudents to the obligation of complying with laws that uphold public order.[36] So no wonder that in its eighth conclave Hizbullah added new political, organizational, media, and cultural units in order to accommodate this new development. The need for drastic organizational changes concomitant with the party's rotation policy, not only in its military structure but also in its civil organs, has been growing ever since the end of the July 2006 War, where great deficiencies have been noted in this regard.[37]

7.3   ANALYSIS OF THE NEW MANIFESTO

HIZBULLAH'S WORLD VIEW

Hizbullah's world view did not drastically alter in its 2009 Manifesto. In line with its 1985 Open Letter, its first Manifesto, it replaced the bipolarity of the West facing the East with Imam Khumayni's ideological bipolarity that divides the world into the Qur'anic notions of 'oppressors' and 'oppressed'. Hizbullah upheld its 'liberation theology' and called for the 'unity of the oppressed':

According to Hizbullah's vision and approach, the criteria of divergence and conflict are based upon political-moral grounds, primarily between the arrogant and wretched, the oppressor and oppressed, the haughty occupier and a pursuer of freedom.[38]

The central goal of the American hegemony resides in dominating the nations politically, economically, culturally and through all aspects… as it is the base of controlling the world economy not to mention resorting to all merciless, inhumane and unethical means including the use of extreme military power whether directly or through a mediator. To achieve this goal, Washington… provided the Zionist entity with stability guarantees, in such a way that allows this entity to play the role of a cancerous gland that absorbs and sucks out all the energies and capabilities of the nation as to destruct its ambitions and aims.[39]

We look with great interest and appreciation at the liberalization, independence and dominance rejection experiences of Latin America countries. We see vast grounds for overlap between the endeavors of these countries and the resistance movements of our region, overlap which should lead to the creation of a more equitable and balanced international order… our motto 'Unity of the Oppressed' shall remain as one of the pillars of political thought, shaping our understanding, relationships and attitudes towards international issues.[40]

Hizbullah neither changed its stance towards the US nor Israel. In rhetoric, although the ideological slogans of the 'Great Satan' and the 'Small Satan' were dropped, the 'Zionist entity' and the 'cancerous gland' remained the most used descriptions of Israel.

The unlimited US support for 'Israel' and its cover for the 'Israeli' occupation of Arab lands, in addition to the American domination of international institutions, the double standards in the criteria of issuing and applying international policies… puts the American administration in the position of the aggressor and holds it responsible for producing chaos in the international political system.[41]

We categorically reject any compromise with 'Israel' or recognizing its legitimacy. This position is definitive, even if everyone recognizes 'Israel'.[42]

In the question-and-answers session of the press conference, Nasrallah was careful to fend off any accusations of anti-Semitism against Hizbullah: "I have clearly stated in the Manifesto that our problem with the Israelis is not that they are Jews; our problem with them is not religious, ethnic, or racial. Rather, the core of the problem is that they are occupiers who are raping our land and holy places."[43]

However, Hizbullah's stance towards NATO's Western European countries and the EU, which now comprises 27 countries, did undergo serious revisions. Nevertheless, based on a common historical experience of war and occupation, Hizbullah wanted to uphold its cherished distinction between 'resistance' and 'terrorism':

> The Bush Administration decided to establish a correlation between 'terrorism' and 'national resistance', and this in order to disarm the resistance of its humanitarian legitimacy and its righteousness of cause, and to justify the waging of all forms of wars against it... 'Terrorism' was transformed into an American alibi for hegemony.[44]
>
> As for the European policies (EU), these hang between being barely effective on one side and being a follower of the American policies on the other, and this actually leads to the hollowing out of the moderate drift in Europe at the expense of and in service to the "Atlantic drift" (NATO) of colonial backgrounds.
>
> The EU's following of US policies constitutes a strategic mistake that will increase the problems of the Middle East and the world and will ultimately lead to more problems and complications in the European-Arab relations.
>
> Europe holds responsibility for the damage it has caused due to the colonial "inheritance" it has left behind – of which our people still suffer the consequences and results.
>
> Since some European people have a history in resisting the occupier, Europe's ethical and humanitarian duty – in addition to being a political duty – is to acknowledge the right of the people to resisting the occupier, on the basis of distinguishing between resistance and terrorism.
>
> The preconditions of stability and cooperation in European-Arab relations require a European approach that is more independent, just, and objective (than that of the US).[45]

THEMATIC ANALYSIS

The 71-page 2009 Manifesto begins with a "Foreword" and is divided into three chapters: "Hegemony and Mobilization"; "Lebanon"; and "Palestine and the Settlement Negotiations." I will highlight the most salient statements in each.

Lashing the US and Israel
Hizbullah contends that the US's unipolar hegemony shatters world balance, security, and stability. The party claims that the US administration's unwaver-

ing support of Israel puts the former in the position of enmity towards the Arab and Muslim nation.

Starting in the "Foreword" Hizbullah admonishes:

> We are witnessing great historical changes that point in the direction of a retreat of the US role and decline in the hegemony of the Zionist Entity (Israel)... The path of resistance and opposition to hegemony, which is based upon military victories and political successes, is gaining ground (p. 11).

In Chapter 1 entitled "Hegemony and Mobilization", Section 1: "The World and Western-American Hegemony", Hizbullah continues lashing the US, and to a lesser extent, Israel.

> Globalization reached a one-time high when it took a military shape through war in Afghanistan, Iraq, Lebanon, and Gaza (p. 18)... American terrorism is the basis of all terrorism in the world (p. 22)... The grave fiasco of the US war on resistance (movements) in Lebanon and Palestine through Israeli hands led to the deterioration of the US credibility on the international scene (p. 22)...

The same trend continues in Chapter 1, Section 2, "Our Region and the American Plot" where Hizbullah contends that the main purpose of US colonialism is to exercise hegemony over the countries and their capabilities (pp. 24-6).

Lebanon and the political system
In Chapter 2: "Lebanon", Section 1: "The Homeland", contrary to its first Manifesto, the Open Letter, Hizbullah stresses that it is against establishing cantons or states within the state and also in opposition to founding an Islamic state in Lebanon. Hizbullah regards Lebanon as its homeland par excellence:

> Lebanon is our country and the country of our fathers and forefathers; it is also the country of our children and grandchildren and all future generations. We want it strong and unified... we reject partition and federalism... Lebanon is the country that we have offered the most precious sacrifices and the most dignified of martyrs for the sake of its sovereignty, honour, dignity, and the liberation of its land... (p. 30).

However, this was not all. After Hizbullah recognized the ultimate sovereignty and territorial integrity of Lebanon stressing the building of a "capable, strong, and just state" (p. 30), in Section 3 entitled, "The State and the Political

System", the party voiced its demand to reform the political system in line with the Ta'if Agreement, Lebanon's 1990 constitution:

> The main ill in the Lebanese political system is political sectarianism... (p. 38) Consensual democracy represents a proper political formula to assure true partnership and contributes in opening the doors for everyone to join the phase of state building... (p. 39) The state that we are looking forward to taking part in is the one that upholds public freedoms and is concerned for national unity... (p. 40)

In Section 2 entitled "The Resistance", Hizbullah exposes what it perceives as the Israeli threat calling for the adoption of a national defense to face it:

> Because of its historical expansionist policy, Israel poses a perpetual existential danger to Lebanon...The Zionist entity, being a racist state, represents a peril to the very concept of multi-religious coexistence that Lebanon uniquely manifests... (p. 32) The perpetual Israeli military threat to Lebanon requires the founding of a national defence strategy... (pp. 35-36)

Lebanese-Palestinian relations

Although in Section 4, entitled "Lebanon and Palestinian-Lebanese Relations" Hizbullah is vehemently against naturalizing the Palestinian refugees in Lebanon, it urgently calls on the Lebanese government to grant them their civil rights so that they can lead a dignified life while awaiting the right of return:

> The Palestinian refugees in Lebanon should be accorded their civil and social rights in such a way to safeguard their identity and just cause, without naturalizing them... Upholding the Palestinians' Right of Return and refusal of their permanent settlement in Lebanon. (p. 46)

Relations with Syria and Iran

In conformity with the Open Letter and Lebanese reality, Hizbullah called on the Lebanese state to have privileged relations with Syria and good relations with Iran.

> Syria has recorded a distinctive and steadfast stance in its struggle against the Israeli enemy. This came through its support of regional resistance movements amidst their most difficult of circumstances, and through seeking to concert Arab efforts towards securing the interests of the region and confronting its challenges.

We hereby emphasize the need to adhere to the distinguished relations between Lebanon and Syria, for this is in the common political, security and economic interest of both countries.[46]

Iran is a central and important state in the Islamic world and it is the main supporter of the causes of the *umma*... Hizbullah considers Islamic Iran to be a focal nation in the Islamic world. For Iran was the country that thwarted the Zionist-American scheme through its national revolution, supported resistance movements in our region, and stood with courage and determination alongside Arab and Islamic causes, at the forefront of which is the Palestinian cause.[47]

Pan-Arabism and pan-Islamism

Like its Open Letter, in its 2009 Manifesto, Hizbullah calls for pan-Arabism and pan-Islamism: "The Arabs should put their hands together in order to transcend conflicts that rupture Arab unity (pan-Arabism)...[48] The Arab and Islamic world are facing challenges whose dangers should not be undermined...[49]

Hizbullah is an ardent advocate of the unity of the Muslims. In both Manifestos it called for the unity of the Muslims invoking Qur'anic verses and religious sensibilities. Section 22 of the Open Letter entitled: "God is with the unity of the Muslims" stressed the need to:

Be aware of the malignant colonial discord (*fitna*) that aims at rupturing your unity in order to spread sedition among you and enflame Sunni-Shi'a sectarian feelings. Be knowledgeable that colonialism was not able to control the natural resources and riches of the Muslims except after breaking up their unity... inciting Sunnis against the Shi'as and vice versa. Later on the colonizer left this mission of spreading dissention among the Muslims to its collaborators, be it the governing elite, the corrupt Muslim religious scholars (state jurists), or the feudal leaders (*zu'ama*). God is with the unity of the Muslims... It is the rock that breaks all the conspiracies of the oppressors; it is the hammer that crushes the evil schemes of the oppressors...

Do not allow the policy of "divide and rule" to be practiced among you; rather fight it by recourse to the Qur'an:

"And hold fast to Allah's bond [His religion], all of you, and do not fall apart. And remember Allah's grace is upon you; how you were enemies, then He united your hearts [by becoming Muslims] so that you have become, by His grace, brethren. You were on the brink of the pit of Fire, but He saved you from it." (3:103)

"Those who have made divisions in their religion and become sects, thou art not of them in anything." (6:159)[50]

In a watered-down version, the 2009 Manifesto reiterates:

> We therefore remind you of the importance of unity among Muslims. The Almighty has said: "And hold on fast, together, to the rope of God, and be not separated." (3:103) We take heed of those causes of division between the people, such as confessional provocations that are instigated especially between Sunnis and Shi'ites. We count on the awareness of all Muslims in addressing what is being contrived against them at this level."[51]

The Arab-Israeli conflict and the peace process
Chapter III entitled, "Palestine and the Settlement Negotiations" repeats the same old story of the Open Letter with the same emphatic terms. Section 1; "The Palestinian Cause and the Zionist Entity" paints a grim picture of the creation of the state of Israel and the displacement of the Palestinians:

> A crime against humanity was committed by the West when this extraneous entity (Israel) was implanted in the heart of the Arab and Muslim world, and was nurtured to become a hostile infiltration, standing as a leading front for Western plots of dominion, and posing as a base for control and dominion over the region (p. 58).

It adds that Israel is supported by the West, especially the US, branding both the US and Israel with 'terrorism':

> The Zionist movement is a racist movement both in terms of thought and practice. It is the product of a despotic, authoritarian mentality the basis of which is founded on a Judaization project of settlement and expansion. The state entity that emerged from the Zionist movement has thrived through occupation, aggression, massacres and terrorism, all with the support and under the custody of colonialist powers, particularly with the aid of the United States of America with which the Zionist state is strategically allied – a true partner in war, massacres and the practice of terrorism. The struggle that we are embarked upon against the Zionist project emanates from the duty of self-defence (p. 59).

In Section 2: "Jerusalem and the *Aqsa* Mosque", Hizbullah warns that the serious attacks against the *Aqsa* Mosque (in Jerusalem) constitute a real and present danger that might lead to serious consequences. Hizbullah adds that supporting Jerusalem and liberating it is a religious duty and a humanitarian and ethical duty (p. 62).

In upholding its own resistance identity and its own model of resistance, Hizbullah gives legitimacy to the Palestinian resistance arguing that it is "sanctioned by heavenly messages and international laws." In the third section entitled, "The Palestinian Resistance", Hizbullah adds that the precepts of practice have proven the efficiency of military resistance to liberate the land and regain lost rights (p. 63):

> Resistance is indeed the only viable alternative... [in 2006] the Lebanese Resistance recorded a divine and historical victory, a strategic success that dramatically changed the shape of the conflict. This was the first defeat of its kind for the Israeli enemy, a gun-down to the all-time myth of an "invincible army." (p. 64)

The fourth and final section entitled, "Settlement Negotiations", reinforces the Open Letter's dictum of no recognition of Israel and no negotiations with it, claiming that this policy embodies the will of the people: "We call upon the Arab rulers to be committed to the choices of their people by reconsidering the options of negotiations." (p. 67)

> Our standpoint towards the settlement process (peace negotiations)... is a position of absolute rejection of the very foundation and principles of the settlement option with the Zionist entity. The settlement option is founded on legitimizing the Zionist entity's existence and relinquishing seized Palestine land, an Arab and Islamic land. This is our immutable, permanent and final standpoint towards the negotiation option, one that is not subject to recoil or compromise, even if the entire world recognized "Israel" as a state (p. 67)... We call on the Arabs and Muslims to reject all schemes for normalization with the Zionist enemy, to uphold the right of return of all Palestinian refugees to their lands and homes from which they were expelled, and to unequivocally reject all presented alternatives for Palestinian resettlement, compensation or relocation (p. 69).

7.4   CONCLUSION

This chapter presents a good example of Hizbullah's identity construction and reconstruction. It compares Hizbullah's first and second manifestos and evaluates the party's eight conclaves, all analyzed from the standpoint of the domestic, regional, and international dynamics. Drastic changes were noted. In 1985, when Hizbullah propagated its first manifesto, the party was a small fighting force whose overall resource mobilization was directed towards its war effort in fighting Israel to make it withdraw from the vast territories it occupied in Lebanon. In 2009, the dynamics changed. Hizbullah has become one of the constituent pillars of the Lebanese political system calling for its reform along the lines of consensual democracy. At the time the party earned an Arab and Islamic recognition for liberating Lebanese territories from the Israeli occupation in May 2000 and for standing its grounds against the Israeli offensive in the 2006 July war. That is why its second Manifesto had to be along the lines of a pragmatic political document, rather than the ideological utopian one propagated in the mid-1980s. Nevertheless, the 2009 Manifesto is not a political document par excellence, as Nasrallah claimed in his 30 November 2009 press conference and as Hizbullah tried to portray it in its extensive media campaign; rather it has important ideological undertones such as the enmity towards Israel and the US. It seems Shaykh Na'im Qasim was right in his 2002 predictions that Hizbullah's hostility towards Israel and the US administration would not witness any change in the new Manifesto. However, this enmity is only in rhetoric and semantics since Hizbullah is a patriotic Lebanese resistance movement and does not operate in the US or Israel; it leaves it to the Palestinians to liberate their land, while granting them all kinds of moral and in-kind support, as I tried to argue in chapter four.

8 Epilogue: Future Prospects – Disarmament and the Peace Process

Islam's ability to dominate a state's identity is highly contested. While powerful Islamic movements exist within several states in the region [Middle East], these groups are encountering alternative definitions of community, based on divisions within Islam (Shia versus Sunni), race and language (Arab versus non-Arab), or clan and tribe... While some of these movements and some states are trying to increase Islamic influence and identity in other countries, the success of these efforts is not assured.[1]

8.1 INTRODUCTION

Hizbullah's specific religious ideology has been based upon mobilization, *Jihad,* and martyrdom, as determined by *al-waliyy al-faqih,* first Imam Khumayni and after his death Imam Khamina'i. Based on the aforementioned and keeping in mind that religious ideology ultimately wields religious capital, one can argue that Hizbullah's religious ideology is both 1): an exclusionary ideological identity based on belief in *wilayat al-faqih,* which is a "novel and almost unprecedented reinterpretation of religious canon"; and 2): a return to the fundamentals of Shi'ite faith as a primary historical identity. "To most Islamists, Islam is the first and key identity [primary historical identity] but not the sole identity... *In other words to grant a certain priority to the Muslim identity is to make a statement about the character of the challenge [problems] that individuals and societies face and about the nature of the solution*"[2], the solution that is provided by Hizbullah's adoption and application of *Wilayat al-Faqih*. In fact, belief and application of *Wilayat al-Faqih* is what distinguishes Hizbullah from other Shi'ite political parties and Islamist movements, in general, thus endowing Hizbullah with a distinct religious identity stemming from its adherence to this specific Islamic cultural sphere that in the first place produced this collective unifying identity. On these grounds, *wilayat al-faqih* seems to be an elitist exclusionary doctrine that unifies the adherents of this distinct Shi'ite religious identity that upholds martyrdom and victory as the expected fruits or rewards of *jihad*. Thus, building on its religious ideology, Hizbullah was able to accumulate religious capital based on the production of religious knowledge (*Wilayat al-Faqih*) through construction, appropriation, dissemination, and adherence to the Islamic cultural sphere which comprises the party's constituencies and followers. In other words, Hizbullah was able to manipulate and transform its religious ideology into religious capital, which commands following and allegiance on a doctrinal basis, by mobilizing its constituency as both a resistance identity and project identity through strengthening the already existing Islamic public sphere by *transforming and changing* the notions of disinherited, downtrodden, and oppressed into empowerment, not only through *jihad* and martyrdom that ultimately lead to victory in Hizbullah's dictionary, but also through a shifting political strategy that upholds doctrinal-ideological foundations.

8.2 HIZBULLAH'S NEW FACE: FROM AL-HALA AL-ISLAMIYYA TO AL-SAHA AL-ISLAMIYYA

The transition from *al-hala al-Islamiyya* (Islamic religious-political sphere) to *al-saha al-Islamiyya* (Islamic cultural sphere) comports with the views of my interviewees from Hizbullah's rank and file.[3] In an interview conducted in August 2009 with Ayatullah Sayyid Muhammad Husayn Fadlallah, the highest ranking Shi'ite religiousus authority in Lebanon, he told me that a noticeable transformation has occurred from *al-hala al-Islamiyya* to *al-saha al-Islamiyya*, arguing that he is a strong advocate of the latter. He noted that the former was a transitory stage that has served its purpose. He explained that *al-hala al-Islamiyya* was mainly concerned with establishing an Islamic state where minorities, such as Christians and Jews, were treated as *ahl al-dhimma*, i.e. residents holding limited rights and required to pay a tax in lieu of alms giving (*zakat*). Ayatullah Fadlallah clarified that in *al-saha al-Islamiyya* notions such as the Islamic state and *ahl al-dhimma* are ideological constructs that do not exist anymore.[4] According to him, *al-saha al-Islamiyya* is a pluralistic Islamic cultural sphere where the concept of citizenship (*muwatana*) reigns; where all people have equal rights and duties and where coexistence and mutual respect is the main norm and asset among Lebanon's eighteen ethno-confessional communities.[5] My other interviewees from Hizbullah's rank and file concur to the letter with Ayatullah Fadlallah's views.

In the 1970s and 1980s, *al-hala al-Islamiyya*, which was fundamentally concerned with doctrinal-ideological Islamization, unified various sectors of the Shi'a community under the banner of an overarching Islamic ideology.[6] Members of *al-hala al-Islamiyya* converged and established Hizbullah in the wake of the victory of the Islamic Revolution. Since its inception, the party has been keen to control the Lebanese political system, initially through a top-down revolutionary process aimed at obtaining power and Islamizing society by military force. *Al-hala al-Islamiyya* portrayed itself primarily through Hizbullah's belief in pan-Islamism and the necessity of founding an Islamic order where the 'oppressed' reign over the 'oppressors'. This radicalism proved futile in the 1980s. Sayyid Muhammad Husayn Fadlallah wielded power and influence over *al-hala al-Islamiyya*, being its godfather since the late 1960s. Many considered him Hizbullah's spiritual leader, a charge both persistently and rightfully denied.[7]

Hizbullah changes as circumstances themselves change. *Al-saha al-Islamiyya* started to emerge in the early 1990s, when Hizbullah changed its political strategy and endeavored to control the political system through post-Islamization or a bottom-up process of a gradual participation in the democratic system, starting with the parliament, the municipal councils, and the council of ministers, the main executive body of the country. Thus, the party shifted to acceptance of, and engagement in, the democratic process under a sectarian-confessional political and administrative system in the wake of the emergence of a pluralist public sphere and mixed confessional space that dictated it to increase its openness toward other communities, political parties, and interest groups in the Lebanese myriad.[8] This led to the gradual waning of *al-hala al-Islamiyya* and contributed to the gradual growth of *al-saha al-Islamiyya*. In *al-saha al-Islamiyya* Hizbullah has repeatedly stated that its electoral campaigns represent a consorted effort between its resistance identity, on the one hand, and its socio-economic, intellectual, and cultural work, on the other. Thus, contrary to many Islamic movements and the way Hizbullah is commonly perceived, the party has been holistic in its orientation by finding a viable solution to the socio-economic and political challenges and problems that its constituencies suffer from through the use of its social, economical, religious, and political capitals as forms of resource mobilization.

Al-saha al-Islamiyya is primarily concerned with Islam as culture and social practice. Iranian reformist president Muhammad Khatami (1997-2005) had a pioneering contribution in this regard since he gave prominence to culture. Khatami argued: "If freedom of thought were to be suppressed then it would continue to be nurtured in the minds and hearts of the people. Therefore, the best system of government would be the one which would allow thought to be expressed without any limitation."[9] Khatami articulates his cultural theory through the development of a 'democratic Shi'ite discourse' on political freedom, pluralism, tolerance, and human rights. Khatami's cultural reforms included the following enhancements of the Iranian public sphere: making civil society the subject of common discourse; easing of censorship on books and films; vigorous press and the releasing of dozens of new magazines and newspapers; and the formation of cultural and political associations. Khatami's domestic policy was directed towards civility and the rule of law, as the most salient pillars of democracy. When Sayyid Hasan Nasrallah, Hizbullah's secretary-general, visited Iran around mid-October 1997, Khatami called on the party to pursue a policy of cultural openness towards the other sectarian-confessional communities in Lebanon and to graduate intellectuals in addition to freedom fighters. Khatami's discourse is paralleled by Nasrallah who argues that upholding 'public freedoms' are priorities that go hand in hand with the party's ideology and Islamic doctrine and are conducive to the service of the Lebanese society at large. According to Nasrallah, the establishment of civil society in Lebanon does not contradict Hizbullah's project, but is concomitant with it because one of the basic tenets of Islam urge the enactment of civil society.[10] These claims have been reiterated in Hizbullah's November 2009 Manifesto.

The crux of Khatami's argument is that Islam is not the normative, essentialist, elusive concept; Islam is culture. From this perspective, it is interesting to note that Khatami's discourse was void of the use of the word 'Islam'; in all his speeches and writings he employed culture (*farhang*), civilization (*tamaddun*), and religion (*din*). Thus, Khatami was recasting Islam in cultural terms.[11] To a lesser extent, the current leader of the Islamic Republic of Iran and Hizbullah's 'spiritual leader' Imam Khamina'i asserted that cultural work is always a precursor to political and military work, and added that the Islamic Revolution needs to have a strong, enriching cultural background. In turn, Khamina'i stressed that any message, or call, or revolution, or civilization, or culture, cannot be successfully disseminated if it is not expressed in artistic form[12], which represents another level of discourse. Khatami identifies Islam as culture, whereas Khamina'i and Khumayni believe that culture is one of the means to achieve the aims of the Islamic revolution; in other words, an instrumentalist concept of culture is portrayed in *al-saha al-Islamiyya*.

Hizbullah's *al-saha al-Islamiyya* is trying to emulate the above concepts and put them into practice. Hizbullah argues that the *shari'a* (Islamic law), as a socially constructed phenomenon, does not fall short of guiding a modern life, does have the flexibility and pragmatism to deal with man's progress, and addresses both the generalities and particularities that have to do with man's needs. From this perspective, one could argue that Hizbullah, as a post-Islamist movement, has been engaging in pragmatic attempts to construct an 'alternative modernity' that incorporates modern democratic and religious principles.[13]

Thus, the old motif of *al-hala al-Islamiyya* gradually gave way to the new theme of *al-saha al-Islamiyya*. I view *al-saha al-Islamiyya* and *al-hala al-Islamiyya* as discourses, or ways of thinking and acting belonging to different time periods. Thus, rather than analyzing *al-saha al-Islamiyya* as a manifestation of *al-hala al-Islamiyya*, I would argue that *al-saha al-Islamiyya* entails a substantial transformation that gives saliency to Hizbullah's new phase.

Linking this analysis to the opening quotation of the chapter, one could argue that Hizbullah's ideology was to a greater extent successful in dominating the Lebanese state's identity at least in Hizbullah's major constituencies, as well as in the Islamic cultural sphere where it wields power. Thus, Hizbullah was triumphant in increasing Islamic influence and identity at the expense of the Lebanese state.

8.3 HIZBULLAH'S FUTURE

Hizbullah made it clear, as early as 2002, that its Resistance identity is a strategic choice, rather than a means for the liberation of a few meters of land.[14] Hizbullah declares that it would remain on guard and would not allow Israel to enforce its hegemony on the Middle East as it pleases. Hizbullah stresses that it did not come into being just to perform for a short while, or to execute a specific project, or to be a tool of policy for regional or international actors; rather, it originated from an immutable belief in God, the Almighty, and from the stance of its religious duty (*taklif*), which made it incumbent to pursue its continuous *jihadi* mission of reforming this world till the end of time. As such, Hizbullah would remain "as long as heaven and earth exist"[15], according to Shaykh Na'im Qasim. Such statements are often considered as rhetoric or propagandist statements. However, they can reflect the mentality that directs the decisions made by Hizbullah, which can be categorized as extremist, aiming at political gains.

Qasim explained what he meant by "the party is here to stay". He clarified that the party decided to work in a holistic manner with the members of society. The party is not only a party for the elite which includes the religious scholars, the cadres, and the educated/cultured; it is not only a military party dedicated to the war effort and fighting; it is not only a party dedicated to public conscience raising and moral education aimed at preaching and guidance (da'wa); it is not only a party for the leader who is the fulcrum that ties the masses to the leadership (Majlis al-Shura: consultative council); it is not a political party that musters people around it without caring for polishing and furthering their religious commitment; the party is all of these combined. It is the party of all the people, where the children, the youth, men, women, educated, and illiterate feel that they belong; they are concerned about its success and are engaged in achieving its purpose. The party is an Islamic party that tries to express all the chief concerns of the umma.[16]

8.4   FUTURE PROSPECTS: DISARMAMENT AND THE PEACE PROCESS

The Western-backed March 14's victory in the 2009 legislative elections and the formation of the first cabinet, the main executive body of the country, headed by Sa'd al-Hariri are turning points in Lebanese history. New dynamics emerged as a result of this eventuality. To the international community's surprise, Hizbullah recognized the results of the 2009 elections, acknowledged defeat, gave away its veto power in the cabinet, trimmed its representation in the parliament and cabinet, and agreed on the political framework of a cabinet in which sensitive issues, such as the UN-backed Hariri tribunal, would be discussed in the national unity consensus cabinet. Knowing that Syria and Iran are Hizbullah's main backers, these new developments came at a time of an international change of heart towards Syria: 1) from regime change, 2) to diplomatic sanctions (in addition to the already imposed US sanctions under Bush's 'Syria Accountability Act'), 3) to world leaders rushing to Syria, including French president Sarkozy. In this atmosphere, Lebanon and Syria established diplomatic relations in 2008, after being the only two Arab countries without diplomatic recognition since the 1940s.[17] Concomitantly, after the international community shunned Hizbullah, it started to knock at its doors. What prompted these changes? Not surprisingly, there has also been a European rush towards Hizbullah, especially after the elections, most notably by the EU foreign policy chief Javier Solana, French Foreign Minister Bernard Kouchner, British lawmakers, etc. and other low-level contacts such as the British, Norwegian, and Danish ambassadors to Lebanon and other EU and US delegations. As MP Hasan Fadlallah put it: "We love this country and its political system. We lose the elections, but we get more than we ask for in the formation of the Cabinet." He added, "Not only that, but the world flocks to our doors to give us recognition!"[18]

The announcement of the formation of the Lebanese cabinet in November 2009 came at a time when the Syrian president Bashar al-Asad was paying a state visit to France. Thus, he reaped political capital in taking credit for its formation; the timing could not have been better for him. In response to PM Netanyahu's call for bilateral talks, al-Asad said that if Netanyahu was serious, he should send a committee of experts to Turkey in order to address the thorny issues, and Syria would do the same. Al-Asad added that shaking hands and posing for the press with Netanyahu were ritual things that lead no where. After the expert meetings solve the thorny issues, then posing for the press does not matter.[19]

The US administration knows that the Palestinian track takes a lot of time because of its complexity and delicacy, which is why it is putting a lot of effort into negotiating a peace deal with Syria first. This is not the main reason. Syria wields enormous power over Hizbullah, Hamas, and the 'ten allied forces' (the ten renegade factions against the PLO and PA). This means that if Syria signs a peace deal with Israel, it goes without saying that these militant organizations will disarm or at least abolish their military wings. Hizbullah fairs better in peace than in war. Its future is independent of the fate of Iran and the peace process. Hizbullah enjoys relative independence from Syria and Iran and has all the financial resources in order to channel its recourse mobilization and struggle to boycott Israeli goods and its cultural influences, while at the same time continuing to boost its NGOs, civil, and media institutions. More than one Hizbullah cadre told me, including two members of the *Shura* council, that the party is prepared for the eventuality of peace, as it is prepared for the eventuality of war; both are strategic concerns for it. Thus, Hizbullah's role does not end when a 'just' peace settlement is reached in the Middle East; on the contrary, its role begins to flourish. Hizbullah does not only aim for the "will to live"; rather the "will to power", as MP Sayyid Nawwaf al-Musawi told me.[20] All this is in line with Qasim's statement that "Hizbullah is here to stay." In the previous section, Qasim even made the claim that Hizbullah will stay forever, till eternity!

On the one hand, the state of Israel is worried about security, an intangible, immeasurable threat, which is subjective in nature and depends on one's own perspective. On the other hand, Arab states, Islamic movements, the Palestinian refugees and the Palestinian Authority (PA) are worried about bread and butter, which is a tangible, measurable thing, although it is relative, i.e. somewhat objective. It is neither totally surprising nor unexpected that Hizbullah will give up its arms once a viable and comprehensive peace treaty is signed between Lebanon and Syria whereby Israel cedes land for peace, although the party's rhetoric in its 1985 Open Letter and its 2009 Manifesto is against such a move. Hizbullah made it clear in more than one occasion that it does not want to 'liberate Jerusalem'. These are only slogans, rhetoric; likewise, the terms 'Great Satan' and 'Little Satan', as I have already pointed out in chapter two. What points to this trend (upholding the security across the Lebanese-Israeli border) is that after the July 2006 war, the Lebanese portion of *al-Ghajar* village remained occupied by the IDF, yet Hizbullah did not fire a single bullet against the IDF stationed there or those present in the occupied Shib'a farms, which are considered Syrian by the international community, pending demarcation of the borders between Lebanon and Syria, a move Syria is not willing to take before an Israeli withdrawal from the Golan.

President Bashar al-Asad is much more pragmatic than his father and the old guard. During the Camp David talks between Syria and Israel, Hafiz al-Asad was uncompromising in his refusal to acknowledge Israel's sense of security by swapping a Syrian portion of the lake of *Tabarayya* with another border area, arguing: "I used to swim there when I was a child." Bashar is ready to compromise on this issue and informed the mediators, especially the Turks, on that issue as soon as he took office after his father died in June 2000, reportedly after his heart failed after seeing Israel withdrawing from Lebanon in May 2000. As one of his doctors and some political analysts claimed, "his heart could not take it after he lost the Lebanon card."[21] At the end of 2009, supposed negotiations between Syria and Israel mediated by the Turks were brought to a halt after Israel insisted on including the elimination of Hizbullah's arms in any deal with the Syrians over the 1967 occupied Golan Heights.

Concerning the role of Turkey in the peace process, it is viewed as a fair negotiator acceptable to both parties: the Syrians and Israelis, as well as the US and the EU. It is a NATO Muslim majority country, but secular in its orientation. This is the perfect model the US wants to promote Islam as: a complete separation between the church and the state, a dichotomy between religion (*din*) and the state (*dawla*) in all aspects of life and the public sphere, yet remaining a modern model of progressive Islam. Turkey has been vocal against the Israeli 'Operation Cast Lead' in Gaza and enjoys good relations with both the Israelis and the Arabs.

What is the DNA of Hizbullah then? In conformity with its policy to change as circumstances themselves change, it is important to keep in mind that Hizbullah is not monolithic. The party's internal structure allows it to operate on a number of levels. Hizbullah is a sophisticated, complex, multifaceted, multilayered organization, composed of at least four main divisions: 1) the 'military wing': the *jihadi* and 'terrorist' branch; 2) the social services, NGOs, and civil institutions branch; 3) the 'political wing'; and 4) the cultural politics branch or 'resistance art'.[22] Hizbullah is speaking the same language the West understands: democracy and culture. Thus, the party engages the West using their own means and language. The rapid evolution of Hizbullah from a marginal splinter group to a dominant group in national and international politics, seems to justify Nasrallah's 2007 statement that the movement was still in its early, and vigorous, youth: "We survived more than a quarter of a century and we are here to stay; the future is ours."[23]

8.5 CONCLUSION: THE SHIFT FROM RESISTANCE IDENTITY TO PROJECT IDENTITY

Although resistance identity is the main trait that characterizes a social movement, its transformation into a mainstream political party aiming at empowering society or exercising control and hegemony over it, depends upon to which extent the social movement is capable of reconstructing its identity by upgrading its resistance identity to a project identity. Castells stresses that integration alone into the system or state structures is not sufficient for a social movement to acquire a project identity since it might content itself with negotiations, bargaining, compromise, and dealings with other actors, thus behaving like any interest group or political party that plays according to the rules of the game as set by the system. He argues that a social movement needs to *transform* the overall society to "dominant interests enacted by global flows of capital, power, and information." (1998: 357) This seems not to be an easy task. Can Hizbullah accomplish that difficult, but not impossible task in the near future?

Hizbullah seems to accommodate and change its identity within the guidelines of Islamic fixities/'immutables' (*thawabit*) and authenticity in order to accompany progress and development, thus constructively working within its humanistic agenda, which allows it to legitimize itself through accumulation, conversion, and transformation of social, economic, and symbolic capitals into political capital and vice versa. When Hizbullah earns political capital, the party spends it by investing it in acquiring, more and more, cultural and socio-economic capitals in line with its civilizational mission of accomplishing social justice according to the tenets of Shi'ite jurisprudence. This is one way of demonstrating how Hizbullah employs its capitals as forms of resource mobilization, as its progressive identity allows it a large margin of maneuver.

As a resisting public, through the resilience of its religious culture and identity, Hizbullah was able to shift from the restrictive politics of a narrow exclusive identity to the more encompassing project identity based upon the mobilization of its intellectual and cultural resources. This new jurisprudence leads to dramatic transformations that translate themselves into an Islamic project identity grounded in dominant interests. As an extension of its project identity on the basis of communal resistance, the Islamic project identity relies upon an interdependent, conducive relationship between the leaders, the catalysts of social transformation, and the populace, the kinetic energy of that transformation. Thus, Hizbullah seems on the way to achieving "dominant interests enacted by global flows of capital, power, and information." And so, for Hizbullah *jihad* not only serves as a medium for the negotiation of power, but also becomes a space for resisting, weakening, and challenging the hegemonic ideology and authority of the state by enforcing the party as a 'resisting public'.

Afterword

PARADIGM SHIFT: A CRY FOR FREEDOM

'There is something in the soul that cries out for freedom.'
Martin Luther King

Did the Arabs finally heed the call of the late Chinese communist leader Mao Tse-tung (who urged them to just march in order to realize their potential and actualize their power)[1]? Or, maybe, they listened to one of their indigenous nationalist leaders Antun S'adé who repeatedly stated, "In you is a power, which if actualized will change the course of history"?[2]

In less than a month, two Arab leaders were deposed by the people's power. Are the 1989 winds of change blowing across the Arab world? As the Middle East is engulfed with protests portraying the affirmation of the will of the people after decades of authoritarian rule, Lebanon does not remain the anomaly; rather change has been instigated by an unexpected actor. The catalyst was Tunisia's Jasmine uprising[3] that ended the 23-year old rule of president bin 'Ali after the army supported the uprising and ousted him into exile in Saudi Arabia on 14 January 2011. This paved the way for the return, on 30 January 2011, of the moderate Islamist intellectual Rashid al-Ghannushi, the leader of the 'Renaissance Movement' (*al-Nahda*), who was forced to flee in the late 1980s.[4] While in Tunisia street politics[5] led to a regime change, its domino effect swept throughout the region with varying degrees of success. In Morocco, Algeria, Sudan, Jordan, Syria, Iran, Yemen, Bahrain, Kuwait, Oman and Saudi Arabia demonstrations were more restrained and did not gain the support of the army, thus failing to initiate regime change. From 25 January to 11 February 2011, after eighteen days of massive demonstrations that claimed the lives of more than 350 people throughout Egypt, the most populous Arab country with the largest army in the Middle East, the social-network revolution succeeded in ousting president Mubarak after 30 years of autocratic rule. In Libya, the '17th of February Revolution' deteriorated into protracted civil war that claimed the lives of thousands. Belatedly, on 17 March 2011, UNSC Resolution 1973 imposed a no-fly zone and took 'all necessary measures' to protect civilians. Two days later, operation 'Odyssey Dawn' was launched by France, Britain, the US, Italy, and Canada in order to impose 1973 by military force. Libya was the third Muslim country the US attacked after Afghanistan and Iraq, but this time not in an anti-terrorism campaign; rather in support of the democratic movement. We are yet to see how this new social movement is going to empower the people of the region and the Arab and Muslim world in general. It is interesting to note that Asef Bayat anticipated many of these sweeping changes in one of his latest books.[6]

Hizbullah issued political declarations blessing the Tunisian and Egyptian people, in particular, and the Arab masses, in general, for their drive for 'freedom and dignity'. Nasrallah added, "This is the true path when people believe in their resolve… this is the new Middle East created by its own people". He concluded, "Your Spring has begun; no one can lead you to another Winter. Your belief, vigilance, and resilience will overcome all difficulties and make you triumphant".[7] Within this regional context, Hizbullah managed to affect a tangible change to the political system by democratic means.

THE WATERSHED: HIZBULLAH GAINS THE MAJORITY IN PARLIAMENT

In all my previous writings, I have repeatedly stated that it is a matter of time before Hizbullah governs Lebanon by democratic means. The main aim of the party's gradual integration into the Lebanese political system and its project of post-Islamism materialized on 25 January 2011: Hizbullah virtually succeeded in ruling Lebanon after it obtained a majority of 68 MPs in the 128-seat legislature, a constitutional move that allowed it to name the next prime minister. How did this take place? How did PM Sa'd al-Hariri lose the legislature's majority after the March 14 victory in the June 2009 elections?

Hizbullah already paralyzed the cabinet on 15 December 2010, when March 14 refused to further the dossier of the 'false witnesses' to the Lebanese Judicial Council, arguing that doing so would interfere with the workings of the Special Tribunal for Lebanon (STL). This coincided with the Lebanese Armed Forces' (LAF) discovery of sophisticated, camouflaged Israeli hi-tech spying material hidden in fake rocks in the highest mountain peaks of Lebanon: in the Druz heartland at the *Baruk* (at a height of 1,715 meters) in the *Shuf*; and in *San-*

nine (at a height of around 2,000 meters) in the Christian heartland. The LAF defused both. Hizbullah prided itself on supplying the information to the LAF, proving that it is on high alert to protect the 'sovereignty and territorial integrity of Lebanon.'

On 16 December 2010, Hizbullah commemorated '*Ashura*'. Nasrallah delivered a fiery, mobilizational speech stressing: 'The STL will become a bygone, like other plots contrived against us; we will abort the aims of the unjust accusation leveled against us.' He asserted that Hizbullah is very careful to safeguard national coexistence and to protect Lebanon from the lurking *fitna*: 'We reject *fitna* between the Sunni and Shi'a and we stand firm against it; we will never have recourse to it since it is the option of the weak and because it serves Israeli interest.'

On 12 January 2011, Sa'd al-Hariri's cabinet fell after more than one third of the ministers resigned: the 10 ministers of the Hizbullah-led opposition and a Shi'ite minister from the centralist coalition of the president. In order to embarrass al-Hariri, this move coincided with his meeting with president Obama in Washington. Why did March 8 absolve itself from the Doha promise of not resigning en mass from the national unity cabinet? It justified its move by blaming the March 14 ruling coalition who, instead of shelving contentious dossiers that failed to gain consensus, insisted on putting them up for the vote when it had the two-third majority. Consequently, the Doha formula fell.

After being united for 11 years, the majority of the Druz veteran politician Walid Jumblatt's parliamentary bloc 'The Democratic Forum' deflected to March 8, thus shifting the balance to Hizbullah. Invoking his father's legacy, Jumblatt dubbed his new bloc 'The Struggle Front' (*Jabhat al-Nidal*), which in addition to Druz includes Sunnis and Christians, very important ingredients, in Jumblatt's eyes, to ward off any sectarian label leveled against it. In addition to Jumblatt, it includes six other MPs: Akram Shihayyib, Elie 'Aun, Ala'eddine Terro, Ghazi al-'Aridi, Nehmé Tu'mé, and Wa'il Abu Fa'ur.

The remnants of the dissolved 'Democratic Forum' joined March 14: Marwan Hamadé, Antoine Sa'd, Henri Helou, Fu'ad al-Sa'd, and Muhammad al-Hajjar. Nevertheless, this did not tip the balance to March 8; rather it resulted in a deadlock: 64 seats for both March 8 and March 14.[8]

Actually, four independents tipped the balance after reviewing their calculations. Sa'd al-Hariri considered the deflection of the March 14 MPs to March 8 as 'treason and rebellion' against the will of the voters. Therefore, al-Hariri lost by eight votes: 60 MPs named him, and 68 named Najib Miqati.[9]

The events in Tunisia and Egypt had already influenced Lebanon when Saad al-Hariri's supporters conducted 'The Day of Rage' on 25 January 2011, the day Miqati was named to form the cabinet. Al-Hariri argued that what seemed a democratic game is really a Hizbullah coup in the name of democracy, a coup that betrays the people's will, which refused to grant a majority to the Hizbullah-led opposition in the 7 June 2009 elections. In turn, Hizbullah gave strict orders to its supporters not to engage the Hariri supporters at any cost, even if their lives were in danger. Although Hariri proved that he has a say in Lebanese street politics (which was dominated for a long time by the Hizbullah-led opposition) and proved that he wields influence and can mobilize 70% to 80% of the Lebanese Sunnis, this public rage, which caused mayhem and violently targeted media outlets such as *al-Jezzera*, has negatively effected his image and portrayed al-Hariri as the 'villain', as Hizbullah's *al-Manar* TV labeled him.

Al-Hariri stressed that he is now the opposition and affirmed that Hizbullah hijacked March 14's victory in the 2009 parliamentary elections with the power of the gun. He avowed that the STL would deliver justice, not only concerning the assassination of his father, but also in relation to the political assassinations that targeted many March 14 politicians, mainly Christians.[10] Although al-Hariri and Miqati reconciled, the situation remained tense.

Since Hizbullah's maneuver occurred within the narrow confines of the Lebanese constitution and the democratic rules of the game that encourage negotiations, bargaining, and compromise, the US, France and the EU did not label what has happened as a 'coup', as al-Hariri and March 14 hoped for.

The British foreign minister, William Hague, said when he visited Syria on 28 January 2011 that he neither views the Miqati cabinet as a Hizbullah cabinet, nor Miqati as a Hizbullah man. Instead, the cabinet will be judged by its deeds, as he said. I think he is right. Miqati agreed to run for the post of the PM as a compromise candidate, benefiting from his centralist position, and does not aim to face the international community and the Security Council, especially since its decisions will be implemented under chapter 7. This would be detrimental to his business, his family, and his overall political career. While al-Hariri has almost 80% of the support of the Sunnis, Miqati is only a ceremonial figure and has hardly any following on the ground. If he is able to form the cabinet, like the 2005 precedent, his presence will be for a short period heading a transitional technocrat government. It is well known in Lebanese politics that a technocrat cabinet cannot accomplish much; only politicians who wield influence and power on the ground can do so.

Beside shielding itself from what it called the politically motivated accusations of the STL, Hizbullah's aim is to shelve the discussions pertaining to its weapons and the national defense strategy. This is concomitant with lending legitimacy to Hizbullah's resistance role and its right to bear arms, as would be reiterated in the new government's policy statement, as all policy statements previously stressed, especially after the Syrian army's withdrawal in April 2005.

Glossary

Ahl al-dhimma, dhimmis	non-Muslim residents within an Islamic state holding limited rights and required to pay a poll tax (*jizya*) in lieu of *zakat*
'Amma	ordinary people
Ajr	remuneration
Arkan al-Islam	the five pillars of Islam: *al-shahadatayyn* (Muslim credo: testimony that there is no god but Allah (God), and that Muhammad is His Prophet), *salat* (prayer), *sawm* (fasting), *hajj* (pilgrimage to Mecca), and *zakat* (alms giving)
Awliya'	saints
Dahiya	the southern suburb of Beirut that houses around 850,000 Shi'ites
Batin	esoteric
Din	religion
Faqih	jurisprudent or jurisconsult: an authority or expert in *fiqh*; in Shi'ism *faqih* is synonymous with *mujtahid*
Fara'id	religious duties
Fatwa	a guiding, non-binding religious edict
Fiqh	religious jurisprudence, elucidation, and application of *Shari'a*
Fitna	discord, internal strife
Fuqaha'	jurists
Hadi	guide

Hadith (Sunna)	traditional accounts of the sayings and doings of Prophet Muhammad, which became an important source for determining Islamic law. They are made up of two parts: the names of the transmitters (isnad); and the text (matn).
Hajj	pilgrimage to Mecca
Al-hala al-Islamiyya	Islamic religious-political sphere
Halal	religiously sanctioned
Haqiqat	truth
Haram	religiously prohibited
Hikma	divine wisdom
Hisbi	(obeying) the religious and moral instructions of Islam. It could also cover a wide range of financial, administrative, political, and social matters. In short, hisbi matters are things that God does not allow us to forsake.
Hizbullah	'Party of God'
Hizbullahi	A member or follower of Hizbullah
Hujja	apodictic proof
Husnayayyn	outcomes or rewards of jihad (martyrdom and victory)
Ijtihad:	making religious decisions on the basis of independent reasoning
Ilgha' al-ta'fiyya al-siyassiyya fi al-nufus, qabla al-nusus	the abolition of political sectarianism in the mentality, before abolishing it in the texts
'Ilm	religious knowledge
Al-'ilm al-muhit or al-ihatah fi al-'ilm	the Imam is the most learned in all branches of religious knowledge
Infitah	'opening-up' or Hizbullah integration into the Lebanese public sphere
'Isma (ma'sum)	entails impeccability, sinlessness, and infallibility of the Imams
Al-istikhlaf bi al-nass wa al-ta'yyin	the Shi'ites consider the Imamate a divine appointment
Al-istikhlaf bi al-shura wa al-bayy'a	the Sunnis consider the caliphate as a political process that is the product of consensus
Istishhad	martyrdom
Jahiliyya	pre-Islamic pagan period in Arabia
Al-Jihad al-asghar	(smaller jihad): struggle (holy war) against the enemies of Islam

Al-Jihad al-akbar	(greater jihad): struggle against the self (*jihad al-nafs*) or individual's service for the cause of religion
Jizya	poll tax
Juhhal	ignorant people
Kafir	infidel
Khass wa 'amm	private and public
Khums (one-fifth)	a religious tax comprising 20% of a person's surplus of income over necessary living expenses. Half is paid to the *marja'* as the representative of the Imam (*sahm al-Imam*), and half to the Sayyids.
Kitman	concealment
Khususiyyat	specificities or particularities
Lebanonization	Hizbullah's enrolment in Lebanese domestic political life
Ma'nawi	moral influence
Madad	support and reinforcement
Marja' al-taqlid/ muqallad	The supreme Islamic legal authority to be emulated or accepted for emulation by the majority of the Shi'a in matters of religious practice and law
Marja'iyya	religious authority
Al-mas'uliyya al-shar'iyya	legitimate and religious responsibility to the *marja'* or *muqallad*
Al-mas'uliyya al-shar'iyya wa al-taklif al-shar'i al-Ilahi (taklif)	is loosely translated as 'legitimate and religious responsibility'
Mubaya'a	homage and pledge of allegiance, usually to God
Mujahidin	those who carry out jihad or freedom fighters
Mujtahid	a *'alim* or a high ranking Shi'ite jurist who exercises *ijtihad* or independent reasoning
Muqallad	see *marja' al-taqlid*
Muqalidin	followers of the *muqallad* in law and ritual
Murshid ruhi	spiritual guide or leader
Mustad'afin	oppressed
Mustakbirin	oppressors
Muwatana	citizenship

Nass	textual designation, or the specific designation of an Imam by the preceding Imam
Al-Qada	leaders
Rahbar	leader of the Islamic Revolution. This title was assumed by Khumayni, and after his death, it was accorded to Khamina'i when he became the official *marja' al-taqlid* in 1995.
Fi sabili Allah	in the way of God
Salat	prayer
Sawm	fasting
Shahada	martyrdom
Shahid	martyr
Shari'a (divine or Islamic law)	The whole set of norms, morals, and laws derived from the Islamic sources (mainly Qur'an and *hadith*) pertaining to the various aspects of life of individual Muslims and the Muslim *umma*
Al-Sirat al-Mustaqim	The 'Straight Path' or the path of the righteous
Sunna (*hadith*)	Traditions: the sayings and doings of Prophet Muhammad, which are considered the second source of Islamic law (*shari'a*), the Qur'an being the first.
Al-ta'a	strict obedience and discipline, which conveys a religious connotation
Ta'bi'a	mobilization
Tafsir	textual, literal, or scriptural interpretation of the Qur'an
Tahkim	arbitration
Taklif	religious-legal obligation
Al-taklif al-shar'i al-Ilahi	delegated responsibility/obligation of the *muqalidin* towards the *muqallad*
Taqiyya	expedient dissimulation
Taqlid	emulation
Taqwa	piety
Ta'wil	Shi'ite hermeneutics or allegorical interpretation of the Qur'an
Thawabit	fixities, immutable principles, established set of values and norms
'Ulama	Muslim religious scholars
Umma	the entire community of Muslims

'Urfan	Shi'ite theosophy
Wajib	religious duty or obligation
Wakilayn shar'iyyan	religious deputies
Wilaya	spiritual guidance
Wilayat al-Faqih	governance of the jurisprudent or jurisconsult.
Wilayat al-umma 'ala nafsiha	the governance of the *umma* by itself
La yughsl wa la yukaffan	neither washed nor wrapped in a burial shroud
Yaqin	strong conviction
Yutashhad/ istashhadu	martyred
Zahir	exoteric
Zakat	alms giving
Zu'ama	feudal leaders

Additional Reading[1]

Why is it that so much of the research on Hizbullah is plagued by factual errors and misinterpretations? From its inauguration till the present Hizbullah has issued seemingly divergent declarations and statements, thus indicating the need to think of its identity in evolutionary terms, rather than regarding it as monolithic. When Hizbullah released its Open Letter or Political Manifesto in 1985, it propagated its political ideology, but hardly any discernable political program. The confusion of equating Hizbullah's political ideology with its political program leads to a problematic in the understanding of Hizbullah's role as a political party, as it developed after the Ta'if Agreement. What adds to the confusion is that Hizbullah states in its Open Letter: "We in Lebanon are neither a closed organizational party nor a narrow political framework. Rather, we are an *umma* tied to the Muslims in every part of the world by a strong ideological, doctrinal, and political bond, namely, Islam." This seems to imply that Hizbullah abides by Imam Khumayni's theory that considers political parties in the Islamic context as a Western phenomenon. Thus, in its political ideology, Hizbullah clearly states that it is not a political party, yet it developed a political program and participated in the national elections. Authors who have adopted this relatively undifferentiated approach with respect to Hizbullah's ideology have misunderstood and misrepresented the party's identity. The confusion arises especially when some authors use quotations from Hizbullah's pre-Ta'if discourse and apply these to the post-Ta'if era trying to generalize them as a whole on Hizbullah, irrespective of the historical period in which they are contextualized from.

For instance, a reading of Smit[2] suggests that he tends to confine Hizbullah's ideology to its religious ideology. He narrows the latter solely to *wilayat al-faqih* (guardianship of the jurisprudent), without referring to the other two components, namely, "belief in *Shi'a* Islam" and "jihad [holy war] in the name

197

of God".[3] Relying mainly on secondary sources, Smit tends to conflate Hizbullah's political ideology with its political program. This seems evident, for example, in his reference to Hizbullah's Open Letter as the party's political program, when it constitutes Hizbullah's political ideology (pp. 249ff). Hizbullah's Open Letter is not an embodiment of the party's political program, rather its religio-political ideology, as Norton and Sobelman already argued. Norton labels the Open Letter as Hizbullah's "ideological framework",[4] and Sobelman[5] explicitly considers the Open Letter as Hizbullah's political ideology or its "first political, ideological platform" (p. 23). Hizbullah's political program appeared for the first time in 1992 when the party contested the parliamentary elections. What adds to the unlikelihood of considering the Open Letter as Hizbullah's political program is that the Open letter rejected any participation in Lebanon's sectarian-confessional political system – which rendered Hizbullah as a rejectionist, seclusionist, and reactionary movement, at the time – while its political program sanctioned such a practice.

Since the end of the civil war in 1990 and its acceptance of the Ta'if Agreement, Hizbullah has been confronting major developments in Lebanon: prominently, the emergence of a pluralistic public sphere and increasing openness toward other communities, political parties, and interest groups in the Lebanese myriad. Due to a new interpretation of *wilayat al-faqih*, Hizbullah altered its discourse, priorities, and overall political outlook. The mixed confessional space in Lebanon led Hizbullah to move from marginalization to *infitah* ('opening up'), through which the party became a major player in the Lebanese public sphere by participating in the parliamentary and municipal elections as well as joining the cabinet. In short, since the early 1990s, Hizbullah started promoting its Islamic identity and agenda by following a pragmatic political program, mainly to lull Christians and other Muslims who were opposed to the Islamic state. In the meantime, Hizbullah remained faithful to its Shi'ite constituency by employing a bottom-up Islamization process through engaging in a pluralistic process, working within the Lebanese state's political and administrative structures, while, at the same time establishing Islamic institutions within the civil society. Thus when the party decided to contest the parliamentary elections of 1992 and subsequent legislative and municipal elections, it had to develop a down-to-earth, pragmatic political program, and concentrated on addressing broad problems and concerns that are deeply embedded in society and that worry the majority of the voters irrespective of their denomination or political orientation.

Harik[6] reiterates Hamzeh's and Norton's premise that Hizbullah is a popular nationalist resistance movement when she rightly argues that "during the course of Hezbollah's seventeen-year struggle with Israel along the Lebanese/Israeli frontier in southern Lebanon, it has never been established by any party directly involved (including the United Nations contingent on the ground) that the Party of God has perpetuated a single terrorist attack against Israeli civilians… Hezbollah made an early strategic decision to exclude terrorist tactics from its jihad against Israeli occupation and stuck to it." (pp. 2; 168). Unlike Hamzeh[7] who relies on a good number of primary sources, Harik makes very scanty and frugal references to primary sources; she takes pride in interviewing Nasrallah, but does not produce any reliable evidence to substantiate her claim (p. 78).

She brags that her book was the product of twenty years of work and research; she also prides herself in situating her book within the terrorism paradigm and within the terrorism-resistance debate or controversy. She claims that other works on Hizbullah fail to do so. She writes,

> *Hezbollah: The Changing Face of Terrorism* differs from other works on Hezbollah by dealing in depth with its strategic and foreign policy thrust and focusing on the interrelationship, dynamics and manifestations of the terrorist/resistance controversy. In contrast most recent books on Hezbollah have focused on the interplay of Shiite religious doctrine on the Party of God's political positions, Hezbollah's origins and development during the first decade of its existence and the party's alleged involvement in the terrorist activities that followed the 1982 Israeli invasion. (pp. 4, 203n2)

Although Harik refers to Norton's earlier article in which she claims he "briefly review[s] Hezbollah's standing in Lebanon and possible directions as a fighting force" (p. 203, n2), she fails to mention his seminal article[8] in which he, as far as I know, initiated the trend of distinguishing between terrorism and resistance as well as offered a general definition of terrorism and applied it to Hizbullah.[9] Norton's definitions circumvented her alleged "focus". Even though Harik's book was published in 2004, her data stops in 2002.[10] In her conclusion, she briefly mentions the US-led invasion of Iraq that occurred on 20 March 2003. It seems that she does not live up to her promise of "dealing in depth" with Hizbullah's "foreign policy thrust and focusing on the interrelationship, dynamics and manifestations of the terrorist/resistance controversy" because she neither discusses the effects of the Iraqi and Afghani crises on Hizbullah's identity construction nor relates these to Hinnebusch's[11] three levels: the global, the regional, and the domestic. Harik's alleged original contribution to the field has been circumscribed by Norton.

Unlike Harik, Hamzeh offers a good typology and discussion on *jihad*. One serious liability is that his tables and statistics are mostly appropriated from Hizbullah's propaganda material, as such unoriginal and unimpressive. On the contrary, Harik's most serious liability is her sketchy treatment of the extremely timely and topical subject of 'martyrdom' or suicide operations as such, and in relation to the resistance/terrorism controversy. Harik just adumbrates what she labels as 'suicide/martyrdom attacks', mainly from the perspective of or in relation to the *Intifada* and the Palestinian resistance (p. 26). However, she neither relates this to Hizbullah's resistance identity as an Islamic *jihadi* movement nor refers to Hizbullah's twelve martyrdom operations. For this and other reasons, Harik's book became dated and unoriginal even before it was launched into the market. On the whole, her book seems a mundane book since it reads like Lebanese daily newspapers' editorials and analyses: in effect, there seems to be nothing fundamentally new in Harik's book.

On the contrary, in spite of his difficulty in obtaining primary sources, Sobelman offers a sound analysis in his monograph. Like Harik, Hamzeh, and Norton, Sobelman's book is free from the Smit fallacy. He conveys important insights on Hizbullah's identity construction and reconstruction. He writes,

> the organization's revolutionary fervor and ideological devotion often clash with the process of establishing political legitimacy and compel Hizbollah to make ideological compromises so it can adapt to the new reality and survive in it. This does not, however, imply in any way that Hizbollah is going through an identity crisis. The organization sees itself as entirely Lebanese, and its leaders are careful to express themselves publicly on domestic socio-economic issues, such as support for the working class and the struggle against corruption and unemployment." (pp. 20-21) He adds, "Today Hizbollah views the original platform [Open Letter] as outdated... [There is] an increasingly apparent metamorphosis in the organization at the declaratory level and in the practical sphere... Hizbullah has traveled from the time of its founding and its more recent decision to choose pragmatic integration into the Lebanese system over pure ideology. (pp. 21, 23)

In commenting on Hizbullah's alliances in the 2000 parliamentary elections, Sobelman argues, "Hizbollah apparently thus agreed to compromise on its principles and ideology, and to cooperate with an individual with previous blatant connections with Israel." (p. 39) Hizbullah is an extension of the Islamic revolution within Lebanese society. Hizbullah is a political party functioning within a non-Islamic state and a multireligious, confessional-sectarian state. While the Iranian Hizbullah was instrumental in building a state, the Lebanese Hizbullah cannot go beyond being a political party operating within the Lebanese public sphere.

* * *

Two recent books by N. Noe[12] and A.R. Norton[13] look at Hizbullah from other angles and perspectives.

According to Nicholas Noe, his *Voice of Hezbollah* "is intended as an introduction to Nasrallah's thinking, and not as any kind of a comprehensive, final word." (p. 17) In this, it represents a laudable effort. Noe provides useful, straight to the point, and sometimes insightful introductions to each of the thirty-two texts included in the volume, thereby attempting to place each of Sayyid Hasan Nasrallah's speeches and interviews in context.

The book is composed of thirty-two speeches and interviews, one of which offers a biography of Nasrallah – it is a bit dated, however, having been written in 1993 (pp. 116-143). The rest delineate Hizbullah's stances concerning domestic Lebanese politics and its position toward regional and international issues ranging from the Arab-Israeli conflict and the status of Palestine to the 2003 US-led invasion of Iraq, to Hizbullah's stance regarding its strategic alliance with Syria and its ideological/religious ties with Iran.

Noe has divided the material into three sections. The first, "Radicalism and Resistance 1986-1999," comprises thirteen statements. Only the first of these deals with the issue of radicalism as such, making explicit that Hizbullah regarded the Lebanese state as an apostate that needed to be toppled by military means in order to establish an Islamic state in Lebanon as part of an overall worldly Islamic order. The second statement highlights the proxy war between Amal and Hizbullah and the efforts to curb it. The remaining eleven statements portray Hizbullah as a political party that has accommodated its protest, recognized the Lebanese state, and contested the legislative and municipal elections.

"Repositioning 2000-2004" offers another thirteen statements, most of which cover the period from what Hizbullah calls 'liberation' – the near-complete Israeli withdrawal from southern Lebanon in May 2000 – until just before the assassination of PM Rafiq Hariri. Finally, "February 14, 2005, and After" contains six statements dating from Hariri's assassination through Nasrallah's August 2006 postwar interview with Lebanon's New TV.

Since its inception, Hizbullah has been keen on controlling the Lebanese political system, initially through a top-down process: "We support a military solution because we do not see a better alternative (…) we do believe in a single Islamic world governed by a central government (…) We do not believe in a nation whose borders are 10,452 square kilometres in Lebanon; our project foresees Lebanon as part of the political map of an Islamic world in which specificities would cease to exist, but in which the rights, freedom and dignity of minorities within it are guaranteed." (pp. 31-2) Starting in the 1990s, Hizbullah endeavored to control the political system through a bottom-up process by means of a gradual participation in the democratic system, beginning in parliament, the municipal councils, and the cabinet.

Reading some statements in light of Hizbullah's May 2008 demonstration of military power in the streets of West Beirut and the *Shuf* region is an interesting exercise. Hizbullah's purpose in May was to attain veto power by force, even at the expense of killing Lebanese citizens; this runs contrary to Nasrallah's earlier assurances that Hizbullah "with its huge military capabilities (…) could have staged a military coup and taken control of the country (…) We were capable of that and still are (…) My weapons are to defend the country, and all Lebanese (…) Have we ever used our weapons as a source of strength in municipal or parliamentary elections, or to impose certain shares and conditions? Never." (pp. 402-403)

Noe, founder of Mideastwire.com and a doctoral candidate at the *Université Libanaise* in Beirut, offers handy, to-the-point, sometimes insightful introductions to each of the statements, positioning each speech and interview in context. He does not satisfactorily address the question of how he selected the speeches and interviews for inclusion, however. In his introduction, he blames the July 2006 Israeli war for having destroyed Hizbullah's think tank, the Consultative Center for Studies and Documentation, and thus limiting access to Nasrallah's speeches. The center's material is well preserved on microfilm, however, and all of Nasrallah's speeches are readily available from Hizbullah's yearly bound volumes of its mouthpiece, *al-'Ahd* (these were displayed at Hizbullah's bookfair, organized by *al-Ma'arif* Institute, immediately after the 2006 war, with each volume priced at about $ 50). *Al-'Ahd* was established in 1984 and renamed *al-Intiqad* in 2001, but Noe describes it as "an invaluable resource that only became accessible to us in November 2006 – bound volumes of Hezbollah's weekly magazine *Al Intiqad*, going back to its founding in the mid-1990s." (p. 16)

Journalist Nicholas Blandford writes a satisfactory introduction to the book, although he appears not to know that Nasrallah was elected for life in the party's sixth conclave, held in the summer of 2001. He further seems unaware of the rule of thumb and precedent that the head of Hizbullah's executive council – the post Nasrallah held from 1987 to 1992 – replaces the secretary-general in case of incapacitation or death. Blanford rightly mentions that Sayyid Hashim Safiyyeddine, the current head of the executive council, will replace Nasrallah in case something happens to him, but he does not offer any explanation for this (p. 13).

Noe also acknowledges that he obtained Hizbullah's approval of the translations: "It is also important to say that Hezbollah was informed at various points about the materials we were interested in obtaining and translating... A final set of proof pages was provided to a third party, approved by Hezbollah, for comment on issues related to the accuracy of the translation, as well as the accuracy of the original text." (pp. 17-18) Such close cooperation creates the appearance of party sponsorship and supervision of Noe's work, which raises serious questions about its overall objectivity.

However, a more significant shortcoming is Noe's failure to subject some of Nasrallah's most important public pronouncements to critical analysis. This is particularly the case with Nasrallah's varying and misleading accounts of Hizbullah's founding and of his whereabouts during the critical period of 1978. Noe reproduces, without comment, Nasrallah's assertions that he was in either "Baalbek" (p. 124) or "Najaf" (p. 110) when Musa al-Sadr disappeared (31 August 1978) and Israel's first invasion of Lebanon occurred (14 March 1978). These seemingly minor details are crucial, for they undermine Hizbullah's official narrative, which states that the party was not founded until 1982, in response to the second Israeli invasion of Lebanon. Again, this raises questions about Noe's objectivity vis-à-vis his subject.

Finally, the five-page concluding section of the book entitled "Further Reading" – in addition to excluding Arabic and French sources – is highly selective in its choice of English sources. Noe again appears to endorse Hizbullah's official narrative by including deputy secretary-general Na'im Qassim's *Hizbullah: The Story from Within* and deeming it "indispensible" due to the presence of party documents in its appendix (p. 412). At the same time, other works that contain these and many more documents, in addition to critical analysis of them – the author's *The Shifts in Hizbullah's Ideology* (2006), for example – do not appear.

A.R. Norton paints another story. The purpose of Norton's 2007 book – authored by the co-editor of the series entitled "Princeton Studies in Muslim Politics" – "is to offer a more balanced and nuanced account of this complex organization [Hizbullah]... an honest account of the leading Shi'i political party in Lebanon – Hezbollah." (pp. 8, 186) Compared to Norton's, Harik's and Hamzeh's books read like a compilation of their earlier works. Norton's book seems original although, on a separate page, he thoroughly acknowledges using some of his earlier publications (p. 187), something that Harik and Hamzeh do not. The book is composed of six chapters and a conclusion. Chapter one surveys the "Origins and Prehistory of Hezbollah"; chapter two deals with "The Founding of Hezbollah". The parachuted chapter three entitled, "Being a Shi'i Muslim in the Twenty-first Century" seems unrelated to the main thrust of the argument. It is basically a summary of Norton's 2001 book *Shi'ism and the 'Ashura Ritual in Lebanon*. Undeniably, the chapter is very well written, but it is very detailed, longwinded, and an unnecessary digression in a book aimed at giving a short history of Hizbullah, not Shi'ite rituals. Thus, removing the chapter would not diminish the value of the book. Chapter four discusses the topics of "Resistance, Terrorism, and Violence in Lebanon"; chapter five "Playing Politics" portrays how Hizbullah abandoned its revolutionary fervour and started integrating into the political system through its participation in electoral processes. Finally, chapter six "From Celebration to War" addresses the July 2006 war and its repercussions.

Norton's book seems a fairly good synopsis of what is known about Hizbullah, even though it does not offer any new startling insights. Nevertheless Norton's elegantly, compact written book has drawbacks in terms of inaccurate facts, which might weaken its overall conclusion and lead to errors in scholarly judgment. My aim is not to highlight the merits of this book, as other reviewers have already done; rather to correct some very basic factual errors, which will give the book a better read. I wonder how the well-versed scholars, who reviewed the book, including the ones who originate from Lebanon, did not notice these trivial mistakes.[14]

Norton's book has some historical gaps. He ignores to mention the seminal 1916 Sykes-Picot Agreement, which carved Lebanon and the current Arab states in the Middle East after the collapse of the Ottoman Empire (p. 11). In a 187-page book, Norton belatedly mentions the Ta'if Agreement on page 83, when he refers to it for the first time on p. 12. He does not refer to the Cairo Agreement and its annulment, which is central to understanding the changing dynamics between the PLO and the Shi'ites (p. 14).[15]

Norton adopted a simple, inconsistent transliteration system that distorts words. For instance, on page 13 he writes "Beqaa" and "Hirmil", not Hermel, for the sake of coherence at least. If he writes "Hirmil", then he should write Biqa'. Another obvious inconsistency appears on pp. 110-111 where he writes "Khomeini" and "Tufayli", instead of Tofeili, or he should have written Khumayni in the first place. On page 15, he writes "Bra'sheet", when it should be Bar'ashit, etc. The book is also plagued with transliteration errors in principle, such as the serious mistake of referring to the Iranian leader as *"rakbar"* (p. 90). Irrespective of which transliteration system one employs, and whether the word is written in Arabic or Farsi, *rahbar* is always spelled with an 'h' not a 'k'.

Even the "Index", which Norton praised[16], lacks some important key terms, such as 'Mustapha Chamran'[17] (p. 30); 'cluster bombs' and 'mines' (p. 63); and most notably 'Samir Kuntar' [sic] the oldest serving Lebanese prisoner (p.

134), whom Hizbullah's integrity and probity depended upon, mainly because, in order to release him and a few others, the party kidnapped the two Israeli soldiers on 12 July 2006, an event that triggered a 34-day war that inflicted enormous devastation on Lebanon's infrastructure and shattered its economy. Although a simple search function would have identified all the pages in which a certain word is mentioned, the list is not exhaustive in many cases. For instance, 'Abd al-Amr [sic] Qabalan is also mentioned on p. 64. ('Amr' means order, while his name is Amir, which is a direct reference to Imam 'Ali, the Amir of the faithful or believers); 'Ali Shariati is also mentioned on p. 29; etc.

Concerning the map on page 1 in the "Prologue", it is true that more than one religious group inhabits most of the areas in Lebanon. That is why, an absolutely accurate map that shows the exact distribution of the eighteen religious groups recognized by the state is almost impossible to draw. However, this does not give Norton license to swap Greek Orthodox representation, in the *Kura* region below Tripoli, with Greek Catholic, when Kura is represented in the legislature by three Greek Orthodox MPs, which unequivocally implies that that region is predominantly Greek Orthodox.

The late PM Hariri was neither "blown to pieces by a bomb that also killed twenty-two of his colleagues" (p. 7) nor "twenty-two others traveling in his entourage" (p. 127) as Norton contends. Rather his body remained intact and many of the 22 victims were innocent civilians who were passing by at the moment of the explosion.

Another trivial mistake appears in his third chapter, in the picture on page 64. The person in the foreground is not Sayyid 'Abbas al-Musawi, as Norton contends, rather Shaykh Raghib Harb, Hizbullah's most influential resistance leader in the south, who was assassinated by the Israeli forces on 16 February 1984. The Open Letter is dedicated to him, among other ideologues. Shaykh Raghib had a white turban, while Sayyid Abbas had a black turban. Sayyid Abbas was assassinated on 16 February 1992, on his way back from commemorating the eighth anniversary of the assassination of Shaykh Raghib. Anyone researching Hizbullah should know the difference between the two.

Imam Musa al-Sadr did not establish *Harakat Al-Mahrumin* (the Movement of the Deprived) on his own, as Norton seems to suggest (p. 19). In 1974, al-Sadr, together with Grégoire Haddad, a Greek Catholic archbishop, founded *Harakat Al-Mahrumin* in a bid to alleviate the suffering of the deprived people regardless of their sectarian or ethnic affiliations. As such it was open to all the 'downtrodden' from every sect, and not only restricted to Shi'ites. However, this intercommunity openness did not last long enough, as the ruling elites were afraid this would undermine the community's patronage system. With the outbreak of the civil war, *Harakat Al-Mahrumin* soon developed into a Shiʻite based movement under the leadership of al-Sadr. Furthermore, the main aim behind al-Sadr's visit to Libya was not "to attend ceremonies commemorating the ascent of the Libyan leader" Qadhaffi to power (p. 21). He went to Libya in an attempt to put an end to the Lebanese civil war, after the Algerian president told him that Qadhaffi was funding the militias across the sectarian divide, as repeatedly stated by al-Sadr's sister Rabab, "one of the most admired woman [sic] in the Lebanese Shiʻi community." (p. 19)

Norton's statements on Khaminaʼi and Sistani seem to suffer from errors in scholarly judgment and errors of attribution. Although Sistani is mentioned at least three times before in the course of the book (pp. 31, 100, 101), only in the conclusion on p. 151, does Norton make an unsubstantiated claim based on his 'impression', rather than on reliable surveys or scientific statistics based on representative samples of the Shiʻite population: "… as of November 2006, at least 60 percent of all Lebanese [Shiʻites] follow Sistani, with the rest following Fadlallah. Very few consider themselves 'imitators' of Khamenei." It is worth noting that Khaminaʼi or al-Sayyid al-Qaʼid, 'The Religious Leader', as Hizbullah supporters call him, is the *marjaʻ al-taqlid* (official authority of emulation) in the Islamic Republic, and Hizbullah's official *marjaʻ* (religious authority), not *marjaʻi* [sic] (p. 100). Without producing scientific evidence, Norton's claim should be taken with a grain of salt. Keeping in mind that both Fadlallah and Sistani are vehemently against *wilayat al-faqih*, Norton seems to contradict himself when he writes that "Nayif Krayem" [sic], a Hizbullah cadre, fell out of favor after the Hizbullah establishment suspected that he was emulating Fadlallah (p. 118).

Another mistake of principle surfaces on p. 100. It is too simplistic and factually wrong to write that Khaminaʼi "gave his blessings" to Hizbullah's participation in the electoral process. This is reductionism. As discussed earlier, Hizbullah requested Khaminaʼi's formal legal opinion (*istifta'*) on the legitimacy of participating in the 1992 elections. As soon as Khaminaʼi authorized and supported (*ajaza wa 'ayyada*) participation, Hizbullah embarked on drafting its election program and officially announced its participation in the elections.

Norton writes that the 2006 July war ended with a "cease-fire" (p. 113). Even after one year, UNSC Resolution 1773, which renewed UNIFIL's mandate till 31 August 2008, only reiterated what was achieved a year ago by UNSC Resolution 1701, namely, a cessation of hostilities, rather than a cease-fire, as Norton contended, misleading the reader and implying that the war is over.

Norton does not refer to the national dialogue sessions (pp. 132-133), which started in March 2006 and lasted till June. Keeping in mind that the war broke out in July, it is not a coincidence that the last two sessions of 8 and 29 June 2006 were dedicated to addressing the controversy regarding Hizbullah's weapons and Lebanon's defense strategy.[18]

Norton's conclusion reads like a chronology of events, which seem to serve as an update to the main text of his book. He mistakenly refers to general Michel 'Aun's Free Patriotic Movement (FPM) as the 'Free Political Movement' (pp. 153; 175). Based on a wrong name, Norton draws wrong conclusions. He writes, "'Aounists' and the Shi'a share a profound sense of victimization in what they see as a corrupt and unresponsive political system."[19] (p. 153) This is an error in scholarly judgment. Although victimization and the desire to stamp out corruption might be some common factors between FPM and Hizbullah, these factors are marginal and not central to forging an understanding, let alone an alliance based on mutual interest. A more plausible explanation is that the Christian nationalists (FPM) and the Muslim nationalists (Hizbullah) put their hands together, in a church across the old 'green line', and signed a historic ten-point Understanding – addressing political, economic, administrative, security issues, and relations with Syria – after the 5 February 2006 civil unrest threatened to spark a civil war.[20]

Only on the last two pages or so of the conclusion Norton offers some analytical insights, which, by the precept of practice, proved to be far off the mark and contradictory. This applies to his insistence that "half-solutions and compromise usually prevail, just as they will likely prevail in the 2006 crisis" (pp. 157-8) and his forecast of "pragmatic compromises" (p. 159) to the political deadlock. How could Norton argue along these lines, when he contends that the FPM and Hizbullah are working "together to expand their share of power in significant measure at the expense of the Sunni Muslims"? (p. 153) Norton writes: "Following the resignation of an allied Sunni member and in conjunction with these demands [veto over all government measures], all five Shi'i members of the government resigned from the cabinet..." (p. 156) This is factually wrong. The five Shi'ite ministers resigned on 11 November 2006, and after a few days Jacob Sarraf, the Minister of Environment, followed suit. Sarraf is a Greek Orthodox and not a Sunni Muslim; he is allied with the ex-president Lahud, and thus only indirectly allied with Hizbullah.

On the whole, in addition to its merits, Norton's book contains numerous errors and contradictions, ranging from very basic factual errors, to errors in scholarly judgments, to errors of attribution. In some instances, the book reads more like a defense and justification of Hizbullah's performance, rather than a scholarly analysis of it. For instance, Norton seems to exonerate Hizbullah from some acts of terrorism, blaming these on Iran (p. 78). In the conclusion, Norton takes care to advertise Hizbullah's point of view regarding the

July 2006 war by writing, "…it was utterly predictable that the Shi'a would emerge from the war as a mobilized, assertive, and more militant community." (p. 158)

* * *

The fifth 2009 printing of Norton's book is no exception. It is true some mistakes were corrected in the subsequent reprints, but many mistakes of principle were left unattended. For instance, the map on the first page in the "Prologue" remains deeply flawed. In fact, the latest figures in light of the June 2009 elections reveal the composition of the *Kura* population as: 60 percent Greek Orthodox, 17 percent Maronite, 21 percent Sunni, and 2 percent Shi'a. So where did the overwhelming majority of Greek Catholics come from?

Other inaccuracies remain. This also applies to the new facts and information added afterword (pp. 161-172). He asserts, "although Hezbollah has tried to downplay the hostility of the Sunni groups, it is noteworthy that the party's attempts to reach a rapprochement with the most powerful Sunni Islamist groups have failed, at least through the summer of 2008 [sic]" (p. 171). Norton seems to be unaware of the 18 August 2008 eight-point Understanding between Hizbullah and Salafi movement, where, for instance, article five calls for mutual defense in case of any foreign or domestic aggression.

Not being well-informed, Norton comes up with a flawed conclusion: "It is a good bet that new parliamentary elections in May [sic] 2009 will only replicate the divisions and animosities represented in the post-Doha government." (p. 171) By the concession of international observers and election watchdogs, the 7 June 2009 elections were the most successful elections after the end of the civil war in 1990, unprecedentedly held on one day without any bloodshed or serious feuds. So reading Norton's statement in light of the 2009 legislative elections reveals just the opposite: the elections were neither an epitome of disorder nor did Hizbullah close the door to compromise with its opponents. On the contrary, one day after the elections, the party's secretary-general, Sayyid Hasan Nasrallah conceded defeat, put his differences aside with the March 14 ruling coalition and called for the formation of a national unity government. Rapprochement between Nasrallah, the March 14 Druz leader and seasoned politician Walid Jumblatt, and the parliamentary majority leader Sa'd al-Hariri seemed to be inevitable after the elections. In marathon meetings, after a freeze of almost three years, many misunderstandings and mutual fears were addressed.

This culminated in the formation of a national unity cabinet on 9 November 2009, where, as previously agreed, five seats went to the FPM; two for

Hizbullah, two for Amal, and one for a 'neutral'/technocrat Shi'a personality. On 25 November, a reconciliatory meeting at the presidential palace in B'abda between 'Aun and Jumblatt took place, the first since Jumblatt's visit to 'Aun in Paris mid-April 2005. On 30 November, in this atmosphere of optimism (national unity and reconciliation), Hizbullah released its new Manifesto which dropped any mention of the Islamic state and *wilayat al-faqih*, stressing Lebanon as the homeland, calling for the establishment of a strong, capable, and just state, while working within the narrow confines of the political system through upholding its consensual democracy formula. On 2 December 2009, 'Aun held a reconciliatory meeting with Cardinal Sfeir, while the cabinet officially approved the policy statement that sanctioned Hizbullah's weapons by stressing "the right of Lebanon, its government, its people, its army, and its resistance (Hizbullah) to employ all legitimate means in order to liberate all Lebanese territory." On 12 December, after a three-day parliamentary debate, the cabinet received an overwhelming vote of confidence from 122 MPs out of 128: one MP voted against, one abstained, and four were absent. The air of optimism continued when on 19 and 20 December Sa'd al-Hariri performed a watershed visit to Damascus, where president Bashar al-Asad compromised the protocol and hosted him in the *Tishrin* presidential palace that is reserved for presidents and kings. The meeting resulted in "positive and constructive talks" that diffused around five years of tensions between the two countries. Ironically, the visit and rapprochement between Syria and Lebanon not only put the cabinet's policy statement into effect but also enforced Hizbullah's Manifesto that called for an urgent need to resume 'brotherly' relations between the two countries.

Norton seems to reform his position of constantly defending Hizbullah's actions by contending that the party's "recent 'victories' have been costly on every level that matters. The Shi'i party is as much constrained by its successes as its adversaries have been enlivened by its rise." (p. 172) Nevertheless, this future prospect in the closing paragraph of his book seems also far off the mark. It is most likely that Hizbullah's reconciliatory discourse and strategy of reaching out to allay the fears of the other after its defeat in the 2009 elections were conducive in defusing chronic tensions that had almost succeeded earlier in igniting another civil war.

In the fifth reprint of his book, it seems Norton only corrected some embarrassing mistakes that might tarnish his reputation as an authority "for close to three decades"[21] on the Lebanese Shi'a and Hizbullah, but also committed other factual and analytically short-sighted blunders, which seem to downgrade the overall value of his book and scholarship.

* * *

In short, the critique of the literature conveys an important weakness and apparent difficulty in construing the way Hizbullah's identity has been permanently under reconstruction, thus failing to reveal its new multifaceted, complex face. These misconceptions give free reign to picture and depict Hizbullah in a stereotyped, monotonous distorted pattern.

Notes

INTRODUCTION AND ANALYTICAL FRAMEWORK

1   For more details, refer to Joseph Alagha, *The Shifts in Hizbullah's Ideology*. Amsterdam: Amsterdam University Press, 2006, 19-67.

2   *"Identity and Goals" is Hizbullah's 2004 self-description. My reliance on publicly available primary sources has its own inevitable limitations in exposing Hizbullah's clandestine nature, given the largely secretive nature of the party and its operations.*

3   Musa al-Sadr, one of Hizbullah's ideologues, was a charismatic and distinguished leader, who mobilized the Lebanese Shi'ites in the 1960s and 1970s and was able to channel their grievances into political participation. Al-Sadr never called for an Islamic state, rather for equality and social justice among the various denominations within the Lebanese multiconfessional system.

4   Tawfiq Al-Madini, *Amal wa Hizbullah fi Halabat al-Mujabahat al-Mahaliyya wa al-Iqlimiyya [Amal and Hizbullah in the Arena of Domestic and Regional Struggles]*. Damascus: Al-Ahli, 1999, 172.

5   At the time, he was head of the Islamic Amal, and later served as Nasrallah's aide for municipal affairs.

6   Amal, the Lebanese secular Shi'ite political party with a military wing, was founded by Imam Musa al-Sadr at the outset of the Lebanese civil war in 1975.

7   Nabih Berri, the current leader of Amal and the Speaker of the Lebanese parliament, has repeatedly stated that Amal birthed Hizbullah.

8   Established in 1966. (See Waddah Sharara, *Dawlat Hizbullah: Lubnan Mujtama'an Islamiyyan [The State of Hizbullah: Lebanon as an Islamic Society]*. Fourth edition. Beirut: Al-Nahar, 2006, 87ff). It is worth mentioning that Shaykh Na'im Qasim, Hizbullah's current deputy secretary-general, was one of its leading founding members.

9   Talal Salman, *Sira Dhatiyya li Haraka Muqawina 'Arabiyya Muntasira: Hizbullah [An Autobiography of a Victorious Arab Resistance Movement: Hizbullah]*. Beirut: *Al-Safir*, June 2000, 7.

10 For security reasons, Hizbullah remained operating underground and anonymously till 1984.

11 'Ali Al-Kurani, a Hizbullah middle rank cadre, was the first to expose the social movement's mobilization strategies in his book entitled, *Tariqat Hizbullah fi Al-'Amal Al-Islami [Hizbullah's Method of Islamic Mobilization]*. Tehran, Maktab Al-I'lam Al-Islami: Al-Mu'assa Al-'Alamiyya, 1985, 183-203.

12 The now defunct 'Islamic Jihad' was at the time the spearhead of radical Shi'ite military factions mobilized on the ideology of fighting Israel, the US, and the West. This Shi'ite 'Islamic Jihad' should not be conflated with the Sunni Islamic Jihad, a Palestinian organization founded by Fathi al-Shaqaqi and Abd al-Aziz Awda in Syria during the 1970s.

13 According to US political analysts, this incident served as a blueprint for the Marine's bombing six months later. On this basis, it ought to have served as an omen to the CIA to try to prevent the Marine's bombing. (Brent Sadler, CNN, 11 GMT News, 23 October 2003). The death toll of the US Embassy in West Beirut was 63 people, out of whom 17 were Americans, including the entire Middle East contingent of the CIA. Ann Byers, *Lebanon's Hezbollah (Inside the World's Most Infamous Terrorist Organizations)*. London: Rosen Publishing Group, 2003, 26-35.

14 The same sources claim that the 12,000 ton explosion was the largest non-nuclear device that resulted, in one instance, in the largest number of US casualties since WWII. Till now, the US holds Iran and Hizbullah responsible for the incident. Ibid., 28-33.

15 In retaliation to Israel's assassination of Sayyid Abbas al-Musawi, Hizbullah's second secretary-general, on 16 February 1992.

16 Shaul Shay, *The Axis of Evil: Iran, Hizbullah, and the Palestinian Terror*. London: Transaction Publishers, 2005, 89-100; Byers, op. cit., 36-49; Ely Karmon, *Fight on all Fronts: Hizbullah, the War on Terror, and the War on Iraq*. Policy Focus, no. 46. Washington, DC: The Washington Institute for Near East Policy, December 2003, 1-29.

17 Back then, the deputy president of the National Liberal Party (*Hizb al-Wataniyyin al-Ahrar*). See http://www.ahrar.org.lb/news.asp?id=120

18 *Al-Masira* last week of March 1986.

19 As to the borders of the alleged Maronite state, Z'aytir claims they are constantly expanding. (Muhammad Z'aytir, *Al-Mashru' Al-Maruni fi Lubnan: Juzuruhu wa Tatawwuratuhu [The Maronite Project in Lebanon: Roots and Development]*. Beirut: Al-Wikala Al-'Alamiyya lil-Tawzi', 1986, 14). Since this book contains 1136 pages of severe political-ideological bashing against the

Maronites, it is officially banned in Lebanon. (The book's cover portrays a blue map of Lebanon with a black cross situated in its midst).

20 See respectively http://www.lebanese-forces.com/ and http://www.psp-lb.org/

21 *Al-'Ahd* 95 (9 *Sha'ban* 1406/ 18 April 1986), 11.

22 Ra'd meant to say that Hizbullah neither clashed with the Christian militias nor kidnapped, car-bombed or sniped Lebanese civilians.

23 Personal interview, 4 August 2009.

24 In painting a rosy picture about the Party, these cadres ignore to mention Hizbullah's bloody campaign against the Lebanese Communist Party from 1984 to 1986; its war of attrition against Amal from 1988 to 1990; and, most importantly, its unprecedented uprising in May 2008 when it stormed West Beirut and Mount Lebanon in order to impose, by force, its will of attaining veto power in the Lebanese cabinet. The latter move, which almost brought Lebanon back to the brink of civil war, resulted in the 21 May Doha Accord, which granted Hizbullah its will in a political settlement that ultimately barred the Lebanese from using weapons in settling domestic feuds. (Elaborated later in chapter 6). Hajj Muhammad Ra'd insinuated to me in the same interview that he regrets Hizbullah's show of force in May 2008.

25 Personal interview, 19 January 2010.

26 See 'Victory Speech' *Bint Jubayl* marking the nearly complete Israeli withdrawal on 25 May 2000; *Al-Safir*, 11 July 2001; *Al-Intiqad* 1428 (13 April 2007), 10-14; see also Nasrallah's televised speech in *Bint Jubayl* on 28 July 2007; his speech on 26 May 2008, see *al-Intiqad* 1267 (30 May 2008); and, most importantly, his press conference on 30 November 2009, in which he announced the Party's new Manifesto.

27 Personal interview, 2 November 2004. He is currently a member of the Executive Council.

28 Shaykh Muhammad Yazbik, Hizbullah's *Shura* council member and the head of the religio-judicial council.

29 Joshua S. Goldstein, *International Relations*. Fifth Edition. New York: Longman, 2003.

30 Shibley Telhami and Michael Barnett (eds.), *Identity and Foreign Policy in the Middle East*. Ithaca: Cornell University Press, 2002, 4.

31 Ibid., 182.

32 Alexander Wendt, "Collective Identity Formation and the International State", *American Political Science Review*, 88 (June 1994), 385.

33 Manuel Castells, *The Power of Identity. (The Information Age: Economy, Society, and Culture, Volume II)*. Oxford: Blackwell Publishers Ltd., 1998, 6.

34 Ibid., 9.

35 Ibid., 8. See also Craig Calhoun, (ed.), *Social Theory and the Politics of Identity*. Oxford: Blackwell Publishers, 1994, 17.

36 Castells, *The Power of Identity*, 356. Resistance identities incorporate an array of various movements, which dwell upon religious fundamentalism, nationalism, socialism, ethnic identity, and territorial identity (urban movements and local communities). Georg Sorensen and Robert Jackson, *Introduction to International Relations: Theories and approaches*. Second Edition. Oxford: Oxford University Press, 2003, 219.

37 Castells, *The Power of Identity*, 8.

38 Ibid., 10, 12.

39 Telhami and Barnett (eds.), *Identity and Foreign Policy…*, 7, 63.

40 Chris Barker and Dariusz Galasinski, *Cultural Studies and Discourse Analysis: A Dialogue on Language and Identity*. London: Sage Publications, 2001, 30-31.

41 Raymond Hinnebusch and Anoushiravan Ehteshami (eds.), *The Foreign Policy of Middle East States*. Boulder, Co.: Lynne Rienner Publishers, 2002, 2.

42 Ibid., 2, 45.

43 Telhami and Barnett (eds.), *Identity and Foreign Policy...*, 169.

44 Irredentism refers to the "dissatisfaction with the incongruity between territorial borders and [Benedict Anderson's] 'imagined communities.'" See Hinnebusch and Ehteshami (eds.), *The Foreign Policy…*, 7.

45 Hinnebusch and Ehteshami (eds.), *The Foreign Policy…*, 22.

46 Ibid., 336.

47 Ibid., 7ff.

48 Ibid., 7.

49 Ibid.

50 Ibid., 8.

51 Richard T. Schaefer and Robert P. Lamm, *Sociology*. Sixth Edition. New York: McGraw-Hill, Inc., 1998, 584-5.

52 Ousmane Kane, *Muslim Modernity in Postcolonial Nigeria: A Study of the Society for the Removal of Innovation and Reinstatement of Tradition*. Leiden: Brill, 2003, especially his "Theoretical framework" on pp. 20-23, and his "Conclusion" on "Accumulating and Converting Capital" on pp. 227-31.

53 Bourdieu used the term religious capital in "Genèse et structure du champ religieux", *Revue française de sociologie*, (12), 1971, 295-334. See also the English translation "Genesis and Structure of the Religious Field", Comparative Social Research, 13 (1991), 1-44.

54 This corresponds to a few of Hizbullah's leading religious scholars (*'ulama*), cadres, and the elite, who are the product of religious seminaries (*al-hawzat al-'ilmiyya*).

55 Kane, *Muslim Modernity…*, 22. This corresponds to middle-rank Hizbullah cadres who are mostly the product of the European system of education.

56 Brigit Fowler, "Pierre Bourdieu's sociological theory of culture". *Variant*, 2 (Summer 1999) 8, 2.

57 Pierre Bourdieu, *The Field of Cultural Production*. Cambridge: Polity Press, 1993, 7; *In Other Words: Essays Towards a Reflexive Sociology*. Cambridge: Polity Press, 1990, 22. 111, as cited in Kane, *Muslim Modernity…*, 21.

58 "Hizbullah also sees itself committed to introducing the true picture of Islam, the Islam that is logical. Committed to introduce the civilized Islam to humanity". Hizbullah's "Identity and goals". http://www.hizbollah.org/english/frames/index_eg.htm (Last accessed August 2004).

59 Kane, *Muslim Modernity…*, 22. It is worth mentioning that (4:95) is not the only Qur'anic verse that conveys the idea of symbolic capital. There are so many others, which are frequently quoted by Hizbullah; here, I refer to the most salient. *Jihad* as a means of accumulating symbolic capital is warranted in (61:11-12) and in (9: 111). 'Martyrdom' as a means of accumulating symbolic capital is merited in (3:169).

60 See http://www.theaesthetic.com/NewFiles/capital.html (Accessed 5 July 2005).

61 Fowler, "Pierre Bourdieu's…", 2.

62 Pierre Bourdieu, *Sociology in Question*. London: Sage Publications, 1995, 32-33, as quoted by Kane, *Muslim Modernity…*, 23.

63 Fowler, "Pierre Bourdieu's…", 2.

64 Kane, *Muslim Modernity…*, 22.

65 Ibid., 21.

66 Neera Chandhoke, *State and Civil Society: Explorations in Political Theory*. London: Sage Publications, 1995, 230.

67 Ibid., 233, 225.

68 Castells, *The Power of Identity*, 3.

69 Graham E. Fuller, *The Future of Political Islam*. New York: Palgrave, Macmillan, 2003, 24.

70 Ibid., 193.

71 For instance, in July 2003, Hizbullah celebrated the Lebanese government's acquiescence to its demand to create a separate governorate in *B'albak-Hirmal* – one of its basic constituencies and strong holds – as it used to celebrate successful *jihadi* operations against the Israeli forces. Out of this move, Hizbullah is expected to accumulate more political, and socio-economic capitals.

1 TOLERANCE AND DISCRIMINATION: AHL AL-DHIMMA IN THE ISLAMIC ORDER

1 This chapter is a revised, updated, and modified version of my article: "*Ahl Al-Dhimma* in Hizbullah's Islamic State: Acceptance and Tolerance". *Shia Affairs Journal* 1 (Winter 2008): 23-39.

2   Residents within an Islamic state holding limited rights and required to pay a poll tax in lieu of *zakat*.

3   Established in the wake of the Israeli invasion in June 1982.

4   From a historical perspective, "Lebanon's Christians… are not a monolithic but a collection of distinctive groups possessing marked diversities. They broadly divide into three major denominational groups – the Maronites and the Melkites, both Roman Catholic, and Greek Orthodox, who are part of the Eastern Orthodox church… The Maronites reject inclusion in the Arab world outright; the Greek Orthodox accept their status as part of that world; and the Melkites vacillate between the two attitudes. However, all Lebanese Christians perceive themselves as imperiled since their survival is as a religious minority trapped in a sea of Islam." Sandra Mackey, *Lebanon: Death of a Nation*. New York: Congdon and Weed Inc., 1989, 30.

5   I prefer to translate *da'wa* as Islamic propagation or call, which is closer to its lexical origin than 'Islamic indoctrination' as some authors choose. See for instance, Uriah Furman, "Minorities in Contemporary Islamist Discourse". *Middle Eastern Studies* 36.4 (October 2000): 1-20.

6   Muslim attitudes towards the Maronites might have been influenced, in part, by the Maronite role outlined by the French colonial mandate following the Sykes-Picot Agreement of 1916, which partitioned the Levant between the French (Lebanon and Syria) and the British (Palestine, Jordan, and Iraq). By political Maronism Hizbullah means the leading Maronite notables and their retinue, which constitute the symbols of the Lebanese political system. Their retinue included the Sunni prime minister (PM) and the Shi'a speaker who were completely under their command, blindly exercising their political whim and will. The late PM Sami al-Solh said that the PM was only "ketchup" in the hands of the president. Thus, from 1943 to 1990 the Muslims, in general, and the Shi'ites, in particular, had been politically marginalized since the Maronites wielded economic and political power and had absolute control over the country's resources and riches. The National Pact of 1943, which is an oral agreement not drafted in the 1926 Constitution, stipulated that the PM be Sunni Muslim, the Speaker Shi'ite, and the following Maronites: the President of the Republic; the Commander of the Army; the Governor of the Central Bank (BDL); and the head of the Labor Unions (GLC). However, article 95 of Section 6 of the 1943 Constitution – which was amended by a constitutional law issued on 9 November 1943 – gave some hope for the Shi'ites of a fairer representation in the future: "Temporarily and from the stance of justice and national reconciliation, the sects are represented in a just manner in public employment and in the formation of the Council of Ministers, without harming state interest". Alagha, *The Shifts in Hizbullah's Ideology*, 23.

7 Hasan Fadlallah, *Al-Khiyar al-Akhar: Hizbullah: al-Sira al-Dhatiyya wa al-Mawqif [The Other Choice: Hizbullah's Autobiography and Stance].* Beirut: Dar al-Hadi, 1994, 137.

8 See Section 13: "Words to the Christians in Lebanon".

9 Ibid.

10 In other words, *jizya* has been used since the Caliphal period as a penalty for not being Muslim. It seems that its original intention was to ensure a non-Muslim contribution to the public purse, i.e. a measure in the Prophetic period to include non-Muslims as shareholders in a plural society.

11 Similar to those who agreed to the Constitution of Medina but had secret alliances with Mecca and other enemy causes.

12 See Hizbullah's Political Declaration of 31 May 1986. It is most likely that Hizbullah's attitude to the Maronites was informed by more than recent and contemporary events. Their actions from the Civil War to date might be explained as a minority overreacting in its defence. However, when this is considered in the context of their single-minded drive to carve out a Maronite state at the cost of their Muslim neighbors terms like hypocrisy seem not too radical. See Z'aytir, *Al-Mashru' Al-Maruni*...

13 Ayatullah Fadlallah was the highest ranking religious authority in Lebanon and the local authority of emulation (*marja'*) who still has following among the Shi'ite community in Lebanon and who wielded power and influence over the Islamists. Many considered him Hizbullah's spiritual leader, a charge which he persistently denied. It is interesting to note that Fadlallah's declaration of *'id al-fitr* at the end of Ramadan in 2002, which coincided with that of the (Sunni) Mufti of the Lebanese Republic, split the *Dahiya*, Hizbullah's main constituency in Beirut, between Hizbullah's adherents of the Iranian religious authority and Fadlallah's followers who celebrated the *'id* a day before the Hizbullahis. Such eventualities increase the tensions between Hizbullah and the Iranians, on the one hand, and Fadlallah and his followers, on the other hand.

14 For the connection between the good political order (Islamic state) and the application of justice to all groups, including minorities, see the following Qur'anic verses: (4:28); (42:15); (5:8); (5:42); (6:152); and (16:90).

15 Sayyid Fadlallah was referring to one of the maxims of Islamic jurisprudence (*qawa'id al-fiqh*), which states that the warding off of vices is preferable to obtaining interests.

16 See the section entitled, "Power and its Relationship to the Sovereignty and Islam", in: Sayyid Muhammad Husayn Fadlallah, *Al-Islam wa Mantiq Al-Quwwa [Islam and the Logic of Power]*, Beirut: Dar Al-Huruf, 1987, 245-259.

17 Kurani added that neither Israel nor the US care about the Lebanese Christians, since they have cost them too much and given too little benefit in return. *Tariqat Hizbullah...*, 181, 191.

18 He was a strong advocate of establishing an Islamic State in Lebanon along the Khumaynist ideology but, to my knowledge, he did not occupy a prominent role in Hizbullah's leadership. See his book entitled, *Nazra 'ala Tarh Al-Jumhuriyya Al-Islamiyya fi Lubnan [A Look at the Proposal of the Islamic Republic in Lebanon]*. Beirut: Al-Wikala Al-Sharqiyya lil-Tawzi', 1988.

19 Z'aytir, *Nazra'ala Tarh Al-Jumhuriyya Al-Islamiyya...*, 106.

20 *Al-Safir* (7 September 1985).

21 Q. 3:64

22 Z'aytir, *Nazra 'ala Tarh Al-Jumhuriyya Al-Islamiyya...*, 60-61.

23 See Section 13: 'Words to the Christians in Lebanon'. Kurani interprets this as a clear reference to the Jews who did not honor their covenant with the Prophet as stipulated by the Constitution of Medina. Al-Kurani, *Tariqat Hizbullah...*, 160.

24 Q. 2:256. See Section 9 of Open Letter: "We are committed to Islam, but we do not impose it by force".

25 Q. 5:51 Literally 'oppressors'.

26 Q. 2:120

27 Q. 6:121

28 Due to perpetually fighting the Islamists and manipulating the Muslims.

29 Z'aytir, *Nazra 'ala Tarh Al-Jumhuriyya Al-Islamiyya...*, 103-104.

30 See Hizbullah's political declaration in the anniversary of the annulment of the 17 May 1983 Agreement with Israel. *Al-'Ahd* 100 (15 *Ramadan* 1406/ 23 May 1986), 11.

31 Sharara, *Dawlat Hizbullah...*, 348.

32 'Arif Al-'Abd, *Lubnan wa Al-Ta'if: Taqatu' Tarikhi wa Masar Ghayr Muktamil [Lebanon and the Ta'if: A Historical Crossroad and an Unfinished Trajectory]*, Beirut: Markaz Dirasat Al-Wihda Al-'Arabiyya, 2001.

33 Al-Madini, *Amal wa Hizbullah*, 172-173.

34 Cooptation refers to the 'disarming' of opposition by the invitation of opposition leaders to become part of a ruling elite or structure.

35 Contestation refers to "opportunities to oppose the government, form political organizations, express oneself on political matters without fear of government reprisals, read and hear alternative points of view, vote by secret ballot in elections in which candidates of different parties compete for votes and after which the losing candidates peacefully yield their claim to office to the winners, etc." Robert A. Dahl, *Polyarchy: Participation and Opposition*. New Haven: Yale University Press 1971, 20.

36 Empowerment describes a process in which a marginalized group experiences an accretion to its power without continuously setting out to do so at the expense of others. However, the key term here is 'power' which is a much debated term.

37 The header of Hizbullah's now defunct website www.hizbollah.org referred to the following Qur'anic verse: "We wish to favor the downtrodden [oppressed] in the land and make them leaders [Imams] and make them the inheritors; And establish (*numakin*) them firmly in the land..." (28:5-6).

38 Rather than attributing this policy change to pragmatism, Hizbullah legitimizes this line of thinking through references to Qur'anic verses such as 3:26, which stress that 'all good is from Allah', in order to validate the idea of an Islamic state that develops by acceptance of good, rather than by any form of stereotypical imposition. Thus, there is a rational theological basis for believing that all good is from Allah; that good will ultimately shape government; and that the resultant society is inherently Islamic. In fact, the adoption of the concept of *'amal al-ihsan* (action of excellence under God's guidance) and texts which promote them as Islamic is established in Shi'ite thinking and traditions.

39 The National Pact of 1943 remained intact after Lebanon's 1990 Constitution and the Doha Accord of 21 May 2008, which granted veto power to the Hizbullah-led opposition in the Council of Ministers, the main executive body of the country.

40 John Paul II, 1997, "On numerous occasions, from the beginning of my Pontificate, I have urged the international community to help the Lebanese people once again to live peacefully within a national territory recognized and respected by all, and to foster the rebuilding of a society of justice and brotherhood."

41 During the latter days of the 2006 Israeli incursion, John Simpson in a live interview broadcast by BBC News 24 with the Bishop of Tyre was told of the cooperation between Christians and Muslims in peace and their united Lebanese opposition to intruders.

42 Some party members label him as the 'minister of culture'. *Fi Al-Mamnu'* [*Discussing Taboos/Prohibitions*], with Katrin Hanna, a *New TV* show aired in March 2007.

43 Personal Interview with Sayyid Abd al-Halim Fadlallah (16 March 2007). Fadlallah, a researcher in sociology, is also currently the president of Hizbullah's think tank the Consultative Center of Studies and Documentation (CCSD).

44 Q. 2:256

45 Personal recollection.

46 Jaradi was deriding the stance of Hizbullah's ideological enemies, in particular the *takfiri* Salafi's doctrine of: "Covert or die". As mentioned earlier, in its 1980s discourse, the Hizbullah establishment called for conversion through peaceful means.

47 Personal Interview, 4 December 2007. Al-Musawi worked at al-Manar TV as a political program's editor, was the editor-in-chief of Hizbullah's weekly mouthpiece *al-Intiqad*, and is currently the party's spokesman. He holds a Ph.D. in

Islamic studies from Birmingham University.

48 *The Garden of the Prophet* 1933, via the Internet at:http://leb.net/gibran/ (Accessed 6 July 2007).

49 *Hizbullah's Political Manifesto*, Chapter 11: "Lebanon", Section 6: "Lebanon and Islamic Relations". First edition. Beirut: Media Relations Office, 2009, 50. It is worth mentioning that Hizbullah distributed among the audience of Nasrallah's 30 November 2009 press conference a 32-page preliminary document of the Manifesto. A few weeks later, the party published the Manifesto in a 71-page polished short book, elegantly printed on expensive paper. Throughout my book, I refer to the latter.

2 INTERPRETATION AND AUTHORITY: WILAYAT AL-FAQIH

1 This chapter is a revised, updated, and modified version of my article "*Wilayat Al-Faqih* and Hizbullah's Relations with Iran", *Journal of Arabic and Islamic Studies* 10 (Winter 2010): 24-44.

2 "We emphasize the need to adhere to the distinguished relations between Lebanon and Syria as a common political, security, and economic need, dictated by the interests of the two countries and two peoples, by the imperatives of geopolitics and the requirements for Lebanese stability and facing common challenges. We also call for an end to all the negative sentiments that have marred bilateral ties in the past few years and urge these relations to return to their normal status as soon as possible." Hizbullah's 2009 Political Manifesto, Chapter 11: "Lebanon", Section 5: "Lebanon and the Arab Relations", 49.

3 "Hizbullah considers Iran as a central state in the Muslim world, since through its revolution it ousted the Shah's regime and its American-'Israeli' projects. Iran is also the state that supported the resistance movements in our region, and stood with courage and determination at the side of the Arab and Islamic causes and especially the Palestinian one… The response to such actions should be cooperation, brotherhood, and a center of awakening and strategic weight as well as a model for independence and liberty that supports the Arab-Islamic project. Iran should be viewed as a power that boosts the strength and might of the people of our region." Ibid., Chapter 11, Section 6: "Lebanon and Islamic Relations", 51-2.

4 The Ta'if Agreement, Lebanon's new 1990 constitution, is a 'bill of rights' or a blueprint for national reconciliation and reform aimed towards a more equitable political system for all sectarian-confessional groups.

5 Peter Mandaville aptly argued that post-Islamism is bottom-up Islamization in disguise. See *Global Political Islam*. New York: Routledge 2007, 343-8.

6   J. Z. Smith, To Take Place: Toward Theory in Ritual. Chicago: The University of Chicago Press, 1987.

7   In 1978 Foucault reported on the Iranian Revolution by writing articles for *Corriere della serra*.

8   Authority is power that has been institutionalized and is recognized by the people over whom it is exercised.

9   Georg Stauth, *Revolution in Spiritless Times: An Essay on the Inquiries of Michel Foucault on the Iranian Revolution*. Singapore: National University of Singapore, 1991.

10   See Nasrallah's speech delivered in Southern Beirut in order to mark the fortieth anniversary following the death of Imam Husayn.

11   From now on *al-waliyy al-faqih* will be referred to as *faqih*.

12   10 *Jumadi al-Awwal* 1409 AH.

13   See Khumayni's letter to Khamina'i concerning the latter's Friday speech on the absoluteness of *wilayat al-faqih*. Published in Farsi in *Kayhan* 13223, 16 *Jamadi Al-Awwal* 1409/ 6 January 1989.

14   Personal interview with Sayyid Ibrahim Al-Musawi, 12 July 2004.

15   Personal interviews with Mahdi N. and 'Abdallah S., respectively on 21 and 25 October 2004.

16   AL-*'Ahd* 8 (21 *Dhul-Qadah* 1404/ 17 August 1984), 6.

17   Nasrallah, NBN, 21 July 2002.

18   Al-Kurani, *Tariqat Hizbullah…*; and Z'aytir, *Nazra 'ala Tarh Al-Jumhuriyya Al-Islamiyya…*

19   Z'aytir, *Al-Mashru' Al-Maruni…*

20   One should keep in mind that the concepts of *jahiliyya* and *hakimiyya* constitute a common denominator among many Islamic movements, and, as such, are not exclusively a Hizbullah notion.

21   Based on inside sources and fieldwork observations by the author, it could be fairly stated that the majority of Hizbullah's cadres consider disagreements in religious and political opinions and viewpoints of the leaders to be a phenomenon, which represents a healthy 'democratic' atmosphere. However, strict obedience and discipline prevents disagreements from festering into discord, al-Tufayli's case being an exception.

22   Since *wilayat al-faqih* was being applied in a multiconfessional, multireligious society.

23   Al-Tufayli held a high post in the leadership of Hizbullah in the early 1980s. But he later created a minor dissent in the party for reasons that, apparently, were social but, in fact, were for control of the B'albak region. Al-Tufayli today represents that category of Hizbullah which still upholds the Iranian revolutionary ideology of the 1980s.

24 Na'im Qasim, *Hizbullah: Al-Manhaj, Al-Tajriba, Al-Mustaqbal [Hizbullah: The Curriculum, the Experience, the Future].* Seventh revised and updated edition. Beirut: Dar Al-Mahajja Al-Bayda', 2010, 337-343.

25 For a detailed account of Hizbullah's social services see Joseph Alagha and Myriam Catusse, "Les services sociaux de Hezbollah: Effort de guerre, ethos religieux et ressources politiques", in: *Le Hezbollah: État Des Lieux*, ed. Sabrina Mervin. Paris: Actes Sud, 2008, 117-140. For an illuminating discussion on the role of social services for Islamic movements, see Jonathan Benthall and Jerome Bellion-Jourdan. *The Charitable Crescent: Politics of Aid in the Muslim World.* London: I.B. Tauris, 2003. Paperback edition with new preface, 2008.

26 Nasrallah, NBN, 4 August 2002.

27 For information on the Lebanese prisoners in Israeli jails in English, Arabic, Hebrew, and French, see http://www.samirkuntar.org/, which was officially launched on 19 April 2007.

28 *Al-Intiqad* is Hizbullah's official mouthpiece and weekly newspaper. It was established on 18 June 1984 as *al-'Ahd*, but changed its name and orientation in 2001, thus conveying a 'secular' image by dropping the Qur'anic substantiation (5:56), on the right side, and removing the portrait of Khumayni and Khami-na'i, on the left side. The last issue of *al-'Ahd* was number 896, dated 6 April 2001 or 12 *Muharram* 1422 AH; the first issue of *al-Intiqad* was number 897, dated 20 April 2001 or 26 *Muharram* 1422 AH. The last hard-copy issue of *al-Intiqad* was number 1267, dated 30 May 2008. Since number 1268, dated 6 June 2008, *al-Intiqad* has been only available electronically and initially was publis-hed bi-weekly on Fridays and Tuesdays, until it settled as a Friday weekly once more, but with only the date, no number. See http://www.alintiqad.com/

29 *Al-Manar* literally means 'The lighthouse'. It is probably named after the Leb-anese reformist Shaykh Muhammad Rashid Rida's (1865-1935) journal, which circulated from Indonesia to Morocco without interruption for 37 years (1898-1935). It was an influential platform for Muslims to vent their ideas on moder-nity and modernism in the form of *fatwas*. *Al-Manar* was a treasure house of Islamic subjects where almost every problem of modernity was discussed. As such, it was the most influential instrument of modern change. Hizbullah's *al-Manar* aspires to achieve the same standing.

30 This number reflects legitimate cable subscribers. It is estimated that at least eight million watched *al-Manar* through pirated techniques.

31 Nabulsi is not a Hizbullah member, rather a local influential cleric revered by the party. In 1982, he was one of the participants in the 'Conference of the Oppressed' presided by Khumayni. It is worth mentioning that after the five Shi'ite ministers – including the two from Hizbullah – suspended their membership of the Lebanese cabinet for seven weeks as of 12 December 2005, Nabulsi, not Nasrallah, issued a *fatwa* barring any other Shi'ite from joining

the cabinet in their absence. (See Lebanese daily newspapers of 21 December 2005).

32 Jabal 'Amil – the den of Shi'ism in Lebanon and an important Shi'ite center of higher learning – has an important moral significance being the birth place of imminent *hadith* scholar al-Hurr al-'Amili (died 1104 AH/1692 AD), who complied the canonical volumes of Shi'ite *hadith*. See Al-Shaykh Muhammad Bin Al-Hasan Al-Hurr Al-'Amili, *Wasa'il Al-Shi'a [Shi'ite Rituals]*. Beirut: Mu'assat Al-Hulul, Bayt Ihya' Al-Turath, 1993. For a closer look at the instrumental role of the *Jabal 'Amil 'ulama* in converting the majority of the Iranians from Sunnism to Shi'ism at the outset of the Safavid period, see Alagha, *The Shifts in Hizbullah's Ideology*, 20ff.

33 Based on interviews I have conducted with high ranking cadres, including members of the *Shura* council.

34 In order to preserve the calm with Israel, Hizbullah neither hesitates to apprehend Palestinian fighters or *al-Qa'ida* affiliated militants who attempt to target northern Israel with rockets nor to stop anyone attempting to attack Israel, even by force. Also, Hizbullah informs UNIFIL and the Lebanese Army of any rocket it discovers set to be fired at Israel, so that it can be defused immediately. On these grounds, Subhi al-Tufayli mocked Hizbullah for protecting the borders of Israel and criticized Iran for serving the interests of the US, as he contended. See Tha'ir 'Abbas's interview with Subhi al-Tufayli in *al-Sharq al-Awsat* 9067 (25 September 2003). Interestingly, Hizbullah has erected two pillars (like the one in *Mina*, Saudi Arabia where Muslims perform the symbolic, ritual stoning of Satan during the *hajj*) near the Fatima Gate bordering Israel for the ritual stoning of the 'Little Satan' (Israel) and the 'Great Satan' (US), so that people will not throw rocks at the Israeli soldiers across the border. In order to preserve the status quo ante, Hizbullah does not even tolerate the throwing of rocks across the broader. It is noteworthy that Hizbullah's 2009 Manifesto makes no mention of the ideological concepts of the 'Little Satan' and the 'Great Satan'.

35 According to Hizbullah's discourse, Lebanonization refers to the party's integration in the Lebanese public sphere, including the political system and state structures.

36 *Al-Harakat Al-Islamiyya fi Lubnan [Islamic Movements in Lebanon]*. Beirut: Al-Shira', 1984, 323-336.

37 Imam Khumayni, *Al-Hukumat Al-Islamiyya [Islamic Government]*. Tehran: The Institute of Coordinating and Publishing Imam Khumayni's Heritage, 1996, 60ff.

38 Al-Madini, *Amal wa Hizbullah…*, 162-163; Sharara, *Dawlat Hizbullah…*, 342.

39 Hizbullah's 30 November 2009 Manifesto, Chapter II: "Lebanon", Section 1: "The Homeland", 30.

40 Dale Eickelman and Jon Anderson, eds. *New Media in the Muslim World: The Emerging Public Sphere*. Bloomington, IN: Indiana University Press, 2003, 2.

41 Nasrallah as cited by Hasan 'Izzeddine, "How is Hizbullah looked upon and how does it introduce itself?", *Al-Safir*, 12 November 2001.

42 *Al-Intiqad* 1267, 30 May 2008.

43 Nasrallah, AL-JAZEERA TV, 24 September 1998; Qasim, *Hizbullah: Al-Manhaj...*, 51-52; and MP Ali Fayyad, as cited in Fadeel M. Abun-Nasr, *Hizbullah: Haqa'iq wa Ab'ad [Hizbullah: Facts and Dimensions]*. Beirut: World Book Publishing, 2003, 127.

44 Nasrallah's press conference was broadcast live on *Al-Manar* TV, 30 November 2009, at 1:30 GMT.

45 Nasrallah's 2001 call for the abolition of political sectarianism in mentality, before abolishing it in the texts (10 July 2001 Speech; *al-Safir* 11 July 2001) bears a striking resemblance to the Maronite bishops' declaration that cautioned that deleting political sectarianism from legal texts before wiping it out from Lebanese people's mentality – through an efficient education of coexistence and mutual respect – is hazardous (*Daily Star* 5 February 2004). See Alagha, *The Shifts in Hizbullah's Ideology*, 160.

46 A few days before revealing Hizbullah's Manifesto.

47 Idem., Chapter II: "Lebanon", Section 3: "The State and the Political System", 38-39.

48 Idem., Nasrallah's press conference, 30 November 2009.

49 See NBN, 7:30pm News, and the Lebanese newspapers of 14 January 2010.

50 LBCI, 8:00 pm news, 14 January 2010.

51 LBCI, 3:00 pm news, 16 January 2010; Future News, 3:00 pm, 17 January 2010.

52 If this move is ratified in the new election law, then calculating the number of voters between the ages of 18 and 21 reveals that the Muslim voters will number 75%, while the Christian voters will number 25%, as the latest statistics indicated. In order to create a balance, the Lebanese Forces and their allies are calling for linking this move with granting suffrage to the Lebanese Diaspora, the majority of whom are Christians.

53 *Al-Safir* and *al-Nahar* (15 June 2005); Shaykh Ja'far Hasan 'Atrisi, *Hizbullah: Al-Khiyar Al-As'ab wa Damanat Al-Watan Al-Kubra [Hizbullah: The Difficult Choice and Lebanon's Greatest Guarantee]*. Beirut: Dar Al-Mahajja Al-Bayda', 2005, 435-439; *Hizbullah: Al-Muqawama wa Al-Tahrir [Hizbullah: Resistance and Liberation]*, Volume11, Beirut, Edito International, 2006, 200-206. (A thirteen volume encyclopedia on the party).

54 The 34-day war, from 12 July to 14 August 2006, between Israel and Hizbullah led to the death of around 1,200 Lebanese, one-third of whom were children under the age of 12; wounded and handicapped 4,000; displaced more than one million; and caused around $ 15 billion in damages and revenues. Accor-

ding to Israeli media sources, more than two-thirds of the 159 Israeli dead were soldiers: 118 soldiers and 41 civilians. *Daily Star* and *AFP* (Agence France-Presse). See http://www.dailystar.com.lb/July_War06.asp (Accessed 5 September 2006).

55   Formed on 11 July 2008. According to the deal of power-sharing, Hizbullah was supposed to obtain three ministerial seats, but it waived two to its allies the FPM, thus making a considerable concession.

56   As mentioned in chapter one, the National Pact of 1943 remained intact after the ratification of the 1990 Ta'if Agreement and the 2008 Doha Accord.

57   International observers and election watchdogs conceded that the 7 June 2009 elections were the most successful elections after the end of the civil war in 1990, unprecedentedly held on one day without any bloodshed or serious feuds.

3 POLITICAL VIOLENCE: TERRORISM AND 9/11

1   This chapter is a revised, updated, and modified version of my earlier article "Hizbullah, Terrorism, and Sept. 11." *ORIENT: Deutsche Zeitschrift für Wirtschaft und Kultur des Orients*. 44.3 (September 2003): 385-412.

2   The OIC was established in 1969 in the wake of setting ablaze the Al-Aqsa Mosque in Jerusalem. In addition to promoting social, economic, and political solidarity among its members, since its founding, the OIC has been an ardent defendant of the Palestinian cause. See http://www.oic-oci.org/main-body. htm.

3   See "Islamic nations pledge to fight terrorism, soft-pedal on Iraq, Mideast", *AFP* 17 October 2003; and Lebanese daily newspapers of 18 October 2003.

4   Shafiq Masri, "*Al-Irhab fi Al-Qanun Al-Duwali* [Terrorism in International Law]". *Shu'un al-Awsat*, 105 (Winter 2002), 46-56.

5   *Al-Safir* 26 August 2003.

6   See Qaradawi's viewpoint regarding this issue in Section 6.3.

7   Unlike most works on Hizbullah that focus on secondary literature, the part and parcel of my research is based on Hizbullah's primary sources.

8   Raymond Hinnebusch and Anoushiravan Ehteshami (eds.), *The Foreign Policy of Middle East States*. Boulder, Co.: Lynne Rienner Publishers, 2002, 2.

9   Hizbullah uses the term '*infitah*' to describe its post-Ta'if political role. See Qasim, *Hizbullah: Al-Manhaj…*, 356, 363, 389, 396. The Ta'if Agreement of 1990 ended the 16-year Lebanese civil war and became Lebanon's new constitution.

10   (Personal interview with Hajj Abdo Saad, 24 December 2001. See his article in *al-Intiqad* 911, 27 July 2001). It is worth mentioning that the abolition of poli-

tical sectarianism is stipulated in article 95 of the Ta'if Agreement. Hajj Abdo Saad is the election and political analyst of the party. He heads an independent research center called the 'Beirut Center for Research and Information' (*Markaz Beirut lil Abhath wa Al-Ma'lumat*).

11   In an attempt to curtail Hizbullah, from 11 to 18 April 1996, Israel launched a massive attack against southern Lebanon killing more than 150 civilians – including 102 civilians seeking shelter in the UN headquarters in the Lebanese village of Qana – and displacing around half a million others. Also, Israel heavily bombed the Lebanese infrastructure. (See Hasan Fadlallah, *Harb al-Iradat: Sira' al-Muqawama wa al-Ihtilal al-Isra'ili fi Lubanan [The War of Volitions: The Resistance's Struggle and the Israeli Occupation in Lebanon*. Beirut: Dar al-Hadi, 1998, 181-202). The 'Grapes of Wrath' resulted in an unprecedented national solidarity with Hizbullah. Thus, along with other denominations, Christians, most notably, donated gold and money so that Hizbullah can buy Katyusha rockets to be fired at Israel as a deterrent strategy in an endeavor to halt the attack.

12   MP Sayyid Husayn al-Musawi, back then Nasrallah's Executive Aide, argued that a "terrorist is by their [US's] definition anyone who is against the US policy" (*al-Manar*, 7:30 pm News, 30 June 2002).

13   Nicholas Blanford, "Hizballah in the Firing Line". *MERIP*, (28 April 2003), 2. This is clearly stated in Hizbullah's Open Letter or Political Manifesto, which forms the party's political ideology.

14   Amal Saad-Ghorayeb, *Hizbullah: Politics and Religion*. London: Pluto Press, 2002, 191.

15   I suggest that before 1992, there was no clear distinction between Hizbullah's political ideology and political program. The dichotomy occurred when Hizbullah decided to participate in the parliamentary elections of 1992, thus propagating for the first time an election program. For a distinction between Hizbullah's political ideology and political program, see my article entitled "Hizbullah's Gradual Integration in the Lebanese Public Sphere", *Sharqiyyat: Journal of the Dutch Association for Middle Eastern and Islamic Studies* 13 (2001), 1, 47, 54 and my book *The Shifts in Hizbullah's Ideology*. It seems that Sobelman concurs with my analysis when he explicitly labels the Open Letter as Hizbullah's political ideology or its "first political, ideological platform". See Daniel Sobelman, *Rules of the Game: Israel and Hizbullah After the Withdrawal from Lebanon*. Memorandum no. 69. Tel Aviv University: Jaffee Center for strategic Studies, January 2004, 23. Via the Internet at: http://www.tau.ac.il/jcss/memoranda/memo69.pdf.

16   Augustus Norton, "America's Approach to the Middle East: Legacies, Questions, and Possibilities", *Current History*, (January 2002), 5. Norton, the Hizbullah authority, is professor of International Relations and Anthropology at

Boston University. He has been a consultant to the National Security Council, the US State Department, and the government of Norway.

17 Joshua S. Goldstein. *International Relations*. Fifth edition. New York: Longman, 2003, 214.

18 Ibid.

19 See for instance, Gerhard von Glahn, *Law among Nations: An Introduction to Public International Law*. Seventh edition. Boston: Allyn & Bacon, 1996, 276-277ff.

20 See section 6 of this article.

21 Bruce Russett, Harvey Starr, and David Kinsella, *World Politics: The Menu for Choice*. New York: Bedford/St. Martin's, 2000, 228-233.

22 Gerd Baumann, *Contesting Culture: Discourses of identity in multi-ethnic London*. Cambridge: Cambridge University Press, 1996.

23 "Today bookstores in the US are filled with shabby screeds bearing screaming headlines about Islam and terror, the Arab threat and the Muslim menace, all of them written by political polemicists pretending to knowledge imparted by experts who have supposedly penetrated to the heart of these strange oriental peoples. CNN and Fox, plus myriad evangelical and rightwing radio hosts, innumerable tabloids and even middle-brow journals have recycled the same unverifiable fictions and vast generalisations so as to stir up 'America' against the foreign devil… In the demonisation of an unknown enemy for whom the label 'terrorist' serves the general purpose of keeping people stirred up and angry, media images command too much attention and can be exploited at times of crisis and insecurity of the kind that the post-September 11 period has produced… terror pre-emptive war, and unilateral regime change… are the main ideas debated endlessly and impoverishly by a media that assigns itself the role of producing so called 'experts' who validate the government's general line. Reflection, debate, rational argumentation and moral principle based on a secular notion that human beings must create their own history have been replaced by abstract ideas that celebrate American or western exceptionalism, denigrate the relevance of context, and regard other cultures with contempt". (See Edward Said, "A window on the world", *The Guardian* 2 August 2003, Guardian Unlimited Books: http://books.guardian.co.uk; and the author's introduction to the 2003 Penguin edition of *Orientalism*).

24 Ahmad Moussalli, *Historical Dictionary of Islamic Fundamentalist Movements in the Arab World, Iran, and Turkey*. London: The Scarecrow Press, Inc., 1999, 154.

25 Dennis Ross – a former US diplomat and a Middle East expert, during his press conference at the "Lebanese Press Office Centre" in January 2003 – reiterated that the US distinguishes between resistance and terrorism, the best example being the 1993 and 1996 "Understandings" brokered by the US,

France, and Syria between Hizbullah and Israel, legitimizing Hizbullah's right to resist the Israeli occupation.

26 Daniel Byman, "Should Hezbollah Be Next?", *Foreign Affairs*, 82 (November/December 2003), 6, 58.

27 Hizbullah ironically notes that the name 'IDF' is itself a euphemism since the 'aggressor' is being labeled as the 'defender'. By Hizbullah, I mean Hizbullah's official policy – as conveyed by its Central Press Office and media institutions – which is usually based on the discourse and policy of its leaders.

28 The first Israeli invasion of Lebanon took place on 14 March 1978; the second invasion occurred on 5 June 1982.

29 Hinnebusch and Ehteshami (eds.), *The Foreign Policy…*, 31.

30 Byman, "Should Hezbollah Be Next?", 58.

31 Mattew A. Levitt, "Hezbollah's West Bank Terror Network", *Middle East Intelligence Bulletin*, 5 (August-September 2003), 8-9, via the Internet at: http://www.meib.org/articles/0308_l3.htm (Accessed 12 January 2004).

32 After the Israeli withdrawal, Hizbullah continued its resistance and military operations in the Lebanese Shib'a farms, a small strategic strip of land – bordering Lebanon, Israel, and Syria – situated near the Golan Heights. See my article entitled: "Successen Hezbollah bij 'kleine oorlog' om Shib'a [Hizbullah's Successes in the 'Small War' in Shib'a]", Soera 9.2 (July 2001), 34-38.

33 Sayyid Ibrahim al-Musawi argues that branding Hizbullah with terrorism is "slander", specifically a "dysphemism" using the language of critical thinking: "The opposite of a euphemism is a dysphemism. Dysphemisms are used to produce a negative effect on a listener's or reader's attitude toward something or to tone down the positive associations it may have. Whereas 'freedom fighter' is a euphemism for 'guerrilla' or 'rebel,' 'terrorist' is a dysphemism. Euphemisms and dysphemisms are often used in deceptive ways, or ways that at least hint at deception… Hence, [the] *purpose* for using euphemisms and dysphemisms determines whether or not those uses are legitimate". See Brooke Noel Moore and Richard Parker, *Critical Thinking: Evaluating Claims and Arguments in Everyday Life*. Fifth Edition. CA: Mayfield Publishing Company, 1998, 101.

34 These being the following: the US; Israel; Canada as of 11 December 2002; and Australia as of 5 June 2003.

35 In April 2001 a communiqué issued by the US Department of State kept Hizbullah's classification as a 'terrorist organization'.

36 *Bidnayyil's* Speech, 20 May 2001; Interview with *al-Jazeera*, 25 May 2001.

37 Byman argues that Hizbullah is "… legitimate, because of its participation in Lebanese parliamentary politics". Byman, "Should Hezbollah Be Next?", 55.

38 Their assets were frozen and they were barred from travel to the US, a move that was only partially enforced in 2009, instead of immediately materializing

after 9/11.

39 Byman, "Should Hezbollah Be Next?", 60.

40 See his article entitled, "Hizballah: The Calculus of Jihad" in *Bulletin: The American Academy of Arts and Sciences* 47 (May 1994), 8, 20-43. See also Kramer's two articles entitled: "The Moral Logic of Hizballah" in Walter Reich (ed.), *Origins of Terrorism, Psychologies, Ideologies, States of Mind*, New York: Cambridge University Press, 1990, 131-151; and "Redeeming Jerusalem: The Pan-Islamic Premise of Hizballah" in David Menashri (ed.), *The Iranian Revolution and the Muslim World*. Boulder, Co: Westview Press, 1990, 105-130.

41 A conference held in Paris entitled "Vingt Ans Après" from 22-24 June 2000.

42 A Hizbullah media cadre who served as *al-Manar* T V editor and *al-Intiqad* weekly newspaper columnist.

43 Al-Musawi is accusing Israel of state terrorism, where states "use terror against their own populations to gain or increase control through fear. Tactics include expulsion or exile, failure to protect some citizens from the crimes of others (as in state-tolerated vigilante groups [right-wing Jews], arbitrary arrest, beating, kidnappings ('disappearances'), torture, and murder". (Bruce Russett et al, *World Politics...*, 207). Making use of 9/11 discourse, Nasrallah labeled Israel as a "terrorist state" because of the "massacres" it committed, and is still committing against the Palestinian and Lebanese civilians. (See Nasrallah's speech commemorating the first anniversary of the Intifada, 28 September 2001). For similar reasons, Salim al-Hoss, the ex-Lebanese prime minister, accused the US of supporting and sponsoring terrorism through its policy of continuously buttressing Israel come what may. Al-Hoss questioned till when is the US going to pursue its double standard policy, namely, its war against terror, on the one hand, and its backing of 'Israeli state terrorism', on the other hand? Al-Hoss claimed that the Arabs and Muslims consider Israel as a terrorist state. (*Al-Safir* 8 October 2003). Affirming al-Hoss's stance, OIC slammed Israel with state terrorism. (See "Islamic nations pledge to fight terrorism, soft-pedal on Iraq, Mideast", *AFP*, 17 October 2003).

44 Augustus Richard Norton, "Hizballah of Lebanon: Extremist Ideas vs. Mundane Politics", *Council on Foreign Relations*, February 2000, 25.

45 Ibid., 27.

46 Augustus R. Norton, "Hizbullah and the Israeli Withdrawal from Southern Lebanon", *Journal of Palestine Studies*, 30 (Autumn 2000), 1, 27.

47 Norton, "Hizballah of Lebanon", 15.

48 Magnus Ranstorp, "The Strategy and Tactics of Hizbullah's Current 'Lebanonization Process'", *Mediterranean Politics*, 3 (Summer 1998) 1, 110 as quoted by Eric Husem, *The Syrian Involvement in Lebanon: An analysis of the role of Lebanon in Syrian regime security, from Ta'if to the death of Hafiz al-Asad (1989-2000)*. Kjeller, Norway: Norwegian Defense Research Establishment, 2002, 63.

49 Husem, *The Syrian Involvement...*, 63-64.

50 A paper delivered at the American University of Beirut (AUB) 2 May 2000, quoted by the *Daily Star*, 3 May 2000. The 'Lebanese nationalists par excellence' premise is reiterated in one of Norton's articles entitled "Hizbullah and the Israeli Withdrawal...", 35. See also Alagha, *Sharqiyyat*, op. cit., 53.

51 Paul Viotti and Mark Kauppi, *International Relations and World Politics: Security, Economy, Identity*. New Jersey: Prentice-Hall, 1997, 164-165.

52 Hinnebusch and Ehteshami , *The Foreign Policy...*, 33.

53 Husem, *The Syrian Involvement...*, 64.

54 Norton, "Hizbullah and the Israeli Withdrawal", 32.

55 The late Imam Shamseddine (died 2001) argued that all the Lebanese people, not the Shi'ite sect, liberated Lebanon. He also remarked that the Israeli backed-up SLA was made up of all sects: Shi'a, Druz, Christians, etc. He said that the 6,000 Lebanese, or so, who sought refuge in Israel are considered as misguided (*dallu*) and will soon return (MBC 21:00 GMT News 24 May 2000). Echoing the official Hizbullah position, Norton remarks that it was a "national victory, not a victory by one sect or militia." "Hizbullah and the Israeli Withdrawal", 32.

56 Hasan Fadlallah, *Al-Khiyar al-Akhar...*, 136.

57 Norton, "Hizballah of Lebanon", 31-2.

58 Norton, "Hizbullah and the Israeli Withdrawal", 26.

59 *Al-Safir* 15 December 2001.

60 See United States Department of State, *Patterns of Global Terrorism*. Washington, D.C.: USGPO, 2002. Cuba, Libya, Sudan, Syria, Iran, Iraq, and North Korea were listed as states sponsoring terrorism. It is worth mentioning that earlier President Bush classified the last three as "The Axis of Evil".

61 *Al-Safir* 22 May 2002; *Daily Star* 22-23 May 2002.

62 Noteworthy, Hizbullah's political ideology does do not warrant such a relationship with *al-Qa'ida* since they are ideological enemies.

63 Most likely, Nasrallah was alluding to Artimage's accusations (See section 6.3). As Byman puts it, "Deputy Secretary of State Richard Armitage has warned of Hezbollah's lethality, noting that 'Hezbollah may be the A team of terrorists,' while 'al Qaeda is actually the B team'". Byman, "Should Hezbollah Be Next?", 55.

64 Byman, "Should Hezbollah Be Next?", 63-64.

65 This trait is attributed to Imam Husayn and Imam Ali. See the manual on jihad and martyrdom entitled, *Al-Jihad wa Khisal Al-Mujahidin [Jihad and the Martyrs' Traits]*. Beirut: Markaz Baqiyyat Allah, 1999, 54. I interpret this statement as a reference to symbolic capital.

66 The US National Security Advisor at the time.

67 Donald Rumsfeld and Dick Cheney had bitter experiences with the Lebanon of the 1980s. See my article in *Sharqiyyat*, op. cit., 38.

68 "Actors can find themselves bound by their public discourse, and conforming to discourse over time can lead to internal adjustments". Marc Lynch, "Jordan's Identity and Interests", in: Telhami and Barnett (eds.), *Identity and Foreign Policy...*, 33. In Nasrallah's speech on the third anniversary of the liberation on 25 May 2003, Nasrallah addressed Bush as "Mister", but referred to Israel as the "idiotic enemy". Walid Jumblat, the Progressive Socialist Party leader in Lebanon and a member of the Lebanese parliament, repeatedly remarked, "Bush has a naïve mind".

69 *Al-Manar* and *al-Nour*; *al-Intiqad* 954 (24 May 2002). Nasrallah's speech was attended by the three representatives of the Lebanese government's Troika, namely, the President, the Prime Minister, and the Speaker of the Parliament.

70 Before the ratification of the Ta'if Agreement in 1990 – that ended the 16-year Lebanese civil war and became Lebanon's new constitution – Hizbullah employed a confrontational discourse in international and regional politics, mainly with the US and Israel. Also, in domestic politics Hizbullah anathematized the whole Lebanese political system, considering the Lebanese state as an apostate.

71 See *al-Intiqad* 956 (7 June 2002), 14; and Nasrallah's speech in the "13th Anniversary of the Death of Imam Khumayni", 6 June 2002, www.nasrollah.org

72 See Abun-Nasr, *Hizbullah: Haqa'iq wa Ab'ad...*, 80-81, 95. See also my article entitled, "Hizbullah, Iran and the Intifada", *ISIM Newsletter*, 9 (January 2002), 35.

73 The slogan labeling Israel as the "Absolute Evil" was also used by Imam Musa al-Sadr. According to Hizbullah, "even if hundreds of years pass by, Israel's existence will continue to be an illegal existence" (Saad-Ghorayeb, *Hizbullah: Politics and Religion*, 135). Ayatullah Fadlallah concedes that the Liberation of Palestine will not materialize during the current Muslim and Arab generations' times (Personal Interview, 27 December 2001).

74 Hizbullah considers the Jews as members of the "People of the Book".

75 Al-Mufti Al-Ja'fari al-Mumtaz, Shaykh Abd al-Amir Qabalan, the Deputy of the Islamic Shi'ite Higher Council, considers Zionism "the worst terrorism". (*Daily Star* 23 May 2002).

76 On 10 and 13 December 2001, Norman Finkelstein gave two lectures in Beirut entitled, "The Middle East and America After Sept. 11" and "U.S. Foreign Policy and the Jewish-American Lobby". The first lecture was delivered at *Masrah Beirut [Beirut Theatre]*, a leftist gathering place. Finkelstein was denied the right to deliver his second lecture at AUB, at *Issam Fares Hall*. After a row between the Student Faculty Association (SFA) and the administration, a compromise was reached: the title was modified to "The American Foreign

Policy in the Middle East: The Palestinian-Israeli Conflict", and the place was changed to the student's cafeteria.

77 He is vocal against "Zionism" and he accuses the Jews of exploiting the holocaust. For instance, see his book entitled *The Holocaust Industry: Reflections on the Exploitation of Jewish Suffering*. London: Verso, 2000.

78 Amin F., personal interview, 13 December 2001.

79 Saad-Ghorayeb, *Hizbullah: Politics and Religion*, 168.

80 See his book entitled *Cult, Ghetto, and State: The Persistence of the Jewish Question*. London: Al Saqi Books, 1983. [Translated from French by Jon Rothschild].

81 Saad-Ghorayeb, *Hizbullah: Politics and Religion*, 169.

82 Qasim, *Hizbullah: Al-Manhaj...*, 322, and the section entitled "The Legitimacy of Targeting Israeli Civilians", 321-325.

83 This stance, as radical as it seems, is neither new, nor is it confined to Hizbullah or Islamic movements. Even before the creation of Israel, Antun S'adé, the Syrian Social Nationalist Party (SSNP) Leader, as early as the 1930s (The party was officially established in November 1932), employed an uncompromising discourse, namely, "Our contact with the Jews is a contact of a foe to a foe". S'adé's statement is clearly anti-Semitic because he discriminates against the Jews as a race. Unlike S'adé, Hizbullah discriminates against the Jews as a religion, not as a race, thus Hizbullah is not anti-Semitic in its overall orientation. (See Saad-Ghorayeb, *Hizbullah: Politics and Religion*, 171 ff.). It is worth mentioning that the abolished UN Resolution 3379, which stipulated Zionism as a form of racism, was clearly anti-Semitic. Hizbullah exploited the knesset's (Israeli parliament's) passing of a bill stopping Palestinians from obtaining Israeli citizenship in order to accuse Israel of being "racist and discriminatory". (See http://www.knesset.gov.il/main/eng/home.asp; AFP 31 July 2003; and "'Communal Punishment and Racial Discrimination': Knesset Approves Barring the Palestinians from Obtaining the [Israeli] Nationality"; *Al-Safir* 1 August 2003).

84 Nasrallah concedes, "I know that this talk has its heavy price from the perspective of the overall *shar'i*, moral, and *jihadi* responsibilities".

85 Nasrallah's speech on the commemoration of "The Jerusalem (Quds) Day", Beirut, 14 December 2001.

86 Saad-Ghorayeb, *Hizbullah: Politics and Religion*, 143.

87 Nasrallah's speech on the commemoration of "The Jerusalem (Quds) Day", Beirut, 14 December 2001.

88 Saad-Ghorayeb, *Hizbullah: Politics and Religion*, 145-6.

89 Again, a reference to dignity as the opposite of humiliation: symbolic capital.

90 See http://media.manartv.com/clips/clip25.ram (Last accessed 25 August 2003).

91 October 2001: Nasrallah's speech commemorating the 'Day of the Wounded' of the Islamic Resistance; 14 December 2001: Nasrallah, 'The Quds Day'.

92 See Levitt, "Hezbollah's West Bank…"

93 Byman, "Should Hezbollah Be Next?", 59.

94 Beirut, *LBCI*, 8:00 pm News, 30 May 2002.

95 Husem, *The Syrian Involvement…*, 69-70.

96 Ibid., 66.

97 Byman, "Should Hezbollah Be Next?", 55.

98 In Western discourse, James Kitfield has coined the term "[the export] of 'the Hezbollah model' to the Israeli-Palestinian conflict". See Byman, "Should Hezbollah Be Next?", 58-59.

99 As repeatedly stated by Nasrallah on various occasions. See Imad Rizq, *Al-Sharq Al-Awsat fi Mizan Al-Ruʻb [The Middle East in the Balance of Terror]*. Beirut: Naufal Group, 2003, 288-291, (Chapter 34 entitled "Export of the Lebanese Resistance [Hizbullah's resistance] – The Model").

100 Byman, "Should Hezbollah Be Next?", 59.

101 Personal interviews, 31 December 2001 and 4 August 2009. Raʻd is *Shura* council member and the head of Hizbullah's parliamentary bloc. Nasrallah also affirmed this stance in his 28 September 2001 speech in commemoration of the first anniversary of the *Intifada*.

102 Interview with Brent Sadler on CNN, 10:00 a.m. News (Beirut time), in the wake of the 10th *Muharram* commemorations, 1423 AH- Sunday, 24 March 2002.

103 Hinnebusch and Ehteshami (eds.), *The Foreign Policy…*, 16.

104 Belatedly, on 21 June 2002, the late Yasir Arafat announced that he had just accepted Clinton's vision, which was based on both the July 2000 Camp David II and the breakthrough achieved later on in Taba. His announcement fell on deaf ears (*Radio Monte Carlo*, 5 GMT News).

105 The Arabs pledged $ 55 million as a monthly aid to the Palestinians, but only delivered 47% of it, i.e. $ 26 million (*Radio Monte Carlo*, 5 GMT News, 13 July 2002).

106 In November 2003, Shaykh Ahmad Yasin contended that the number of Palestinian refugees was five million. However, UNRWA sources estimated that at least a million of these had obtained another nationality, thus being permanently crossed out from UNRWA lists as refugees.

107 At its tenth summit in October 2003, the OIC affirmed the right of return of Palestinian refugees according to UN resolution 194. See George ʻAlam, "What Lebanon Has Gained from the Islamic Summit", *Al-Safir* 20 October 2003.

108 On 16 August 2003, Avi Pazner, the Israeli government spokesman, said: "Israel has no intention, under any circumstance and within any framework, of accepting the return of [Palestinian] refugees in Israeli cities… The (refu-

gee) Palestinians, if they want, can return to their future state". Earlier Sharon affirmed, "I will not allow any Palestinian refugee to come back to Israel, never… I was clear in the past and I repeated in Aqaba: the question of the Palestinian refugees cannot be solved on Israeli territory". See "Israel categorically rejects refugee right of return", AFP 16 August 2003.

109 Blanford, "Hizbullah in the Firing Line", 2.

110 Stephen Saideman, "Thinking Theoretically about Identity and Foreign Policy", in: Telhami and Barnett (eds.), *Identity and Foreign Policy…*, 191.

111 For instance, during the fifty-day cease-fire in the summer of 2003 between Israel and the Palestinians, Hizbullah turned its resource mobilization, domestically threatening the Lebanese government to vehemently oppose its taxation policy. On a theoretical level, this is warranted by the following logic: "Transnational identities, while quite important, may be very limited in their long-term impact because politicians [Nasrallah] respond more strongly to domestic audiences than to opinions held by citizens of other countries". Saideman, "Thinking Theoretically…", 194.

112 Hizbullah refers to the Middle East peace process as the "peace settlement".

113 This is a standard Hizbullah policy iterated by Qasim and Nasrallah on several occasions, some of which are the following: Qasim's speech of 28 May 2002 at AUB entitled, "The Experience of the Resistance and the Future of the *Intifada*", and Nasrallah's speech of 18 June 2002 on the occasion of the "First Convention of the Parliamentarians who are Defending the Palestinian Cause". See *al-Intiqad* 955 (31 May 2002), 16; *al-Intiqad* 958 (21 June 2002), 6-7.

114 Belatedly, after 36 years of occupation, on 26 May 2003 Sharon conceded that Israel could not continue occupying 3.5 million Palestinians living in the West Bank and Gaza forever. For the first time since 1967, Sharon used the term "occupation"; however, this precedent was short-lived since he retrieved the term a day later as a result of judicial advice and under the pressure of a relentless political campaign from the Likud Party and the extreme right. (*Al-Safir* 27 May 2003). On 17 July 2003 the knesset put an end to the debate by officially affirming that the West Bank and Gaza are non-occupied lands. (See http://www.knesset.gov.il/main/eng/home.asp; and *al-Nour*, 5 GMT News, 18 July 2003). Nevertheless, Norton continues to refer to "the Israeli occupation of Gaza and the West Bank". Augustus Richard Norton, "Making War, Making Peace: The Middle East Entangles America", *Current History*, (January 2004), 7.

115 Israel labeled its operation as the "April 2002 West Bank counterterrorism offensive". See Levitt, "Hezbollah's West Bank…"

116 Hizbullah is playing its cards clearly on the table so that Sharon will weigh his options. Nasrallah used the "if" theory, thus falsifying Norton's theory of "calculated ambiguity". See Norton, "Hizballah of Lebanon…", and Nicholas Blanford, "South expert says prospects for peace are 'good'", *Daily Star* 3 May

2000.

117 For a detailed explanation see: 'Abd Al-Husayn Al-Hasan, *Al-Transfer Al-Sahyuni: Al-Mafhum wa Al-Mukhatatat [The 'Zionist' Transfer: Concepts and Tactics]*. Beirut: Markaz Bahith Lil-Dirast, 2003.

118 The same threat was reiterated by Nasrallah on 8 April 2002, in his Speech to Hizbullah's 'Educational and Cultural Cadres'. *Al-Safir* and *Daily Star*, 9 April 2002; *Al-Safir* 11 April 2002.

119 See http://media.manartv.com/palastine/11_ya_shaabi_fi_aldafa-2.ram (Accessed 2 August 2003).

120 Three Hizbullah fighters were arrested by the Jordanian authorities when they were smuggling weapons to the Palestinians. During the Arab Summit in Beirut, attempts were not fruitful at releasing them; however, through a special intervention from the Syrian and Lebanese presidents, they were eventually released. See *al-Safir* 31 May and 3 June 2002. Nasrallah officially thanked the Lebanese president for his efforts. See *Al-Intiqad* 955, (31 May 2002), 2.

121 Brent Sadler's interview, CNN 10:00 a.m. News, 24 March 2002.

122 *Al-Safir* and *Daily Star*, 9 April 2002.

123 Qasim concedes that the operations were a show of solidarity with the *Intifada* and were dedicated to the "pains and sufferings of the Palestinian people". Qasim, *Hizbullah: Al-Manhaj...*, 209.

124 In connection with this, Maloney argues "... Iran's support for resistance groups in Lebanon is another case in point; Iran's present choices are governed by its past professions, despite the changing circumstances of Hezbollah's effective autonomy and the June 2000 Israeli withdrawal". Suzanne Maloney, "Identity and Change in Iran's Foreign Policy", in: *Identity and Foreign Policy...*, 108. "Maloney shows that the identity choices made by Iranian elites constrained them later, so supporting groups in Lebanon was not an easy decision to reverse". Stephen Saideman, "Thinking Theoretically about Identity and Foreign Policy", in: *Identity and Foreign Policy...*, 171. Interpreting Maloney, Saideman labels the Iranian involvement in Lebanon as a "costly polic[y]". Ibid., 179.

125 IRNA 12 April 2002; *Al-Safir* and *Daily Star*, 13 April 2002.

126 *Al-Safir* 15 April 2002.

127 Various Lebanese daily newspapers in the month of April 2002, especially *al-Safir* of 18, 20, and 23 April 2002.

128 Interview with CNN, 17 April 2002. In relation to this, James Abu Rizq, an ex-US Senator, accused the US media of hiding the truth about the Shib'a Farms affirming that they were Lebanese, not Syrian. He decried the US policy that supports Israel; Rizq conceded that Hizbullah played a positive role in Lebanon. (*Al-Nour*, 13 GMT News, 13 June 2002; *al-Safir* and *Daily Star*, 13-14 June 2002).

129 See Ha'aretz 25 June 2002, quoted by *al-Safir* 26 June 2002, and *Daily Star* 28 June 2002. Kaufman is a professor at the Truman Institute at Jerusalem Hebrew University. Mirroring *Ha'aretz* the *Daily Star* writes, "'all the documents found by Kaufman from the period of the French Mandate over Syria and Lebanon, and which was supposed to mark the border between Lebanon and Syria back up the Lebanese argument'... The documents, mostly French maps and arbitration documents from the period, position the Shebaa Farms 'about a kilometer or two inside Lebanon' ... the evidence suggests that locals in the area during the period consistently fell under the jurisdiction of Lebanese authorities." For more details see Kaufman's article entitled "Who Owns the Shebaa Farms?" in *The Middle East Journal*, 56 (Autumn 2002), 4, 576-595.

130 *Al-Nour* and the Lebanese National News Agency; 17 April 2002.

131 See Lebanese daily newspapers of 17 April 2001.

132 The student was referring to Nasrallah's 28 September 2001 speech commemorating the first anniversary of the *Intifada*, in which he affirmed that Hizbullah was ready for direct military intervention in the *Intifada* when the benefit of the Palestinian resistance really would dictate recourse to such an option.

133 Israel adopts the US policy of 'collateral damage' that justifies the 'destruction of civilian life' for the achievement of military aims. The US practiced the collateral damage theory in WWII, when it dropped the atomic bombs on Japan; it also used it in its war against Vietnam, Afghanistan, and Iraq. Concerning Iraq, Hinnebusch quotes Brzezinski: "Our policy is either strike them or starve them, and neither accomplishes our objectives". See Hinnebusch and Ehteshami, *The Foreign Policy...*, 75. It is ironic to note that al-Qa'ida used the same theory for 9/11. Dr. Shafiq Masri argues, "What happened in Jinin is a criminal genocide, and it is incumbent upon the International Court of Justice to look into it". See *al-Intidad* 952 (10 May 2002), 8; and Masri's discussion of crimes against humanity and the fourth Geneva convention of 1949, in 'Terrorism in International Law', 46-47, 55.

134 *Al-Safir*, 25 April 2002.

135 This remark should be viewed in comparison to other Arab countries – where "state control of the media imposes identities from above" – but certainly not in comparison to Western Democracies. "The existence of media is not alone sufficient to constitute a public sphere. For a public sphere to be said to exist, actors must use media to engage in public arguments... An open public sphere offers the structural possibility for public deliberation that might change conceptions of identity and interests." Marc Lynch, "Jordan's Identity and Interests", 30-31. For an overview of Lynch's argument, see his book entitled, *State Interests and Public Spheres*. New York: Colombia University Press, 1999.

136 Saad-Ghorayeb, *Hizbullah: Politics and Religion*, 133.

137 Fadlallah, a Press Release, 12 September 2001, (www.bayynat.org.lb); *al-Safir*, 14 September 2001; Interview by Sarkis Na'um in *al-Nahar*, published in instalments in issues from 19-26 September 2001; Interview with *al-Zaman Magazine* 27 November 2001.

138 A few days after 9/11, Ayatullah Khamina'i condemned the attacks, "Our stance is that of Islam: we denounce the massive killing of people... these calamities are condemned in whichever place they occur". See http://www.nasrollah.org/arabic/khaminai/khitabat/2001/khitabat007.htm (Last accessed 2 July 2004).

139 A Political Declaration issued by the Central Press Office, 16 September 2001, www.hizbollah.org. (English mistakes are not corrected). (Accessed on the same date).

140 Interview with Sayyid Ibrahim Al-Musawi, 7 July 2002.

141 See Saad-Ghorayeb, *Hizbullah: Politics and Religion*, 93-95.

142 Qasim, *Hizbullah: Al-Manhaj...*, 438-440.

143 Hinnebusch and Ehteshami, *The Foreign Policy...*, 76-77.

144 William Blum, *Rogue State: A Guide to the Word's Only Superpower*. Monroe, ME: Common Courage Press, 2000, 30.

145 Samuel P. Huntington, "The Clash of Civilizations?", *Foreign Affairs*, 72 (Summer 1993), 3, 36.

146 Muhammad Yunis, "The Standard of Justice", *Al-Intiqad* 1010 (20 June 2003).

147 This statement was made by President Gerald Ford's envoy to Lebanon in 1976. See "Al-Irhabiyyum al-Judud [The New Terrorists]", *Al-Mustaqbal Magazine*, 410 (29 December 1984), 23.

148 Byman, "Should Hezbollah Be Next?", 56.

149 A Political Declaration issued by the Central Press Office, 1 May 2002. (English mistakes not corrected).

150 See Masri, "Terrorism in International Law", 48-49.

151 On 21 June 2002, GAFI, "Financial Action Task Force on Money Laundering", removed Lebanon from its black list. (*Al-Manar*, 2:30 pm English News, 22 June 2002; *al-Safir* 22 June 2002). Although the decision was supposed to reinforce Lebanon's economic stance, it came at a time when Lebanon was suffering from an estimated $ 30 billion public debt by the end of April of that year (a statement released from the Central Bank, http://www.bdl.gov.lb/; reiterated by *al-Manar*, 7:30 pm News, 29 June 2002). In spite of GAFI's decision and Paris II Conference, held on 23 November 2002 in order to reduce Lebanon's public debt, Riad Salamé, the current governor of the Lebanese Central Bank (BDL), remarked that by November the public debt reached $ 31.3 billion and was estimated to reach $ 31.5 billion by the end of 2002. (See the program entitled "Kalam Al-Nas [People's Talk]", *LBCI*, 28 November 2002, 9: 30 pm). On 24 July 2003, the BDL issued a statement announcing that Lebanon was admitted as a new member to the "Egmont Group of Financial Intelligence

Units", which is an international cooperation group against money laundering. (See http://www.bdl.gov.lb/; *al-Safir* and *Daily Star*, 25 July 2003).

152 CNN, 9:00 pm News local Beirut time, 12 September 2001.

153 *Al-Afkar*, 1006 (26 November 2001), 5. Almost two years later, the CIA director George Tenet remarked, "Hezbollah, as an organization with capacity and worldwide presence, is [al Qaeda's] equal if not far more capable organization. I actually think they're a notch above in many respects". Byman, "Should Hezbollah Be Next?", 57.

154 "In a rare strong defense of Lebanon by a European envoy, Italian ambassador Giuseppe Cassini... termed as 'laughable' allegations that the Bekaa Valley housed bases or members of the notorious Al-Qaeda organization... [Cassini said] Lebanon was the target of 'a series of Israeli rumors.' The Bekaa... 'is neither Afghanistan nor Baluchistan,' referring to the large expanses there that offer perfect hideouts. 'The Bekaa is a small area where everybody, including myself, knows everything... I can escort those who wish to go into the Bekaa to show me where anyone can hide there. It is impossible to hide in the Bekaa, such statements are truly laughable... There's a war raging in the world which is accompanied by nonsensical press reports whose authors don't know what they're talking about'... " *Daily Star* 9 February 2002; LBCI 8:00pm News, 8 February 2002.

155 It seems that Chirac was swayed by Hariri who argued that if Hizbullah is a terrorist organization because it resisted the Israeli occupation of Lebanon, then by the same token De Gaulle and the French resistance as well as George Washington were 'terrorists' because the former fought the German occupation, and the latter the British one.

156 Interview with Riad Salamé. *Al-Afkar*, 1004 (12 November 2001), 34-37.

157 It seems that the Lebanese state has been taking measures to appease the US's financial onslaught on Lebanon. A case in point was the big row that aroused on 8 September 2003 when BDL asked Lebanese banks to disclose the assets of six Hamas leaders, in an attempt to freeze these assets later on. (See Lebanese daily newspapers of 22-26 September 2003). It is worth mentioning that on 16 September 2003, Jordan backed off from a move aiming to freeze Hamas' assets.

158 Lebanese law does not allow the extradition of Lebanese citizens, whatever the criminal charge; rather, it stipulates their trial in Lebanon.

159 Interview with Edmond N'im, the former governor of the Lebanese Central Bank, *Al-Afkar*, 1005 (19 November 2001), 14-15.

160 Masri, "Terrorism in International Law", 50-53.

161 *Al-Safir* 14 December 2001; See also Masri, "Terrorism in International Law", 50.

162 The visit of the four US Congressmen (two of Lebanese origin) as well as Bush's letter to president Lahud in the wake of the commemorations of Lebanese Independence Day constituted an indirect recognition that Shib'a Farms are occupied Lebanese land since the US administration admitted, in that letter, that UNSC Resolution 425 was not completely implemented. See *al-Afkar*, 1006 (26 November 2001), 5; 8.

163 -18 February 2002: 'The Second Meeting of the Trustees of the Jerusalem Foundation' in Beirut (*Majlis Umana' al-Quds*). Qaradawi, the ex-dean of the 'Shari'a College' in Qatar and the head of The European Council of Edicts (*Ifta'*)", is also the president of the 'Jerusalem Foundation'.

164 West Bank and Gaza.

165 *Masa'il Jihadiyya wa Hukm Al-'Amaliyat Al-Istishhadiyyah [Jihadi Issues and the Judgement of Martyrdom Operations]*. Beirut: Dar Al-Wihda Al-Islamiyya, 2002, 83.

166 "Armitage's antipathy for Hizbullah is well known and likely stems from his service in the Reagan administration between June 1983 and May 1989. He served as assistant secretary of defense for international security affairs and was involved with counter terrorism, special operations and Middle East security policies. Armitage's term in office coincided with the suicide bombing of the US Marine barracks in Beirut and the hostage crisis, acts which successive US administrations have blamed on Hizbullah". Nicholas Blanford, "Nasrallah warns US not to seek Hizbullah's end", *Daily Star* 1 August 2003. (http://daily-star.com.lb/01_08_03/art23.asp).

167 A Political Declaration issued by the Central Press Office, 6 September 2002.

168 Contrary to the US stance, the EU did not classify Hizbullah as a terrorist organization; rather, it referred to Lebanese citizens wanted by the US. (*Al-Safir* 29 December 2001). Israel argues, "The EU has banned Hizbullah's military arm but continues to recognize its political wing". (See http://www.knesset.gov.il/lexicon/eng/mia.htm).

169 *Daily Star* 30 August and 6-7 September 2002; *Al-Safir* 30 August and 6 September 2002; LBCI 8:00pm News, 29 August and 5 September 2002. Mistretti reiterated the same stance on 12 November 2002. See *Daily Star* and *Al-Safir*, 13 November 2002. It is worth mentioning that both Italy and France have economic interests and benefits in Lebanon, and both participated in the NATO forces that came to Lebanon in 1983. However, the Italians were unharmed, while the French paratroopers suffered 58 fatalities due to a suicide operation in October.

170 "Previously the EU proscribed... what it calls the Hizbullah External Security Organization (ESO) in December 2001... Hizbullah, the political party represented by MPs in the [Lebanese] Parliament which pursues a broad social agenda and retains a military wing called the Islamic Resistance, was left of the

list… For several years, Hizbullah's efforts have been confined to South Lebanon and the Israeli-Palestinian conflict." Nicolas Blanford, "Hizbullah could end up on EU terrorist list", *Daily Star* 13 September 2003.

171 See Hizbullah's Political Declaration entitled "Hizbollah denounces the Canadian Government's decision for adding the party on its list of terrorist organizations" issued by the Central Press Office, 12 December 2002; *Al-Intiqad* 983 (13 December 2002), 5; *Al-Safir* and *Daily Star*, 13 December 2002.

172 See Nasrallah's speech, and *Al-Intiqad* 981-2 (29 November 2002), 12-13.

173 See the program entitled "*Ahzab Lubnan: Al-Hiwar* [Lebanese Parties: The Dialogue]", *NBN*, 5 January 2003, 8:15 pm.

174 "Shortly after attending the opening ceremonies of the October 2002 Francophone summit in Beirut, Canadian Prime Minister Jean Chrétien was asked by reporters about Hezbollah Secretary-General Hasan Nasrallah, who had been seated nearby at the event. 'Who is he?' Chrétien replied, 'I don't know him.' Minutes later, he was asked if Hezbollah was a terrorist organization. 'Well, I don't know,' he answered. Canadian officials later explained that Chrétien had not been adequately briefed, but the gaffe-prone prime minister's remarks signified precisely the Canadian government's policy toward Hezbollah prior to December 2002". Ziad K. Abdelnour, "The Lebanese-Canadian Crises", *Middle East Intelligence Bulletin* 5, (January 2003), 1, 1. http://www.meib.org/articles/0301_l3.htm

175 Blanford, "Hizbullah in the Firing Line", 4.

176 Byman, "Should Hizbollah Be Next?", 64.

177 *Al-Safir* 27 June 2003.

178 As early as May 2003, the Lebanese government and Hizbullah tried to counter the Australian move; however, their efforts were of no avail.

179 *Al-Nour*, 5 GMT News, 17 June 2003; *al-Safir* 18 June 2003.

180 *Al-Liwa'* 24 June 2003.

181 "The Story of US Contacts with Hizbullah: Unofficial Dialogue for Years in Arab and European Capitals", *Al-Mustaqbal* 1982 (19 July 2005), 3. *Al-Mustaqbal* is the newspaper of the Western allied March 14 Sa'd al-Hariri, the son of the late PM Rafiq al-Hariri.

182 Josie Ensor, "Britain open to contacts with Hizbullah", *DailyStar* 1 December 2009.

183 See *al-Akhbar*, Press Secrets (23 September 2009): www.al-akhbar.com/.

184 Chapter II: "Lebanon", Section 7: "Lebanon and International Relations", 55-56.

185 Chapter I: "Hegemony and Mobilization", Section 1: "The World and Western-American Hegemony", 21.

186 Chapter II: "Lebanon", Section 7: "Lebanon and International Relations", 56.

187 See the program entitled "Ahzab Lubnan: Al-Hiwar [Lebanese Parties: The Dialogue]", *NBN*, 5 January 2003, 8:15 pm. On 28 September 2001, Nassrallah

stressed, "Sept. 11 might change the US and the face of the world, but not us [Hizbullah]". On 2 October 2001 Nasrallah repeated that nothing has changed since September 11: "Our culture is that of *jihad*, resistance, and martyrdom". He added that Hizbullah still opts for the "military, *jihadi* option" to liberate Lebanon from Israeli occupation and to support the Palestinian *Intifada* with all its might. On 22 October 2001, while commemorating the "Day of the Wounded of the Islamic Resistance" Nasrallah affirmed, "Nothing will change at all for us after September 11: the resistance continues as long as Shiba is occupied, our prisoners of war are detained in Israeli prisons, and the Palestinian people are slaughtered. The Great Satan [the US] that issues terrorist lists is a terrorist state that has no right to classify people as terrorists or not".

188 Lynch, "Jordan's Identity and Interests", 31.

189 'The Muslim Council of *Ulama*' acknowledged that in points seven and eight of its final declaration: "Hizbullah in Lebanon is the vivid embodiment of the will of the *umma*". See *Masa'il Jihadiyya*…, 83.

190 Saad-Ghorayeb, *Hizbullah: Politics and Religion*, 191.

191 Directly after the end of Cast Lead, A Hizbullah cell, whose mission was to smuggle weapons and aid to Gaza, was uncovered in Egypt. Nasrallah not only admitted the charge but also took pride in portraying Hizbullah as the only Arab party who came to the aid of the under siege Palestinians, calling on other Arab regimes to do the same. See Nasrallah's speech of 11 April 2009 on "Answering the Egyptian Accusations (*radd 'ala al-ittihamat al-masriyya*)": http://www.youtube.com/watch?v=7Oe_K2TJdp4&feature=related.

192 International Crisis Group (ICG) refers to the 'Palestinianization' of Hizbullah. Reinoud Leenders, "Hizbullah: Rebel Without a Cause?" *ICG Middle East Briefing Paper*, 30 July 2003, 9. (http://www.crisisweb.org/projects/middleeast/arab-israeliconflict/reports/A401070_30072003.pdf).

193 "The goal of ridding the region of militant and armed non-state actors no longer is seen as a by-product of US peacemaking, as it has been at times in the past – but as a priority objective in and of itself that is likely to be pursued relentlessly." "Hizbullah: Rebel Without a Cause?", 6.

194 In July 2003, a European diplomat, stationed in Lebanon, argued, "By branding Hizbollah entirely as a terrorist organisation, the US shot itself in the foot: This way one excludes a dialogue and one ends up with no direct influence over the party and with less credibility among many Lebanese who see, instead of terrorism, the party's hospitals and social services." "Hizbullah: Rebel Without a Cause?", 19, note 138. Byman seconds this analysis by arguing, "Even some government officials in Europe and Asia see Hezbollah as more of a social movement than a terrorist organization". Byman, "Should Hezbollah Be Next?", 64.

4 POLITICAL VIOLENCE: SUICIDE OPERATIONS

1   This chapter is a revised, updated, and modified version of my earlier article
    "Hizbullah and Martyrdom." ORIENT: *Deutsche Zeitschrift für Wirtschaft und
    Kultur des Orients*. 45.1 (March 2004): 47-74.

2   "Identity and Goals" is Hizbullah's 2004 self-description, which could be
    considered as an abridged, updated, and modified version of Hizbullah's 1985
    Open Letter or Manifesto.

3   Zvi Mazel, the Israeli ambassador in Stockholm, destroyed an artwork – fea-
    turing her as Snow White swimming in a pool of blood – because he consi-
    dered it "a monstrous glorification of suicide bombers and an incitement to
    genocide against the Israeli people." Even though the artwork was produced by
    an Israeli-born Jew (Dror Feiler, and his wife, Gunilla Skoeld Feiler), Sharon
    commended Mazel's reaction "in the face of this fresh outbreak of anti-Semi-
    tism." See "Israeli ambassador kicked out of Swedish museum after vandalizing
    art", and "Sweden and Israel in furious diplomatic row over art scandal", AFP,
    17 and 18 January 2004.

4   See "Majority of the Palestinians Support Martyrdom Operations", *al-Safir* 20
    October 2003.

5   See *al-Sharq Al-Awsat* 2 February 2002 as cited by Joyce M. Davis, *Martyrs:
    Innocence, Vengeance and Despair in the Middle East*. New York: Palgrave
    Macmillan , 2003, 79.

6   She had a son and a daughter: 'Abida, 3 years old, and Duha, 18 months. Reem
    Al-Riyashi originated from a wealthy family who owns a battery factory. See
    Salih Al-Masri, "Reem Al-Riyashi: An Ideal Wife and a Mother Who Adores
    her Children", *al-Intiqad* 1041 (23 January 2004).

7   See Lebanese daily newspapers of 15 January 2004.

8   See "Israel Seals Off Gaza Strip after Hamas Suicide Attack", AFP 15 January
    2004.

9   *Al-Manar* 7:30 pm News, 14 January 2004.

10 *Al-Nour* 6:00 GMT News, 20 January 2004. See also Imad 'Id, "Shaykh Ahmad
    Yasin in a Special Dialogue with *Al-Intiqad*: The Palestinian Woman was in the
    Army of Substitutes and its Role has Come", *Al-Intiqad* 1041 (23 January 2004).
    Shaykh Yasin made the analogy between prayer and *jihad* as two religious
    duties binding for both genders.

11 See "Hamas declarers 'open' war on Israel after slaying of spiritual leader
    Sheikh Ahmed Yasin" and "Israel kills Sheikh Yasin, Hamas pledges all-out
    war", AFP, 22 March 2004.

12 Hizbullah substantiated its words with deeds through a symbolic support
    of and solidarity with the *Intifada*, when 'the Brigades of the Great Martyr
    and Leader, Shaykh Ahmad Yasin' targeted all the Israeli posts in Shib'a with

massive fire power (65 rockets and mortar shells). Hizbullah even trespassed the 'redline', for the second time since March-April 2002, when it 'silenced' an Israeli artillery gunship, which was shelling Lebanese territory from the Syrian Golan Heights. (See Lebanese Daily Newspapers of 23 March 2004; *Al-Manar* and *Al-Nour* 22 March 2004).

13   See *al-Intiqad* 1054 (23 April 2004).

14   http://english.bayynat.org.lb/se_002/news/rantese19042004.htm

15   For instance, see "IDF releases Cast Lead casualty numbers", by Yaakov Lappin at: http://www.jpost.com/servlet/Satellite?cid=1237727552054&pagename=JPOS t%2FJPArticle%2FshowFull (Accessed 26 March 2009).

16   See "Medics identify 1,505th victim of Gaza assault", at: http://www.maannews. net/en/index. php?opr=ShowDeta ils&ID=39171 (Accessed 11 July 2009).

17   Juan Cole and Nikki Keddie (eds.), *Shiʻism and Social Protest*. New Haven: Yale University Press, 1986, 28.

18   Fouad Ajami, *The Vanished Imam: Musa al-Sadr and the Shia of Lebanon*. Ithaca: Cornell University Press, 1986.

19   "Prologue in Heaven": cf. J.W. von Goethe, *Faust*. Baltimore, MD: Penguin Books, 1983. The Martyr's Mother: cf. Hala Jaber's "Introduction" in *Hizbullah: Born with a Vengeance*. New York: Colombia University Press, 1997; and cf. Amal Saad-Ghorayeb, *Hizbullah: Politics and Religion*. London: Pluto Press, 2002, 127-133.

20   For a distinction among the 'four senses of martyrdom' employed in this chapter, see Section 4.3.

21   In its war of attrition against the Israeli forces occupying southern Lebanon, Hizbullah conducted twelve martyrdom operations *(ʻamaliyyat istishadiyya)* targeting only Israeli military and intelligence personnel occupying south Lebanon. See Hasan Fadlallah, *Suqut al-Wahim: Hazimat al-Ihtilal wa Intisar al-Muqawama fi Lubnan [The Collapse of the Illusion: The Defeat of the Occupier and the Victory of the Resistance in Lebanon]*. Beirut: Dar al-Hadi, 2001, 233.

22   This trait is attributed to Imam Husayn and Imam Ali. See the manual on *jihad* and martyrdom entitled, *Al-Jihad wa Khisal Al-Mujahidin*, op. cit., 54. I interpret this statement as a reference to symbolic capital.

23   This bears a striking resemblance to Nasrallah's political discourse, especially his speeches – on 20, 22 and 25 May 2001; and 23 May 2002 – commemorating the first and second anniversaries of the Israeli withdrawal. Cf. André Malraux, *Man's Fate*. New York: Vintage Books, 1990.

24   Compiled from Nasrallah's speech delivered after his son's death on 13 September 1997. See *'Irs Aylul:Qissat al-Shahid Hadi Hasan Nasrallah [September's Wedding: The Story of the Martyr Hadi Hasan Nasrallah]*. Beirut: Dar Al-Amir, 2001; and *Sjil Al-Nur: Qanadil Ila Al-Zaman Al-Akhar [Al-Nur's Record: Lanterns to the Hereafter]*. A book by Hizbullah's Central Information Office,

October 1998.

25 *Al-Jihad wa Khisal Al-Mujahidin*, 31-37.

26 See Farhad Khosrokhavar, *Les Nouveaux Martyrs D'Allah [God's New Martyrs]*.
Paris: Flammarion, 2002, 12-20

27 Ahmad Moussalli, *Historical Dictionary of Islamic Fundamentalist Movements
in the Arab World, Iran, and Turkey*. London: The Scarecrow Press, Inc., 1999,
98, 154-155.

28 See Nasrallah's speech on the first day of *Muharram* 1425 AH, 20 February
2004.

29 See Nasrallah's speech in the weekly commemoration of the martyrdom of
Youssef Mer'i, 14 March 2004.

30 For instance, Russett et al. argue, "terrorism is indeed the weapon of groups
that are relatively weak." See Bruce Russett, Harvey Starr, and David Kinsella,
World Politics: The Menu for Choice. New York: Bedford/St. Martin's, 2000,
209. Hinnebusch also concedes that terrorism is the "weapon of the weak". See
Raymond Hinnebusch and Anoushiravan Ehteshami (eds.), *The Foreign Policy
of Middle East States*. Boulder, Co.: Lynne Rienner Publishers, 2002, 77. The
same view is shared by Paul Viotti and Mark Kauppi, *International Relations
and World Politics: Security, Economy, Identity*. New Jersey: Prentice-Hall, 1997,
162.

31 See Stephan C. Wright and Linda R. Tropp, "Collective Action in Response
to Disadvantage: Intergroup Perceptions, Social Identification, and Social
Change", in: Iain Walker and Heather J. Smiths (eds.), *Relative Deprivation:
Specification, Development and Integration*. Cambridge: Cambridge University
Press, 2002, 203, 200-201.

32 Al-Musawi worked in *al-Manar* TV as the political program's editor, was the
editor-in-chief of Hizbullah's weekly mouthpiece *al-Intiqad*, and is currently
the party's spokesman. He holds a Ph.D. in Islamic studies from Birmingham
University.

33 Psychological approaches to revolution formulate a frustration-aggression
hypothesis that propounds that the phenomenon of 'relative deprivation' is
primarily responsible for revolution. According to proponents of this theory,
"the individual's perception of a discrepancy between his value expectations – economic, political, social – and gratification of those expectations" is
the reason behind a 'persisting deprivation'. This 'persisting deprivation' is a
motivating state for anger that leads to aggression as its inherently satisfying
response (James Davies (ed.), *When Men Revolt and Why?* New York: The Free
Press, 1971, 294). Thus, theorists such as Ted Gurr and James Davies under-
score this discontented 'state of mind' as the chief determinant of revolution
rather than the actual supply (or lack of) of material needs, social and political
equality, etc. (Ibid., 136). More specifically, Gurr considers religious cleavages

to be one of the chronic sources of deprivation – inducing conflict. Such a source intensifies social conflict, especially when basic values are at stake that raises the potential for extremist political movements (Ibid., 299).

34 See al-Musawi's article entitled "Despair, oppression and faith are midwives to martyrdom", *Daily Star*, 8 April 2002, 7.

35 Moojan Momen, *The Phenomenon of Religion: A Thematic Approach*. Oxford: Oneworld Publications, 1999, 230.

36 According to Khamina'i, "martyrdom constitutes the highest level of jihad in the name of God". See Al-Imam Al-Khamina'i, *'Itr Al-Shahada [The Perfume of Martyrdom]*. Beirut: Al-Dar Al-Islamiyyah, 2001, 16-17.

37 Moussalli, *Historical Dictionary…*, 185-6. Antoun concurs with Moussalli that "martyrdom is the ultimate evidence of the activist orientation of fundamentalism–action to the point of death." See Richard T. Antoun, *Understanding Fundamentalism: Christian, Islamic, and Jewish Movements*. Oxford: Altamira Press, 2001, 147.

38 Based on fieldwork conducted three times in Lebanon: from 27 September 2001 till 26 February 2002; from 20 June 2002 till 6 March 2003; and from 9 November 2003 till 6 December 2003.

39 As previously stated, she labeled her son as "an anti-Destin, a bronze hawk, *a hard-core altruist*, whose greatest duty and source of *pride [honor and dignity]* is to sacrifice himself for the well-being of his country"; "This is the greatest *pride* that can befall a mother". (Italics added for emphasis).

40 Pierre Bourdieu, *The Field of Cultural Production*. Cambridge: Polity Press, 1993, 7; *In Other Words: Essays Towards a Reflexive Sociology*. Cambridge: Polity Press, 1990, 22, 111, as cited in Kane, *Muslim Modernity…*, 21.

41 See Hizbullah's "Identity and goals".

42 "Hezbollah also sees itself committed in introducing the true picture of Islam, the Islam that is logical. Committed to introduce the civilized Islam to humanity". Hizbullah's "Identity and goals".

43 Kane, *Muslim Modernity…*, 22. It is worth mentioning that (4:95) is not the only Qur'anic verse that conveys the idea of symbolic capital. There are so many others, which are frequently quoted by Hizbullah; here, I refer to the most salient. *Jihad* as a means of accumulating symbolic capital is warranted in (61:11-12) and in (9: 111). Martyrdom as a means of accumulating symbolic capital is merited in (3:169).

44 Dignity is defined as "the opposite of humiliation" at the hands of the enemy; and "death [is preferable] to humiliation". As will be demonstrated later, Nasrallah uses the same discourse of 'dignity', or symbolic capital in order to justify martyrdom operations against the Israeli occupying army, so do the relatives of martyrs when they endeavor to offer a rationale and justification for martyrdom.

45 The SSNP martyrdom operations and resistance to Israel are based on its political ideology as stipulated by S'adé. Antun S'adé, the Lebanese Christian founder of the secular SSNP argued, "Our martyrs are the indication of our victory"; "Our contact with the Jews is a contact of a foe to a foe." S'adé formed a brigade to fight Israel, and, in 1949, he was executed by the Lebanese state by a firing squad. For a discussion on the ideology of SSNP see, for instance, Labib Z. Yamak, *The Syrian Social Nationalist Party: An Ideological Analysis.* Harvard: Center for Middle Eastern Studies, 1966; Haytham A. Kader, *The Syrian Social Nationalist Party: Its Ideology and Early History.* Beirut: Dar Fikr, 1990; and Christoph Schaumann. "The Generation of Broad Expectations", *Die Welt Des Islams*, 41 (2001), 2, 174-205.

46 Although the Muslim tradition distinguishes among eight categories of martyrdom all referring to 'premature or violent death', in this chapter I mainly confine myself to the fist category, namely, martyrdom in the name of God or *jihad*. Basing himself on the concordance of *hadith*, Wensinck writes that in the Muslim tradition "The martyrs are seven, apart from death in Allah's way [*jihad*]. He that dies as the victim of an epidemic is a martyr; he that dies by being drowned, is a martyr; he that dies from diarrhoea, is a martyr; he that dies by fire, is a martyr; he that dies by being struck by a house or a wall falling into ruins, is a martyr; the woman who dies in childbed, is a martyr". A. J. Wensinck, "The Oriental Doctrine of the Martyrs", in: *Mededeelingen der Koninklijk Akademie van Wetenschappen, Afdeeling Letterkunde; dl. 53, nr. 6.* Amsterdam: Koninklijk Akademie van Wetenschappen (KNAW publications), 1922, 172-73.

47 Momen, *The Phenomenon of Religion...*, 554. The book entitled *Al-Jihad wa Khisal Al-Mujahidin* cites on page 54 two other *hadiths* that convey a similar meaning, namely, "the martyr longs to return to this world to be martyred again". So does Wensinck, "The Oriental Doctrine of the Martyrs", 149, 152.

48 Wensinck, "The Oriental Doctrine of the Martyrs", 147-48.

49 Ibid., 150.

50 Compiled from an extended dialogue with Hizbullah's deputy secretary-general, Shaykh Na'im Qasim, on the subject of '*Al-Shahada wa al-'Ithar*' [*Martyrdom and 'Preference'*] in the program entitled "*Al-Din wa Al-Hayat [Religion and life]*", Al-Manar, 10 October 2002; Al-Khamina'i, '*Itr Al-Shahada...*; and *Al-Jihad wa Khisal Al-Mujahidin...*; Al-Shaykh Ahmad Al-Nasiri, *Al-Mawt Al-Muqadas: Dirasa 'an Al-'Amaliyyat Al-Istishhadiyya 'inda Al-Shi'a [Divine Death: A Study on the Martyrdom Operations of the Shi'a].* First edition. Beirut: Dar Al-Mahajja Al-Bayda', 2005.

51 Prophet Muhammad said: "The martyrs have certain dignities [*karamat*] that are not ascribed to the Prophets including me. If I die, I am washed and wrapped in a burial shroud; however, the martyr is neither washed nor wrapped in

a burial shroud… The Angels wash him." Wensinck quotes Bukhari, *Jana'iz*, b.74: "In the works on law and tradition it is expressly said that martyrs may not be washed." Wensinck, "The Oriental Doctrine of the Martyrs", 171. For more details see Al-Shaykh Muhammad Bin Al-Hasan Al-Hurr Al-'Amili, *Wasa'il Al-Shi'a [Shi'ite Rituals]*. Beirut: Mu'assat Al-Hulul, Bayt Ihya' Al-Turath, 1993, 506-511, *hadith*s 1 to 12, *abwab ghusl al-mayyit* (sections of the washing of the dead), specifically *ghusl al-shahid* (the washing of the martyr), in *bab* 14 (section 14), *hadith* 7.

52 Although Imam Husayn did not blow himself up (simply because there were no explosives at the time), he is classified in this category. According to Shi'ite religious doctrine, Imam Husayn is considered *sayyid al-shuhada*, the 'Lord of the Martyrs' and 'The Immortal Maryr', as Enayat puts it, since he faced a superior army in the battlefield knowing for sure that he was going to die. See Hamid Enayat, *Modern Islamic Political Thought: The Response of the Shi'i and Sunni Muslims to the Twentieth Century*. London: Macmillian, 1982, 181-194. Enayat includes martyrdom as one of the three 'aspects of Shi'i modernism', the other two being constitutionalism and *taqiyya* (expedient dissimulation).

53 Al-Khamina'i, *'Itr Al-Shahada...*, 17.

54 Wensinck, "The Oriental Doctrine of the Martyrs", 153. Nasrallah seconds this analysis in his speech on the first day of *Muharram* 1425 AH, 20 February 2004.

55 Since it is not every citizen's duty to fight the enemy on the battlefield.

56 *Al-Nour*, "Paper Views", 5:30 GMT, 15 January 2004.

57 Antoun, *Understanding Fundamentalism...*, 100.

58 See "Bush adviser Condoleeza Rice peddles democratic blueprint for Middle East", AFP 7 August 2003.

59 See her book entitled: *Army of Roses: Inside the World of Palestinian Women Suicide Bombers*. PA: Rodale Press, 2003. See also the article entitled, "Equality in death – Barbara Victor lifts the veil on the world of the women suicide bombers", *The Observer*, (25 April 2004). Guardian Unlimited © Guardian Newspapers Limited 2004, at: http://observer.guardian.co.uk/magazine/story/0,11913,1200794,00.html (Accessed on the same day).

60 Judith Palmer Harik, *Hezbollah: The Changing Face of Terrorism*. London: I.B. Tauris, 2004, 26.

61 Momen, *The Phenomenon of Religion...*, 231.

62 "Toward an Islamic Liberal Theology: Muhammad Husayn Fadlallah and the Principles of Shi'i Resurgence", in: Ibrahim M. Abu-Rabi', *The Intellectual Origins of Islamic Resurgence in the Modern Arab World*. Albany, N.Y.: State University of New York, 1996, 242.

63 Fadlallah's views stand in sharp contrast to Antoun and Khosrokhavar who offer a psychological explanation of martyrdom.

64 Muhammad Husayn Fadlallah, *Min Ajl Al-Islam [For The Sake of Islam]*. Beirut: Dar Al-Ta'arruf, 1989, 49, as cited by Abu-Rabi', *The Intellectual Origins...*, 242.

65 Antoun, *Understanding Fundamentalism...*, 101.

66 Khosrokhavar, *Les Nouveaux Martyrs D'Allah*, 230. In an earlier work, Khosrokhavar discussed "the four modalities of a martyr": (1) "The martyr's languishing of the self"; (2) "The martyr as potlatch"; (3) "The martyr's body as an obstacle to the desire of totality"; and (4) "The death of the body and the adoration of the 'Guide' [*Rahbar*]". See Farhad Khosrokhavar, *L'Islamisme et la Mort: Le Martye Revolutionnare en Iran [Islamism and Death: The Revolutionary Martyrs in Iran]*. Paris: L'Harmattan, 1995, 258-267.

67 Abu-Rabi', *The Intellectual Origins...*, 242.

68 Council of Muslim Ulama, *Masa'il Jihadiyya wa Hukm Al-'Amaliyat Al-Istishhadiyyah [Jihadi Issues and the Judgement of Martyrdom Operations]*. Beirut: Dar Al-Wihda Al-Islamiyya, 2002, 27-28.

69 Antoun, *Understanding Fundamentalism...*,43.

70 As quoted by Davis, *Martyrs: Innocence...*, 45. I take this as a reference to symbolic capital: "Dignity is the opposite of humiliation, and death to humiliation".

71 See the program entitled "*Al-Din wa Al-Hayat [Religion and Life]*", Al-Manar, 10 October 2002.

72 IRNA 14 April 2002.

73 *Masa'il Jihadiyya...*, 37-38.

74 Sayyid Muhammad Husayn Fadlallah, *Al-Islam wa Mantiq al-Quwwa [Islam and the Logic of Power]*. Third edition. Beirut: Dar Al-Malak, 1985, preface.

75 Abu-Rabi', *The Intellectual Origins...*, 242.

76 Ibrahim Mousawi, "Fadlallah Explains Religious Basis for Suicide Attacks", *DailyStar* 8 June 2002.

77 Ibid.

78 Ibid.

79 "It is the pilgrimage especially which for women is the substitute of warfare". Wensinck, "The Oriental Doctrine of the Martyrs", 154.

80 *Al-Safir* 2 April 2002. Cf. Amal-Saad's contention that "Fadlu'llah never did issue a *fatwa* in support of the martyrdom operation..." in: *Hizbullah: Politics and Religion*, 132.

81 Musawi, "Fadlallah Explains...", *Daily Star* 8 June 2002.

82 Al-Nasiri, *Al-Mawt Al-Muqadas...*, 53.

83 *Masa'il Jihadiyya...*, 82-83.

84 Ibid., 35-36. This could be viewed as a retributional measure to Israel's adoption of the theory of collateral damage.

85 A similar view emerged, in April 2002, when Israel invaded the West Bank and exchanged gunfire with Hizbullah in the occupied part of south Lebanon. In the wake of these events, Christian religious and political leaders voiced their support for the Intifada and Hizbullah's resistance. For instance, the Maronite Cardinal argued that what is happening to the Palestinians is "abhorrent", and that Hizbullah has the right to liberate Lebanese occupied land. He added that he has great confidence in Hizbullah and its rationalization in managing the conflict. (Various Lebanese daily newspapers in the month of April 2002, especially *al-Safir* of 18, 20, and 23 April 2002). Even the banned Christian rightist 'Lebanese Forces' issued a declaration supporting the *Intifada* and Hizbullah's resistance. (See Lebanese daily newspapers of 17 April 2001).

86 A *fatwa* is a non-binding religious edict. Thus, a Christian cannot give a *fatwa* to the Muslims; he can only issue an opinion. See "Edmond N'im Gives a 'Fatwa' Legitimising Martyrdom Operations: There is No Distinction Between a Settler and an Israeli Military", *Al-Safir* 19 April 2002.

87 Ibid. This resembles Fadlallah's notion, "One must face power with equal or superior power."

88 For definitions on 'terrorism' from the perspective of public international law see Von Glahn, *Law among Nations...*, 275-277ff.

89 *Yadi'ot Ahronot* 7 June 2002, as quoted by *Al-Safir* 8 June 2002.

90 As quoted in Davis, *Martyrs...*, 70-71. See also Boaz Ganor, "A New Strategy Against the Terror" at: http://www.ict.org.il/articles/articledet.cfm?articleid=4 (Accessed 12 December 2003).

91 Al-Nasiri, *Al-Mawt Al-Muqadas...*, 60-69.

92 See Tom L. Beauchamp, *Philosophical Ethics: An Introduction to Moral Philosophy*. Second edition. New York: McGraw-Hill, Inc., 1991, 68-79, 241-244, 246-248; and Peter Singer, *Practical Ethics*. Second edition. Cambridge: Cambridge University Press, 1999, 243, 321, 334.

93 Etan Kohlberg, "Medieval Muslim Views on Martyrdom" in: *Mededeelingen der Koninklijk Akademie van Wetenschappen, Afdeeling Letterkunde; dl. 60, nr. 7*. Amsterdam: KNAW publications, 1997, 303.

94 Ibid., 305.

95 Ibid., 306.

96 Ibid., 307.

97 Ibid., 306. At the time of writing his article, all the suicide bombers, in Israel, for instance, were males.

98 Fadlallah, a Press Release, 12 September 2001, (www.bayynat.org.lb); *al-Safir*, 14 September 2001; Interview by Sarkis Na'um in *al-Nahar*, published in instalments in issues from 19-26 September 2001; Interview with *al-Zaman Magazine* 27 November 2001.

99 'Self-sacrifice' is a euphemism for martyrdom.

100 This is corroborated by Wensinck: "suicide, under whatever circumstances, is forbidden in Islam". Wensinck, "The Oriental Doctrine of the Martyrs", 153.

101 Mousawi, "Fadlallah Explains Religious Basis…"

102 Qasim insinuates that Islamic movements and Hizbullah employ upbringing on the concept of martyrdom; that is why they were and still are victorious. While nationalistic movements use upbringing on the concept of victory, reaping nothing but defeat and treason. Qasim, *Hizbullah: Al-Manhaj…*, 71.

103 Strict obedience and discipline is labeled by Hizbullah as *al-ta'a*, which conveys a religious connotation (Nasrallah, Interview with *al-Safir*, 28 June 2000; Hasan Fadlallah, *Al-Khiyar al-Akhar…*, 125). Shaykh Nabil Qawuq, Hizbullah's representative in the south, repeatedly stated: "When the *umma* comes closer to *al-ta'a*, it comes closer to victory."

104 "And they give food, despite their love of it, to the destitute, the orphan and the captive. [They say]: 'We only feed you for the sake of Allah; We do not want from you any reward or gratitude.'" (76:8-9) Qasim broadens the mandate of *ithar* – from fasting for three days and preferring to feed others, rather than the self – to include the giving of blood for the sake of the *umma*.

105 Qasim, *Hizbullah: Al-Manhaj…*, 74-77.

106 See the program entitled "*Al-Din wa Al-Hayat [Religion and Life]*", Al-Manar, 10 October 2002.

107 See http://media.manartv.com/clips/clip11.ram (Accessed 10 January 2004).

108 Harik, *Hezbollah: The Changing Face of Terrorism*, 26.

109 See Sayyid Hasan Nasrallah's speech delivered in *Nabi Shit* on 16 February 2003 in commemoration of the martyrdom of Sayyid Abbas al-Musawi and Shaykh Raghib Harb, as well as the 18th anniversary of the inauguration of the party.

110 Saad-Ghorayeb, *Hizbullah: Politics and Religion*, 133.

111 Harik, *Hezbollah: The Changing Face of Terrorism*, 26.

112 Harik, *Hezbollah: The Changing Face of Terrorism*, 2; 168.

113 Again, a reference to dignity as the opposite of humiliation: symbolic capital.

114 See http://media.manartv.com/clips/clip25.ram (Accessed 12 January 2004).

115 Symbolic capital as *jihad* and martyrdom.

116 See Rohan Gunaratna, "Suicide Terrorism: A Global Threat", in: Pamela L. Griset and Sue Mahan, *Terrorism in Perspective*. London: Sage Publications, 2003, 220-225; and Gus Martin, *Understanding Terrorism: Challenges, Perspectives, and Issues*. London: Sage Publications, 2003, 131, 259-262.

117 For instance, Anton Balasingham is one of the LTTE Christian leaders.

118 According to Martin, the act was conducted by a girl in May 1991. *Understanding Terrorism…*, 131.

119 Gunaratna, "Suicide Terrorism…", 221.

120 Ibid.

121 Khosrokhavar, *Les Nouveaux Martyrs D'Allah…*, 221.

122 In line with the stipulations of the Ta'if Agreement, which ended the Lebanese civil war and became Lebanon's new constitution in 1990, all militias were disbanded with the exception of the Islamic Resistance, Hizbullah's military wing, because it was and still is classified as a resistance movement, and not as a militia. Thus ever since 1990, Hizbullah virtually monopolized the resistance against Israeli forces occupying southern Lebanon.

123 Hizbullah's *istishhadiyyin* listed chronologically: 1 Ahmad Qasir (11 November 1982); 2 'Ali Safiyyeddine (13 April 1983); 3 Ja'far Al-Tayyar (14 October 1983); 4 Aborted operation killing 2 Hizbullahis (1983); 5 'Amer Kalakish (11 March 1988); 6 Haytham Dbuq (19 August 1988): 7 Abdallah 'Atwi (19 October 1988); 8 Shaykh As'ad Birru (9 August 1989); 9 Ibrahim Dahir (21 September 1992); 10 Salah Ghandur (25 April 1995); 11 'Ali Ashmar (20 March 1996); 12 'Ammar Husayn Hammud (30 December 1999). See Amin Mustapha, *Al-Muqawama fi Lubnan: 1948-2000 [The Resistance in Lebanon: 1948-2000]*. Beirut: Dar Al-Hadi, 2003, 459-463; *Kawakib Al-Nasr: Qisas Shuhada' Al-Muqawama al-Isla-miyya [Lanterns of Victory: The Stories of the Martyrs of the Islamic Resistance]*. 2 Volumes. Beirut: Dar Al-Amir, 2001; and *Al-'Amaliyyat Al-Istishadiyya: Al-Maqawama Al-Wataniyya Al-Lubnaniyya (1982-1985) [Martyrdom Operati-ons: Lebanese National Resistance (1982-1985)]*. Introduction by the late Syrian president Hafiz Al-Asad. Beirut: Al-Markaz Al-'Arabi lil Ma'lumat, 1985.

124 Hizbullah placed safeguards on martyrdom operations; the most important is that the number of Israeli soldiers killed should be 30 and above. (See Mus-tapha, *Al-Muqawama fi Lubnan…*, 461). However, not all Hizbullah martyrs could accomplish this goal; only Ahmad Qasir, the first Hizbullah martyr, did. Qasir detonated himself in the Israeli headquarters in Tyre, in southern Lebanon, killing around 76 military officers and wounding 20 others. Begin, the Israeli Prime Minister at the time, declared a three-day mourning in Israel arguing that this was Israeli's worst calamity since its creation in 1948. (See Nasrallah's speech on 28 December 2000, on the 'Jerusalem Day Celebration'). In Qasir's honor, Hizbullah celebrates 'Martyrdom Day' annually on the ele-venth of November.

125 Khosrokhavar, *Les Nouveaux Martyrs D'Allah*, 228.

126 *Al-'Amaliyyat Al-Istishadiyya: Al-Maqawama Al-Wataniyya…*, 120-140.

127 In her farewell address, which Khosrokhavar quotes, Sana Muhaydli dedicated her martyrdom operation to the first SSNP martyr, Wajdi al-Sayegh (Khosrok-havar, *Les Nouveaux Martyrs D'Allah*, 330).

128 Ibid., 229-231.

129 SSNP *istishhadiyyin* listed chronologically: 1 Wajdi Al-Sayegh (13 March 1985); 2 Sana Muhaydli (9 April 1985); 3 Malek Wehbé (20 April 1985); 4 Khaled Al-Azraq (9 July 1985); 5 Ibtissam Harb (9 July 1985); 6 Ali Ghazi Talib (31

July 1985); 7 Mariam Kheireddine (11 September 1985); 8 Ammar al-A'sar (4 November 1985); 9 Muhammad Qana'a (10 July 1986); 10 Norma Abi Hassan (17 July 1986); 11 Zahr Abi 'Assaf (18 June 1987): 12 Fadwa Hasan Ghanim 'Suryana' (25 November 1990). See *Al-Bina': Sabah Al-Khayr* 1039 (March 2001), 21-23.

130 Khosrokhavar, *Les Nouveaux Martyrs D'Allah*, 330. Khosrokhavar already contradicted himself when he mentioned that the LCP martyrs, Lola Abboud and Jamal al-Sati (a Christian female and a Muslim male) came from the *Biqa'* (Ibid., 229). Jamal al-Sati blew himself up on 6 August 1985 in the Israeli Military Governor's residence in *Zaghlé*. For an overview of the LCP operations against the Israeli forces, see Mustapha, *Al-Muqawama fi Lubnan…*, 345-349.

131 Augustus Richard Norton argues along similar lines as myself: "The party's [Hizbullah's] gradual entry into the political arena in 1992 and its subsequent attraction to middle class members of the Shiite community has led Hizbullah's members to become 'Lebanese nationalists par excellence'". Nicholas Blanford, "South expert says prospects for peace are 'good'". The *Daily Star* 3 May 2000.

132 Interview with Elie Sa'adé, an SSNP middle-rank cadre, 29 November 2003.

133 SSNP believes in Syrian nationalism, opting to form a 'Syrian Nation' in 'Natural Syria', which comprises the following present-day countries: Lebanon, Syria, Palestine [Israel], Jordan, Iraq, Kuwait, Sinai in Egypt, Cyprus, and southern parts of Turkey.

134 After 23 years, Israel returned her remains – along with the remains of 187 Lebanese, Palestinian, and Arab fighters – on 16 July 2008 in a groundbreaking prisoner swap with Hizbullah. Her mother Fatima – Umm Haytham – was very happy to finally bury her. See *al-Safir* (25 July 2008). The swap included the notorious Samir al-Quntar – who served 29 years in prison out of a life sentence – and the four Hizbullah fighters who were kidnapped by Israel during the July 2006 war: Khudr Zaydan, Maher Kawtharani, Husayn Sulayman, and Muhammad Srur. With the swap, Israel aimed at closing this contentious file with Lebanon.

135 One year before Hizbullah standardized the practice of videotaping the martyrdom operations and the farewell addresses of the martyrs, the SSNP only videotaped the farewell addresses of the martyrs, starting with Sana.

136 2 July 1988. It is worth mentioning that, in recognition of Sana's 'great feat', her family was given a house as well as work in Libya by the Libyan leader Mu'ammar al-Qadhaffi.

137 This bears a sticking resemblance to Dr Abboud's remark that, "each of us is free to worship God the way he wishes, but we are not free to treat our country any way we want." Dr Abboud is the brother of the martyr Lola Abboud. See Davis, *Martyrs: Innocence…*, 83.

138 *Kuluna Muslimun, fa minna man aslama Allah bi al-Qur'an, wa minna man alma Allah bi al-Injil, wa minna man alma Allah bi-alhikma.* (It is difficult for an English translation to capture the exact meaning).

139 *Al-'Amaliyyat Al-Istishadiyya: Al-Maqawama Al-Wataniyya...*, 258-271.

140 Her mother acknowledged that Lola was "a religious girl, who used to attend church, pray and light candles for the Lebanese soldiers fighting Israelis." See Davis, *Martyrs: Innocence...*, 76.

141 Ibid., 68.

142 Ibid., 68, 77-79.

143 Ibid., 69.

144 Defensive *jihad*.

145 Ibid., 69-70.

146 Ibid., 70.

147 Ibid., 72.

148 Ibid., 81.

149 Ibid., 84.

150 See the episode "Hizbullah: Identity and Role" of the program entitled "Hot Spot" (*Nuqta Sakhina*), al-Jazeera TV 24 September 1998; *Kawakib Al-Nasr: Qisas Shuhada'...*, Volume 2, 23-35.

151 Saad-Ghorayyeb refers to the 'dignity' that the martyr upholds by his sacrifice, as opposed to the 'humiliation' under the occupation. Saad-Ghorayeb, *Hizbullah: Politics and Religion*, 128-129.

152 Khosrokhavar, *Les Nouveaux Martyrs D'Allah*, 331.

153 See Christoph Reuter, *My Life as a Weapon: A Modern History of Suicide Bombing*. Translated from German by Helena Ragg-Kirkby. Princeton, NJ: Princeton University Press, 2004.

154 See "Shireen and Others Like Her", *The Economist* (22 May 2004), 88-89.

155 The word *husnayayyn* in verse (9:52) is taken to refer to martyrdom (of the self) and victory (for the *umma*): "Say: 'Do you expect for us anything other than one of the two fairest outcomes (martyrdom and victory); while we expect that Allah will smite you with a punishment, either from Him, or at our hands?' So wait and watch, we are waiting and watching you."

5   FROM COOPTATION TO CONTESTATION TO POLITICAL POWER

1   Craig Calhoun, "The Democratic Integration of Europe: Interests, Identity, and the Public Sphere". In: *Europe without Borders: Re-Mapping Territory, Citizenship and Identity in a Transnational Age*, M. Berezin and M. Schain, eds. Baltimore: Johns Hopkins University Press, 2003, 244.

2   Qasim, *Hizbullah: Al-Manhaj...*, 356, 363, 389.

3   Ibid., 396.

4   The Lebanese myriad or mosaic refers to the ethnic composition of the Lebanese communities that comprise Lebanon, including the officially recognized eighteen sects.

5   Unlike the parliamentary elections law, the municipal elections law is not drawn along sectarian lines, which leaves a large margin for the grassroots to voice their opinion in the ballot box and make their subaltern voices heard.

6   Qasim, op. cit., 342-343.

7   Calhoun, op. cit, 255.

8   Hizbullah participated in all the elections in the post-Ta'if era. It contested the parliamentary elections of 1992, 1996, 2000, 2005, and 2009 as well as the municipal elections of 1998, 2004, and 2010. For the election programs and their results up to 2005, refer to Alagha, *The Shifts in Hizbullah's Ideology*, 42-62; 247-277.

9   'Ali Ammar, Ibrahim Bayan (Sunni), Muhammad Berjawi, Muhammad Fnaysh, Munir al-Hujayyri (Sunni), Rabi'a Kayruz (Maronite), Muhammad Ra'd, Sa'ud Rufayyel (Greek Catholic), Sayyid Ibrahim Amin Al-Sayyid, 'Ali Taha, Khudr Tlays, Muhammad Yaghi.

10   Here is a list of the names with (O) and (N) beside the names to denote old [i.e. previously elected] and new respectively Abdallah Qasir (N), Ammar al-Musawi (N), Nazih Mansur (N), Husayn al-Hajj Hasan (N), Ibrahim Bayan, Sunni (O), Muhammad Fnaysh (O), Isma'il Sukariyyé, Sunni (N), Rabi'a Kayruz, Maronite (O), Muhammad Ra'd (O), Sayyid Ibrahim Amin Al-Sayyid (O).

11   'Ali Ammar (O); Muhammad Berjawi (o); Abdallah Qasir (O); Muhammad Fnaysh (o); Nazih Mansur (O); Muhammad Ra'd (O); Husayn al-Hajj Hasan (O); Ammar al-Musawi (O); Husayn Yaghi (o); George Najm, Maronite (N); Ibrahim Bayan, Sunni (o); Mas'ud al-Hujayyri, Sunni (N).

12   Hizbullah's 2009 Manifesto, Chapter II: "Lebanon", Section 1: "The Homeland", 30-31.

13   Calhoun, op. cit., 248.

14   The following social indicators are telling: 24.3% of the LMCB were between 20-25 years old, 46.1% between 25 and 30, and 29.3% older than 30. 17.2% had elementary education, 24.3% had intermediate education, 35.7% had secondary education, 35.7% had high school education, 16.9% had university education, and 5.9% had MAS and PhDs. 69% were bachelors, 25.8% married with children, and 5.2% married without children. The following political indicators are telling: 51% were ex-political parties' members, 6.8% were affiliated with various political parties, and 42.2% were non-members of political parties. A further 38% were Sunni, 25% Shi'a, 25%, Druz 20%, and 17% Christians. In addition, 40% came from Beirut, 20.6% from the north and *Kisirwan* (predo-

minantly Christian areas), *Biqa'* 13.4%, Mount Lebanon 8.6%, and the south and *Iqlim al-Karrub* 17.4%. See Ali Fayyad, "*Al-Saraya Al-Lubnaniyya Limuqa-wamat Al-Ihtilal Al-Israeli: Al-Tarkiba Al-Ijtima'iyya-Al-Siyassiyya wa Afaq Al-Dawr* ["Lebanese Multiconfessional Brigades: The Socio-political Makeup and Future Role]". Beirut: CCSD, 22 November 1999.

15 Benedict Anderson "refers to a growing sense of reading together, the public sphere emerges less from associations, more strictly the domain of civil society, than from ways of dealing confidently with others in an expanding social universe of shared communication." Eickelman and Anderson, op. cit., 16.

16 Hariri was assassinated by a massive suicidal truck bomb attack in the predominantly Muslim West Beirut. The explosion killed MP Basil Flayhan and 22 other people from Hariri's motorcade and innocent pedestrians. An unknown group by the name of "The Organization for Victory and Jihad in the Levant" claimed responsibility through a video message read by the Palestinian Abu 'Adas. Lebanese security forces at the time tried to implicate the Salafis with the assassination. The UNSC formed the Special Tribunal for Lebanon (STL) to put the perpetrators to justice.

17 Hizbullah is not only allied with leftist political parties such as the SSNP, the LCP, the *Ba'th* Party, the Naserite Social Party, etc., but also with prominent Sunni organizations and political parties, including the Islamic Association (*Al-Jama'a Al-Islamiyya*); the Islamic Unity Movement (*Harakat al-Tawhid al-Islami*); the Association of Islamic Charitable Projects (*al-Ahbash*); the Islamic Work Front (*Jabhat al-'Amal al-Islami*); and interestingly, the Palestinian *jihadi* Salafi *Ansar Allah*, who fought the IDF alongside Hizbullah during the July 2006 war.

18 http://www.14march.org/.

19 UNSC Resolution 1559 called on the Lebanese state to have absolute monopoly over the use of force, calling on it to disband and disarm all militias, which is an indirect reference to Hizbullah and the Palestinian factions in Lebanon. See Shaykh Ja'far Hasan 'Atrisi, *Hizbullah: Al-Khiyar Al-As'ab wa Damanat Al-Watan Al-Kubra [Hizbullah: The Difficult Choice and Lebanon's Greatest Guarantee]*. Beirut: Dar Al-Mahajja Al-Bayda', 2005, 309-311; Rif'at Sayyid Ahmad, *Hasan Nasrallah: Tha'ir min Al-Janub [Hasan Nasrallah: A Rebel from the South]*. Cairo: Dar Al-Kitab Al-'Arabi, 2006, 215-230.

20 See my article: "Hizbullah After the Syrian Withdrawal". *Middle East Report.* (Winter 2005) 237: 34-39.

21 Muhammad Ra'd (O); Muhammad Fnaysh (O); Muhammad Haydar (N); Hasan Fadlallah (N); Hasan Huballah (N); Amin Sherri (N); Ali Ammar (O); Pierre Serhal, Maronite (N); Isma'il Sukariyyé, Sunni (N); Kamel al-Rifa'i, Sunni (N); Ali al-Miqdad (N); Husayn al-Hajj Hasan (O); Jamal al-Taqsh (N); Nawwar al-Sahili (N).

22 *Hizbullah: Al-Muqawama wa Al-Tahrir...*, op. cit.

23 Interview with *Al-Safir* (29 July 2005).

24 *Al-Safir* (17 August 2005).

25 *Al-Safir* (11 June 2005); *Hizbullah: Al-Muqawama wa Al-Tahrir*, op. cit., 178-184.

26 The Ta'if Agreement stripped the president of his powers and rendered them to the cabinet.

27 Previously, Hizbullah argued that its prospective representatives in the cabinet could do nothing to alter these decisions. However, in the parliament and in municipality councils, Hizbullah's members can voice their opinion freely and act in favor of the masses or the social base that they represent. Hizbullah controlled municipal councils act as advocacy groups, employing a kind of empowerment mechanism, in order to lobby the government to pursue a course of balanced development as well as to live up to its promises and perform its developmental projects.

28 See Lebanese daily newspapers of 21 December 2005.

29 See http://www.tayyar.org/files/documents/fpm_Hizbullah.pdf; *Mawsu'at Nasrallah [Nasrallah's Encyclopedia]*, Volumes II & III, Beirut: Manshurat Al-Fajir, 2007, 16-24.

30 The official Syrian position is that demarcating the borders between Lebanon and Syria is possible, but only as a part of comprehensive peace settlement, by which Israel would return the Golan Heights to Syria, as a first priority. In turn, Al-Mufti Al-Ja'fari al-Mumtaz, Shaykh 'Abd al-Amir Qabalan, the Deputy of the Islamic Shi'ite Higher Council, said in his Friday speech on April 20, 2007, that Hizbullah would only relinquish its arms as part of an overall regional settlement, whereby , in addition to founding a Palestinian state, the IDF would relinquish both Shib'a and the Golan. *LBCI* News Bulletin, 18.00 GMT. In a similar vein, on May 2, 2007, president Lahud affirmed that even if Israel withdraws from Shib'a and keeps the water resources, then Hizbullah would not give up its arms unless a comprehensive, just, and lasting peace is reached in the Middle East.

31 With the establishment of the March 14 Group, Qrnet Shahwan Group became defunct.

32 'Aun makes all the difference in the tug of war between March 14 and March 8. If he changes his alliance to March 14, then they will have the 2/3-majority in the parliament, in addition to the 2/3-majority in the cabinet, which they already have. (The FPM parliamentary bloc had more than 21 MPs).

33 For the past two decades, Hizbullah embarked on an open, peaceful, and constructive dialogue with all sects, political parties, and civil society groups and organizations in order to tackle the source or origin of cultural, political, theoretical, and practical differences.

34 The August 2006 UNSC Resolution 1701 gave a one-month time table to solve this issue, which did not materialize.

35 'Internal debates' surrounding the tribunal, and other issues, take place in the public sphere.

36 *Mawsu'at Nasrallah*, Volume II, 25; Amin Mustapha. *Al-I'sar [The Tornado]*, Beirut, Dar Al-Hadi, 2006, 273-276.

37 I was in the Netherlands before the war started, but I sensed that something drastic was going to happen. So I boarded a KLM flight and landed in Beirut on 6 July. My presence in the field gave me the first-hand privilege to observe, witness, and document the 34-day war.

38 Eldad Regev and Ehud Goldwasser. The war led to the death of around 1200 Lebanese, one-third of whom were children under the age of 12; wounded and handicapped 4000; displaced more than one million; and caused around $ 15 billion in damage and revenues. *Daily Star* and AFP. See http://www.dailystar. com.lb/July_War06.asp (Accessed: 2 August 2006). Due to Hizbullah's 4000 rockets, Israel lost 158, more than two-thirds of whom were soldiers: 119 soldiers and 39 civilians; 5000 were wounded; 12,000 houses were destroyed; 750, 000 trees were burned; and 5 aircrafts/helicopters crashed. Also, Israel incurred a financial loss of 25 billion shekels (around $ 6 billion). See "The War in Figures", in *Yadi'ot Ahronot* (15 August 2006).

39 Sharara, *Dawlat Hizbullah…*, 389-442; Abdallah Balqaziz. *Hizbullah min Al-Tahrir ila Al-Radi' [Hizbullah from Liberation to Deterrence]*. Beirut, Markaz Dirasat Al-Wihda Al-'Arabiyya, 2006, 73-107; Joseph Alagha, "Hizbullah's Promise". *ISIM REVIEW* 18 (Autumn 2006), 36 and "The Israeli-Hizbullah 34-Day War: Causes and Consequences." *Arab Studies Quarterly* 30.2 (Spring 2008): 1-22.

40 It is remarkable to note that although Hizbullah knew about Avi Jorisch, they gave him free access trusting that he would portray their own point of view. It is ironic to note that Jorisch's book *The Beacon of Hatred* is one of the main reasons the US Administration branded *al-Manar* as a "terrorist organization." Abiding by the democratic rules of the game in an open society, Hizbullah assigned Stanley L. Cohen-- a famous US Jewish lawyer, who successfully defended the militant Hamas member Musa Abu Marzuq, where he was extradited to Jordan, and not to Israel, as the Israeli government demanded --to defend al-Manar in front of US courts. Since in addition to his $ 5000 fee per hour, he charged an additional $ 2 million in order to take the case, the party dismissed the case as a matter of beating a dead horse, preferring to use that money for the cause of the Resistance and to boost its already thriving NGOs.

41 Reached through a lit dungeon made by a long line of small lights till one arrived at the broadcasting room, where everything was manually operated, with very limited equipment and resources.

42 Exceptionally on Monday, 17 July, issue 1171, right after Haifa was bombed; and regularly on Friday, 21 July, issue 1172.

43 http://www.lebanonundersiege.gov.lb/english/F/eNews/NewsArticle. asp?CNewsID=61. (Accessed: 2 August 2006). The release of the Lebanese and Israeli prisoners and detainees; the withdrawal of the IDF behind the Blue Line; placing the *Shib'a* Farms under UN jurisdiction, and Israel surrendering all remaining landmine maps to the UN; a robust UNIFIL force to guarantee stability and security in the south; putting the 1949 Armistice Agreement between Lebanon and Israel into effect; the international community's support to Lebanon on all levels.

44 The first since 1969.

45 Calhoun, op. cit., 251.

46 Idem, 244.

47 Many areas in the south remain uninhabitable, which resulted in an estimated 200,000 internally displaced or refugees. See http://www.lebanonundersiege. gov.lb/english/F/Main/index.asp? for official Lebanese government figures and statistics (Accessed: 2 August 2006).

48 The US banned dealings and froze the assets of the state-run Iranian *Sadirat* Bank, as well as, the following two companies: *Bayt Al-Mal* ['The House of Money'] and *Al-Yusr Lil-Tamwil wa Al-Istithmar* ['Al-Yusr Financing and Investing'] accusing these of financing Hizbullah's institutions. See *AFP*, *AP*, *Reuters*, and *Al-Safir* (8-9 September 2006).

49 Author's estimates are based on fieldwork and Hizbullah's primary documents. For instance, see http://www.waad-rebuild.com/Home/index.php (Accessed: 14 January 2007).

50 *Al-Intiqad* 1228 (17 August 2007), 4.

51 *Al-Manar*, 7:30pm News, 14 January 2010.

52 Aired on December 27, 2006.

53 *See http://www.haaretz.com/hasen/spages/846423.html* "The IDF's Lost Honor," Haaretz, *9 April 2007.*

54 Interview with *New TV*.

55 See *Al-Intiqad* 1181 (23 September 2006), 11-15, and Lebanese daily newspapers. The front page of *al-Intiqad* issue 1176 of 18 August showed a red page, symbolizing the blood of the martyrs, with on the right side, the words 'Divine Victory', the word 'victory' in green, the color of Islam. On the left side, it portrayed Khamina'i's letter addressed to Nasrallah and entitled: "Your Victory is an Apodictic Proof (*Hujja*)".

56 Although Hizbullah already took precautions and dug elaborate dungeons, it would have sufficed if Israeli planes caused a sonic boom, which would have resulted in stampede and chaos. Fearing the worst the party canceled its annual show of force on 'Jerusalem Day', the last Friday of Ramadan.

57 *Mawsu'at Nasrallah*, Volume III, 151-177.

58 The pun is that his name means 'Victory of God'.

59 Calhoun, op. cit., 251.

60 Speaker Nabih Berri refused to convene the parliament for more than 10 months after the resignation of the six ministers. Also, like the Lebanese opposition, the outgoing president considered the cabinet as unconstitutional after the resignation took place on 11 November 2006, thus refusing to ratify any bill submitted to him by it.

61 67% of the Christian voters voted for the FPM.

62 He is the vice-president of Hizbullah's political council and the head of Hizbullah's committee on Christian-Muslim dialogue. *Salun Al-Sabt, Sawt Lubnan* (Radio Voice of Lebanon), 6 May 2007.

63 Calhoun, op. cit., 252.

64 In Lebanon, the Muslims include Shi'ites, Sunnis, Druz, and 'Alawis.

65 Had a parliamentary bloc of fourteen members.

66 Composed of four big blocs and a few independents.

67 Naturally Hizbullah benefited from the Understanding and its alliance with the FPM, before, during, and after the war. Before the war, by saving Lebanon from plunging again into civil war after the 5 February 2006 civil unrest, thus boosting Hizbullah's image as a nationalist Lebanese political party. During the war, the Christian areas were no more off-limits to the Hizbullahis, where the Shi'ite displaced were well treated and received all the aid they needed by members of the FPM (along other regional and international NGOs), which is unprecedented since the outbreak of the civil war on 13 April 1975. After the war, Hizbullah aspired for veto power through political alliance.

68 Calhoun, op. cit., 249.

69 This is reminiscent of the 19 August assertion of the Lebanese Minister of Defense that the decision to wage war and peace should be the sole prerogative of the Lebanese government.

70 Mustapha, *Al-I'sar...*, 276-278.

71 Hizbullah's psychological warfare is not only confined to the battlefield; rather, as masters of public relations and publicity, Hizbullah exploit its media to such ends.

72 For instance, see *al-Intiqad* 1189 (17 November 2006): 1-2, and 1191 (1 December 2006): 2.

73 *Salun Al-Sabt, Sawt Lubnan* (Radio Voice of Lebanon), 6 May 2007.

74 Hizbullah's MPs approved laws dealing with prostitution, gambling (casinos), drinking, etc. See Alagha, *The Shifts in Hizbullah's Ideology*, op. cit., 161-165.

75 The position of the Egyptian street seemed to be in accordance with its government, after it was at odds with it during the war supporting Hizbullah through popular demonstrations.

76 The security arm of the Lebanese state killed thirteen Hizbullah supporters – including two women – and wounded 40 because they took to the streets when the Hariri government imposed a ban on demonstrations on 13 September 1993, when the party was protesting peacefully against the Oslo Agreement. On 27 May 2004, demonstrations spread all over the country in protest of the pressing socio-economic situation. In Hizbullah's southern suburb of Beirut, the Lebanese army fired at the demonstrators killing five and wounding several others.

77 Some Hizbullah cadres bragged that the government would resign in 33 hours; others affirmed that it would resign before 33 days. Neither materialized.

78 See his 1 and 10 December 2006 speeches. This is another morally charged statement, which puts Hizbullah and its reputation and credibility at stake.

79 At a time when Lebanese public debt reached a high of 180% of the GDP, in the presence of 33 countries and international organizations, Lebanon received pledges of $ 6.7 billion in loans and $ 1 billion in donations.

80 Al-Intiqad 1199 (26 January 2007), 3. This was Nasrallah's first *fatwa* in the political sphere.

81 The Lebanese army imposed a curfew from 8:30 pm to 6:00am, which was the first measure since the May 1973 curfew, before the civil war erupted.

82 Quoting a *hadith* by Prophet Muhammad, *Al-Safir*'s front page editorial admonished against discord: "*Fitna* is slumbering; God damn [Those] who wake it up." See *al-Safir* 10611 (26 January 2007).

83 Symbolizing the color of blood, the cover page of *al-Intiqad* portrayed the map of Lebanon surrounded by the color red, and the main slogan in yellow, Hizbullah's color, "The Government of the Militias Confronts the Republic of the Opposition", and a small headline in black, symbolizing the color of death, "The Wisdom of the Opposition and the [Tactical] Moves of the Lebanese Army Warded off *Fitna*". *Al-Intiqad* 1199 (26 January 2006).

84 Sayyid Hani Fahs is a member of the legislative council of the Islamic Shi'ite Higher Council in Lebanon and a founding member of the Arab team for the Muslim-Christian dialogue and the permanent committee for the Lebanese dialogue.

85 Because of his views, on 16 May 2008, he was stripped of his position by the Islamic Shi'ite Higher Council and was replaced by Shaykh Hasan Abdallah. During his meeting with Shaykh Muhammad Al-Hajj Hasan on 19 July 2009, the latter condemned the decision arguing that the council is not a private property for a certain family or party (in reference to Hizbullah), warning them to carefully read into the wave of condemnations that occurred in Iran after the elections against the 'unjust' rulers. Al-Hajj Hasan questioned that since turbans have a certain sanctity, then why discriminate and differentiate among religious scholars on the basis of their views and opinions, in a country

where the freedom of expression is supposed to be sacred? Al-Hajj Hasan condemned the killing of one of his followers in the *Biqaʻ* calling on the Lebanese authorities to administer justice in this regard. See Lebanese daily newspapers of 20 July 2009 and http://www.lebanonfiles.com/news_desc.php?id=107657 (Accessed 19 July 2009).

86 On 15 April 2007, he accused Hizbullah of preventing him from holding a press conference in his home town, *Shmistar*, in the *Biqaʻ*. He also claimed that Hizbullah intended to get rid of him by fueling a family feud, whereby he would be the victim.

87 He continuously criticized Hizbullah's 'miscalculated adventure' in the 2006 July War. In defiance to Hizbullah, his rapprochement to the March 14 Christians led him to go to church and participate in the funeral service of MP Pierre Jumayyel.

88 For instance, al-Amin's elder son is finishing an 11-years study in Qum to become a *mujtahid*. His cousin Muhammad Hasan al-Amin is the chief judge in the southern city of Sidon; his nephew is also establishing a seminary, etc.

89 Al-Amin and Sharafeddine families constitute the two main pillars of *Jabal ʻAmil*.

90 From 1994 till his death in 2001. See http://www.shamseddine.com/ and http://www.shiitecouncil.com/ (Accessed 5 June 2008).

91 The more followers a *marjaʻ* has, the more powerful he is, both financially and religiously. See Alagha, *The Shifts in Hizbullah's Ideology*, op. cit., 73-75.

92 He has a distinguishably big turban.

93 Khaminaʼi boasted that he would make Lebanon the place of defeat and humiliation for the US and Israel.

94 On 13 July 2007, Ahmad al-Asʻad, the son of the ex-speaker Kamel al-Asʻad, founded another marginal Shiʻite opposition group to Hizbullah known as '*Tayyar Lubnan Al-Kafaʼat*' (Lebanese Merit Movement). Later the name was revised to '*Tayyar Al-Intimaʼ Al-Lubnani*' (Lebanese Belonging Movement).

95 *Al-Intiqad* 1428 (13 April 2007), 10-14.

96 From a demographic viewpoint, Nasrallah might be right. He stressed the idea of rebirth, not on the commemoration of the Prophet's birthday; but waiting until Easter. The analogy between a movement's rebirth after years of struggle and the Christian theology of resurrection was not accidental.

97 Most US media outlets referred to it as, 'The pro-American government of Sanyura'.

98 Jeffry Feltman was the US ambassador to Lebanon at the time.

99 Dr Dawud al-Sayegh, a veteran political aide to the late ex-PM Rafiq Hariri and to his son Saʻd, conceded that states have interests, but refused to use the term 'foreign tutelage' preferring instead 'foreign attention' (*al-ihtimam al-khariji*). As examples to support his argument, he cited the visits of the

Spanish PM José Luis Rodríguez Zapatero and the Italian PM Romano Prodi in support of the French presidential candidate Ségolène Royal against Nicolas Sarkozy, and Vladimir Putin's visit in support of Gerhard Schröder against Angela Merkel.

100 Which, as mentioned earlier, reflects the power base in the parliament.

101 One political commentator argued that the precept of practice seemed to suggest that Sanyura proved to be a statesman, rather than a tax collector.

102 Calhoun, op. cit., 254.

103 Currently Nawwaf Al-Musawi is an MP and Muhammad Fnaysh is the Minister of Administrative Reform.

104 Lebanese daily newspapers the next day, especially *al-Nahar* no. 22994.

105 During a talk show with the Iranian Satellite TV 'Al-'Alam' (The World) on 5 May 2007.

106 For instance, on 9 August 2006, Nasrallah appeared on Lebanese TV stations *unequivocally* endorsing the Seven Points.

107 In the morning talk show 'Naharkum Sa'id' ('Good Morning') on LBCI on 27 April 2007.

108 On 30 May 2007, the UNSC Resolution 1757 established, under chapter seven, the International Tribunal (STL) of the Hariri murder, effective 10 June 2007.

109 Berri's initiative on the occasion of the 29th anniversary of the disappearance of Imam Musa al-Sadr seemingly eroded the Hizbullah-led opposition's demand of the formation of a national unity cabinet, even "half an hour before the presidential elections", and apparently shelved such a demand till the election of a new president, as the March 14 Trend has repeatedly requested. (See Lebanese daily newspapers of 1 September 2007). Unfortunately, this was also a tactical move, and not a genuine policy shift.

110 The tenure of the outgoing president Lahud ended on 24 November 2007, with the failure of the parliament to elect a new president during the constitutional period between 24 September and 23 November 2007. Before the election of president Michel Sulyman on 25 May 2008, the speaker delayed the vote nineteen times.

111 Calhoun, op. cit., 258.

112 Ibid., 259.

113 Back then BDL funded both cabinets. This possibility seems out of the question these days because of the estimated $ 55 billion public debt that is rupturing Lebanon.

114 Although the patriarch stressed that the president should be elected by a two-third majority in the parliament (as the Hizbullah-led opposition argued), he cautioned that boycotting the parliamentary session to electing the president is tantamount to boycotting Lebanon.

115 *Une guerre pour les autres*. Preface by Dominique Chevallier. Paris: Jean-Claude Lattès, 1985.

116 *Al-Safir* 10876 (29 August 2007), 4.

117 Although Hizbullah does not work on the basis of speculations, this does not mean that the party does not have contingency measures and well-contrived anticipatory plans.

118 MP Walid 'Ido was assassinated on 13 June 2007, in a car bomb in West Beirut, the Muslim sector of the Lebanese capital. On 19 September, a powerful explosion ripped the Eastern sector of Beirut killing the Phalangist MP Antoine Ghanem. Hizbullah vehemently condemned both explosions. Like the case of the six previously politically motivated assassinations, which all targeted anti-Syrian politicians, March 14 pinned the blame directly on the Syrian regime.

119 Six other deadly explosions and the annihilation of four terror cells and the arrest of many others ripped the fragile peace that Lebanon was witnessing. According to the Lebanese Minister of Defense, after the Lebanese army took total control of the *Nahr al-Barid* camp on 2 September 2007, at least 150 Fatah al-Islam militants were killed and around 300 were arrested, while 170 Lebanese soldiers were killed and more than 1,000 were wounded. Also, a total of 42 civilians died, including those who passed away as a result of the militants' rockets that were fired on nearby villages (32 Palestinian civilians and 10 Lebanese civilians).

120 On 12 December 2007 al-Hajj, the chief of military operations and the presumed successor to Lebanese army commander, was killed by a car bomb in *B'abda*, a Christian area where the presidential palace, many Western embassies, and at the nearby Yarzé, the headquarters of the LA are located. Al-Hajj headed the ground operations at *Nahr al-Barid*. Also, Fatah al-Islam targeted UNIFIL three times with roadside bombs, fatally injuring three Spanish soldiers on 24 June 2007, and a US embassy reconnaissance vehicle on 15 January 2008.

121 In the above piece, which I wrote in September 2007, I rightfully predicted Hizbullah's show of force in May 2008.

6 THE DOHA 2008 ACCORD AND ITS AFTERMATH

1   It is Ironic to note that Wafiq Shuqayr submitted his resignation to the Minister of Interior after the 20-year old Firas Husayn Haydar, who used to live two kilometres away in the *Dahiya*, was found dead on 10 July 2010 in the wheel compartment of *Nasair*, a Saudi airliner that was carrying important Saudi personalities, including high-ranking military officials. Since Haydar had a picture of Imam Khumayni in his wallet, some media outlets claimed that he

was either a Hizbullah member or a sympathizer, implying an attempted 'terrorist attack'. (NNA, 13 July 2010).

2   And also more than 200 wounded according to AFP estimates, while Reuters reported the death toll as 80.

3   See Nasrallah's speech of 26 May 2008.

4   The vacant seat of assassinated MP Antoine Ghanem was not filled because the parliament failed to conduct partial elections.

5   See the editorial of *al-Akhbar* 524 (15 May 2008).

6   See *al-Intiqad* 1290 (15 August 2008); *al-Intiqad* 1291 (18 August 2008), 5; *al-Intiqad* 1294 (29 August 2008): 3; Qasim, *Hizbullah: Al-Manhaj...*, 275-9; NNA, 18 August 2008.

7   NNA.

8   Yakan was the pioneer of Sunni Islamism in Lebanon and a principal founder of the Islamic Association (*Al-Jama'a Al-Islamiyya*). In August 2006, Yakan established the Islamic Work Front (*Jabhat al-'Amal al-Islami*), an umbrella organization that aims to coalesce Lebanese opposition Sunni groups and personalities.

9   March 14 won 55% of the parliamentary seats, and March 8 appropriated the remaining 45%. Whereas in terms of public mandate, demographic factors weighed in: March 8 earned 55% of the votes, and March 14 got 45% of the votes.

10 Muhammad Ra'd (O); Muhammad Fnaysh (O); Husayn al-Musawi (N); Hasan Fadlallah (O); Ali Ammar (O); Walid Sukariyyé, Sunni (N); Kamel al-Rifa'i, Sunni (O); Ali al-Miqdad (O); Husayn al-Hajj Hasan (O); Ali Fayyad (N); Nawwaf Al-Musawi (N); Nawwar al-Sahili (O).

11 http://www.moqawama.org/essaydetails.php?eid=15765&cid=199 (Accessed 15 September 2009).

12 Al-Hariri congratulated Barud for fulfilling his promise, extolled the 'unprecedented accomplishment' of successfully holding the elections in one day without any tangible security threat or infraction.

13 See Lebanese daily newspapers of 17 September 2009.

14 See the editorials of *al-Safir* 11398 and *al-Nahar* 23818 dated 17 September 2009.

15 *Al-Sharq Al-Awsat* 11255 (21 September 2009). *Tazkiya* literally means a pronouncement of someone's integrity or credibility. (Hans Wehr, *A Dictionary of Modern Written Arabic*. Beirut: Librairie du Liban, 1980, 380).

16 http://www.moqawama.org/essaydetails.php?eid=16050&cid=199 (Accessed 19 September 2009).

17 http://arabic.bayynat.org.lb/ (Accessed 9 September 2009).

18 Arend Lijphart, *Democracies in Plural Societies: A Comparative Evaluation*. New Haven: Yale University Press, 1977.

19 Personal interview, 18 January 2010. See also his book: *Fragile States: Dilemmas of Stability in Lebanon and the Arab World*. Oxford: International NGO Training and Research Centre (INTRAC), 2008 (ISBN 878-1-905240-13-5) (95 pages). In order to inculcate democratic experience and practice among its members, in addition to Lijphart, Hizbullah indoctrinates them with the likes of *The Federalist Papers*, Alex de Tocqueville's *Democracy in America*, David Held's *Theories of Democracy*, Carl Schmitt's *The Crisis of Paliamentary Democracy*, Marcel Gauchet's *Situations de la democratie* [*The Conditions of Democracy*] and *Madness and Democracy*, as well as other theoreticians on Western democracy, especially in the US.

20 NNA, 29 October 2009.

21 He vehemently criticized Hizbullah's May 2008 'bloodbath'. In a show of solidarity with the Sunnis of Beirut, al-Amin prayed behind the Sunni Mufti of the Republic in the *'Id al-Fitr* prayer service commemorating the end of the fasting in the holy month of *Ramadan* 2009.

22 As he contended, Hizbullah and Amal stormed the headquarters of the Islamic Shi'ite Higher Council (*Dar al-Ifta'*) in Tyre and destroyed his library and confiscated his publications.

23 He referred to the Qur'an (4: 93): "And he who kills a believer intentionally will, as punishment, be thrown into Hell, dwelling in it forever; and Allah will be angry with him, curse him and prepare for him a dreadful punishment."

24 "Mufti of Tyre Sayyid 'Ali Al-Amin: The state does not beg, rather it [should] extend its authority and sovereignty on all Lebanese soil." Interview with Hasan Shalha and Muhammad Mizhir, *Al-Liwa'* 12719 (26 October 2009).

25 NNA, 8 November 2009.

26 After May 2008, the ministry of interior was classified as a security ministry along side the ministry of interior.

27 See Lebanese daily Newspapers of 10 November 2009.

28 Mainly the residence of the party's leading cadres and its security institutions.

29 In Abrahamic religions, including Islam, ten is a perfect number.

30 A reference to the *Shib'a* Farms and the occupied part of the *Ghajar* village.

31 See *al-Nahar* 23887 (27 November 2009), 1, 6-7.

32 NNA, 22 November 2009.

33 See "'Aun Breaks the Barriers with *Bkirké* and Explains his Stance: A new page for the Christians and the Lebanese and a very successful visit", *al-Intiqad* (4 December 2009), 9.

7 THE EIGHTH CONCLAVE: A NEW MANIFESTO (NOVEMBER 2009)

1   Since 'Islamic state' and 'relations with Christians' were discussed in chapters one and two, I will not refer to these again below.

2   Hizbullah is not monopolizing the use of religion, as Roy seems to imply, rather the party employs the word Hizbullah in an extended, inclusive, and progressive sense, which includes all believers from all religious denominations. Hajj Muhammad Al-Jammal, Hizbullah's spokesman, argued along these lines on the occasion of receiving a Danish delegation – composed of students, researchers, and faculty, mainly from Aarhus University and the University of Southern Copenhagen, and some Danish journalists – at the Central Information Office, 30 March 1999. Cf. Olivier Roy, *Globalised Islam: The Search for a New Umma*. Revised and updated edition. London: Hurst and Company, 2004, 249, 329.

3   Cf. As'ad Abu Khalil, "Ideology and Practice of Hizbollah in Lebanon: Islamization of Leninist Organizational Principles", *Middle Eastern Studies*, 27 (July 1991), 3, 395; and Roy, op. cit., 247-248.

4   'The Union of Muslim *'Ulama'* was established in the wake of the Israeli invasion in June 1982.

5   See *Al-Harakat al-Islamiyya fi Lubnan* and Al-Kurani, *Tariqat Hizbullah…*, especially 147-163.

6   Imam Khumayni, *Al-Kalimat Al-Qisar: Al-Islam wa A'malina [Short Words: Islam and our Words]*, 193, as cited in: Rafiq Sulayman Fidda, *Athar Al-Imam Al-Khymayni ala Al-Qadiyya Al-Filastiniyya [Imam Khymayni's Impact on the Palestinian Cause]*. Beirut: n.d., 170.

7   Westoxification, a term coined in the 1960s by an Iranian intellectual called Jalal al-Ahmad, denotes the venomous Western civilizational influence and hegemony on other civilizations and cultures.

8   The UK has replaced France, which is classified by Hizbullah as a neutral state, rather than the original position of being regarded as a foe. It is worth noting that France was on Iraq's side during the 1980-1988 Iraq-Iran war.

9   Abun-Nasr, *Hizbullah: Haqa'iq wa Ab'ad…*, 72-73.

10 Al-Madini, *Amal wa Hizbullah…*, 172; and documents collected by the author from the party's think tank the Consultative Center of Studies and Documentation (CCSD).

11 Hasan Fadlallah, *Al-Khiyar al-Akhar…*, 137.

12 Al-Madini, *Amal wa Hizbullah…*, 172-4; and documents collected by the author from the CCSD.

13 Nasrallah's cousin from the mother's side (*ibn khaltu*).

14 See Hizbullah's political declaration of 7 July 1995; Al-Madini, *Amal wa Hiz-bullah…*, 174-5; *al-Safir* 8 July 1995: "Hizbullah Reelects Sayyid Nasrallah as Secretary General", and *al-Nahar* 29 July 1995: "Leadership Changes in Hizbullah."

15 *Al-Safir* 6 August 1998; Al-Madini, *Amal wa Hizbullah…*, 178-9; and Imad Marmal, "The Results of Hizbullah's Conclave", *al-Safir* 1 August 1998. Marmal is *al-Safir* columnist and *al-Manar* political talk show presenter.

16 According to documents collected by the author from the CCSD.

17 Interview with *Al-Bilad* 12 October 1994.

18 Hizbullah is careful to clarify that its animosity is towards the US administration, and not the US people. (This seems to be in conformity with Khumayni's discourse on *hakimiyyat Allah* or 'God's Sovereignty', which is tolerant towards the populace, but not the ruling elite. This stands in sharp contrast to Bin Laden's nihilist discourse that does not distinguish between the two).

19 See Nicholas Blanford, "Hizbullah to issue updated version of manifesto: New 'Open Letter' will reflect changes", *Daily Star* (28 October 2002), 2.

20 Reinoud Leenders, "Hizbullah: Rebel Without a Cause?" *ICG Middle East Briefing Paper*, 30 July 2003, 19. (http://www.crisisweb.org/projects/middleeast/arab-israeliconflict/reports/A401070_30072003.pdf).

21 Interviewee wishes to remain anonymous. This person contended that 16 February was the intended date of launching the new document.

22 Sobelman, *Rules of the Game…*, 21, 23.

23 Ibid., 103.

24 Two leading cadres in the Islamic Resistance were assassinated by blowing up their cars: Ghalib Awali on 19 July 2004 and Ali Husayn Salih on 2 August 2003. The Lebanese government and Hizbullah accused Israel of being behind these assassinations; Israel repeatedly denied any involvement or responsibility in these attacks.

25 See " *'Abna' Al-Tufayli' Yuhajimun Nasrallah [Tufayli's Followers Chastise Nasrallah]*", *Al-Safir* 5 July 2004.

26 Compiled from *Al-Safir* 17 and 18 August 2004; Lebanese daily newspapers of 18 August 2004; and "Hizbullah's Seventh Conclave: Vivid Organization, Stability of Leadership, and A follow up on Recent Events", *Al-Intiqad* 1071 (20 August 2004).

27 At the time of the appointment, Rima Fakhry was a 38-year old mother of four. She has been a Hizbullah member since the age of eighteen. She also holds a BSc in Agriculture from the American University of Beirut. *Al-Safir* 5 January 2005; *Daily Star* 6 and 7 January 2005; *al-Intiqad* 1091 (7 January 2005).

28 This seems to suggest, more and more, the credibility of Hizbullah's *infitah* policy.

29 See Lebanese daily newspapers of 20 November 2009, especially *al-Safir* 11452; and *al-Safir* 11454 (24 November 2009).

30 No wonder the conclave took a lot of time; a new manifesto was also in the works.

31 http://www.moqawama.org/essaydetails.php?eid=16230&cid=199; http://english.moqawama.org/essaydetails.php?eid=9567&cid=214

32 The leadership realized that the pen name of Jawad Nureddine did not save Imad Mughniyyé from assassination. So, they decided not only to keep the name a secret, but also not to announce the eighth member at all.

33 After the Manifesto was released it attracted a lot of media coverage to the extent that it was item number one on the news and Nasrallah's press conference took center stage by being portrayed on the front page and in editorials of most Lebanese dailies.

34 Personal interview, 23 November 2009.

35 Most of these rhyme in Arabic; so it is difficult to capture the exact meaning and implications/connotations in an English translation. See "Order Stems from Religious Belief and its Manifestations on the Street", *al-Intiqad* (20 November 2009), 4.

36 http://www.almanar.com.lb/NewsSite/NewsDetails.aspx?id=116716&language=ar [Accessed 24 December 2009]

37 See Lebanese daily newspapers of 20 November 2009, especially *al-Safir* 11452; and *al-Safir* 11454 (24 November 2009). Although in its 17 November 2009 copy under "Press Secrets" *al-Akhbar* was the first to announce the end of the conclave, it is interesting to note that it is perhaps the only Lebanese daily that did not mention anything on the issue in its 20 November editorial. *Al-Safir* showed the most extensive coverage, but it mistakenly stated the seventh conclave instead of the eighth.

38 Chapter II, Section 7: "Lebanon and International Relations", 54.

39 Chapter I, Section 2: "Our region and the American Scheme", 24-25.

40 Chapter II, Section 7: "Lebanon and International Relations", 56.

41 Chapter II, Section 7: "Lebanon and International Relations", 54-55.

42 Chapter III, Section 1: "Palestine and the Zionist entity", 60.

43 Chapter III, Section 1: "Palestine and the Zionist entity", 58.

44 Chapter I, Section 1: "The World and Western-American Hegemony", 21.

45 Chapter II, Section 7: "Lebanon and International Relations", 55-56.

46 Chapter II, Section 5: "Lebanon and Arab Relations", 49

47 Chapter II, Section 6: "Lebanon and Islamic Relations", 51-2.

48 Chapter II, Section 5: "Lebanon and Arab Relations", 47.

49 Chapter II, Section 6: "Lebanon and Islamic Relations", 50.

50 *Al-'Ahd* (Friday 3 *Jamadi al-Thani* 1405 AH), 8, as cited in: *The Shifts in Hizbullah's Ideology*, 236.

51 Chapter II, Section 6: "Lebanon and Islamic Relations", 53.

1   Stephen Saideman, "Thinking Theoretically about Identity and Foreign Policy", in: *Identity and Foreign Policy...*, op. cit., 191.

2   (Italics in original). See Graham E. Fuller, *The Future of Political Islam*. New York: Palgrave, Macmillan, 2003, 18.

3   Some notable figures I interviewed in August and October 2009 and January and June 2010 are the following: Hajj Muhammad Ra'd, member of Hizbullah *Shura* council and the head of the party's parliamentary bloc; Sayyid Abd Al-Halim Fadlallah, the head of the party's think tank the Consultative Center of Studies and Documentation (CCSD); Hajj Ghalib Abu Zaynab, party officer for Muslim-Christian dialogue; Shaykh Shafiq Jaradi, the Rector of *Al-Ma'arif Al-Hikmiyya College*; Shaykh 'Ali Daher, the head of Hizbullah's cultural unit; MP Hasan Fadlallah; MP 'Ali Fayyad; MP 'Ali Ammar; MP Sayyid Nawwaf al-Musawi; Shaykh Akram Barakat, the head of the *Cultural Islamic Al-Ma'arif Association*; Sayyid Muhammad Kawtharani, political council member and responsible for the Iraqi file; Sayyid Ibrahim Amin Al-Sayyid, chairman of the political council; and the party spokesman Sayyid Ibrahim al-Musawi.

4   In fact, there is no mention of these concepts in Hizbullah's 2009 Manifesto.

5   Personal interview, 4 August 2009.

6   The Hizbullah leader, Nasrallah defines Islamists as fervent Muslim believers or pious (religious) youth.

7   For more details see *The Shifts in Hizbullah's Ideology*, 33-36.

8   The Lebanese myriad or mosaic refers to the ethnic composition of the Lebanese communities that comprise Lebanon, including the officially recognized eighteen sects.

9   Joseph Alagha, "Hizbullah's Gradual Integration in the Lebanese Public Sphere", *Sharqiyyat*, op. cit., 40.

10 Ibid., 40-42.

11 Ibid., 41.

12 Imam Khamina'i, *Al-Kalimat Al-Qisar [Aphorisms]*. Beirut: Cultural Islamic Al-Ma'arif Association, 2006, 147-167; 221-226.

13 See Asef Bayat, *Making Islam Democratic: Social Movements and the Post-Islamist Turn*. Stanford: Stanford University Press, 2007, 13; and "The Coming of a Post-Islamist Society". In *Critique: Critical Middle East Studies*, 9 (Fall 1996): 43-52.

14 Na'im Qasim, *Al-Safir* 20 May 2002.

15 *Al-Nour*, 6:00 GMT News, 9 February 2004; *Al-Safir* 9 February 2004.

16 Shaykh Na'im Qasim, *Mujtama' Al-Muqawama: Iradat Al-Shahada wa Sina'at Al-Intisar [The Society of Resistance: The Will to Martyrdom and the Making of Victory]*. Beirut: Dar Al-Ma'arif Al-Hikmiyya, 2008, 84.

17   Lebanon declared its independence on 22 November 1943; while Syria declared it on 17 April 1946, the year French soldiers evacuated both countries since they could not leave earlier because France was occupied by Germany.

18   Personal interview, 19 January 2010.

19   "Netanyahu: Syria drops key precondition for peace talks with Israel." By Jonathan Lis, Haaretz Correspondent http://www.haaretz.com/hasen/spages/1133396.html [Accessed 6 December 2009].

20   Personal interview, 19 January 2010. Al-Musawi was quoting Schopenhauer and Nietzsche respectively.

21   See Dennis Ross, *The Missing Peace: The Inside Story of the Fight for Middle East Peace.* Farrar, Straus, and Giroux, 2005; Dennis Ross and David Makovsky, *Myths, Illusions, and Peace: Finding a New Direction for America in the Middle East.* Viking Adult, 2009.

22   See the author's forthcoming two articles: "Pious Entertainment: Hizbullah's Islamic Cultural Sphere", in: *Muslim Rap, Halal Soaps and Revolutionary Theater: Artistic Developments in the Muslim World,* edited by Karin van Nieuwkerk. Austin: University of Texas Press, 2011, 289-353; and "Jihad With 'Music': The Taliban and Hizbullah". *Performing Islam.* 1 (2012):. ISSN 2043-1015 http://www.intellectbooks.co.uk/journals/view-Journal,id=209

23   *Al-Intiqad* 1428 (13 April 2007), 10-14.

AFTERWORD

1   Either there was no intention, or simply the fear of a crackdown by the hegemon dominating the scene.

2   "*Inna fikun quwwa law fu'ilat, laghayarat majjra al-tarikh.*" Antun S'adé, a Christian by birth and the founder of the secular Syrian Social Nationalist Party (SSNP), was executed by a firing squad in 1949 in Beirut.

3   The trigger was the 17 December 2010 self-immolation of Muhammad Buazizi, a Tunisian street vendor, in protest for the confiscation of his wagon. He succumbed to his wounds on 4 January 2011.

4   He had been in exile for the past 22 years in London.

5   Asef Bayat, *Street politics: Poor People's Movements in Iran.* New York: Columbia University Press, 1997.

6   *Life as Politics: How Ordinary People Change the Middle East.* Stanford: Stanford University press, 2010.

7   See Nasrallah's 7 February 2011 speech delivered at the 'Lebanese Political Parties' Festival in Support of Egypt's Arabism' at: http://www.moqawama.org/essaydetails.php?eid=19822&cid=142; and his 19 March 2011 speech in support of Arab revolutions at: http://www.moqawama.org/essaydetails.php?eid=20205&cid=142.

8   According to the results of the June 2009 elections, March 8: $57 + 7 = 64$ seats; March 14: $71 - 7 = 64$ seats.

9   Actually 67 since one MP from the FPM was out of the country during the parliamentary vote.

10 See his groundbreaking speech at the sixth anniversary of the assassination of his father on 14 February 2011.

ADDITIONAL READING

1   This section is mainly a revised and updated compilation of the following: "Hizbullah: An Islamic Jihadi Movement." *Arab Studies Quarterly* 30.1 (Winter 2008): 61-70; A book review of Nicholas Noe's *Voice of Hezbollah: The Statements of Sayyed Hassan Nasrallah. Journal of Palestine Studies* 38.2 (Winter 2009): 94-95; "Hizbullah: The Islamic Resistance in Lebanon." (April 2008): https://www.h-net.org/reviews/show rev.cgi?path=238301210371469; & "Hizbullah: From Radicalism to Accommodation." (January 2009): http://www.h-net.org/reviews/showpdf.php?id=23746

2   Ferdinand Smit, *The Battle for the South: The Radicalisation of Lebanon's Shi'ites 1982-1985*. Amsterdam: Bulaaq, 2000.

3   Na'im Qasim, *Hizbullah: Al-Manhaj...*, 40-90.

4   See the following by Augustus Richard Norton: *Hizballah of Lebanon: From Radical Idealism to Mundane Politics*. New York: Council on Foreign Relations, 1999, 12; *Hezbollah: A Short History*. Fifth Printing. Princeton: Princeton University Press, 2009, 35-41.

5   Sobelman, *Rules of the Game: Israel and Hizbullah After the Withdrawal from Lebanon*. Memorandum no. 69. Tel Aviv University: Jaffee Center for strategic Studies, 2004.

6   Judith Palmer Harik, *Hezbollah: The Changing Face of Terrorism*. London: I.B. Tauris, 2004, 2006.

7   A. Nizar Hamzeh, *In the Path of Hizbullah*. Syracuse: Syracuse University Press, 2004.

8   Augustus Norton, "America's Approach to the Middle East: Legacies, Questions, and Possibilities", *Current History*, (January 2002).

9   Ibid., 5.

10 Although her book was published in a second edition in 2006 one year after the Syrian withdrawal, the irony is it doesn't say anything about that issue because she didn't update the book, satisfying herself with a one-page preface to the second edition. So, it was just a publisher's propaganda since all the page numbers and content remained the same as the original 2004 edition.

11 It is worth noting that although Hinnebusch reviewed her book, she neither refers to him nor to his "analytical framework." See Raymond Hinnebusch

and Anoushiravan Ehteshami (eds.), *The Foreign Policy of Middle East States*. Boulder, Co.: Lynne Rienner Publishers, 2002.

12 Nicholas Noe, *Voice of Hezbollah: The Statements of Sayyed Hassan Nasrallah*. London: Verso, 2007.

13 Augustus Richard Norton, *Hezbollah: A Short History*. First edition. Princeton: Princeton University Press, 2007.

14 Of course, I will not mention typos and the like.

15 The Cairo Agreement (CA) was signed on 3 November 1969 between Lebanon and the PLO granting the latter license to launch attacks from south Lebanon against Israel. The CA and all its corollaries were annulled by the Lebanese parliament and published in the Official Gazette on 18 June 1987 under law number 87/25.

16 "Tobiah Waldron prepared a comprehensive, even perceptive index, which I am confident readers will find unusually useful." (p. 187)

17 The late Iranian Minister of Defense who was instrumental in the founding of Amal and Hizbullah.

18 The last session was scheduled on 25 July, which naturally did not take place because of the war.

19 Hizbullah does not monopolize Shi'ite representation; Amal also has its share of the pie.

20 See http://www.tayyar.org/files/documents/fpm_hezbollah.pdf (Acessed 6 July 2008).

21 As mentioned on the book's back cover.

Selected Bibliography

Abun-Nasr, Fadeel M. (2003). *Hizbullah: Haqa'iq wa Ab'ad [Hizbullah: Facts and Dimensions]*. Beirut: World Book Publishing.

Ahmad, Rif'at Sayyid. (2006). *Hasan Nasrallah: Tha'ir min Al-Janub [Hasan Nasrallah: A Rebel from the South]*. Cairo: Dar Al-Kitab Al-'Arabi.

Alagha, Joseph. (2011). *Hizbullah's Documents: From the 1985 Open Letter to the 2009 Manifesto*. Amsterdam: Pallas Publications.

— (2008). *Hizbullah: Al-Tarikh Al-Aydiyulugi wa Al-Siyasi 1978-2008 [Hizbullah: The Ideological and Political History]*. Beirut: Institute for Strategic Studies.

— (Spring 2008) "The Israeli-Hizbullah 34-Day War: Causes and Consequences". *Arab Studies Quarterly* 30.2: 1-22.

— (2006). *The Shifts in Hizbullah's Ideology*. Amsterdam: Amsterdam University Press.

— (Autumn 2006). "Hizbullah's Promise". *ISIM Review* 18: 36.

— (Winter 2005). "Hizbullah After the Syrian Withdrawal". *Middle East Report* 237: 34-39.

— (March 2004). "Hizbullah and Martyrdom". *ORIENT: German Journal for Politics and Economics of the Middle East* 45.1: 47-74.

— (September 2003). "Hizbullah, Terrorism, and Sept. 11". *ORIENT: German Journal for Politics and Economics of the Middle East* 44.3: 385-412.

— (January 2002). "Hizbullah, Iran and the *Intifada*". *ISIM Newsletter* 9: 35.

— (July 2001). "Successen Hezbollah bij 'kleine oorlog' om Shib'a [Hizbullah's Successes in the Small War in Shib'a]". *Soera: Midden-Oosten Tijdschrift*. 9.2: 34-38.

— (2001). "Hizbullah's Gradual Integration in the Lebanese Public Sphere". *Sharqiyyat: Journal of the Dutch Association for Middle Eastern and Islamic Studies* 13.1: 34-59.

Alagha, Joseph and Myriam Catusse. (2008). "Les services sociaux de Hezbollah: Effort de guerre, ethos religieux et ressources politiques", in: *Le Hezbollah: État Des Lieux*, edited by Sabrina Mervin. Paris: Actes Sud.

Anderson, Benedict. (1991, 2006). *Imagined Communities: Reflections on the Origin and Spread of Nationalism*. London: Verso.

Anon (2007). *Mawsu'at Nasrallah [Nasrallah's Encyclopedia]*. Three Volumes. Beirut: Manshurat Al-Fajir.

Anon (2006). *Hizbullah: Al-Muqawama wa Al-Tahrir [Hizbullah: Resistance and Liberation]*. Beirut, Edito International (A thirteen volume encyclopedia).

Antoun, Richard T. (2001). *Understanding Fundamentalism: Christian, Islamic, and Jewish Movements*. Oxford: Altamira Press.

'Atrisi, Shaykh Ja'far Hasan. (2005). *Hizbullah: Al-Khiyar Al-As'ab wa Damanat Al-Watan Al-Kubra [Hizbullah: The Difficult Choice and Lebanon's Greatest Guarantee]*. Beirut: Dar Al-Mahajja Al-Bayda'.

Balqaziz, Abd Al-Ilah. (2006). *Hizbullah min Al-Tahrir ila Al-Radi' [Hizbullah from Liberation to Deterrence]*. Beirut, Markaz Dirasat Al-Wihda Al-'Arabiyya.

— (2000). *Al-Muqawama wa Tahrir Al-Janub: Hizbullah min Al-Hawza Al-'Ilmiyya ila Al-Jabha [The Resistance and the Liberation of the South: Hizbullah from the Religious Seminary to the Battle Front]*. Beirut: Markaz Dirasat Al-Wihda Al-'Arabiyya.

Barker, Chris and Dariusz Galasinski. (2001). *Cultural Studies and Discourse Analysis: A Dialogue on Language and Identity*. London: Sage Publications.

Baumann, Gerd. (1996). *Contesting Culture: Discourses of Identity in Multi-Ethnic London*. Cambridge: Cambridge University Press.

Bayat, Asef. (2010). *Life as Politics: How Ordinary People Change the Middle East*. Stanford: Stanford University Press.

— (2007) *Making Islam Democratic: Social Movements and the Post-Islamist Turn*. Stanford: Stanford University Press.

— (1997). *Street Politics: Poor People's Movements in Iran*. New York: Columbia University Press.

— (Fall 1996) "The Coming of a Post-Islamist Society". Critique: Critical Middle East Studies 9: 43-52.

Bourdieu, Pierre. (1994). *Language and Symbolic Power*. Oxford: Polity Press.

— (1994). "Structures, Habitus, and Practices", in: *The Polity Reader in Cultural Theory*. Cambridge: Cambridge University Press, 95-110.

— (1993). *The Field of Cultural Production*. Cambridge: Polity Press.

— (1990). *In Other Words: Essays Towards a Reflexive Sociology*. Cambridge: Polity Press.

— (1991). "Genesis and Structure of the Religious Field". *Comparative Social Research* 13: 1-44.

— (1980). *The Logic of Practice*. Cambridge: Polity Press.

— (1971). "Genèse et structure du champ religieux". *Revue française de sociologie*, 12: 295-334.

Byers, Ann. (2003). *Lebanon's Hezbollah (Inside the World's Most Infamous Terrorist Organizations)*. London: Rosen Publishing Group.

Calhoun, Craig. (2003). "The Democratic Integration of Europe: Interests, Identity, and the Public Sphere." In: *Europe without Borders: Re-Mapping Territory Citizenship and Identity in a Transnational Age*, M. Berezin and M. Schain, eds. Baltimore: Johns Hopkins University Press, 243-274.

— (1994). *Social Theory and the Politics of Identity*. Oxford: Blackwell.

Castells, Manuel and Martin Ince. (2003). *Conversations with Manuel Castells*. Cambridge: Polity Press.

Castells, Manuel. (2000). *The Rise of the Network Society. (The Information Age: Economy, Society, and Culture, Volume I)*. Second edition. Oxford: Blackwell Publishers Ltd.

— (2004). *The Power of Identity. (The Information Age: Economy, Society, and Culture, Volume II)*. Second edition. Oxford: Blackwell Publishers Ltd.

— (2000). *End of Millennium. (The Information Age: Economy, Society, and Culture, Volume II)*. Second edition. Oxford: Blackwell Publishers Ltd.

Chandhoke, Neera. (1995). *State and Civil Society: Explorations in Political Theory*. London: Sage Publications.

Cobban, Helena. (1986). "The Growth of the Shi'i Power in Lebanon and its Implications for the Future", in: Juan Cole and Nikki Keddie (eds.). *Shi'ism and Social Protest*. New Haven: Yale University Press, 137-155.

— (1985). *The Shia Community and the Future of Lebanon*. Washington, D.C.: American Institute for Islamic Affairs.

— (1985). *The Making of Modern Lebanon*. London: Hutchinson.

Deeb, Yusuf. (February 2001). *Mazari' Shib'a: Dirasa Watha'qiyya Li-Marahil Al-Ihtilal wa Al-Iqtila' wa Al-Atma' wa Ta'kid Al-Haq Al-Lubnani [Shib'a Farms: Documented Research on the Stages of the Occupation, the Withdrawal, the Greed, and the Insistance on the Lebanese Right (of Ownership)]*. Beirut: Lebanese Parliament.

Dishum, Ramzi and Muhammad Jarbu'a. (2001). *Al-'Amama Al-Sawda': Hizbullah wa Al-Mu'adala Al-Iqlimiyya [The Black Turban: Hizbullah and the International Equation]*. Beirut: Al-Nida' lil Nashr wa Al-Tawz'i.

Eickelman, Dale F. and Jon W. Anderson (eds). (2003). *New Media in the Muslim World: The Emerging Public Sphere*. Second edition. Bloomington: Indiana University Press.

El-Ezzi, Ghassan. (1998). *Hizbullah: Min Al-Hulm Al-Aydiyuluji ila Al-Waqi'iyya Al-Siyasiyya [Hizbullah: From Ideological Dream to Political Realism]*. Kuwait: Qurtas Publishing.

Fadlallah, Hadi. (1999). *Fikr al-Imam Musa al-Sadr al-Siyasi wa al-Islahi [The Political and Reformist Thought of Imam Musa al-Sadr]*. Beirut: Dar al-Hadi.

Fadlallah, Hasan. (2001). *Suqut al-Wahim: Hazimat al-Ihtilal wa Intisar al-Muqawama fi Lubnan [The Fall of the Illusion: The Defeat of the Occupation and the Victory of the Resistance in Lebanon]*. Beirut: Dar al-Hadi.

— (1998). *Harb al-Iradat: Sira' al-Muqawama wa al-Ihtilal al-Isra'ili fi Luban-an [The War of Volitions: The Struggle of the Resistance and the Israeli Occu-pation Forces in Lebanon]*. Beirut: Dar al-Hadi.

— (1994). *Al-Khiyar al-Akhar: Hizbullah: al-Sira al-Dhatiyya wa al-Mawqif [The Other Choice: Hizbullah's Autobiography and Stance]*. Beirut: Dar al-Hadi.

Fadlallah, Ayatullah Al-Sayyid Muhammad Husayn. (2001). *Al-Haraka Al-Islamiyya: Humum wa Qadaya [The Islamic Movement: Worries and Causes]*. Fourth edition. Beirut: Dar Al-Malak.

— (2001). *Fiqh Al-Shari'a [The Jurisprudence of the Shari'a]*. Volume I, fifth edition. Beirut: Dar Al-Malak.

— (2000). *Iradat Al-Quwwa: Jihad al-Muqawama fi Khitab al-Sayyid Fadlal-lah. [The Will to Power: The Jihad of the Resistance in Fadlallah's Discourse]*. First edition. Beirut: Dar Al-Malak.

— (17 June 1995). *"Fi Hiwar Al-Din wa Al-Mar'a wa Al-Siyasa wa al-Mufawa-dat [Dialogue on Religion, Women, Politics, and the Peace Talks]"*. *Al-Majal-la*: 23-26.

— (1994a). *Al-Ma'alim Al-Jadidat lil-Marja'iyya Al-Shi'iyya [The New Features of the Shi 'ite Religious Authority]*. Compiled by Salim Al-Husayni.Third Edition. Beirut: Dar Al-Malak.

— (1994b). *Al-Marja'iyya wa Harakat Al-Waqi' [Religious Authority and the Contemporary World Transformation]*. Beirut: Dar Al-Malak.

— (1985). *Al-Islam wa Mantiq al-Quwwa [Islam and the Logic of Power]*. Third Edition. Beirut: Dar Al-Malak.

Fakhry, Majid. (1998). *The Qur'an: A Modern English Version*. Reading: Garnet Publishing.

Fayyad, Ali. (22 November 1999). *"Al-Saraya Al-Lubnaniyya Limuqawamat Al-Ihtilal Al-Israeli: Al-Tarkiba Al-Ijtima'iyya-Al-Siyassiyya wa Afaq Al-Dawr"* ["Lebanese Multiconfessional Brigades: The Socio-Political Make-up and Future Role"]. Beirut: CCSD.

Fuller, Graham E. (2003). *The Future of Political Islam*. New York: Palgrave Macmillan.

Fuller, Graham E. and Rend Rahim Francke. (1999). *The Arab Shi'a: The Forgotten Muslims*. New York: St. Martin's Press.

Foucault, Michel. (1972). *Power/Knowledge*. C. Gordon (ed.). New York: Pantheon.

Goldstein, Joshua S. (2003). *International Relations*. Fifth Edition. New York: Longman.

Gunaratna, Rohan. (2003). "Suicide Terrorism: A Global Threat", in: Pamela L. Griset and Sue Mahan. *Terrorism in Perspective*. London: Sage Publications, 220-225.

Habermas, Jürgen. (1989). *The Structural Transformation of the Public Sphere: An Inquiry into a Category of Bourgeois Society*. Cambridge: Polity Press.

— (1987). *Theory of Communicative Action*. 2 Vols. Cambridge: Polity Press.

— (1979). *Communication and the Evolution of Society*. Boston: Beacon Press.

— (Fall 1974). "The Public Sphere". *New German Critique* 1.3: 49-55.

Halawi, Majed. (1992). *A Lebanon Defied: Musa al-Sadr and the Shi'a Community*. Boulder: Westview Press.

Hamade, Shaykh Hasan. (2001). *Sirr Al-Intisar: Qira'a fi Al-Khalfiyyah Al-Imaniyya Al-Jihadiyya li Hizbullah [The Secret of Victory: A Reading in the Religious, Jihadi Background of Hizbullah]*. Beirut: Dar al-Hadi.

— (2000). *Ayyam Al-Intisar [Days of Victory]*. Beirut: Dar Al-Hadi.

Hamzeh, Nizar A. (2004). *In the Path of Hizbullah*. Syracuse: Syracuse University Press.

Harik, Judith Palmer. (2004, 2006). *Hezbollah: The Changing Face of Terrorism*. London: I.B. Tauris.

Hinnebusch, Raymond and Anoushiravan Ehteshami (eds.). (2002). *The Foreign Policy of Middle Eastern States*. Boulder: Lynne Rienner Publishers.

Hiro, Dilip. (1985). *Iran Under the Ayatollah*. First edition. London: Routledge and Kegan Paul.

Hizbullah's Political Manifesto. (2009). First edition. Beirut: Media Relations Office, (71 pages). Translated into three languages: English, French, and Spanish (59 pages each and all published in 2009).

Hizbullah's Central Press Office. (16 July 2002). *Mu'tamar Al-Baladiyyat Al-Awwal [The First Municipal Conference/Convention]*. Beirut: Hizbullah's Central Press Office.

— (2000). *Malahim Al-Butula: 'Amaliyyat Al-Muqawama Al-Islamiyya Al-Naw'iyya [Heroic Epics: The Islamic Resistance's Major Operations]*. (A Videotape and a CD). Beirut: Hizbullah's Central Press Office.

— (1992-2000). *Safahat 'Izin fi Kitab Al-Umma: 'Ard wa Tawthiq Li-'Amaliyat Al-Muqawama Al-Islamiyya [Pages of Dignity in the Book of the Nation: Portrayal and Documentation of the Islamic Resistance's Operations]*. Beirut: Hizbullah's Central Press Office.

— (1998). *Kawkab Al-Shahada: Sirat, Hayat, wa Jihad Sayyid Al-Muqawama Al-Islamiyya, Al-Sayyid Abbas Al-Musawi [The Planet of Martyrdom: Biography, Life, and Jihad of the Leader of the Islamic Resistance, Al-Sayyid Abbas Al-Musawi]*. Beirut: Hizbullah's Central Information Office.

— (October 1998). *Sjil Al-Nur: Qanadil Ila Al-Zaman Al-Akhar [Al-Nur's Record: Lanterns for the Hereafter]*. Beirut: Hizbullah's Central Press Office.

Hizbullah's Central Internet Office. (2002). *Saykh Al-Shuhada': Raghib Harb [The Shaykh of Martyrs: Raghib Harb]*. CD-ROM.

— (2001). *Fajr Al-Intisar [The Dawn of Victory]*. (Documents the Israeli Withdrawal). CD-ROM.

— (2001) *Mu'taqal Al-Khiam [Al-Khiam Detention Center]*. CD-ROM.

— (2000). *Wa Kanat Al-Bidaya: Imam Musa Al-Sadr [And It was the Beginning: Imam Musa Al-Sadr]*. CD-ROM.

— (2000). *Tahrir Asra Mu'taqal Al-Khiyam [The Liberation of the Khiam Detainees]*. CD-ROM.

"Hizbullah: Identity and Role". (24 September 1998). In "Hot Spot" (*Nuqta Sakhina*). AL-JAZEERA TV.

Hizbullah's Politburo: The Committee of Analysis and Studies. (1989). *Wathiqat Al-Ta'if: Dirasat fi Al-Madmun [The Ta'if Document: A Study of its Content]*. First edition. Beirut.

Husem, Eric. (2002). *The Syrian Involvement in Lebanon: An Analysis of the Role of Lebanon in Syrian Regime Security, from Ta'if to the Death of Hafiz al-Asad (1989-2000)*. Kjeller, Norway: Norwegian Defense Research Establishment.

Al-Hurr Al-'Amili, Al-Shaykh Muhammad Bin Al-Hasan. (1993). *Wasa'il Al-Shi'a [Shi'ite Rituals]*. Beirut: Mu'assat Al-Hulul, Bayt Ihya' Al-Turath.

Ibrahim, Fu'ad. (1998). *Al-Faqih wa Al-Dawla: Al-Fikar Al-Siyasi Al-Shi'i [The Jurisprudent and the State: Shi'ite Political Thought]*. Beirut: Dar Al-Kunuz Al-Adabiyya.

Idris, Nisreen. (2001). *'Irs Aylul:Qissat al-Shahid Hadi Hasan Nasrallah [September's Wedding: The Story of the Martyr Hadi Hasan Nasrallah]*. Beirut: Dar Al-Amir.

Jaber, Hala. (1997). *Hezbollah: Born with a Vengeance*. New York: Colombia University Press.

Jafri, Husain M. (1979). *Origins and Early Development of Shi'a Islam*. London:Longman Group Ltd.

Jorisch, Avi. (2004). *Beacon of Hatred: Inside Hizballah's Al-Manar Television*. Washington, D.C.: Washington Institute for Near East Policy.

Al-Jam'iyya Al-Ijtima'iyya Al-Thaqafiyya Li-Abna' Al-Qura Al-Sabi'. (November 2003). *Al-Qura Al-Sabi'Al-Lubnaniyya Al-Muhtalla: Dirasa Qanuni-yya-Ijtima'iyya [The Seven Lebanese Occupied Villages: A Legal-Social Study]*. First edition. Beirut: Al-Markaz Al-Istishari Lil-Dirasat.

Kader, Haytham A. (1990). *The Syrian Social Nationalist Party: Its Ideology and Early History*. Beirut: Dar Fikr.

Kadivar, Shaykh Muhsin. (2000). *Nazariyyat Al-Dawla fi Al-Fiqh Al-Shi'i: Buhuth fi Wilawat Al-Faqih [The Theory of the State in the Shi'ite Jurisprudence: Research on the Rule of the Religious Jurist]*. Beirut: Dar al-Jadid.

Kane, Ousmane. (2003). *Muslim Modernity in Postcolonial Nigeria: A Study of the Society for the Removal of Innovation and Reinstatement of Tradition*. Leiden: Brill.

Karmon, Ely. (December 2003). *Fight on all Fronts: Hizballah, the War on Terror, and the War on Iraq*. Policy Focus, no. 46. Washington, D.C.: The Washington Institute for Near East Policy.

Kashshafat Al-Imam Al-Mahdi. (2003). *Sayyid Shuhada Al-Muqawama, Abbas Al-Musawi: Nash'tahu, Jihadahu, Shahadatahu [The Leader of the Martyrs of the Resistance, Abbas Al-Musawi: His Childhood, Jihad, and Martyrdom]*. Beirut: Kashshafat Al-Imam Al-Mahdi.

Kaufman, Asher. (Autumn 2002). "Who Owns the Shebaa Farms? Chronicle of a Territorial Dispute". *The Middle East Journal* 56.4: 576-595.

Keddie, Nikki and Juan Cole (eds). (1986). *Shi'ism and Social Protest*. New Haven: Yale University Press.

Kepel, Gilles. (2008). *Beyond Terror and Martyrdom: The Future of the Middle East*. Translated by Pascale Ghazaleh. Cambridge: The Belknap Press of Harvard University Press.

— (2002). *Jihad: The Trial of Political Islam*. Translated by Anthony F. Roberts. London: I.B. Tauris Publishers.

Khalidi-Beyhum, Ramla. (1999). *Economic and Social Commission for Western Asia, Poverty Reduction Policies in Jordan and Lebanon: An Overview*. Eradicating Poverty Studies (Series number 10). New York: United Nations.

Al-Khamina'i, Al-Imam. (2002). *Al-Sira wa Al-Masira [Biography and Path]*. Beirut: Al-Dar Al-Islamiyya.

— (2001). *'Itr Al-Shahada [The Perfume of Martyrdom]*. Beirut: Al-Dar Al-Islamiyyah. (A series of lectures delivered by Khamina'i before the victory of the Islamic Revolution in 1979 and in the early years of the Iraq-Iran war).

— (2000). *Al-'Awda ila Nahj Al-Balagha [The Return to the Peak of Eloquence]*. Beirut: Markaz Baqiyyat Allah.

— (2000). *Al-Wilaya [Guardianship]*. Beirut: Dar Al-Hadi.

— (1999). *Al-Imama wa Al-Wilaya: Qiyadat Al-Mjtama' Al-Islami wa Mas'uliyyat Al-Muslim [The Imamate and Guardianship: The Leadership of the Muslim Community and the Responsibilities of the Muslim]*. Beirut: Markaz Baqiyyat Allah. (A series of lectures delivered by Khamina'i before the victory of the Islamic Revolution in 1979, collected and published in 1980).

— (1999). *Shams Al-Wilaya [The Sun of Guardianship]*. Beirut: Markaz Baqiyyat Allah.

— (1998). *Al-Khutut Al-'Amma lil Fikr Al-Islami [The General Guidelines of Islamic Thought]*. Beirut: Markaz Baqiyyat Allah.

— (1997). *General Concepts of Islam in the Quran*. Tehran: Department of Translation and Publication, Islamic Culture and Relations Organization.

— (1995). *Al-Hukuma fi Al-Islam [Islamic Government]*. Translated by Ra'd Hadi Jaber. Beirut: Dar Al-Rawda. (A series of lectures delivered during Friday prayers by Khamina'i between 1983 and 1995 during his appointment by Imam Khumayni as the leader of prayers in Tehran University).

Khatami, Muhammad. (2000). *Madinat Al-Siyasat: Fusul min Tatawwur Al-Fikr Al-Siyasi fi Al-Gharb [The City of Politics: Sections in the Development of Political Thought in the West]*. Beirut: Dar al-Jadid.

— (1999). *Al-Islam wa al-'Alam [Islam and the World]*. Cairo: Maktabat al-Shuruq.

— (1998a). *Mutala'a fi al-Din wa al-Islam wa al-'Asr [A Reading in Religion, Islam, and Modern Times]*. Beirut: Dar al-Jadid.

— (1998b). *Bim Muj [In the Commotion]*. Beirut: Dar al-Jadid.

Al-Khatib, Munif. (2001). *Mazari' Shib'a: Haqa'iq wa Watha'iq [Shib'a Farms: Facts and Documents]*. Beirut: Sharikat Al-Matbu'at Lil-Tawzi' wa Al-Nashr.

Khatun, Al-Shaykh Muhammad Ali. (2002). *Amir Al-Qafila: Al-Sira Al-Zati-yya Li-Sayyid Al-Muqawama Al-Islamiyya, Al-Sayyid Abbas Al-Musawi [The Autobiography of the Leader of the Islamic Resistance, Al-Sayyid Abbas Al-Musawi]*. Introduction by Sayyid Hasan Nasrallah. Beirut: Dar Al-Wala.

El-Khazen, Farid. (2003). "The Postwar Political Process: Authoritarianism by Diffusion", in: Thoedor Hanf and Nawaf Salam (eds.). *Lebanon in Limbo: Postwar Society and State in an Uncertain Regional Environment*. Baden Baden: Nomos, 53-74.

— (Autumn 2003). "Political Parties in Postwar Lebanon: Parties in Search of Partisans". *Middle East Journal* 57.4: 605-624.

— (2000). *The Breakdown of the State in Lebanon: 1967-1976.* London: I.B. Tauris Publishers.

— (2000). *Intikhabat Lubnanma Ba'd Al-Harb:1992, 1996, 2000: Dimuqratiyya Bila Khiyar [The Lebanese Elections After the War: 1992, 1996, 2000: Democracy without Choice].* Beirut: Dar Al-Nahar.

— (Spring 1992). "Lebanon's Communal Elite-Mass Politics: The Institutionalization of Disintegration". *Beirut Review.* 3.

Khosrokhavar, Farhad. (2002). *Les Nouveaux Martyrs D'Allah [God's New Martyrs].* Paris: Flammarion.

— (2000) "Le Hezbollah, de la Société Révolutionnaire a la Société Post Islamiste [The Hizbullah: From a Revolutionary Society to a Post-Islamist Society]". CURAPP, *Passions et Sciences humaines,* PUF, 129-144.

— (1995). *L'Islamisme et la Mort: Le Martyre Revolutionnaire en Iran [Islamism and Death: The Revolutionary Martyrs in Iran].* Paris: L'Harmattan.

Khumayni, Ruhallah. (1996). *Al-Hukumah Al-Islamiyyah [The Islamic Government].* Tehran: The Institute of Coordinating and Publishing Imam Khumayni's Heritage.

— (1996). *Al-Imam Al-Khumayni wa Thaqafat 'Ashura [Al-Imam Al-Khumayni and 'Ashura Culture].* Tehran: The Institute of Coordinating and Publishing Imam Khumayni's Heritage.

— (1992). *Kashf al-Asrar [The Revelation of Secrets].* Beirut: Dar wa Maktabat Al-Rasul Al-Akram.

— (1989). *Sahifat Al-Thawra Al-Islamiyya: Nass Al-Wasiyya Al-Siyasiyya Al-Ilahiyya Lil-Imam Al-Khumayni, Qa'id Al-Thawra Al-Islamiyya [The (Religious) Book of the Islamic Revolution: The Text of the Political-Divine Will of Imam Khumayni, the Leader of the Islamic Revolution].* Beirut: Iranian Cultural Center.

— (1981). *Tahrir Al-Wasila.* Volume 1. Beirut: Dar Al-Ta'aruf. [*Tahrir Al-Wasila* is Imam Khumayni's practical treatise (*risala 'amaliyya*)].

— (1981). *Islam and Revolution: Writings and Declarations.* Translated by Hamid Algar. Berkeley: Mizan Press.

— (1980). *Al-Jihad Al-Akbar [Greater Jihad].* Translated by Husayn Kurani. Tehran: Islamian Grand Library.

Kohlberg, Etan. (1997). "Medieval Muslim Views on Martyrdom", in: *Mededeelingen der Koninklijke Akademie van Wetenschappen, Afdeeling Letterkunde; dl. 60, nr. 7.* Amsterdam: KNAW publications, 281-307.

Kramer, Martin. (1997). "The Oracle of Hizbullah", in: R. Scott Appleby (ed.) *Spokesmen for the Despised.* Chicago: The University of Chicago Press, 83-181.

— (1997). *The Islamism Debate*. Tel Aviv: The Moshe Dayan Center for Middle Eastern and African Studies.

— (1993). "Hizbullah: The Calculus of Jihad", in: *Fundamentalisms and the State: Remarking Polities, Economics, and Militance*. Vol. III. Chicago: The University of Chicago Press, 539-56.See: http://www.martinkramer.org/pages/899528/index.htm

— (Autumn 1991). "Sacrifice and 'Self-Martyrdom' in Shi'ite Lebanon". *Terrorism and Political Violence* 3.3: 30-47.See: http://www.geocities.com/martinkramerorg/Sacrifice.htm

— (1990). "Redeeming Jerusalem: The Pan-Islamic Premise of Hizbullah", in: David Menashri (ed.). *The Iranian Revolution and the Muslim World*. Boulder, 105-130.

— (1989). *Hizbullah's Vision of the West*. Washington, D.C.: Washington Institute for Near East Policy.

— (ed.). (1987). *Shi'ism, Resistance and Revolution*. Boulder: Westview Press.

— (August 1987). *The Moral Logic of Hizbullah*. The Dayan Center for Middle Eastern and African Studies. Occasional Papers. 101: 1-28. Tel Aviv University: The Shiloah Institute.

Krayyem, Nayef. (1997). *Hawla Al-Dawla Al-Mansuba li Hizbullah [On Hizbullah's Alleged State]*. Beirut: Hizbullah's Educational Mobilization Unit.

Al-Kurani, 'Ali. (1985). *Tariqat Hizbullah fi Al-'Amal Al-Islami [Hizbullah's Method of Islamic Mobilization]*. Tehran, Maktab Al-I'lam Al-Islami: Al-Mu'assa Al-'Alamiyya.

The Lebanese Council of Muslim 'Ulama. (2002). *Masa'il Jihadiyya wa Hukm Al-'Amaliyat Al-Istishhadiyyah [Jihadi Issues and the Judgment of Martyrdom Operations]*. Beirut: Dar Al-Wihda Al-Islamiyya.

Leenders, Reinoud. (30 July 2003). "Hizbullah: Rebel Without a Cause?" *ICG Middle East Briefing Paper*. http://www.crisisweb.org/projects/middleeast/arab_israeliconflict/reports/A401070_30072003.pdf

Levitt, Mattew A. (August-September 2003). "Hezbollah's West Bank Terror Network". *Middle East Intelligence Bulletin*, 5.8-9. http://www.meib. org/articles/0308_l3.htm

Lynch, Mark. (1999). *State Interests and Public Spheres*. New York: Colombia University Press.

Mackey, Sandra. (1989). *Lebanon: Death of a Nation*. New York: Congdon and Weed Inc.

Al-Madini, Tawfiq. (1999). *Amal wa Hizbullah fi Halabat al-Mujabahat al-Mahaliyya wa al-Iqlimiyya [Amal and Hizbullah in the Arena of Domestic and Regional Struggles]*. Damascus: Al-ahli.

Al-Manar. (2003). *Shu'a' Al-Nasr [The Bean of Victory: A Collection of Works in Support of the Intifada and the Palestinian People].* Beirut: Dar Al-Manar Li-Intaj Al-Mar'i wa Al-Tawzi'. (VHS).

— (2003). *Amir Al-Qafila [The Autobiography of the Leader of the Islamic Resistance, Al-Sayyid Abbas Al-Musawi].* Beirut: Dar Al-Manar Li-Intaj Al-Mar'i wa Al-Tawzi'. (VHS).

— (2002). Al-Harb Al-Sadisa: Al-Ijtiyah Al-Sahyuni Li-Lubnan 1982 [The Sixth War: The Zionist Invasion of Lebanon 1982]. Beirut: Dar Al-Manar Li-Intaj Al-Mar'i wa Al-Tawzi'. (VHS).

— (2001). *Qudwat Al-Tha'rin [The Leaders of the Revolutionaries].* Beirut:Dar Al-Manar Li-Intaj Al-Mar'i wa Al-Tawzi'. (VHS).

— (2000). *'Urs Al-Nasr: Tahrir Qura Al-Janub wa Al-Biqa 'Al-Gharbi wa Dahr Al-Ihtilal Al-Sahyuni [The Wedding of Victory: The Liberation of the South and the Western Biqa' and the Defeat of the Zionist Occupier].* (Documents the Israeli Withdrawal in May 2000). Beirut: Dar Al-Manar Li-Intaj Al-Mar'i wa Al-Tawzi'. (VHS and three CD-ROMs).

Mandaville, Peter. (2007) *Global Political Islam.* New York: Routledge.

Markaz Baqiyyat Allah. (1999). *Al-Jihad wa Khisal Al-Mujahidin [Jihad and the Martyrs' Traits].* Beirut: Markaz Baqiyyat Allah.

Martin, Gus. (2003). *Understanding Terrorism: Challenges, Perspectives, and Issues.* London: Sage Publications.

Masri, Shafiq. (Winter 2002). "Al-Irhab fi Al-Qanun Al-Duwali [Terrorism in International Law]". *Shu'un al-Awsat* 105: 46-56.

Al-Muqawama Al-Wataniyya Al-Lubnaniyya. (1985). *Al-'Amaliyyat Al-Isti-shadiyya: Watha'iq wa Suwar [Martyrdom Operations: Documents and Pictures] (1982-1985).* Damascus: Al-Markaz Al-'Arabi li al-Ma'limat.

Mustapha, Amin. (2006). *Al-I'sar [The Tornado].* Beirut: Dar Al-Hadi.

— (2003). *Al-Muqawama fi Lubnan [The Resistance in Lebanon] (1948-2000).* Beirut: Dar Al-Hadi.

Al-Nabulsi, Al-Saykh Al-'Allama 'Afif. (2003). *Mushahadat wa Tajarib: Laqa-tat mi Sirat Al-Imam Al-Sadr [Sightings and Experiences: Glimpses from Imam Al-Sadr's Biography].* Beirut: Dar Al-Mahajja Al-Bayda'.

Al-Nasiri, Al-Shaykh Ahmad (2005). *Al-Mawt Al-Muqadas: Dirasa 'an Al-'Amaliyyat Al-Istishhadiyya 'inda Al-Shi'a [Divine Death: A Study on the Martyrdom Operations of the Shi'a].* First edition. Beirut: Dar Al-Mahajja Al-Bayda'.

Nasr, Seyyed Hossein, Hamid Dabashi, and Seyyed Vali Reza Nasr (eds.). (1988). *Shi'ism: Doctrines, Thought, and Spirituality.* New York: State University of New York Press.

— (1989). *Expectation of the Millennium: Shi'ism in History*. New York: State University of New York Press.

Nasrallah, Fida. (1992). *Prospects for Lebanon: The Questions of South Lebanon*. Oxford: Centre for Lebanese Studies.

NBN (21, 28 July and 4 August 2002). *Ahzab Lubnan: Hizbullah [Lebanese Parties: Hizbullah, Parts I, II, III]*. (VHS).

Noe, Nicholas (ed.). (2007). *Voice of Hezbollah: The Statements of Sayyed Hassan Nasrallah*. London: Verso.

Norton, Augustus R. (2007, Fifth edition: 2009). *Hezbollah: A Short History*. Princeton: Princeton University Press.

— (January 2002) "America's Approach to the Middle East: Legacies, Questions, and Possibilities". *Current History* 101.651: 3-7.

— (Autumn 2000) "Hizbullah and the Israeli Withdrawal from Southern Lebanon", *Journal of Palestine Studies*, 30.1: 22-39.

— (February 2000). "Hizballah of Lebanon: Extremist Ideas vs. Mundane Politics". *Council on Foreign Relations*. See: http://www.foreignrelations.org/public/resource.cgi?pub!3586

— (January 1998). "Hizballah: From Radicalism to Pragmatism". *Middle East Policy Council* 5.4. www.mepc.org/journal/9801norton.html

— (1987). *Amal and the Shi'a Struggle for the Soul of Lebanon*. Austin: University Press of Texas.

Olmert, Joseph. (1987). "The Shi'is and the Lebanese State", in: Martin Kramer (ed.). *Shi'ism, Resistance, and Revolution*. Boulder, CO.: Westview Press.

Picard, Elizabeth. (1993). *The Lebanese Shi'a and Political Violence*. UNRISD: Discussion Paper 42.

— (1986). "Political Identities and Communal Identities: Shifting Mobilization Among the Lebanese Shi'a Through Ten Years of War, 1975-1985", in: Dennis L. Thompson and Dov Ronen (eds.) *Ethnicity, Politics and Development*. Boulder, Co.: Lynne Riener Publishers, 157-78.

Piscatori, James. (2000). *Islam, Islamists, and the Electoral Principle in the Middle East*. Leiden: ISIM.

Qasim, Shaykh Na'im. (2010). *Hizbullah: Al-Manhaj, Al-Tajriba, Al-Mustaqbal [Hizbullah: The Curriculum, the Experience, the Future]*. Seventh revised and updated edition. Beirut: Dar Al-Mahajja Al-Bayda'.

— (2008). *Mujtama' Al-Muqawama: Iradat Al-Shahada wa Sina'at Al-Intisar [The Society of Resistance: The Will to Martyrdom and the Making of Victory]*. Beirut: Dar Al-Ma'arif Al-Hikmiyya.

Interview with Shaykh Na'im Qasim. (10 October 2002). *Al-Manar TV*. "Al-Shahada wa al-'Ithar" [Martyrdom and "Preference"] in the program entitled "*Al-Din wa Al-Hayat [Religion and life]*".

Ranstorp, Magnus. (Summer 1998). "The Strategy and Tactics of Hizbullah's Current 'Lebanonization Process'". *Mediterranean Politics* 3.1: 103-134.

— (1997). *Hizb'allah in Lebanon: The Politics of the Western Hostage Crises.* London: Macmillan Press Ltd.

Reuter, Christoph. (2004). *My Life as a Weapon: A Modern History of Suicide Bombing.* Translated from German by Helena Ragg-Kirkby. Princeton, NJ: Princeton University Press.

Rizq, Hiyan. (2002). *Sayyid Al-Qada: Qissat Sayyid Shuhada Al-Muqawama Al-Islamiyya [The Leader of the Leaders: The Story of the Leader of the Islamic Resistance].* Beirut: Dar Al-Amir.

Rizq, Imad. (2003). *Al-Sharq Al-Awsat fi Mizan Al-Ru'b [The Middle East in the Balance of Terror].* Beirut: Naufal Group.

Roy, Olivier. (2004). *Globalised Islam: The Search for a New Umma.* Revised and updated edition. London: Hurst and Company.

Al-Ruhaimi, Abdul-Halim. (2002). "The Da'wa Islamic Party: Origins, Actors and Ideology", in: *Ayatollahs, Sufis and Ideologues: State, Religion and Social Movements in Iraq.* Edited by Faleh Abdul-Jabar. London: Saqi books, 149-160.

Ruhani, Muhammad Mahdi. (2002). *Thawrat Al-Faqih wa Dawlatuhu: Qira'at fi 'Alamiyyat Madrasat Al-Imam Al-Khumayni [The Revolution of the Juris-prudent and his Government: Readings in the Global Nature of Imam Khu-mayni's School].* Second edition. Beirut: Mu'assat Al-Balagh.

Saad, Abdo. (2005). *Al-Intikhabat Al-Niyabiyya li-'Am 2005: Qira'at wa Nata'ij [The Parliamentary Elections of 2005: Readings and Results].* Beirut: Markaz Beirut lil Abhath wa Al-Ma'lumat (The Beirut Center for Research and Information).

Saad-Ghorayeb, Amal. (September 2003). "Factors Conducive to the Politici-zation of the Lebanese Shi'a and the Emergence of Hizbu'llah". *Journal of Islamic Studies* 14.3: 273-307.

— (2002). *Hizbu'llah: Politics and Religion.* London: Pluto Press.

Sachedina, Abdulaziz. (2001). "The Rule of the Religious Jurist in Iran", in: John L. Esposito and R.K. Ramazani (eds.). *Iran at the Crossroads.* New York: Palgrave, 123-147.

— (1991). "Activist Shi'ism in Iran, Iraq and Lebanon", in: Martin E. Marty and Scott R. Appleby (eds). *Fundamentalism Observed.* Vol. I. Chicago: The University of Chicago Press, 403-56.

— (1980). *Islamic Messianism: The Idea of Mahdi in Twelver Shiism.* Alabany: State University of New York Press.

Hayy'at Nasrat Al-Imam Al-Sadr wa Rafiqayh. (2003). *Qalu fi Al-Imam Al-Sadr [What Has Been Said About Al-Imam Al-Sadr]*. Beirut: Dar Al-Mahajja Al-Bayda'.

Al-Sadr, Imam Musa (1969). *Minbar wa Mihrab [A Podium and a Shrine]*. Beirut:Dar Al-Arqam.

Salman, Talal. (June 2000). *Sira Dhatiyya li Haraka Muqawina 'Arabiyya Muntasira: Hizbullah [An Autobiography of a Victorious Arab Resistance Movement: Hizbullah]*. Beirut: Al-Safir.

Schaefer, Richard T. and Robert P. Lamm. (1998). *Sociology*. New York: McGraw-Hill, Inc.

Schaumann, Christoph. (2001) "The Generation of Broad Expectations". *Die Welt Des Islams* 41.2: 174-205.

Shami, Hajj Husayn. (Fall 1997). "*Hizbullah In Haka* [Hizbullah Speaks Out]". *Hurriyat* (CRED, Beyrouth) 9: 34- 41.

Shamran, Mustapha. (2004). *Qudwat Al-Qada [The Lead of the Leaders]*. Beirut: Al-Mustashariyya Al-Thaqafiyya Lil-Jumhuriyya Al-Islamiyya Al-Iraniyya fi Lubnan.

Shanahan, Rodger. (June 2004). "The Islamic *Da'wa* Party: Development and Future Prospects". *Meria Journal* 8.2.

Sharafeddine, Hasan. (1996). *Al-Imam Al-Sayyid Musa Al-Sadr, Mahatat Tarikhiyya: Iran, Al-Najaf, Lubnan [Al-Imam Al-Sayyid Musa Al-Sadr, Historical Moments: Iran, Al-Najaf, Lebanon]*. Beirut: Dar Al-Arqam.

Sharara, Waddah. (2006). *Dawlat Hizbullah: Lubnan Mujtama'an Islamiyyan [The State of Hizbullah: Lebanon as an Islamic Society]*. Fourth edition. Beirut: Al-Nahar.

Shatz, Adam. (29 April 2004). "In Search of Hezbollah". *The New York Review of Books* 51.7.

Shay, Shaul. (2005). *The Axis of Evil: Iran, Hizballah, and the Palestinian Terror*. London: Transaction Publishers.

— (2004). *The Shahidas: Islam and Suicide Attacks*. Translated by Rachel Lieberman. London: Transaction Publishers.

Al-Shira'. (1984). *Al-Harakat al-Islamiyya fi Lubnan [Islamic Movements in Lebanon]*. Beirut.

Smit, Ferdinand. (2000) *The Battle for South Lebanon: The Radicalisation of Lebanon's Shi'ites (1982-1985)*. Amsterdam: Bulaaq.

Sobelman, Daniel. (January 2004). *Rules of the Game: Israel and Hizbullah After the Withdrawal from Lebanon*. Memorandum no. 69. Tel Aviv University: Jaffee Center for strategic Studies.

Sorensen, Georg and Robert Jackson. (2003). *Introduction to International Relations: Theories and approaches*. Second Edition. Oxford: Oxford University Press.

Telhami, Shibley and Michael Barnett. (Eds.) (2002). *Identity and Foreign Policy in the Middle East*. Ithaca: Cornell University Press.

Victor, Barbara. (2003). *Army of Roses: Inside the World of Palestinian Women Suicide Bombers*. Philadelphia, Pennsylvania: Rodale Press.

Viotti, Paul and Mark Kauppi. (1997). *International Relations and World Politics: ecurity, Economy, Identity*. New Jersey: Prentice-Hall.

— (1993). *International Relations Theory: Realism, Pluralism, Globalism*. Second Edition). Boston: Allyn and Bacon.

Walbridge, Linda S. (ed.). (2001). *The Most Learned of the Shi'a: The Institution of Marja' Taqlid*. Oxford: Oxford University Press.

Walker, Iain and Heather J. Smiths (eds.). (2002). *Relative Deprivation: Specification, Development and Integration*. Cambridge: Cambridge University Press.

Waltz, Kenneth N. (2001). *Man, the State and War: A theoretical Analysis*. (New edition with a new introduction). New York: Colombia University Press.

Warm, Mats. (May 1999). *Staying the Course: The "Lebanonization"of Hizbullah -the integration of the Islamist movement into a pluralist political system*. Stockholm University: Department of Political Science. www.almashriq. hiof.no/lebanon/300/320/324/324.2/hizballah/warn2/index.html

— (May 1997). A Voice of Resistance: the Point of View of Hizbullah;-perceptions, goals and strategies of an Islamic movement in Lebanon. Stockholm University: Department of Political Science: Advanced Course in *Political Science*. www.almashriq.hiof.no/lebanon/300/ 320/324/ 324.2/ hizballah/ warn/

Wasfi, Muhammad Rida. (2000). *Al-Fikar Al-Islami Al-Mu'asir fi Iran: Jadaliyyat Al-Taqlid wa Al-Tajdid [Contemporary Political Thought in Iran: the Dialectics of Traditionalism and Innovation]*. Beirut: Dar Al-Jadid.

Weber, Max. (1976). *The Protestant Ethic and the Spirit of Capitalism*. London: Allen and Unwin.

— (1963). *The Sociology of Religion*. Boston: Beacon.

Wendt, Alexander. (1999). *Social Theory of International Politics*. New York: Cambridge University Press.

— (June 1994). "Collective Identity Formation and the International State". *American Political Science Review* 88.2: 384-396.

— (1992). "Anarchy Is What States Make of It: The Social Construction of Power Politics". *International Organization* 46.2: 391-426.

Wensinck, A.J. "The Oriental Doctrine of the Martyrs", in: *Mededeelingen der Koninklijke Akademie van Wetenschappen, Afdeeling Letterkunde; dl. 53, nr. 6*. Amsterdam: Koninklijke Akademie van Wetenschappen (KNAW publications), 1922, 147-174.

Wiktorowicz, Quintan (ed). (2004). *Islamic Activism: A Social Movement Theory Approach*. Bloomington: Indiana University Press.

Yamak, Labib Z. (1966). *The Syrian Social Nationalist Party: An Ideological Analysis*. Harvard: Center for Middle Eastern Studies.

Z'aytir, Muhammad. (1988). Nazra 'ala Tarh Al-Jumhuriyya Al-Islamiyya fi Lubnan [A Look at the Proposal of the Islamic Republic in Lebanon]. Beirut: Al-Wikala Al-Sharqiyya lil-Tawzi'.

— (1986). *Al-Mashru' Al-Maruni fi Lubnan: Juzuruhu wa Tatawwuratuhu [The Maronite Project in Lebanon: Roots and Development]*. Beirut: Al-Wikala Al-'Alamiyya lil-Tawzi'.

Index

Praise for *Hizbullah's Identity Construction (1978-2010)*

✳✳✳

ALAGHA OFFERS A NUANCED AND SOPHISTICATED LOOK AT HOW Hizbullah's ideology and political tactics have evolved. His work sheds light on an important, but to Western audiences mysterious and opaque, political force in Lebanon.

Daniel L. Byman, Director of Georgetown's Security Studies Program and the Center for Peace and Security Studies and Associate Professor at the School of Foreign Service

✳✳✳

JOSEPH ALAGHA'S BOOK IS TO DATE ONE OF THE MOST SCRUPULOUS and meticulously researched works on Hizbullah. Articulate, and devastatingly accurate, Alagha's work is a refreshing departure from the bland panegyric hagiographies that have defined the canon of those plodding the marshes of Hizbullah's murky history.

Franck Salameh, Assistant Professor of Near Eastern Studies, Arabic, and Hebrew, Boston College, USA. Author of *Language, Memory and Identity in the Middle East: The Case of Lebanon* (2010)

✳✳✳

JOSEPH ALAGHA HAS WRITTEN THE MOST UP-TO-DATE STUDY OF THE Shi'i organization, Hizbullah. Through an analysis of Hizbullah's identity, Alagha carefully follows the evolution of the organization's political ideology as it has changed to respond to the challenges of the time. His book underscores the dynamism of Hizbullah and demonstrates the extent of the organization's successes as well as predicaments and possible future challenges. To the best of my knowledge, there is no work that covers the evolution of Hizbullah's ideology all the way to 2010, so extensively and meticulously.

Professor Asher Kaufman, a leading specialist on the tri-border area of Israel, Lebanon and Syria, and a Lebanon Identity expert, Notre Dame University, USA

ALAGHA'S BOOK ON HIZBULLAH'S IDEOLOGY AND HISTORY IS A must-read for anyone interested in the politics of Islam and the modern Middle East. Based in part on fieldwork among Hizbullah's members, the author offers a nuanced and original reading of the movement's inner workings and ideological developments as well as the unvarnished views of many Hizbullahis.

Bernard Haykel is Professor of Near Eastern Studies and Director of the Institute for the Transregional Study of the Contemporary Middle East, North Africa and Central Asia (TRI) at Princeton University, USA

✶✶✶

THIS IS A THOROUGH ANALYSIS BASED ON DEEP KNOWLEDGE OF Hizbullah and Lebanese politics in its regional context. Hizbullah's transformation and performance undergoes a rigorous critique that debunks main myths about the Party and demonstrates its phenomenal influence in Lebanese politics and its significant regional role. The work points out Hizbullah's structural limitations despite its proven adaptability to changing circumstance. The methodology that the author employs and his painstaking research, allows him to reach conclusions that make the work a corrective to previous scholarship on Hizbullah.

Ibrahim G. Aoude, Professor and Chair, Department of Ethnic Studies, University of Hawai'i, USA, and Editor of *Arab Studies Quarterly*

✶✶✶

SINCE ITS BIRTH IN THE EARLY 1980S, HIZBULLAH HAS EMERGED NOT only as the preeminent Shia organization in Lebanon and the Arab world, but also as the most effective link in the chain of 'resistance' to Israel and pro-Western Arab forces. For an organization that is so outwardly radical, it is extraordinary that it also behaves so pragmatically – joining the Lebanese government, on the one hand, and cultivating close links with militant Lebanese Maronite elements, on the other. Hizbullah then is an enigma, and its ability to successfully navigate the Middle East's complex power relationships is mystifying. Hence the importance of Joseph Alagha's new book on Hizbullah, for in this major new study he provides the most comprehensive account of the rise and staying in power of Hizbullah to date. This is a compelling read which demystifies Hizbullah and also the Middle East's apparently contradictory relationships. A must-read.

Anoush Ehteshami, Professor of International Relations, Durham University

JOSEPH ALAGHA'S LATEST BOOK IS A MAJOR CONTRIBUTION TO THE
understanding of Hizbullah's position not only in Lebanon or the Shi'ite
world, but also in world politics. It combines the mastery on Hizbullah's
ideology through its major thinkers and its relation to the Shi'ite intellectual
production in Iran and elsewhere. It shows in particular the change within
Hizbullah's major political and ideological stances and their flexibility in
terms of modernization, opening up the Islamic views to many modern
ones, which were once thought as antagonistic to Islam. Alagha displays a
rare mastery of ideological and socio-political analysis, combining them in
a scholarly view that makes this book indispensable for understanding this
movement within the Muslim world.
**Farhad Khosrokhavar, Professor of Sociology at the École des Hautes
Études en Sciences Sociales (EHESS), Paris; Yale and Harvard Visiting
Professor. Author of *Inside Jihadism: Understanding Jihadi Movements
Worldwide* (2009) and *Suicide Bombers: Allah's New Martyrs* (2005)**

✷✷✷

JOSEPH ALAGHA REMAINS ONE OF THE MOST THOROUGH AND
careful analysts of Hizbullah's political ideology and practice. Scholars,
analysts, and policymakers will find in this work a veritable treasure trove of
research and insights into this complex organization.
**Michaelle Browers, Associate Professor of Political Science,
Wake Forest University, North Carolina, USA. Author of *Political Ideology
in the Arab World* (2009) and *Democracy and Civil Society in Arab Political
Thought* (2006)**

✷✷✷

JOSEPH ALAGHA'S *HIZBULLAH'S IDENTITY CONSTRUCTION* IS A
fresh perspective on Hizbullah, whose hydra-like nature has perplexed and
confounded laymen and scholars alike. Based on an expansive, impressive
use of primary and secondary sources, the study offers an in-depth analysis,
in theory and practice, on Hizbullah's construction and reconstruction of its
identity unrivalled in its minute details and exposition.
**Robert G. Rabil, Associate Professor of Political Science and Director of
Graduate Studies, Florida Atlantic University, USA. Author of *Syria, the
United States and the War on Terror in the Middle East* (2006) and *Embat-
tled Neighbors: Syria, Israel, Lebanon* (2003)**

THE POLITICAL LANDSCAPE OF LEBANON IS REMARKABLE IN ITS constant flux which keeps the country and its citizens in an enduring 'emergency' mode, while at the same time maintaining an equally remarkable stability in its political groupings and their internal dynamics. The exception to this rule has been Hizbullah which introduced a new and powerful factor into Lebanese politics in the 1980s and which has also undergone extensive internal evolution in the three decades since its formation. This new book by Joseph Alagha continues his earlier work in carefully dissecting Hizbullah's inner workings and transformations as well as its impact on the wider Lebanese public sphere. Meticulous in its detail and documentation, this is a must-read for anyone interested in Lebanon and in socio-religious movements in general.

Seteney Shami, Director of the Program on the Middle East and North Africa at the Social Science Research Council of America (SSRC)